RURAL DEVELOPMENT in INDIA

VOLUME I

Edited by

K.R. GUPTA

ATLANTIC
PUBLISHERS & DISTRIBUTORS

Published by
ATLANTIC PUBLISHERS AND DISTRIBUTORS
B-2, Vishal Enclave, Opp. Rajouri Garden, New Delhi-27
Phones : 5413460, 5429987, 5466842

Sales Office
4215/1, Ansari Road, Darya Ganj, New Delhi-02
Phones : 3273880, 3285873, 3280451
Fax : 91-11-3285873
e-mail : info@atlanticbooks.com
web : www.atlanticbooks.com

ISBN 81-269-0182-9

Typeset at
APD Computer Graphics, Delhi

Printed in India at
Nice Printing Press, Delhi

PREFACE

Since Independence India has made a significant progress in various sectors of rural development. Efforts have been made to bring about rapid and sustainable development and socio-economic transformation in rural India with an integrated approach towards improving the quality of life of rural poor and ensuring equity and effective people's participation. The thrust of rural development programmes has been to make a frontal attack on poverty through special employment generation programmes, productive asset transfer through institutional credit and subsidy programmes and programmes of rural housing, drinking water and sanitation. Strong thrust has been given to social security programmes for providing assistance to the destitutes and poor families. The Government has undertaken development of wastelands, desert and drought prone areas and land reforms in the country. Assistance and encouragement to voluntary agencies and training of functionaries of rural development forms part of the emphasis on accelerated rural development.

Any strategy for rural development must involve the people themselves and their institutions at all levels. The need for revitalising Panchayati Raj Institutions has, therefore, been recognised as an instrument for participative planning and implementation of various development programmes at grassroot level. The Government is constantly endeavouring to empower the Panchayati Raj Institutions in terms of functions, powers and finance. The Gram Sabha being potentially the most significant institution for participatory democracy and decentralisation, it was decided to observe 1999-2000 as the "Year of Gram Sabha".

Agriculture plays an important role in the rural development. The Agricultural Sector provides livelihood to about sixty-four per cent of the labour force, contributes nearly twenty-six per cent of Gross Domestic Product and accounts for about eighteen per cent share of the total value of country's exports. It supplies bulk of wage goods required by the non-agricultural sector and raw materials for large section of industry.

The Volume has a wide coverage and includes papers written by experts spread over the whole country.

It is hoped that the book will prove very useful to the researchers and students of Economics, government executives concerned with the formulation and execution of policies for rural development, parliamentarians and legislators, and the common readers interested in rural development.

I express my deep gratitude to all contributors who have worked hard to present their papers.

K.R. GUPTA

CONTENTS

LIST OF ANNEXURES

LIST OF STATISTICAL TABLES

ACRONYMS

ARWSP	—	Accelerated Rural Water Supply Programme
AARRO	—	Afro-Asian Rural Reconstruction Organisation
AIR	—	All India Radio
APO	—	Assistant Project Officer
BLBC	—	Block Level Bankers Committee
BLCC	—	Block Level Coordination Committee
BMTPC	—	Building Material Technology Promotion Council
BPL	—	Below Poverty Line
CAPART	—	Council for Advancement of People's Action and Rural Technology
CBRI	—	Central Building Research Institute
CBS	—	Commercial Broadcasting Station
CGWB	—	Central Ground Water Board
CIRDAP	—	Central for Integrated Rural Development for Asia and the Pacific
CLCC	—	Central Level Coordination Committee
CLIC	—	Computerised Library and Information Clearing House
COSAMB	—	Council of State Agricultural Marketing Board
CRISP	—	Computerised Rural Information System Project
CRSP	—	Central Rural Sanitation Programme
CBCS	—	Community Based Convergent Services

CCA	—	Child Care Activities
CEO	—	Chief Executive Office
CSIR	—	Council for Scientific and Industrial Research
DANIDA	—	Danish International Development Agency
DAVP	—	Directorate of Advertising and Visual Publicity
DDUSIRD	—	Deen Dayal Upadhyay State Institute of Rural Development
DDP	—	Desert Development Programme
DFID	—	Department for International Development
DFP	—	Directorate of Field Publicity
DIC	—	Documentation Information Centre
DLO	—	District Link Officer
DPAP	—	Drought Prone Areas Programme
DWCRA	—	Development of Women and Children in Rural Areas
DRDA	—	District Rural Development Agency
DLCC	—	District Level Coordination Committee
DSMS	—	District Supply and Marketing Society
DWD	—	Department of Wastelands Development
EAS	—	Employment Assurance Scheme
EDP	—	Enterpreneurship Development Programme
EFC	—	Expenditure Finance Committee
ESCAP	—	Economic and Social Commission for Asia and the Pacific
ETC	—	Extension Training Centre
ETTC	—	Exclusive TRYSEM Training Centre
FCP	—	Family Credit Plan
GKY	—	Ganga Kalyan Yojana
GPCD	—	Generic Project Concept Document

HLCC	—	High Level Committee on Credit
HADP	—	Hill Areas Development Programme
HRD	—	Human Resource Development
HSMI	—	Human Settlement Management Institute
HUDCO	—	Housing and Urban Development Corporation
HCMRIPA	—	Harish Chander Mathur Rural Institute of Public Administration
IAY	—	Indira Awaas Yojana
ICOR	—	Incremental Capital Output Ratio
INSDOC	—	Indian National Scientific Documentation Centre
IPS	—	Investment Promotional Scheme
IRDP	—	Integrated Rural Development Programme
ICAR	—	Indian Council for Agricultural Research
IGNOU	—	Indira Gandhi National Open University
IJRY	—	Intensified Jawahar Rozgar Yojana
IIT	—	Indian Institute of Technology
IWDB	—	Integrated Wastelands Development Board
ITI	—	Industrial Training Institute
IIPA	—	Indian Institute of Public Administration
IIM	—	Indian Institute of Management, Anand
ITN	—	Indian Training Network
IWSU	—	Internal Work Study Unit
JRY	—	Jawahar Rozgar Yojana
JGSY	—	Jawahar Gram Samridhi Yojana
KERAMS	—	Kerala Rural Development and Marketing Society
KESNIK	—	Kerala State Nirmithi Kendra
LAN	—	Local Area Newwork

LBSNAA	—	Lal Bahadur Shastri National Academy of Administration
LR	—	Land Reforms
MADA	—	Modified Area Development Approach
MIS	—	Management Information System
MLO	—	Ministry Link Officer
MNP	—	Minimum Needs Programme
MPDC	—	Marketing Planning and Design Centre
MWS	—	Million Wells Scheme
NICNET	—	National Informatics Centre Network
NIRD	—	National Institute of Rural Development
NIAM	—	National Institute of Agricultural Marketing
NIUA	—	National Institute of Urban Affairs
NABARD	—	National Bank of Agriculture and Rural Development
NC	—	Not Covered
NMBS	—	National Maternity Benefit Scheme
NOAPS	—	National Old Age Pension Scheme
NFBS	—	National Family Benefit Scheme
NFRD	—	National Fund for Rural Development
NGO	—	Non-Governmental Organisation
NHRDP	—	National Human Resource Development Programme
NREP	—	National Rural Employment Programme
NSAP	—	National Social Assistance Programme
NWDB	—	National Wastelands Development Board
NIBM	—	National Institute of Bank Management
NICD	—	National Institute of Communicable Diseases
NERC	—	North East Regional Centre

OB	—	Organisation of Beneficiaries
OBB	—	Operation Black Board
ODA	—	Overseas Development Agency
ODI	—	Overseas Development Institute
ODR	—	Other District Roads
OTC	—	Organisation of Training Courses
PC	—	Partially Covered
PEO	—	Programme Evaluation Organisation
PIA	—	Project Implementation Agency
PIB	—	Press Information Bureau
PLO	—	Programme Link Officer
PRIs	—	Panchayati Raj Institutions
QFE	—	Qualifying Financial Entitlement
RAC	—	Research Advisory Committee
RBI	—	Reserve Bank of India
RGNDWMA	—	Rajiv Gandhi National Drinking Water Mission Authority
RGNDWM	—	Rajiv Gandhi National Drinking Water Mission
RLEGP	—	Rural Landless Employment Guarantee Programme
RPDS	—	Revamped Public Distribution System
RSM	—	Rural Sanitary Marts
SAARC	—	South Asian Association for Regional Cooperation
SCP	—	Special Component Plan
SCR	—	Subsidy Credit Ratio
SHG	—	Self-Help Group
SIDA	—	Swedish International Development Corporation Agency

SITRA	—	Supply of Improved Toolkits to Rural Artisans
SDC	—	Swiss Development Corporation
SIRD	—	State Institute of Rural Development
SLBC	—	State Level Bankers Committee
SLCC	—	State Level Coordination Committee
SRA & ULR	—	Strengthening of Revenue Administration and Updating of Land Records
SRS	—	Software Requirement Specification
SSRC	—	Screening Sanctioning and Review Committee
SFC	—	State Finance Commission
STAC	—	Science and Technology Advisory Committee
TDET	—	Technology Development Extension and Training
TRYSEM	—	Training of Rural Youth for Self-Employment
TSP	—	Tribal Sub Plan
VO	—	Voluntary Organisation
WA	—	Watershed Association
WC	—	Watershed Committee
WDA	—	Wastelands Development Agency
WDT	—	Watershed Development Team
WDTF	—	Wastelands Development Task Force
WP	—	Watershed Projects
YPs	—	Young Professionals
ZP	—	Zila Parishad

1

Reforming Rural Credit Institutions in Uttar Pradesh

*Awadhesh Kr. Singh**

The role of credit and credit institutions in augmenting production and productivity is well recognised. Moreover, credit is the most important input for any development — be it agriculture, industrial or commercial. The main thrust of Indian Public Policy towards rural credit has, therefore, been to ensure that sufficient and timely credit, at reasonable rates of interest, is made available to as large segment of rural population as possible. The strategy of developing rural financial services was thus a three pronged one, consisting of[1] : (i) expansion of institutional structure, (ii) directe lending and (iii) concessional or subsidized credit. This approach has resulted in an impressive growth of rural banking in India over the years in terms of its outreach, credit disbursement and support to the poverty alienation programmes. It is to be noted that agricultural credit is a diversified and complex one. Despite of significant expansion of the formal sector, non-institutional agencies continued to play a dominant rule. Although the formal agencies levy high rates of interests, it is observed that rural people continued to borrow from money lenders, the rate of interest being charged as high as

*Faculty Member, Institute of Development Studies, Lucknow University, Lucknow.

23 per cent, 21 per cent and 24.7 per cent in the case of small farmers, marginal farmers and other farmers, respectively and no records/documents are required to be produced to them[2]. However, the share of the non-institutional sector of the total borrowings has recorded a decline, mainly due to the adoption of multi-agency approach. Institutional credit in the early 1950's formed only 4 per cent of total credit, which has now increased to 65 per cent in India. The co-operatives play an important role in influencing people towards social and economic changes and offer unlimited possibilities of participation in economic resurgencies.

In this paper, an attempt has been made to analyse the co-operative credit reforms in India and revitalisation of co-operative credit structure in Uttar Pradesh. Interestingly, perspective of rural credit has been discussed in the context of new agricultural policy of state.

Co-operative Credit and Banking

The co-operatives in India by now have expanded, both vertically and horizontally. It is embracing wider and wider fields of action and is considered as one of the biggest and most diversified movements in the world. Today, with about 175 million membership, a network of 3,53,000 co-operatives of various types working at different levels, there is hardly any field of economic activity that remains untouched by it. The paid up share capital of all co-operatives is estimated at over Rs. 7000 crore and working capital nearly Rs. 89,000 crore. Almost all the villages in the country have been covered by 95,200 primary agricultural co-operatives with about 67 per cent coverage of rural households[3]. The three-tier co-operative credit structure has come of age and is made up of 95,000 PACS (Primary Agricultural Co-operative Societies) functioning at the village level with a membership of about 8.8 crore farmers, 35 district central co-operative banks with a network of about 11,000 branches spread out mainly in the rural areas and 28 state co-operative banks functioning at the state level with about 700 branches. Parallel to short-term and medium-term three-tier co-operative credit structure geared mainly to the dispensation of agricultural production credit and other agro-inputs, a long-term co-operative credit structure on flow of investment credit or agriculture and allied activities has also emerged as the only specialised institution providing term loans in the rural credit field. This structure, as it stands today, is made up of 20 state co-operative land/agriculture development banks and 2841 primary land development banks supervised by about 290 offices of the SLDB's at district/divisional levels. The membership of this structure is about 18 million and in 20 states, a little over 50 per cent of about 5000 blocks have been covered by operational units[4].

The growth in Primary Agricultural Credit Societies has been truly staggering. The number of PACS stood at 90,783 in 1994-95 with a membership of around 890 lakhs. These apart, 2200 Primary Land Development Banks also came up in the co-operative sector. The position of Uttar Pradesh in all India co-operative credit has been reported very poor, constituting a share of 8.50 per cent in loans/advances during 1994-95 while share of state in total members of PACS was reported as high as 17.29 per cent. Moreover, state constitutes 9.51 per cent in total number of PACS in country during 1995. The share of state in total deposits in PACS was reported to be just 2.70 per cent.

In the state of Uttar Pradesh, 8384 Primary Agriculture Co-operative Societies were reported during 1997. Lucknow, Faizabad, Agra, Varanasi, Allahabad, Azamgarh and Gorakhpur division were reported having a large number of PACS while smaller number of PACS were reported in Chitrakoot Dham and Mirzapur division. The disbursement of loans/advances in different regions was also found uneven.

The co-operative credit institutions accounted for a preponderance share of nearly 56.9 per cent in total direct institutional credit disbursed for agriculture and allied activities during 1994-95 and the amount of loans issued by the co-operative rose from Rs. 743.8 crore during 1970-71 to Rs. 12.120 crore during 1994-95 and it was expected to reach Rs. 14,000 crore by 1995-96 in India. Against this, the position of the state of Uttar Pradesh is found to be pathetic since a comparison of PACS with all India shows almost dismal picture of state. During 1991-92, members per society in Uttar Pradesh was reported to be 1426 against national average of 995 members. Similarly working capital per society in the state was reported lower than national average. Similar is the case with share capital per society and share capital per member. It is a startling fact that deposits per society in the state was reported at Rs. 44805 against Rs. 247788 at national level. Moreover, deposits per member of society in the state was computed at Rs. 31 against Rs. 248 at national level. However, loans and advances per active society in the state was found slightly higher as compared to national average.

During 1980-81 to 1990-91 highest growth was recorded in deposits (9.05 per cent per annum) followed by working capital (8.97 per cent per annum) and share capital (6.96 per cent per annum) while lowest growth was recorded in medium-term loans/advances (1.32 per cent per annum). During the corresponding period disbursement of total loans and advances grew by 5.51 per cent per annum while disbursement of short-term loans grew by 6.05 per cent per annum. Similarly, during 1990-91 to 1996-97, disbursement of loans and advances made by PACS in the state grew by 16.34 per cent per annum which is quite high growth rate while disbursement of medium-term loans and advances declined by 5.69 per cent per annum. Moreover, disbursement of short-term credit grew by 17.86 per cent per annum, recording comparatively higher growth rate. The recovery position of credit provided by PACS in the state shows a nominal improvement. It grew just 0.69 per cent per annum during 1980-81 to 1990-91 and 0.17 per cent per annum during 1990-91 to 1996-97.

Outstanding and Overdue Syndrome

The outstanding loans, under the head direct institutional finance for agriculture and allied activities, of the co-operative institution is less than that of the schedule commercial banks. The total outstanding loan for 1993 was Rs. 33,666.90 crore of which the share of co-operatives was Rs. 13,243.90 crore (39 per cent), scheduled commercial banks Rs. 18,8,287.80 crore (54 per cent) and the share of regional rural banks was Rs. 2,132.80 crore (7 per cent). In providing direct financial assistance to agriculture, co-operative institutions occupy the first place and the same position is also retained by them in recovering the loan. It is evident from the fact that share of direct financial assistance of the co-operative institutions was 53 per cent and the share of scheduled commercial banks was 39 per cent in total, but the share of outstanding loans of the co-operatives was 39 per cent and the share of scheduled commercial banks was 54 per cent in total. Importantly, out of the 369 District Central Co-operative Banks, only 171 (46.34 per cent) were operating in profit as on March 31, 1994. The overdues at Rs. 3874 crore constituted 33 per cent of the demand. As regards PACS, out of 90,783 units, only 52211 (58 per cent) had been identified as being viable as on March 31, 1994. Overdues of PACS at Rs. 3,875 crore constituted 38 per cent of their outstanding loans. The pictures as regards the Regional Rural Banks was no better. During 1994-95, 32 RRBs had made profit while 164 RRBs showed a loss aggregating Rs. 423.21 crore. The annual loss increased from Rs. 94.05 fcrore in 1991 to Rs. 425.65 crore in 1994-95 while the accumulated losses of RRBs aggregated at Rs. 1686.61 crore as on 31st March, 1995.

The recovery position of SCBs and PACS is relatively better than that of the DCCBs and state/Central LDBs. In terms of total loans outstanding the overdues of DCCBs stood at 24.2 per cent at the end of the year 1988-89 and further it had gone upto 33 per cent at the end of 1989-90. In case of demand, the overdues of DCCBs increased from 36.7 per cent in 1988-89 to 51.7 per cent at the end of 1988-90. The percentage of overdues to demand in the case of state/central LDBs stood at 55.9 per cent in 1988-89. These went up further to 66.8 per cent of demand in 1989-90. In the state of Uttar Pradesh, recovery percentage of credit provided by PACS was recorded highest in 1989-90 (71.70 per cent) followed by 1994-95 (70.89 per cent), 1995-96 (70.41 per cent) and 1992-93 (62.26 per cent) while lowest recovery was recorded in 1988-89 (48.21 per cent). It shows that recovery position of PACS is increasingly better during the reforms period.

The causes of poor recovery identified by the Agricultural Credit Review Committee (1989) are as follows : (i) internal causes relating to credit system directly affecting recoveries, including defective loan policies and procedures, inadequate supervision over credit and unsatisfactory management; (ii) external factors related to credit agency comprise natural calamities like floods and droughts, absence of backward and forward recoveries through legal measures and socio-political environment in which the credit agencies are required to function.[5]

Importantly, the strategies followed have undoubtedly helped to build up a broad-based institutional infrastructure for the delivery and deployment of credit. However, the emphasis throughout has been on achieving certain quantitative targets. As a consequences, inadequate attention was paid to the qualitative aspects of lending resulting in loans defaults and virtual erosion of repayment ethics, to a grater or lesser extent, by all categories of borrowers. The end result was the disturbing growth in overdues which not only hampered the recycling of scarce resources of banks, but also affected the profitability and viability of the financial institutions[6].

Strengthening of Rural Credit Institutions

The new agricultural policy of state, 1999 presents a frame work for progress and prosperity of agriculture and allied sectors in the state. Keeping in view the requirements of agricultural credit, policy has pinpointed to strengthen micro finance for sustaining rural economic activities and agricultural operations. It has proposed to increase the availability of rural credit for shortterm and longterm investment. In order to achieve the objectives, co-operative credit institutions are to be strengthened and special efforts are to be initiated to wipe out the deficit, and reforming co-operative credit structures. Importantly, self-help groups and non-governmental organizations are also to be encouraged to achieve the targets of agricultural credit. Thus, micro-credit for agricultural operations has been equally emphasised in the new policy. Again, issuing of kisan credit cards to obtain agricultural credit and other facilities are needed and these may be promoted through initiatives taken by bank officials and co-operative credit institutions. Significantly, centrally sponsored Integrated Co-operative Department Progammes (ICDP) has been introduced in the policy for strengthening co-operative institutions and widening of their programmes. It is expected that co-operative credit societies will prepare a development action plan and will ensure its implementation. Though the policy has emphasised important aspects of agricultural credit, it has not focused on agenda for reforms in rural credit. With the changed economic and business environment, it is high time that rural credit institutions should be thoroughly reviewed and process of reforms for revitalising the rural credit institutions should be accelerated.

Reform in Co-operative Sector Lending

The foundations for the building of a broad credit infrastructure for rural credit were laid by the Report of All India Rural Credit Survey in 1954. The main attempt was to expand rural credit and displace the money lender. It viewed rural credit in India as being 'inadequate and unsuitable.' The Committee, therefore, recommended an integrated scheme of rural credit based on the co-operatives. The Committee envisaged development of co-operative credit system as an exclusive agency for providing agriculture credit supplanting the money lender. The merit of the co-operative banking structure was observed to be in fulfilling the twin objectives of (i) providing a credit delivery system operating at the door steps of the farmer and (ii) making such credit available at relatively cheaper rates in view of the economy in operating costs. Moreover, the All India Rural Credit Review Committee (1966) undertook a comprehensive review of the agricultural credit system and recommended for a substantial contribution to come from the commercial banking sector in order to provide credit for both current production and long-term development. With the nationalisation of the major commercial banks in 1969, branch banking in the rural areas acquired a new momentum. Narasimham Working Group (1975) made a recommendation for setting up of Regional Rural Banks. The concept of 'Priority Sector' was evolved in the later sixties to focus attention on the credit needs of the neglected and under privileged sector. Public sector banks were asked to extend credit to the priority sector to the extent of at least one third of their total credit outstanding by March 1979. The target was raised further to 40 per cent to be achieved by March 1985. It was also stipulated that the advances to the weaker sections should reach a level of 25 per cent of the total credit outstanding by March 1985. The target for lending for agriculture and allied activities was set at 15 per cent of the total credit to be achieved by March 1985, 16 per cent by March 1987, 17 per cent by March 1989, and 18 per cent by March 1990. The refinance facility was ensured directly by the RBI until the establishment of NABARD in 1982. Since then, the facility has been routed through NABARD. The refinance facility is given both in relation to short-term and long-term credit.

The co-operative credit system is far from a healthy situation. The system suffers from a number of problems, such as : — (i) excessive reliance on funds from higher level structure, (ii) undue state control, (iii) poor deposit mobilization and (iv) poor recovery of loans and advances. It is to be noted that in the co-operative structure, the weakest link in the chain is the PACS. A major weakness of the co-operative system lies in the weakness of the base level institutions. These societies have neglected the basic responsibility of mobilizing deposits. About 68 per cent of the funds of PACS come in the form of borrowings. Over the years, progressive officialization has caused considerable damage to the co-operative system[7].

The financial sector reform that is currently underway encompasses the institutional rural credit delivery system as well. The essence of these measures is to improve the efficiency and productivity of all credit institutions including rural credit institutions whose financial health is far from satisfactory. Institutional development is an evolutionary process. The progress of rural financial institutions will have to reflect the trends towards greater efficiency and effectiveness. Importantly, the rural financial sector is still not an integrated one. Despite the growth of formal institutional agencies, informal institutions continue to play a role in the market. Moreover, the experience of NABARD with their Pilot Project launched in 1992, linking Self-Help Groups with formal credit institutions, has also been found to be immensely successful, particularly, in the case of groups formed by women. A measure of the success of Pilot Project is that in 1997, 2112 Self Help Groups were linked with banks supported by NABARD refinance assistance of around Rs. 2.4 crore. The repayment performance of members has been found to be overwhelmingly satisfactory, at around 95 per cent, compared with roughly 50 per cent in the case of normal banks lending. Apart from helping to improve levels of income and savings, Self-Help Groups have also been able to bring about positive improvement in a number of social indicators such as literacy and health.

Notwithstanding the increase in the flow of credit to the agricultural sector in recent years, there is perception that investments in agriculture have not kept pace with demand. In this backdrop and also in the context of priority accorded to the flow of credit to agriculture, one-man High Level Committee on Agriculture Credit through commercial banks, headed by Shri R.V. Gupta, was set up by the Reserve bank of India in December 1997 to suggest measures for improving the credit delivery systems as well as simplication of procedures for agricultural credit. The Committee submitted its report on April 21, 1198 and recommended the following policy measures[8] :

(1) The focus of credit appraisal should be on evaluation of the income stream of the borrower and a comprehensive assessment of credit needs taking into account track record, credibility, capability as well technical viability of the proposal;

(2) To ensure quick disposal, at least 90 per cent of loan applications should be decided at the branch level;

(3) Short-term credit needs of the farmer should include all requirements directly and indirectly related to production, post-harvest and household expenses. Repayment capacity should be assessed on the basis of aggregate household income from all sources including crop production and ancillary activities.

(4) In order to foster an environment of trust, banks may disburse loans for agricultural activities on cash basis only and discontinue the practice of obtaining bills/ receipts of inputs/assets purchased;

(5) Banks should design appropriate incentives systems including interest benefit or rebate to borrowers who repay their dues promptly;

(6) State Government may initiate steps to abolish stamp duty on mortgage of agricultural land for obtaining loans from banks;

(7) The internal supervision system of banks should provide for visits to a few service area villages;

(8) To bring about the desired behavioural change in rural lending and to strengthen the sense of mission of bank staff, a package of incentives encompassing foreign exposure, training in prestigious institutions within the country, weightage in promotion, posting to centre of choice, etc. is recommended;

(9) Banks training institutions need to design training programmes emphasising borrower appraisal including techniques for assessing the needs of the rural household in a holistic way *vis-à-vis* the income stream repayment capacity;

(10) Banks should give wide publicity to their preference for financing Self-Help Groups (SHGs), sensitize regional heads and branch managers to the potential for good lending through their route.

Need for Qualitative Change and Reforms

The quantitative growth of co-operatives depict impressive performance in key areas of the economy, *viz.*, agriculture credit, marketing and processing, retail distribution, housing, weaker sections and others. However, the benefits of co-operative development programmes and projects have not percolated to the extent desired to the large sections of the rural population, which apparently are not in a position to make use of the services and facilities provided by co-operative societies. Importantly, states are increasingly becoming aware of the need to undertake legislative measures to remove restrictive provisions from the co-operative legislation in their respective areas. The co-operators believe and rightly so, that the essence of co-operative organisation precludes control and interference by any outside agency. It has to be ensured that co-operatives develop as voluntary, autonomous, democratic bodies and not as appendage of the government. Significantly, the measures such as programmes for business development planning in PACS, strengthening the role of the federal co-operatives in relation to primaries, formation of Model Co-operative Societies Act, declaration of government policy on co-operation, professionalisation of management and human resources development are needed to revitalise the co-operatives in the state of Uttar Pradesh as well as in India.

It is to be noted that 'Model Co-operative Law' analysed by an Expert Committee (Brahm Prakash as its chairman) set up by the Planning Commission was circulated in 1991 and was pending upto mid 1995 before Parliament. The model law aims at restoring the spirit of self-reliance and member participation in the affairs of the co-operatives and the role of the government is restructured so as to 'minimise' government control and interference to enable co-operators and co-operatives to exercise power of decision making. It is hoped that necessary amendments in the state co-operative legislation in the framework of Model Co-operative Societies Act will not only strengthen the co-operative character but will also help eliminate bureaucratic control and politicization[9]. Similarly, functional and operational autonomy of the Rural Financing Institutions is a major issue, particularly, for the co-operative sector. This needs to be granted to the institutions either through legislation or through self-denial by government so that these institutions can truly function as financial intermediaries with professional ethos and orientation[10]. Significantly, strengthening of human resources needs to be carried out in Rural Financing Institutions. This has been highlighted by the Committee headed by K.N. Ardhanareswaran (1987). The Committee focused on the significance and relevance of professional management and has suggested comprehensive measures on a professionalization of management and human resource development in the co-operative sector[11]. Moreover, appropriate and adequate attention by all concerned will have to be paid to training of personnel and technical upgradation.

Given the present institutional health of the co-operatives, it would not be an exaggeration to say that future of rural credit depends much on the appropriations and the degree of response to the measures already taken. They are likely to be strengthened if appropriate amendments to the Banking Regulation Act 1949 are carried out so as to make the compliance of the recommendations of institutions reports mandatory, and ensure strict compliance with prudential financial norms, professionalization of Boards of Management and non-interference of state government. Empowerment of NABARD under the Banking Regulation Act would significantly enhance the effectiveness of its institutional development initiatives.

Self-Help Groups should be further strengthened through sustained financial support and establishing linkages between banks and Self-Help Groups. Banks can also work through NGOs or voluntary organisations, which can provide credit to Self-Help Groups to be passed on the members. The route chosen by a bank will depend upon the strength of the Self-Help Groups and the support they may need from voluntary organisations/NGOs. Importantly, Self-Help Groups will need to move to the second phase of providing credit for supporting economic activities and help their members to increase their income levels. In this regard NGOs/voluntary organisations will have to play a much greater role. Productive activities will require stronger support in terms of marketing distribution, etc.

Conclusion

The role of co-operatives especially PACS in agricultural development in terms of agricultural inputs and micro-credit has been well recognised. The rural credit system stands today at an important stage in evolution. It needs to meet the growing requirements of agriculture especially diversified agriculture which is becoming input intensive and getting increasingly commercialised. Thus, the demand of agricultural credit well necessarily increase. Since a majority of the farmers are small and marginal and they are in dire need of micro-credit for sustaining procurement of agricultural inputs and consumer expends. Therefore, the only hope from Rural Financing Institutions is of PACS for sustained availability of credit. Obviously, the strategy and approach of the credit delivery system to meet the needs of the various segments of rural society has to be different. However, attitutional change on the part of lending institutions and healthy environment of repayment are needed. Moreover, changes including structuring of Rural Financing Institutions especially co-operative will lead towards efficiency, autonomy, accountability and competitiveness in rural credit sector.

REFERENCES

1. Rangarajan, C., 'Role of Credit in Rural India' in *Banking and Financial Sector Reforms in India*, Vol. 3, (ed.) Raj Kapila & Uma Kapila. Academic Foundation, New Delhi, 1998, p. 89.
2. State Bank of India, *Monthly Review*, March, 1988, p. 32.
3. Shah, U.M., 'Co-operative Development — Progress and Trends', *Kurukshetra*, November, 1995, p. 3.
4. *Ibid.*, p. 4.
5. *Report of the Agricultural Credit Review Committee*, 1989, RBI, pp. 556-582.
6. *Report of the Committee on the Financial System*, Reserve bank of India, 1991.
7. *Report of the Agricultural Credit Review Committee*, RBI, 1987.
8. *Report of the High Level Committee on Agricultural Credit through Commercial Banks*, RBI, 1998.
9. Shah, Uma, *op. cit.,* p. 8.
10. Rangaranjan, C., *op. cit.,* p. 100.
11. Shah, Uma, *op. cit.,* p. 30.

2

Marine Product Exports from India Under Economic Liberalization Policy

*J.M. Talathi** and *M.G. Joshi***

The fisheries sector occupies a significant place in Indian economy because it contributes to the national income, generate employment, provides nutritious food and earns foreign exchange. This sector consists of two types of fisheries, Inland fisheries and marine fisheries. Inland fisheries include fishing and fish culture in rivers, ponds, swamps, canals, reservoirs and lakes. While marine fisheries includes fishing in sea, brackish water fisheries and fishing in estuaries. The nature of marine fisheries is quite different from agriculture or mining industry in relation to resources and their utilization. By the year 1979, a new regime for marine fisheries has arisen with the declaration of the Exclusive Economic Zone (EEZ) by most of the littoral countries. The EEZ gives the right to these countries to extend their jurisdiction over the living and non-living resources within a 200 miles of zone of the oceans from their shores.

With a coast line of about 7517 kms., a shelf area of about 4.5 lakh sq. kms., an Exclusive Economic Zone about

* Professor, Department of Agril. Economics, College of Agriculture, Kokan Krishi Vidyapeeth, Dapoli, Maharashtra.

** Suprintendent, Mahatma Phule Krishi Vidyalaya Asond Tal-Dapoli, Maharashtra.

2 million sq. km., and fisherman population of about 8 milllion, India is one of the major fish producing nations of the world. Indian sea food industry ranks seventh in the world in marine production while it is second largest in Inland fish production both from culture and capture fisheries. With the declaration of the Exclusive Economic Zone, India got monopoly over the living and non-living resources of a vast area of 2.02 million sq. kms. in the Arabian sea, Bay of Bengal and Indian ocean. So far as the estimation of marine resource potential is concerned no systematic efforts have been made to locate fishing grounds and asses the resource potential. However, Fishery Survey of India and Expert Groups did some efforts. As per Fishery Survey of India, total fishery resources potential of India was estimated 9 million tonnes, comprising the marine sector's potential of 4.5 million tonnes and Inland sector's potential of 4.5 million tonnes.

In the context of identifying products of high growth potential for export, marine products satisfy almost all requirements of being an ideal exports-oriented products.

Objective

It is to analyze the performance of marine product export from India and constraints in development of marine sector.

Methodology

The performance of marine product export was studied by collecting secondary data from the publication *Marine Products Export — Annual Report* (various issues).

RESULT AND DISCUSSION

Growth

In this section an attempt is made to examine the growth performance of marine products during 1950-51 to 1998-99. Total fish production in India was recorded 5.6 million tonnes (Table 1) in 1988-99. Out of this share of marine products had been 3.03 million tonnes which accounted for 54.10 per cent to the total fish production. While Indland fish production was 2.57 million tonnes and occupied 45.90 per cent share. On the basis of estimated potential of fishery resources, actual fish production amounted to 62.22 per cent and thus 37.78 per cent remains untapped. It was 67.33 per cent amd 57.11 per cent in case of marine and inland fisheries respectively. Thus, gap between fish resource potential and actual fish production clearly shows that there is a great scope for increasing fish production in the years to come.

TABLE 1

Fish Production in India

(Figures in lakh tonnes)

Sr. No.	Year	Marine	Inland	Total	Annual Compound Growth Rates (%)		
					Marine	Inland	Total
1.	1950-51	5.3 (70.66)	2.2 (29.34)	7.5 (100.00)	–	–	–
2.	1960-61	8.8 (75.86)	2.8 (24.14)	11.6 (100.00)	5.20	2.44	4.46
3.	1970-71	10.90 (61.93)	6.7 (38.07)	17.6 (100.00)	2.16	9.11	4.26
4.	1980-81	15.5 (63.52)	8.9 (26.48)	24.4 (100.00)	3.58	2.88	3.32
5.	1990-91	23.00 (59.89)	15.4 (40.11)	38.4 (100.00)	4.02	5.63	4.64
6.	1998-99	30.30 (54.10)	25.7 (45.90)	56.00 (100.00)	3.11	5.85	4.28
7.	1950-99	–	–	–	3.62	5.14	4.19

The progress achieved during the last fifty years in exploiting the fish resources has remained note worthy. It is observed from table 1 that total fish production of Inland fisheries was relatively impressive. Inland fish production increased by 5.14 per cent followed by marine production (3.62 per cent) during the same period. A perusal of sub-period-wise growth rates throws more light on the growth of fish production. During 1950-51 to 1960-61, marine fish production increased by 5.20 per cent followed by inland fish (2.44 per cent) which works out to 4.46 per cent in total fish production. While the second period (1960-61 to 1970-71) showed relatively better performance of inland fisheries (9.11 per cent) but not satisfactory for marine fisheries; its output increased at the rate of 2.16 per cent. During 1970-71 to 1980-81 marine production increased by 3.58 per cent and inland production by 2.88 per cent. During 1980-81 to 1990-91 fish production increased by 4.64 per cent as a result of increased production of marine as well as inland fisheries. However, during 1990-91 to 1998-99 fish production increased to the extent of 4.23 per cent. Higher growth rate was observed in the production of inland fisheries (5.85 per cent) as compared to marine production (3.11 per cent). Thus, fisheries sector has registered consistent growth in the production of marine and inland fisheries, along with marginal ups and downs wings in the magnitudes of the growth rates during 1950-51 to 1998-99.

Exports

As compared to inland fisheries, marine products are export-oriented whose contribution to the total value of agricultural exports has been 17 per cent in 1998-99. It was observed that, of the total marine production nearly 13 per cent marine products were exported in 1998-99. Moreover, the growth performance of the marine products showed that there has been substantial increase in the marine products earnings during 1960-61 to 1997-98. It is revealed from the table 2 that the share of marine exports to total agricultural exports from India has remained less than 3 per cent before liberalization and crossed this mark after liberalization. The quantity exported has also increased from 19.9 thousand tonnes in 1960-61 to 385.8 thousand tonnes in 1997-98.

The Trend analysis (Table 3) of marine products export for the period from 1980-81 to 1997-98 indicates that before liberalization (1980-81 to 1989-90) the quantity and value realized at current prices and constant prices and per unit value had compound growth rate of 4.18, 10.60, 0.05, 6.23 and (-)3.87 per cent respectively. This shows that though export had increased in volumetric and in value terms, the prices realized per unit had declined considerably. After liberalization (1990-91 to 1997-98) the compound growth rates were 15.84, 26.15, 17.02, 8.90 and 2.54 per cent. This indicated positive influence of new liberalized policy on marine exports with increasing trend of exports both in volume and value.

TABLE 2

Share of Marine Fish Products Export to Total Export from India

Year	Marine Fish Product			
	Quantity '000' tonnes	Value Rs. in Crores	Total Export Rs. in crores	Percentage Share to Total Exports
	Pre-Liberalization			
1960-61	19.9	5	642	0.78
1970-71	35.9	36	1536	2.28
1980-81	75.6	235	6711	3.50
1989-90	110.8	635	27682	2.29
	Post-Liberalization			
1990-91	139.4	893	32553	2.74
1991-92	171.8	1374	440.41	3.12
1992-93	209.0	1769	53688	3.29
1993-94	244.0	2552	69751	3.66
1994-95	307.3	3575	82673	4.32
1995-96	296.3	3501	106353	3.29
1996-97	378.2	4124	117525	3.51
1997-98	385.8	4697	126286	3.72

At overall level during 1980-81 to 1990-91 the compound growth rates were 11.33, 20.38, 9.83, 8.14 and (-) 1.08 per cent. This revealed that in post-liberalization era more foreign exchange earnings through marine product exports showed positive growth.

TABLE 3

Trends in Export of Marine Fish Product and Per Unit Value realized

Year	Quantity in '000' tonnes	Value at		Per unit Value (Rs/kg)	
		Current Prices Rs. in Crores	Constant Prices (1980-81) Rs. in Crores	Current Prices	Constant Prices
		Pre-Liberalization Period			
1980-81	75.6	234.84	234.84	31.07	31.07
1989-90	10.8	634.99	292.09	57.29	26.36
CGR (%)	4.18*	10.60*	6.23*	0.05*	-3.87*
		Post-Liberalization Period			
1990-91	139.4	893.37	377.00	64.08	27.04
1995-96	296.3	3501.11	952.30	118.97	32.13
1996-97	378.2	4121.36	1055.07	108.97	35.85
1997-98 (P)	385.8	4697.48	1136.79	121.76	29.47
CGR (%)	15.84*	26.15*	8.90*	17.02*	2.54*
Overall CGR (%)	11.33*	20.38*	8.14*	9.83*	-1.08*

P = Provisional. * Significant at 1% level.

CGR = Compound Growth Rate (%).

Market Trend

Table 5 shows the changing pattern of major markets in quantity terms. In 1981-82 Japan was the major importer of the marine products whose share was 57.07 per cent which declined to 22.98 per cent and further to 17.10 per cent in 1996-97. The share of USA also decreased from 15.02 per cent in 1981-82 to 7.88 per cent in 1996-97; on the other hand, the per cent share of European Union and other countries had increased. The other countries emerged as importers of marine products with increase in per cent share from 14.78 (198-81) to 56.20 (1996-97).

TABLE 4

Market-wise Export of Marine Products

(Quantity in tonnes, Value in Rs. Crores)

Sr. No.	Market	Quantity (Triennum Average 1994-95 to 1996-97)		Value Triennum Average 1994-95 to 1996-97	
		Quantity	% Share	Value	% Share
1.	Japan	56648.33	17.31	1702.18	45.60
2.	USA	29320.66	8.96	430.85	11.54
3.	European Union	76542.67	23.39	809.43	21.69
4.	South East Asia	145842.33	44.56	652.6	17.48
5.	Middle East	8831.00	2.7	66.48	1.78
6.	Others	10106.00	3.09	71.05	1.90
7.	Total	327291.00	100	3732.58	100

TABLE 5

Changing Pattern of Markets for Marine Fish Exports

(Quantity in Tonnes)

Year	Japan		USA		E.U.		Other Countries		Total
	Qty.	% share	Qty.	% share	Qty.	% share	Qty.	% share	
1981-82	40011	57.07	10528	15.02	9202	13.13	10364	14.78	70105 (100)
1992-93	39480	22.98	20844	12.13	55604	32.36	55892	32.53	171820 (100)
1996-97	61656	17.10	29792	7.88	71192	18.82	212559	56.20	378199 (100)

Note : Other countries includes South East Asian countries, Middle East countries and countries like Australia, Sri Lanka, South Asia, New Zealand, Kenya etc.

Major Markets

The details of market-wise exports of marine products are given in table 4. Although India had exported marine products to 69 countries during 1994-95 to 1996-97, Japan continued to be the single largest market accounting for 45.60 per cent share in quantity terms and 21.69 per cent share in value terms. South East Asian countries emerged as one of the largest market (new market) realizing 17.48 per cent of value and 44.56 per cent of quantity (mainly of low valued finish items like Ribbon fish, Reef cod, Croakers and Snappers). The European Union continued to be second largest market in terms of volume of marine product exports mainly of cephalopods. Japan has increased its imports from India especially of frozen shrimp.

Port-wise Exports

The port-wise export along with its share in the marine product export during 1994-95 to 1996-97 is given in table 6. Frozen marine products are exported mainly in reefer containers and as such exports are taking place from the ports which have reefer container facilities. Therefore, the shipments are confined to the 9 major ports namely Mumbai, Kandla, Goa, Kochi, Tuticorin, Chennai, Vizag and Calcutta and the minor port of Porbandar. Live and chills marine products have been exported from airports like Chennai, Thiruvanathapuram, Mumbai and Calcutta. It is observed from table 6 that nearly 80 per cent of the marine products have been exported from west cost of our country. Nearly 25 per cent of marine products have been exported form Kochi port of west coast alone. This reveals the commercial importance of our west coast of our country in exports market of fish.

Monthly Export Trend

The triennum average for year 1994-95 to 1996-97 for the monthly export of marine fish product on quantity and value terms is given in table 7. The quantity as well as value of the marine products steadily increased from the month of September to December. The highest price received per metric tonne of marine product was Rs. 1.78 lakhs in the month of August followed by Rs. 1.74 lakhs in the month of July. The lowest price received was Rs. 0.70 lakhs in the month of February. The overall price received per metric tonnes was 1.12 lakhs.

TABLE 6

Port-wise Export of Marine Fish Products

(Qty. in Metric Tonnes)

Name of Port	Trienmum Average (1994-95 to 1996-97)	% Share
Kandala	32502.00	9.94
Porbandar	65083.67	19.90
Mumbai	39932.67	12.21
J.N. Port	25959.33	7.94
Goa	13625.00	4.17
Mangalore/Bangalore	469.33	0.14
Kochi	81624.67	24.96
Karwar	—	—
Thiruvananthapuram	321.00	0.10
West Coast	259517.67	79.35
Calcutta	14413.00	4.41
Vizag	19462.67	5.95
Chennai	20472.00	6.26
Tuticorin	13208.00	4.04
East Coast	67555.67	20.65
Total	327073.34	100.00

TABLE 7

Monthly Export of Marine Products (Triennum Average 1994-95 to 1996-97)

(Rs. in Lakhs)

Months	Quantity in MT	% Share	Value in Rs. lakhs	Price Received per MT in Rs. Lakhs
April	21565	6.59	23682	1.10
May	20057	6.13	23743	1.18
June	15149	4.63	22785	1.50
July	10987	3.36	19131	1.74
August	16037	4.9	28520	1.78
September	22974	7.02	34119	1.49
October	37059	11.32	40029	1.08
November	46084	14.08	44696	0.97
December	43300	13.23	42708	0.99
January	28211	8.62	30015	1.06
February	29678	9.07	20648	0.7
March	36168	11.05	34850	0.96
Total	327271	100.00	364925	1.12

Constraints

1. Post-harvest Intra-structure is grossly Inadequate

Post-harvest infrastructure required before transport and marketing is totally in the hands of private sector which is too inadequate to handle the marine harvest.

2. No organized landing

The landings of marine fishers is totally unorganized and they create problems in post-harvest management.

3. Harvesting operations of marine fish are fructuous

Harvesting operations of marine fish lack in planning for marketing network and hence fructuous.

4. Spoilage in handling and storage

Due to distant marketing spoilage in handling and storage is a very common phenomenon.

5. Diversification and deep sea fishing fleet

Present deep sea fishing fleet needs to be diversified to handle as existing facilities have impact on the management of near shore fisheries, shore based infrastructure and post-harvest activities and specific needs of marine fish harvesting techniques.

6. Resource specific vessels for long-lining, purse-seining and squid-jigging

Specific vessels in Indian offshore to handle long-lining, purse-seining and squid-jigging, are not available.

7. Inadequate modern fishing vessels of intermediate range (15-19m) to exploit areas between 70-200 m depth

Modern fishing vessels in the intermediate range (15-19m) to exploit areas between 70m to 200m depth to exploit both demersal and pelagic resources, are not available.

8. High risk in deep sea fishing

Deep sea fishing is capital intensive and risk prone.

Challenges

In spite of the increase in production, the per capita consumption of fish in the country is a mere 3.5 kgs. as against the world average of 12 kgs. The proportion of fish eating population in India is expected to increase to 50 per cent by 2020. This constitutes about 650 million of the expected population in India of 1.3 billion. Considering a per capita consumption of 11 kgs. we require around 7.2 million tonnes of fish, of which at least 4.3 million tonnes has to be obtained from the marine sector or an additional two million tonnes of marine fish to meet domestic requirement alone. Further to meet increasing demand for exports a total of six lakh tonnes of marine products will be required. Thus, the total increase in marine fish production required to meet the demand by 2020 would be around 2.6 million tonnes over and above the current production level of about 3.00 million tonnes.

The marine fisheries sector has the following options to meet the challenges of the early part of next millennium.

1. Management of exploited stocks to raise sustainable yields through responsible fishing

Some areas of marine fish sector of India's economic zone call for sustainable exploitating of specific marine zones.

2. Exploiting and monitoring the deep sea fisheries resources

Unexploited deep sea fishing resources should be opened up with careful planning and monitoring to avoid over exploitation.

3. Diversification in sea fishing

Marine fish zme exploitation needs to be diversified to meet domestic as well as export demand in the coming years.

4. Increasing production substantially through coastal seafarming and mariculture

Marine fish production can be increased substantially through modern techniques of coastal seafarming and mariculture which will support for sustainable exploitation of marine zones.

5. Addressing the socio-economic, environment and conservation needs

Attention of planners is required towards releasing of affluents and drainage in sea water to safeguard socio-economic, environment and conservation needs of marine section.

6. Fisheries extension programmes need to be strengthened manifold for fishery folk working in the marine sectors

There is need for modern technology transfer through fisheries extensions programmes on target basis to angument income levels of fishing folk working in the marine sectors.

7. Forword and backward linkages through institutional net work

Market intelligence should be strengthened in the area of demand and supply of fish species alongwith markent news on price trends.

8. Development of technology packages in collaboration with SAUs, NGOs, and state Department of Fisheries

The investment climate is ripe enough for rapid growth in sea fishing. However, technological packages coming through SAUs call for proper linkages between SAUs, NGOs, and state Department of Fisheries. These are the key players to bring about significant growth in marine production.

Summary

Marine products in India are almost export-oriented and dependent on overseas market. The last forty-nine years beginning from 1950-51 have witnessed a substantial increase in the marine product export earnings. It was mostly due to the substantial increase in the unit value realization. Moreover, of the total earnings of marine products, shrimps accounted for nearly 67 per cent of overall foreign earnings of marine products.

Even in the shrimp exports, we have not reached the stage of catering to the actual consumer market abroad. We supply only bulk shipment which are reprocessed/repacked as per local demands in these countries. Therefore, consumers abroad are hardly aware of the fact that the product they consume is from India. It is high time that we try to develop our trade to supply consumer packs so as to establish a better image for our brand and our country. The advance scientific technologies like remote sensing satellite is required to locate marine resources to increase the marine production by easy and quick catch and increase export earning of marine products.

REFERENCES

1. Anonymous (1997), *Marine Products Export Review and Annual Report* of 1996-97, publication of the Marine Products Export Development Authority (MPEDA), Kochi.
2. Anonymous (1999), *India 1999*, A Reference annually published by the Ministry of Information and Broad Casting, Government of India, pp. 305-337.
3. Desai B.M. (1997), *Agricultural Development Paradigm for the Ninth Plan under New Economic Environment* published by Oxford & IBH publishing Co. Pvt. Ltd., pp. 273-286.
4. Devaraj M. (1999), "Marine Fisheries — Regaining the Momentum," in the *Hindu — Survey of Indian Agriculture*, pp. 121-123.

3

WTO and India's Export of Agricultural Products : Challenges and Opportunities

*Biswa Nath Singh**

I

Introduction

The export of agricultural commodities earns not only foreign exchange but also provides the much needed competitiveness in production, productivity and quality when compared to its potential of competitive countries in the global market. It helps to realise economies of scale which benefits the domestic consumers also. Sustained export of agricultural sector encourages modernisation of production, post-harvest processing and marketing system. However, the terms of trade for agricultural sector have been unfavourable for India as it has been unprotected in comparison to industrial sector. Now, under the changing world economic scenario as well as global trade agreements and development of institutions like World Trade Organisation (WTO), the emerging world trading system may claim to change the terms of trade in favour of agriculture and traded goods from India (Gulati, 1997). But several studies reveal that terms of trade are still against the low value added agricultural goods of a developing

*Professor of Economics, Magadh University, Bodh-Gaya, Bihar.

economy like India. The country with about 0.6 per cent share in global exports is not in a position to dictate the terms. Besides, as a member of the WTO, we have several commitments to its provisions related to Quantitative Restrictions (QRS), Trade Related Intellectual Property Rights (TRIPs), Patents, Trade Marks etc., and these provisions are likely to harm the cause of our agricultural growth and export promotion. The loopholes in the provisions of WTO also facilitate the developed world to impose certain restrictions or adopt the policy of protectionism in disguise in the name of qualities restrictions, quota, strict hygenic standards, package standards, labelling requirements, subsidies to their products in different forms and above all the efforts for the implementation of the social clause. The implementation of Trade Related Intellectual Property Rights (TRIPs) may further affect adversely the advantageous position of the Third World countries and especially India in the field of agricultural production, surplus generation and export promotion.

But here the question arises that can India opt out of multi-lateral trading system? Or can India ask the WTO to dismantle all the trading blocks? No, certainly we cannot do so. Then what India can do is to make the efforts to derive the maximum benefits from the process of globalisation and get the status of a Most Favoured Nation (MFN). The process of globalisation is a reality which cannot be denied and also should not be avoided (Ninth Plan, 1997-2000, p. 5). It provides a wide range of challenges and opportunities and so far as the case of Indian agriculture is concerned, it calls for a drastic change from subsistence type of farming to commercialisation of agriculture (Ravi Kumar & Krishna Kumar, 1997) and development of agro-processing and allied activities. It also calls for diversification of agriculture and generation of large agricultural surpluses. In the field of agriculture, India is in a better position in comparison to several other countries of the world as it has vast land resources, diversified climatic and soil conditions, good experience in farming, variety of crops and a vast pool of agricultural scientists to boost agricultural output and exports abroad. Therefore, an effort in this paper is being made to analyse the prospects and problems or the opportunities and challenges of agricultural exports from India in the new regime of World Trade Organisation.

II

Agricultural Exports : The Present Scenario

Increasing production on a sustained basis, rising exportable surplus after catering to the domestic needs and quality improvement through proper processing are among the major essential conditions for export promotion of agricultural products. Low level of output and tough market conditions added by the policy of protectionism in disguise (even after the formation of WTO) adopted by the developed countries have been the leading factors for our poor performance on export front. No doubt, the volume of agricultural exports in rupee terms has been increasing, but its share in our total exports has been fluctuating as is evident from table-1. After peaking the share of 20.4 per cent in total exports during 1996-97, it declined to 19.5 per cent in 1997-98 and 18.5% in 1998-99 (*Economic Survey,* 1999-2000, p. 146). It happened mainly due to a decline in these exports in U.S. dollar value by 11.7 per cent on account of both quantum as well as lower value realised in these two years.

So far as India's share in world trade of agricultural and allied products in concerned, the trend has been rising but slowly and sometimes it has shown a downward trend too in case of certain important products as is evident from table-2.

Under the process of globalisation, except for some restrictions on export of wheat and wheat products, coarse grains, sugar and pulses in bulk, almost all other agricultural products are freely being exported. Agricultural products which are presently being exported include rice, spices, tobacco, cashew, oilmeals, sasame and niger seeds, ground nut, spirit and beverages, guargam, meal oil seed extractions, shellac, sugar and molasses, horticulture and floriculture products, processed fruits and juices, meat and meat preparations etc. In 1998-99, India emerged as a major exporter of basmati and non-basmati rice. The recent trend in export of some principal agricultural and allied products is evident from table-3.

TABLE 1

India's Agricultural Exports

(Rs. in thousand crores)

Year	India's Total Exports	Agriculture and Allied Exports	Percentage Share of Agricultural Exports to Total Exports
1994-95	82.7	13.7	16.6
1995-96	106.4	21.1	19.8
1996-97	118.8	24.2	20.4
1997-98	130.1	25.4	19.5
1998-99+	141.6	26.2	18.5
1999-2000++	104.6++	15.1++	—

+ Provisional.

++ April-November.

Source : *Economic Survey,* 1999-2000, Government of India, table-8.27, p. 146.

The following are the interesting features of agricultural exports from India :

(i) A growing demand stands for basmati rice. The recent spectacular production advancement and favourable buffer stock and growing demand for basmati rice in international market has enabled India to step up its export of basmati rice. Rice export from India increased from 5.05 lakh tonnes in 1990-91 to 49.41 lakh tonnes in 1998-99 (*Economic Survey,* 1999-2000, S. 88).

(ii) There exists a good demand for durum type of wheat in Egypt and West Asian markets.

(iii) In cotton, India can boost varieties of staple length. It can produce the best quality cotton. With sound change in export policy, we should be able to export atleast 25 lakh bales of cotton every year (Ravi Kumar and Others, 97).

(iv) Spices play vital role in export of agricultural commodities. The export earning of spices increased from Rs. 239 crores in 1990-91 to Rs. 794 crores in 1995-96 and Rs. 1617 crores in 1998-99 (*Economic Survey,* 1999-2000, S.89) However, their export declined by 7.72 per cent in 1999-2000.

(v) It can be anticipated that Japan, Korea, etc., will open their rice markets and India can take advantage of these despite the competition from Pakistan, which is already losing the market to India in Gulf countries because it could not maintain quality standards of its produce.

(vi) India is the second largest producer of fruits and vegetables in the world. It has a comparative advantage in growing a variety of fruits and vegetables throughout the year because of diverse agro-climatic conditions and availability of skilled and cheap labour, while in many of the countries such opportunities rarely exist and growing fruits and vegetables is a costly enterprise. The export of fruits and vegetables increased from Rs. 216 crores in 1990-91 to Rs. 802 crores in 1995-96 and Rs. 1067 crores in 1997-98. However, it declined to Rs. 912 crores in 1998-99 (*Economic Survey,* 1999-2000, S.89).

But despite these features, a smooth trend of export growth of agricultural and allied products is skill not visible. On the one side, we have fluctuating trend of agricultural products and exportable surplus and on the other, changes in the world market have a definite impact on our exports.

Being tagged with the global market, our exports have also to bear the burnt of international market situation. The slowdown in the world economy has led to a declining trend in our exports in recent years. In 1998-99, exports declined by 3.9% in U.S. dollar value. It was mainly due to decline in world prices especially the prices of primary products. Likewise, the declining share of agricultural exports to our total exports from 20.4 per cent in 1996-97 to 19.5 per cent and 18.5 per cent in 1997-98 and 1998-99 respectively was due to a decline in their exports in U.S. dollar value by 11.7 per cent on account of both quantum as well as lower value realised in 1998-99. This declining trend continued during 1999-2000 too and a decline by 11.6 per cent in export of agricultural and allied products in U.S. dollar terms led to a further reduction in their share in total exports to only 14.4% during April-November 1999 (*Economic Survey,* 1999-2000, table 8.27).

Structural constraints too operating on the demand as well as supply side of our exports contributed to the slowdown/decline in exports during 1996-97 to 1998-99. The recessionary tendencies across the world severely affected the demand side of our exports. The slowdown and contraction of world trade in 1997-98 also resulted in emergence of protectionist sentiments in some sectors including agriculture in the guise of technical standards and social and environmental concerns. Non-trade barriers like anti-dumping duties, countervailing duties, safeguard measures and other such measures adopted by the developed countries have affected market for exports from the developing countries. Our exports of floriculture, marine products and basmati rice, along with other manufactured commodities to European Union, mushroom products to U.S. and meat products to West Asia have suffered much in these two years. The international trade in agricultural products in increasingly being dominated by concerns of quality to safeguard human health. Importing countries are setting higher standards of quality for food products, where the Indian food processing activities are lagging behind.

Thus, even after the setting up of the WTO, the rich and developed nations have several weapons in their hands and directly or indirectly they have been using them in favour of their own socio-economic and political interests. Several clauses of the WTO itself and especially the provisions related to Intellectual Property Rights (IPR) provide enough scope to these countries to hamper the agriculture in developing economics like India. The entry of multinationals into agricultural sector with IPR would mean a substantial control over entire range of seeds, fertilizers, pesticides and research (Ninth Plan, Vol. II, p. 474). They will not only control important inputs and research but also have a command on investment, production, distribution and marketing. Exports will definitely be badly hampered.

III

Agricultural Exports : Challenges and Opportunities

Agricultural exports, however, have to face enormous problems particularly in developing countries like India, mainly due to serious restrictions on market access. The major world food importers are Germany, USA, Japan, UK, Italy, France, Russia, Neatherlands, Belgium, Luxumberg, Spain, Canada, Hong Kong, Switzerland, Saudi Arabia and Egypt. In most of the developed countries, protectionism in all its forms prevails in terms of high tariff, qualities restrictions, quota, strict hygenic restrictions, package standards, labelling requirements etc. Importing countries are much conscious about the human health and are setting higher standards of quality for food products. But our food processing industries with their limited number and poor performance are lagging behind. Further, there are equally greater restrictions on the import of value added food items from the developing nations. The social clause of the WTO provides a major scope for the developed countries to impose serious restrictions on the import from these countries in the name of labour exploitation and other such reasons. It may affect adversely the export opportunities of agricultural and allied products from India.

The Transnational Corporations (TNCs) also play a dominant role in the spheres of production, trade and distribution of agricultural products from the developing nations and the price received by them. TNCs not only exercise control on prices but also influence the agricultural policy of many developing countries. In respect of food items TNCs have strangle hold in Coffee, Cocoa, tobacco, banana, sugar, wheat and rice. Not only the export of agricultural and allied products to the international market, but these multinationals will influence the domestic market as well. The globalisation of agri-business will lead them to enter the domestic market and their free entry will provide both challenges and opportunities to the domestic companies in the competitive market environment. Challenges in the sense that, the multinational companies have a strong financial, technical, market information, administrative network, which will easily compete with our domestic companies and throw them away from the native market. For example, improved and hybrid seed producing MNCs can compete and drive out domestic seed producing companies like National Seed Corporation, etc., and thus can capture the domestic market too. However, despite such challenges, they also provide good opportunities for the domestic companies in improving the quality of production, in setting-up of agro-based industries, in providing employment opportunities and spreading new technology etc. All these opportunities must be timely taken and utilised by domestic companies so that they can compete well in global trade, otherwise they will fail to reap the benefit.

The Trade Related Intellectual Property Rights (IPR) is another weapon in the hands of these MNCs to enter the agricultural sector with enormous investment potential, high technological level, market experience and command over research, production, distribution and marketing. And by this command, they can also command, control and regulate the agro-based industrial sector, agro-trade and agro-services. In other words, in the name of trade liberalisation and globalisation, we are moving towards monopolisation. We, in the name of globalisation have reduced our 'commanding heights (Rao, C.H. Hanumantha, 1994).

Development in the field of bio-technology that is being developed by the West may also pose a serious threat to agriculture, live stock breading, forestry etc. Some of the large multinational companies in the agro-chemicals, seeds, pharmaceuticals and oil industry have purchased bio-technology firms and are carrying out research in the field of tissue culture, monoclonal antibodies and hybriodomas and gene splicing (recombinant DNA Transfer) to innovate new products and processes. Knowledge concerning developments in the field of bio-technology is kept as exclusive pressure of the Western countries which may cause a lot of harm to export of farm products of developing nations like India (Nasurudeen and Balkrishnan, 1996).

The GATT accord and the consequent WTO provisions also compel for phase-wise elimination of subsidies on agricultural inputs along with other commodities. It has been provided to bring down farm subsidies by the end of the 20th century by the developing countries within 10 per cent of the value of output of a product whereas the developed and industrialised economics today have been paying subsidy from 35% to 90% in different ways to their farm products. So, they will decide how the reduction is to be affected. They will exploit this situation to their benefit. The rich nations generally try (or are trying) to increase their foodgrain exports through high subsidy to the deterimental interest of the poor nations. India, being tied with the GATT accord, is also moving in the direction of phasing out of fertilizer and export subsidies which may affect adversely the farm products and their exportable surplus. The small and marginal farmers will be the worst sufferers. The most important problem in export of agricultural commodities is mainly inadequate surplus due to large scale domestic consumption. India exports only 5-10 per cent of its total output of apples, cherries, grapes, basmati rice, mussoor dal, cotton, etc., and if the removal of subsidies affects adversely the output of agricultural products, the quantum of exportable surplus may further be reduced.

Thus, despite the improvements in recent years in the field of agricultural production and exports, there are several challenges posed by the free flow of goods and services under the policy of globalisation adopted by the new GATT accords and the formation of WTO. But even after such possibilities, the process of globalisation is irreversible. In the contemporary world situation, there is no alternative but to adjust to the realities. To move into the international marketing arena cautiously and surely, the following suggestions can be looked into :

(i) Huge investment in agriculture is needed to boost up the productivity and production in general and in particular special emphasis needs to be laid on the promotion of production and productivity of the selected export oriented agricultural crops.

(ii) Government should assume a more dynamic role in the field of agri-marketing.

(iii) Encouragement to the exports of agricultural commodities which are unique in the world (due to geographical features) and identification of the commodities where there is a real surplus for exports is also essential.

(iv) Setting up of export-oriented farms for selected agricultural commodities particularly for plantation crops and spices for offering incentives to small farmers to pool their operational holdings is also necessary.

(v) Promotion of value added products is also the need of the hour. Deliberate planned efforts are necessary to break away from the traditional form of exporting in bulk. Production and promotion of value added products would help in earning more foreign exchange while at the same time efforts should be made to tackle the problem of increasing production and productivity beyond certain levels.

(vi) Encouragement to 100 per cent export-oriented units. With a view to helping development of value added products, the Government of India should encourage the setting up of units for 100 per cent exports by offering duty free import of capital goods and other requirements.

(vii) Emphasis must be given on value addition by giving thrust to agro-processing industries.

(viii) Air cargo transportation facilities need to be stepped up to meet the delivery of scheduled products with speed.

(ix) A common brand name for promotion of all agricultural products and individual logo for specific commodity/ product is highly necessary.

(x) Systematic planning is essential for agricultural export. Product-wise policy is essential to bring out the necessary consistency in export policy over a long term period. An effective system of market intelligence and research on agricultural exports have to be developed.

(xi) Survey and analytical studies on agricultural marketing should be conducted so that appropriate policy adjustments and refinements could be made for better integration with international market forces.

(xii) There is also a need to provide the facilities for testing packages etc., to exporters. Stringent measures have to be adopted to see that the material being exported is of the desired quality. It would do more damage to export in the long run if poor quality material is exported. The Export Inspection Council of India should be involved closely and the organisation needs to be further strengthened.

Besides these recommendations, greater co-operation is needed between Central and State Governments to plan agricultural production in a proper way for domestic production and export purposes. The much awaited comprehensive agricultural policy of the Government of India must be announced without delay and it must contain among other policy measures, the policy of market friendly export-oriented growth strategy. And finally, we can say that the nature of markets and institutions, industrial organisation and structures and social relations of production as well as the principle and policy of international trade have been transformed dramatically and India's role to the new world order is going to be decided by its response to these changes particularly to the increasing globalisation of economic process.

REFERENCES

1. *Economic Survey,* Government of India, 1999-2000, p. 146.
2. *Ibid.,* S. 88.
3. Gulati, A. (1997) : "Effective Protection and Subsidies in Indian Agriculture — A Case of Wheat and Rice," *IJAE,* Vol. 24, October-December.
4. Nasurudeen, P. and Balkrishnan, V. (1996) : "Agricultural Exports : Prospects and Problems," *The Bihar Journal of Agricultural Marketing,* October-December, p. 326.
5. *Ninth Five Year Plan,* Government of India, 1997-2002, Vol. I, p. 5.
6. *Ibid.,* Vol. II, p. 474.
7. Rao, C.H. Hanumantha (1994) : *Agricultural Growth, Rural Poverty and Environmental Degradation in India,* Oxford University Press, New Delhi.
8. Ravi Kumar K.N., Raja V.T. and Krishna Kumar, K.V. (1997) : "Globalisation and Liberalisation of Indian Agricultural Marketing System — A Critical Note," *BJAM,* Vol. V, No. 3, September, p. 346.
9. *Ibid.,* p. 348.

TABLE 2

India's share in World Exports of Agricultural and Allied Products

(US $ million)

Commodity Division/Group	1990			1995		
	World	India	India's Share (%)	World	India	India's Share (%)
1	2	3	4	5	6	7
Meat and meat preparations	34118	77	0.2	47758	183	0.4
Fish, crustaceans and molluscs & preparations	32847	521	1.6	47318	994	2.1
Cereals and cereal preparations	45314	285	0.6	59461	1576	2.7
Rice	3995	254	6.4	7332	1362	18.6
Vegetables and fruits	50225	400	0.8	70819	682	1.0
Sugar, sugar preparations and honey	14236	21	0.1	19389	156	0.8
Coffee, tea, cocoa, spices and manufactures	21131	842	4.0	33762	973	2.9
Coffee and coffee substitutes	8659	148	1.7	16092	448	2.8
Tea and mate	2650	585	22.1	2414	345	14.3
Spices	1415	109	7.7	1903	180	9.5
Feeding stuff for animals	15603	336	2.2	20537	706	3.4
Tobacco and Tobacco manufactures	17860	145	0.8	24130	113	0.5
Unmanufactured tobacco and refuse	5187	107	2.1	5364	113	2.1
Manufactured tobacco	12674	39	0.3	18766	0	0
Oilseeds and oleaginous fruit	10477	83	0.8	12903	158	1.2

(Contd.)

Commodity Division/Group	1996			1997		
	World	India	India's Share (%)	World	India	India's Share (%)
1	2	3	4	5	6	7
Meat and meat preparations	48405	195	0.4	48326	196	0.4
Fish, crustaceans & molluscs & preparation	47686	111	2.3	48605	1116	2.3
Cereals and cereal preparations	67562	1244	1.8	60866	1250	2.1
Rice	7382	894	12.1	7134	898	12.6
Vegetables and fruits	72191	666	0.9	72505	668	0.9
Sugar, sugar preparations and honey	19657	308	1.6	19148	309	1.6
Coffee, tea, cocoa, spices and manufactures	32964	839	2.8	35014	944	2.7
Coffee and coffee substitutes	13999	402	2.9	16768	404	2.4
Tea and mate	2499	284	11.4	2406	286	11.9
Spices	2026	253	12.5	2314	254	11.0
Feeding stuff for animals	24231	997	4.1	24815	1002	4.0
Tobacco and tobacco manufactures	26808	186	0.7	25908	187	0.7
Unmanufactured tobacco and refuse	6599	186	2.8	7058	187	2.6
Manufactured tobacco	20209	0	0	18850	0	0
Oilseeds and oleaginous fruit	15502	188	1.2	17379	189	1.1

Note : A zero in India's share means negligible or no share at all.

Source : 1997 *International Trade Statistics Year Book* : United Nations 1999, Reproduced in *Economic Survey,* Government of India, 1999-2000, S. 95 and 96.

TABLE 3

India's Export of Principal Agricultural and Allied Products

Quantity in Thousand tonne
Value in Rs. crore & US $ million

Commodity	1990-91			1994-95			1995-96		
	Qty.	Rs. Cr.	$ million	Qty.	Rs. Cr.	$ million	Qty.	Rs. Cr.	$ million
1	2	3	4	5	6	7	8	9	10
Agricultural and allied products : of which	...	6317	3521	...	13712	4367	...	21138	6320
Coffee	86.5	252	141	128.5	1053	335	156.1	1503	449
Tea and mate	199.1	1070	596	151.4	975	311	158.7	1171	350
Oil cakes	2447.8	609	339	4150.8	1798	573	4330.9	2349	702
Tobacco	87.1	263	147	53.7	255	81	87.1	447	134
Cashew kemels	55.5	447	249	80.2	1247	397	70.8	1237	370
Spices	103.3	239	133	155.0	612	195	204.1	794	237
Sugar and molasses	191.0	38	21	51.1	62	20	734.4	506	151
Raw cotton	374.4	846	471	70.7	140	45	33.3	204	61
Rice	505.0	462	257	890.6	1206	384	4914.0	4568	1366
Fish and fish preparations	158.9	960	535	320.9	3537	1126	310.1	3381	1011
Meat & meat preparations	...	140	78	...	403	128	...	627	187
Fruits, vegetables and pulses (excl. cashew kemels, processed fruits & juices)	...	216	120	...	606	193	...	802	240
Misc. processed foods (incl. processed fruits and juices)	...	213	119	...	282	90	...	745	223

(Contd.)

Commodity	1996-97			1997-98			1998-99		
	Qty.	Rs. Cr.	$ million	Qty.	Rs. Cr.	$ million	Qty.	Rs. Cr.	$ million
1	2	3	4	5	6	7	8	9	10
Agricultural and allied products : of which	...	24239	6828	...	25419	6840	—	26164	6219
Coffee	163.0	1426	402	160.3	1696	456	190.1	1703	405
Tea and mate	139.5	1037	292	193.7	1876	505	215.1	2302	547
Oil cakes	4787.7	3495	985	4498	3435	924	3566.9	1912	454
Tobacco	117.0	757	213	144.7	1070	288	91.1	779	185
Cashew kemels	70.4	1288	363	81.3	1407	379	76.6	1613	383
Spices	222.1	1202	339	230.5	1410	379	202.7	1617	384
Sugar and molasses	1716.3	1078	304	246.8	255	69	38.8	23	5
Raw cotton	269.5	1575	444	157.5	822	221	46.3	224	53
Rice	2512.0	3172	894	2398	3371	907	4940.8	6201	1474
Fish & Fish preparations	394.5	4008	1129	398.2	4487	1207	316.1	4368	1038
Meat & meat preparations	...	709	200	—	808	217	—	760	181
Fruits, vegetables & pulses (excl. cashew kemels, processed fruits & juices)	...	828	233	—	1067	287	—	912	217
Misc. processed foods (incl. processed fruits & juices)	...	974	274	—	628	142	—	550	131

Source : *Economic Survey,* 1999-2000, S.88 and 89.

4

Agricultural Policy in Tenth Five Year Plan

Agriculture, Food Security and Land Management

The policy approach to agriculture, particularly in the 1990s, has been to secure increased production through subsidies in inputs such as power, water and fertilizer, and by increasing the minimum support price rather than through building new capital assets in irrigation, power and rural infrastructure. This strategy has run into serious difficulties. Deteriorating state finances have meant that subsidies have "crowded-out" public agricultural investment in roads and irrigation and expenditure on technological upgrading. Apart from the inability to create new assets, the lack of resources has eroded expenditure on maintenance of canals and roads. The financial unviability of the State Electricity Boards, partly due to subsidies on agricultural power supply, has made it difficult to expand power supply in uncovered rural areas and contributed to the low quality of rural power. These problems are particularly severe in the poorer states.

The equity, efficiency, and sustainability of this approach are questionable. The subsidies have grown in size and are now financially unsustainable. Some of the subsidies, *e.g.*, the fertiliser subsidy, are really subsidies to cover the high cost of the fertiliser industry. Other subsidies, *e.g.*, under-pricing of power and irrigation, do not improve income distribution in rural areas and may also be environmentally harmful. Excess use of subsidised fertiliser has created an imbalance between N, P and K, whereas excess use of water has produced water logging in many areas.

It is necessary to evolve a new approach to agricultural policy based on a careful assessment of current constraints and possibilities. A sober and careful assessment of our resources indicates that both land and water will be crucial constraints on our efforts to expand production in agriculture. As a nation we already are in a situation where the extent of forest cover has declined alarmingly. Although in recent years there has been some improvement, we are a long way from our eventual target. In such a situation we do not see any possibility of increase in the cultivated area in the country, and indeed perhaps an eventual decline as urban demand and environmental imperatives lead to conversion of some agricultural land. There is, therefore, no alternative but to focus on raising the productivity of our land water in a manner, which is sustainable over the longer term.

Nevertheless, every effort needs to be made to bring existing uncultivated land into productive use, whether in agriculture or in forestry. For this, it will be essential to evolve a comprehensive land-use policy which will lay out the contours of the ownership and institutional framework that will encourage the productive utilisation of such lands. Furthermore, in order to optimise the utilisation of our land resources, state governments may take such initiatives as deemed appropriate to remove impediments coming in the way of productive utilisation of cultivable land, including tenurial reforms. The Tenth Plan must also focus on increasing work opportunities and productivity of women farmers. Increasing women's access to productive land by regularising leasing and sharecropping of uncultivated agricultural land by women's groups, encouraging collective efforts in bringing wastelands under cultivation and providing policy incentives to women in low-input subsistence agriculture, will have immediate benefits in terms of household food security and women's empowerment.

The first, and possibly the most important, area of focus must be to raise the cropping intensity of our existing agricultural land. Climatically, we are fortunate that it is possible for us to have multiple crops practically all over the country. The critical problem here is water. However, our water resources are also under severe strain. Despite large investments in irrigation in the past, only about 40 per cent of our agricultural area are irrigated. The progress on this front has slowed down considerably in recent years, particularly in terms of major and medium irrigation projects.

Public investment in irrigation has fallen significantly over successive Plan periods. This is largely due to resource constraints faced by governments both at the Centre and the states. However, resources are not the only problem. Potential irrigation projects are located in areas which are either more difficult or environmentally more sensitive which makes it difficult to implement irrigation projects. The Tenth Plan must aim at a major revival of public investment in irrigation capacity and water management. The Accelerated Irrigation Benefit Programme is a potentially important instrument for providing resources to state governments in support of ongoing irrigation schemes. Allocations under this programme need to be massively increased. Greater attention will also have to be paid to rain water harvesting and increasing the irrigation potential through scientific watershed development. There is also considerable scope to improve the efficiency of our existing irrigation infrastructure through better and more participative management practices.

Much of the decline in poverty during the 1980s was due to rise in paddy production in the Eastern India. However, collapse in the supply of electric power in this region during the last ten years combined with no new breakthrough in seeds and technology has led to plateauing of yields. Stimulating ground water development is crucial to kick-start the Green

Revolution in this region as only 1/5th of ground water resource is being utilised.

Watershed and wasteland development—Watershed Development programmes are being implemented by several departments of Government of India, often with different and conflicting guidelines. Even when approach or guidelines are common, sanction of funds is done by different departments and each does separate monitoring. The need for 'a Single National Initiative' has been felt for some time, and was also articulated in the 1999-2000 budget speech of the Union Finance Minister, and in the President's address for 2000-01.

Evaluation reports have shown that watershed projects cannot succeed without full participation of project beneficiaries and careful attention to issues of social organisation. This is because success depends on consensus among a large number of users. Moreover, collective capability is required for management of commons and for new structures created during the project.

The second priority must be the development of other rural infrastructure that supports not only agriculture, but all rural economic activities. A number of recent studies have indicated that the rate of growth of rural incomes and reduction in rural poverty are strongly influenced by the provision of rural and district road connectivity. Other forms of rural infrastructure are also important, but the impact of rural roads in widening the opportunities and alternatives available to our people has a dominant effect. Although this is an area which is in the domain of the state governments, the Centre has taken initiative to provide dedicated funding for a significantly accelerated rural roads programme. It is also necessary to reorient the poverty alleviation programmes in a manner that they contribute more efficiently to the creation of rural assets, both private and community.

The third area that needs attention is the development and dissemination of agricultural technologies. Over the years we have developed an extensive system of agricultural research centres and extension services. There is reason to believe that the quality of the agricultural research effort has weakened while the extension system has virtually collapsed. Strengthening of our agricultural research and development system and a significant improvement in the sophistication of the technology dissemination methodologies are essential for achieving rapid and sustained growth in agricultural productivity. A radical overhaul of the extension service is also needed. Specific measures are necessary to ensure that research, technology development and extension services meet the special needs of women farmers. An increased focus on subsistence crops and technologies in rain-fed/dry land areas would be appropriate in this regard.

Fourthly, serious thought should be given to the issue of declining public investment in agriculture. Although private investment in agriculture has grown, this has often involved macroeconomic inefficiencies (such as private investment in diesel generating sets). Instead of seeking low cost options that have a higher capital-output ratio, present policies have resulted in excessive use of capital on the farms, such as too many tubewells in water scarce regions.

Intensity of private capital is in fact increasing for all class of farmers, but at a faster pace in green revolution areas and for large farmers. Thus, the weight of fertilisers, pesticides and diesel that accounted for a mere 14.9 per cent of the total inputs in 1970-71 in the country increased to 55.1 per cent in 1994-95. For a large farmer in commercialised regions it could be as high as 70 per cent. But the proportion of output sold has increased at a much slower rate than the proportion of monetised inputs, including hired labour. The implication of this is a resource squeeze in agriculture. Whereas the need for resources to purchase these inputs has been increasing, the marketable surplus has been increasing at a slower rate to absorb this, as growth in non-farm employment has become very sluggish. It is not surprising that the repayment of loans is such a problem in Indian agriculture and has even led to suicides in some cases. A better strategy would be to concentrate on small and marginal farmers, and on Eastern and rain-fed areas where returns to both capital and labour are high. The need is also for better factor productivity in agriculture or of a new technological breakthrough, which would be more labour intensive and would cut cash costs.

Finally, we need to recognise that the true potential of Indian agriculture can be realised only when we can diversify our agricultural products, both geographically and over time. The food and nutritional requirements of our people for leading healthy lives demand a wider range of food products than are presently consumed on the average. It calls for increasing the production of pulses and oilseeds. Most of the non-foodgrain food products are, however, perishable in nature. In order to encourage this diversification through minimisation of wastage will require considerable focus on post-harvest technologies and marketing infrastructure. It would also require a reconsideration of the various rules and regulations that govern agricultural trade, which frequently act against the interests of the farmers and distort their incentive structure.

An important component of agricultural diversification is animal husbandry, including dairying and poultry, which hold immense promise for increasing not only rural livelihoods, but urban as well. Proper development of this sector will require attention not only to technology, processing and marketing arrangements, but also to issues of animal welfare. In particular, disaster management programmes for livestock need to be devised since such asset loss can drive the poor into destitution.

A complaint often voiced by representatives of farmers is that the process of economic liberalisation has not been extended to the agricultural sector which remains subject to numerous controls which reduce the potential return to farming. There is merit in this criticism and the Tenth Plan could contribute significantly to agricultural growth if it could address these issues.

To sum up, agricultural output increased in the 1990s because of higher output support price and input subsidies. Now it must come from higher investments in irrigation, seeds, power and roads. Therefore, public investment in irrigation, power and roads should be sufficiently stepped up by reducing subsidies on fertilisers, water and power. Canal systems are in poor shape for lack of operations and maintenance outlay. These should be improved by stepping up plan allocations for maintenance, involving users' groups in management, and appropriate pricing of water to cover operation and maintenance costs. Minimum Support Prices for foodgrains and other commodities will be so adjusted as to promote diversification of agriculture, environmental sustainability, and reduction in food subsidies. And lastly, the Eastern and the rain-fed areas of the central region, which have the highest potential for increase in productivity, would be the focus of attention during the 10th Plan.

These measures in the 10th Plan can place agriculture on higher growth trajectory as well as trigger growth in other sectors, besides reducing poverty.

5

Public Distribution System and Food Security

Despite hefty increase in the annual food subsidy from Rs. 2450 crores in 1990-91 to Rs. 9200 crores in 1999-00 and to Rs. 13,000 crores in 2000-01, all is not well with the Targeted Public Distribution System (TPDS) in India. There is 36 per cent diversion of wheat, 31 per cent diversion of rice and 23 per cent diversion of sugar from the system at the national level. TPDS does not seem to be working in the poorest North and North-Eastern states. The allocation of poorer states such as UP, Bihar and Assam was more than doubled, as a result of shifting to TPDS in 1997, yet due to poor off-take by the states and even poorer actual lifting by the BPL families, the scheme has not made any impact on the nutrition levels in these states.

The challenge is to reduce foodstocks to roughly half its present level and use it for reducing malnutrition, without adversely affecting the farmers. This would need the following legal and policy changes, which would enhance the role of private sector and make markets less distorted than these are at present :

- Amendment of the Essential Commodities Act to make it an emergency provision that will have to be formally invoked by notification for a limited period of time.

- Enactment of an agreed upon Central Act to ban controls on movement within and between States.
- Phase out of all forms of monopoly purchase.
- Remove licensing controls and de-reserve all agri-based and food-processing industries, including sugar, its derivatives and milk processing, in a time-bound manner.
- Announce a policy renouncing the use of export restrictions on agricultural commodities. Domestic shortages should be met by imports, but not by imposing export controls.
- Phasing out of controls on sugar and also removal of sugar from the PDS.
- Remove the present restrictions on establishing new milk processing capacity under the MMPO.
- Lift the ban on futures trading and stocking of all agricultural commodities, and on institutional credit and finance for such activities.
- Remove all restrictions on the export of agri-products.

It is important to emphasise that these initiatives are resource neutral. They do not require the investment of significant public resources but they will help improve agricultural income generation. In addition, the proposed changes discussed below will reduce the surplus with the FCI, as well as reduce leakages. There would thus be massive saving in the food subsidy that can be used for direct income transfer to the poorest and for improving land and water productivity in the poorer areas.

New initiatives have been taken in India in the field of decentralised procurement of foodgrains. Some state governments have, for instance, initiated their own food procurement operations. More such initiatives should be encouraged in the future. Under such a situation it is conceivable that some of the FCI godowns (with staff) are transferred to the state governments. In this context the task of maintaining buffer stocks will become the joint responsibility of the central and state governments. Deficit states should be encouraged to buy directly from surplus states, and they should be compensated for transport and storage etc. These states will most probably hire private agencies to do so, which will bring private expertise into this field.

Most storage godowns with the FCI are small scale low quality structures, or food grains are stored in the open called Covered And Plinth storage (CAP), leading to high storage losses. One should consider fiscal concessions to encourage new godown capacity in the private sector.

The present extraction rates for both wheat and rice are about 10 to 30% below the international standards due to reservation of agro-processing units for small sector who use inefficient technologies. Therefore, remove licensing controls on Roller Flour Mills and other food processing industry. De-reserve food processing units, especially rapeseed and groundnut processing units, from the SSI list.

Private transporters get a low priority on railway movement forcing them to rely on more expensive truck transport. Similarly selective credit controls by RBI restrict access to trade financing by the private sector. These problems deserve attention.

Regulated markets were supposed to improve efficiency, but many Mandies make it illegal for farmers to sell through alternative channels (*i.e.*, selling directly to millers). The markets have thus emerged as taxing mechanisms, rather than facilitating farmers to get the best price.

On the whole, laws and controls have repressed private foodgrain marketing resulting in undercutting its potential contribution to long-term food security.

6

Forests Policy in Tenth Five Year Plan

Forests are natural assets and provide a variety of benefits to the economy. Recorded forest area is about 23 per cent of the geographical area of the country but 41 per cent are degraded hence unable to play an important role in environmental sustainability and in meeting the forest produce needs of the people, industry and other sectors.

The problems and constraints in forestry development include lack of awareness about multiple roles and benefits of forests, especially its role in drought proofing and prevention of soil and water run-off, no linkage between management and livelihood security of the people, low level of technology, inadequate research and extension, weak planning capability, wastage in harvesting and processing, market imperfections, overemphasis on government involvement and control, low level of people's participation and NGOs involvement, lack of private sector participation, unwanted restrictions on felling, transport and marketing of forest produce grown by the people, lack of inter-sectoral co-ordination and weakness and conflicting roles of public forest administration.

Existing policy, laws, rules, regulation and executive orders should be reviewed for removing constraints in holistic development of forestry with people's participation. Areas where action by government is needed relate to :

- Focus on farm forestry has been surprisingly diluted since 1991 despite its enormous potential, especially in agriculturally backward areas. There are better social returns in promoting agroforestry models in the rainfed or semi-arid regions, which contain most of India's marginal lands. It is in this sector that we need to take a big initiative. Similarly tree plantation on marginal and waste lands belonging to the poor is not encouraged. Integrated land-use planning is not being attempted, and common lands adjacent to forests get a low priority in the field after 1991.

- Measures to sustain JFM beyond the project period have not been conceptualised. These relate to : building one-to-one correspondence between user groups and forest patch through a new forest settlement, recognition of JFM groups in law and linking them with statutory panchayats, and integrating the activities of such groups with other income generating programmes such as watersheds and marketing of NTFPs.
- Women, particularly in tribal communities, are dependent on forests for meeting many of their survival needs as well as for income. Protecting women's traditional usufruct rights and enabling women's groups to collect and market NTFPs has been proved to be a viable and cost-effective strategy not only for women's empowerment but also for renewal of forests. It is important to acknowledge and recognise women as managers, food gatherers, wage earners and producers. Forestry development policies must be premised on the basis of this realisation.
- Continuing subsidies on government auctions of wood and bamboo to industries, which acts as a disincentive to industry to pay a remunerative price to farmers. Governments need to examine the pattern of subsidy to forest based industries and wipe out that subsidy in a time-bound manner so as to improve valuation of forests. This will also give a big boost to farm forestry.

- Government must review the tariff structure on forest-based products such as timber and pulp keeping in view the incentive effect on farmers.
- Poor understanding of the social implication of technology; old style plantations still continue to be funded despite the 1988 Policy. We should consider changing forest technology by shifting attention from timber to floor management and production of more gatherable biomass.
- Classification of bamboo as NTFP thereby providing rights to the tribal population and other forest dwellers over this resource. Bamboo harvesting policy systematically maximizes dry bamboo output for paper mills rather than green bamboo output for artisans. In fact the present practices ban felling of green bamboo and streamlining the procedure for making green bamboo available directly to the artisans.
- Gregarious flowering of bamboo is expected from 2003 onward. This will result in mass mortality of bamboos, fire, increase of rodents, famine and unrest in tribal areas. Emergency plan should be formulated to face the calamity.
- Forest fire prevention and control should be given top priority to reduce losses and emission of greenhouse gases.
- Conservation and development of medicinal plants should be given priority to meet the local crude drugs requirement and for export.
- Agroforestry, mountain, watershed development, river valleys, arid areas, wastelands afforestation programme should be given priority.
- Research and technological development must increase productivity, production of new products, value addition, improved marketing, export and productive employment generation.

- Promotion of coastal shelterbelt plantations for prevention of natural calamities.
- An integrated system for addressing issues of animal welfare, including ecology, safety and commercial exploitation will need to be evolved.

It is suggested that for marketing NTFPs, Government should not have a monopoly, nor create such a monopoly for traders and mills. The solution is to denationalise NTFPs gradually, starting with mahua flowers and sal seeds, so as to encourage healthy competition. Encouraging setting up of processing units within the tribal areas is also to be recommended. In fact the Forest Department should be given targets for setting up of such units by the tribals and local groups, so that the role of the FD becomes that of a facilitator, and not of regulator.

Government should give up some of its functions to the market, rather than try to do every thing itself. For instance, retail sale of fuelwood and bamboo can easily be done by the open market. There is no need for having controls under the excise laws on mahua flowers. Its processing and sale can be easily left to free market operations.

Nationalisation also distorts administrative priorities. In central Indian states, the entire forest staff is busy with tendu leaf collection for three months in a year from March to June, with no time for JFM or other important forest related work. It is unfortunate that collection of raw material for a health hazardous industry gets top priority at the cost of forest protection.

7

Promotion of Rural Employment

I. AGRICULTURE AND ALLIED ACTIVITIES

Agriculture accounts for just under 60% of total employment and what happens in this sector is, therefore, extremely important for the employment situation in the economy. However, it is important to recognise that this is not a sector where we should be planning for a large increase in total employment. On the contrary, agriculture has traditionally served as a residual employer, and is, therefore, characterised by considerable underemployment with seasonal variation in employment and relatively low real wages. Our longer term employment strategy should, therefore, aim at absorbing as much of the expansion in the labour force as possible in the non-agricultural sector, thus, reducing the pressure of labour on land and thereby tightening the labour market, so that incomes per head in farming and real wages of agricultural labour rise significantly.

This is reflected in the growth scenarios which project GDP in agriculture to grow by 4% in the high growth scenario (8% GDP growth) and 4.5% in the rapid growth scenario (9% GDP growth), but since the elasticity of employment is only 0.1, the growth in agricultural employment is only 0.4 to 0.45% per year. The resulting productivity growth of 3.5 to 4% per year should help to improve the quality of employment in agriculture through faster growth in real wages of agricultural labour and in incomes per head of the self-employed. However, the desired level of growth in agricultural output and labour productivity will only take place if a number of policy issues in this sector are successfully addressed and market based incentives are created to facilitate greater capital, credit and technology flow. These are discussed below :

(a) Public Investment in Agriculture

Agricultural GDP has been growing at rate of about 3.3% per year in the 1990s and the projected acceleration in between 4 to 4.5% per year. It will definitely require higher levels of investment in this sector. While much of the investment needed will be private on farm investment, the role of public investment in agriculture (including especially irrigation) is extremely important. Unfortunately, public investment in agriculture has been declining in real terms in the 1980s and mostly in the 1990s[1], though there has been some increase in the last three years. Private investment in agriculture has been rising but the trend is offset by decline in public investment so that total investment in agriculture has increased at only a modest rate. Accelerated growth in agriculture in future will require a substantial increase in public investment in agriculture related infrastructure such as irrigation and drainage, land development, water conservation, development of rural road connectivity etc. Such investments are especially needed in the poorer, low rainfall areas of the country, which must now play a larger role in achieving rapid agricultural growth since productivity levels in green revolution areas appear to have plateaued.

Public investment in agriculture is the responsibility of state governments and is, therefore, severely constrained by the fiscal problems of state governments. Resolution of these problems is, therefore, critical for accelerating agricultural growth. It is important to note that although some of the solutions lie in a general improvement in fiscal performance there is also room for restructuring the existing allocation of resources to agriculture by reducing implicit subsidies in this area and utilizing the savings thus achieved to increase public investment. For example, undercharging farmers for power and for irrigation is ostensibly designed to benefit farmers, but in practice it only leads to the power and irrigation systems being starved of resources. The net result being poor maintenance of existence assets and an inability to invest to expand the system, both of which reduce agricultural productivity.

The price distortions introduced by some of the present subsidies also have damaging effects. Low irrigation charges and power tariffs lead to excessive use of water, with harmful effects on soil fertility. The excessive subsidization of nitrogen compared with potash and phosphates leads to excessive use of urea. It can also be argued that the subsidy on urea is primarily a subsidy to high cost domestic producers and not to the farmers. Withdrawing or at least substantially reducing these subsidies and spending the resources thus saved on improving irrigation and pursuing watershed development would be much more beneficial for agricultural production and would promote the employment objective.

The lack of resources to finance investment is not, however, the only constraint in this area. Equally serious is the problem of inefficiency in the use of available resources. The tendency to start new irrigation projects when existing projects are underfunded, leads to a thin spread of available resources, with consequent loss of efficiency. Better prioritization of expenditure to focus on completing ongoing projects is urgently needed.

Poor design of public investment in rural areas is also a serious problem. Many rural development programmes are of a "top down" variety, with little participation by the beneficiaries. The effectiveness of public investments in rural areas in improving productivity can be greatly increased if there is effective participation which requires genuine decentralisation and empowerment of panchayats and zila parishads. There has been some attempt at such decentralization in many States but the situation on the ground varies considerably and there are serious deficiencies in most States. It must be emphasised that these are the areas which fall in the purview of State Governments. Much depends upon the political commitment at the top to bring about these changes which are bound to be resisted by vested interests.

(b) Private Investment in Agriculture

Private investment in agricultural at present consists mainly of on farm investment by the farming community itself. The flow of corporate and institutional investment into this sector which is needed now for next stage of agricultural transformation is negligible. It is necessary to encourage the private corporate sector to invest in agriculture and related activities by facilitating the creation of organised and corporatised entities like Integrated Agricultural Complexes and Food Parks that would attract commercial investments. Innovative policies are needed to facilitate large scale investment into the area of agricultural infrastructure, including irrigation by way of public private partnership.

(c) Controls on Agriculture

One of the factors holding back agricultural growth at present is the failure to extend the benefits of decontrol to the agricultural sector. Liberalisation has had beneficial effects in industry but it has bypassed agriculture which continues to suffer from innumerable controls which hamper realization of potential efficiency. We would recommend the following initiatives to remove existing controls which throttle agricultural development :

(i) The Essential Commodities Act is a central legislation which provides an umbrella under which States are enabled to impose all kinds of restrictions on storage, transport and processing of agricultural produce. These controls have been traditionally justified on the grounds that they are necessary to control hoarding and other types of speculative activity, but the fact is that they do not work in times of genuine scarcity and they are not needed in normal times. Besides, they are typically misused by the lower levels of the administration and become an instrument for harassment and corruption. At a time when European countries have integrated their national markets and regard the resulting large European market as a feature which strengthen their position globally, it is an anomaly that we have laws that actually prevent the development of an integrated national market for agricultural products. After full consideration of this issue, we are of the view that the Essential Commodities Act should be repealed.

(ii) Repeal of central legislation may not suffice as States can introduce controls under State laws. In the interest of creating an integrated national market for agricultural produce, there should be a central legislation that would actually ban imposition of any restrictions on the movement, stocking or forward trading in agricultural commodities. The Ministry of Agriculture in the Central Government, in collaboration with the Planning Commission, should undertake a systematic review of State laws and control orders which impose harmful controls on agriculture and actively seek their repeal. Vested interests and inertia will resist such a move, but we feel that it is an essential step for extending the benefits of economic reforms to agriculture.

(iii) Forward trading in agricultural products should be allowed in a systematic manner with suitable regulation. The introduction of forward markets would help farmers obtain price information and would allow hedging of price risks.

(iv) The marketing of agricultural produce, especially fruits and vegetables is governed by laws that stifle the development of agriculture. The existing laws require that wholesalers must purchase agricultural produce only in regulated mandi's controlled by the Agricultural Produce Marketing Committee (APMC). Since most farmers are small farmers, they cannot directly bring vegetables and fruits to the mandis. They typically sell their produce to village commission agents who collect produce on behalf of the market commission agent who sells to wholesalers in the mandi. Although sale in the mandi is supposed to be by open auction to ensure fair pricing, in practice the price is determined in highly non-transparent manner by negotiations between market commission agents and wholesalers. Lack of transparency is perpetuated by the fact that produce is not graded before it is sold. The prices arrived at in this fashion are declared as the mandi price and the farmer receives the residual price after the commission of the village commission agent and the market commission agent is deducted from the declared market price. Not only is the price determination non-transparent, the large number of middlemen, each of whom charges a commission, squeezes the realization of the farmer so that the gap between the farm-gate price and the retail price paid by the consumer is very large. Although originally designed to protect farmers' interests by creating regulated markets, the system has actually created a monopoly situation in which a small group of traders and agents are able to extract huge benefits. It is absolutely essential to liberalise the existing laws and allow competing markets to be set up. The Government of Karnataka has amended the Agricultural Produce Marketing Act by ordinance to allow National Dairy Development Board (NDDB) to set up a modern fruits and vegetable market in Bangalore. This is a welcome development. We would recommend full decontrol so that any group of persons should be allowed to set up modern marketing infrastructure to facilitate marketing of agricultural produce subject to paying the normal mandi tax. The establishment of competing market will help farmers.

(v) In order to improve the transparency in the operation of APMCs, these Committees should publish on the internet in real time, the daily arrivals, maximum and minimum prices as well as balance of stocks available. This will be a first step towards building an integrated national market for agricultural products.

(vi) Another control instrument which operates against the farmer is the reservation of certain agricultural implements for production by small scale industry. Six of these items were dereserved in 1999 but several other items remain reserved such as cultivators, disc harrows, insecticide dusters (manual), forks, hoses, seed treaters, hand shovels, water lifters, sickles and other agricultural implements. Many of these items can be produced efficiently by SSI units serving local markets and will continue to be produced by them. However, it is surely in the interest of the farmer to allow larger scale units to try to produce superior types of agricultural implements and market them in rural areas. It is illogical to regard agriculture as a priority sector and assert primacy of the objective of improving the conditions of living of agricultural workers, but to deny this sector the best implements which could be produced in India.

(vii) The time has come to review the entire gamut of policies governing procurement and distribution of foodgrains, including the role of the FCI. As we move away from the earlier years of a scarcity economy, we need to take initiatives to encourage the development of private traders who can compete freely with existing public sector entities such as FCI. It is impossible to develop modern private sector trading companies as long as the present system with movement restrictions, restrictions on stocks and lack of forward market continues. Our proposal in (i) above deals with this problem. It is also necessary to do away with the present preferential treatment of FCI in the matter of provision of transport and credit.

(d) Liberalising Leasing of Land

The progressive fragmentation of land holdings, leading to proliferation of very small holdings, poses serious problems in transiting to a high productivity agriculture. There is, no doubt, that much of agricultural technology is scale neutral and small holdings, therefore, can be highly productive but this is not necessarily the case for very small or marginal holdings. According to the 1990-91 agricultural census, almost 60% of the operational holdings were less than 1 hectare and these accounted for 15% of the total area operated. Both percentages are likely to have increased since then because of the continued effect of fragmentation. As fragmentation of land continues in rural areas while real incomes in the rest of the economy increase, more and more of the very small holdings will become unviable in the sense that they will not be able to generate sufficient levels of income to encourage the owners to cultivate them as owner cultivators.

It is, therefore, necessary to liberalise the present laws regarding the leasing of land to allow marginal land owners to lease out land to others to create operationally viable holdings. The legal position regarding leasing varies across states, but at present many states *e.g.*, Uttar Pradesh, Orissa, Bihar, Kerala, Telengana area of Andhra Pradesh, Himachal Pradesh, Karnataka restrict leasing. In other states, leasing leads to the acquisition of tenancy rights which effectively discourages leasing by small farmers. These restrictions are an impediment to the evolution of economically viable operational holdings. It is necessary to consider changes in the land laws which can free up the land market and facilitate the development of viable sized operational holdings.

We recognise that changing the leasing laws is a potentially sensitive issue because these laws are perceived as protecting the interest of small cultivators. However, with the growing commercialisation of Indian agriculture and other changes in the economy, some of the safeguards, which were thought necessary under very different conditions 50 years ago may no longer be relevant. There is now an urgent need to develop a well functioning land market if we are to move to the next level of productivity. Marginal farmers must be enabled to lease out very small holdings with no fear of alienation of land. This requires freeing up the restrictions on tenancy in a manner which would promote efficient agglomeration and development of commercial farming. Tenancy laws can also be relaxed in areas such as Western UP and coastal Andhra Pradesh. To protect the rights of farmer owners, recovery of land by the owner could be made legally unchallengeable. As a measure of abundant caution, these changes need not apply to specified areas, which may be classified as feudal or semi-feudal.

Another dimension along which the rural land market can be freed is with respect to degraded and wasteland, including desert land, saline land & ravines. There are 24 million hectares of land characterised as cultivable wasteland and permanent fallows. Commercial leasing of degraded and wasteland could help to exploit available resources better. Concern is sometimes expressed that such flexibility could be misused and that non-degraded forest land will be misclassified and then leased out. However, such problems could be addressed through careful delimitation. After detailed delimitation, genuine wasteland can be taken out of the purview of land ceiling and tenancy laws, and agro-companies allowed to buy, mortgage, develop, cultivate and sell this land. Commercial leasing can also create problems of environmental degradation as in the case of prawn farming in certain areas where land became highly saline. It would be necessary to protect the interests of lessors in such cases.

(e) Development of Non-Cereal Crops

Faster growth in agriculture necessarily requires agricultural diversification away from cereals towards non-cereal crops such as vegetables and fruits and other allied activities such as floriculture, dairying, poultry etc. These activities are much more labour using than cereal agriculture and will, therefore, help to improve the employment situation. The critical constraint for development of such crops is the lack of marketing linkages and also the lack of development of food processing. As far as marketing is concerned, liberalization of restrictions under the Agricultural Produce Marketing Acts is essential. Private & co-operative organisations should be allowed by urban authorities to set up their own marketing yards in urban areas. This will help in breaking the monopolistic/oligopolistic supply structures for fruits and vegetables existing in some metros, introduce competition and benefit both consumers and farmers.

(f) Agricultural Exports

Export markets are a potentially important source of demand for Indian agriculture in future as Indian agriculture diversifies out of cereal production. The potential for agricultural exports has not been adequately exploited in the past and needs priority attention in future. This is especially so if the renewed WTO negotiations on agriculture succeed in opening markets for our products and controlling the very high trade distorting subsidies to agriculture in many industrialised countries. Agricultural exports are particularly important for employment generation since they are typically very labour using and a more rapid growth of agriculture or agriculture based exports would increase the demand for labour in the agricultural sector.

A major constraint on the development of a dynamic agricultural export sector is the uncertainty generated by frequent resort to export restrictions at the first sign of rising domestic prices. This stop-gap approach to agricultural export has created an environment in which no one has an incentive to invest in building export markets for agricultural products and those that attempt to develop such markets can easily lose credibility and be classified as unreliable suppliers. Export restrictions when they are imposed may appear to hurt only traders, but the ultimate burden is borne by farmers who are denied the benefit of steady access to world markets. We recommend that restrictions on export of wheat, rice, dal, cotton, oilseeds, etc., should be lifted and government should announce a policy that it will not resort to bans on exports of agricultural commodities even if there is a domestic shortage.

In times of shortage of exportable agricultural commodities, government policy should aim at enhancing domestic availability by allowing imports more freely rather than by banning exports. We recognise that pressure on domestic prices can also come from increase in world prices and in such a situation imports may not help in containing prices since import prices will be high. However, in such situations, agricultural exporters should not be denied the benefit of high world prices. If vulnerable groups of consumers are to be subsidised, we recommend that this should be done by providing subsidised supplies through the PDS and making provision for the subsidy in the budget. Furthermore, the quantities to be procured for such subsidized supply should not be obtained only by importing at a high price and subsidising the imported supplies for domestic consumers. They should be obtained competitively from the market, leaving it to suppliers to tender either from domestic sources or from imports.

II. FOOD PROCESSING

India is the second largest producer of fruits and vegetables in the world, but the food processing industry remains highly under-developed. Less than 2% of fruit and vegetable production is processed compared with 30% in Thailand, 70% in Brazil, 78% in the Philippines and 80% in Malaysia. These very low processing percentages above mean that wastage and spoilage in India is very high. Tapping the unutilised potential of food processing including fisheries and marine products is an ideal way of bringing industry to rural areas, providing assured markets for farmers enabling them to diversify into higher value horticultural crops and expanding non-agricultural employment by creating new work opportunities in rural areas.

There are many reasons why food processing has not developed in India as it should have. Part of the explanation lies in the lack of assured electric power in rural areas and also high cost of power to industry. Poor road connectivity to urban markets is another important infrastructural constraint. These are areas where generalized improvements in infrastructure would help the development of non-agricultural activity in rural area in general and food processing in particular.

Government policy has also not focussed adequately on the role of the organised sector in the development of food processing. At present the food processing industry is dominated by small-scale producers, including traditional village industries, with a very small segment of large units including MNCs. The small scale sector is, undoubtedly, an important segment of the economy and and they deserved full support. However, this should not lead to neglect the role of the corporate sector in developing a modern food processing industry. Food processing industry is not a simple matter of taking agricultural products currently grown by farmers and using them as raw material to produce a standard processed product. In fact it is necessary to restructure the food chain from production to consumption keeping in mind the special requirements of the processed food market.

Traditional varieties may not be suitable for processing because the particular requirements of the processed food market are different from food for direct home consumption, or because of the requirements of processing itself. For example, potatoes with high sugar content are not suitable for frying because they change colour. Tomatoes required for making tomato paste need a different solid content than tomatoes for direct consumption. Corporations or modern co-operative organisations are needed to manage the entire chain from farming to food processing to marketing. They have to develop institutionalized relationships with farmers providing them with seeds and other inputs for the varieties needed for the processed food industry along with extension services to overcome technical difficulties which may arise in growing these varieties. They must develop modern storage facilities at the processing stage and also develop methods of handling produce which minimize damage. The identification of varieties that meet the requirements of different markets is obviously crucial since consumer tastes vary across markets, including especially export markets. Standards of quality are also extremely important especially in accessing export markets, though this aspect will become increasingly important even domestically, as consumers become conscious of quality and hygiene standards.

Some of the important policy initiatives that are needed to help promote food processing are the following :

(i) Although government policy allows the entry of larger units including foreign investment into food processing, it is necessary to adopt a more pro-active attitude. Major national and international food processing companies should be approached to ascertain the nature of the problems which limit their activities and interest in India and consideration should be given to making changes in policy which would encourage expanded investment by these companies.

(ii) Government should focus on R&D, information dissemination, extension & training and development of rural industrial estates (food parks). It should also create a policy environment, which supports both private sector and co-operative sector development of post-harvest preservation, quality testing & control labs, silos & warehouses, cold storage facilities, air-conditioned transport and agro-processing.

(iii) A major impediment to the development of a modern food processing industry is the present legal framework which is characterized by a multiplicity of laws and regulations related to food processing which are administered by different ministries and which are often inconsistent with each other. These disparate laws should be integrated into a single Food Act, and a single Food Regulatory Authority should be set up to regulate all the health and safety aspects of food processing, handling etc.

(iv) The Prevention of Food Adulteration Act, which is administered by the Ministry of Health and Family Welfare exemplifies the problem with existing legislation. The Act dates back to 1954 and is extremely restrictive in the category of permitted additives which do not reflect technological options which are now available and widely used internationally. Although changes are possible, the procedure for making changes is extremely complicated and the authorities concerned have shown little flexibility in these matters. The Act is also rigidly administered in the sense that any deviation from what is prescribed, even in the matter of the descriptive content of labels, is treated as an offence equivalent to adulteration which can invite criminal prosecution. There have been instances when smudged labels have been treated as mislabeling and made a basis of criminal prosecution. In one case a label indicated the weight in "kg." whereas the prescribed form under the rule was "kg" and the mere addition of a dot at the end of "kg" was regarded as a material deviation from the prescribed rules! Such provisions clearly deter organized sector companies from expanding in this area while leaving the unorganized sector, which is not effectively policed at all, largely unaffected. We would recommend repeal of the Prevention of

Food Adulteration Act and its replacement by a modern Act in line with prevailing international practice.

(v) The Central level and State level implementation agencies lack adequate manpower and training with the result that implementation is not uniform across states. There needs to be uniformity.

(vi) The present taxation system constitutes a significant disincentive for food processing because the agricultural sector is not subjected to excise taxation and excise taxes are first applied at the food processing stage. Ideally, only the value added at each stage should be taxed. However, since agricultural products are not taxed, no credit can be given for excise paid on these inputs as would happen in a normal modvat chain. Sudden application of the tax rate at the stage of food processing clearly discourages moving up the value chain. The Budget for 2001-02 has exempted processed food based on fruits and vegetables from excise duties but this leaves other processed food (*e.g.*, cereal and dairy based foods unaffected). One way of achieving a more rational tax structure would be by granting a notional excise set off on agricultural inputs. If that is not possible, then a lower rate of tax on the output is desirable.

NOTE

1. This assessment of trends in public investment in agriculture may need to be modified if we take account of the fact that investment in agriculture in national accounts include investment in the form of irrigation but does not include investment in rural roads or development of markets, which are extremely important for agricultural production. It is possible that if these investments are included the decline in total investment may be less than it appears otherwise.

8

Special Employment Programmes for the Rural Poor

1. EMPLOYMENT PROGRAMMES FOR THE RURAL POOR

The major ongoing employment programmes for the rural poor are : (a) the Employment Assurance Scheme (EAS) which is a wage employment programme, (b) the Swarnjayanti Gram Swarozgar Yojana (SGSY), which is a self employment programme involving merger of the erstwhile IRDP and its various component programmes, (c) the Jawahar Gram Samriddhi Yojana (JGSY), which is now conceived as a rural infrastructure development scheme, but which also provides employment to the rural poor.

(a) Employment Assurance Scheme

The Employment Assurance Scheme (EAS) is the only major wage employment programme for rural areas. It was launched in 1993 and was initially limited to the 1778 economically most backward blocks. The scheme was designed to provide supplementary wage employment for the unskilled rural poor in these specially backward blocks where incomes were low and employment opportunities were lacking. The programme was administered by the district administration. In order to ensure that only persons from households below the poverty line obtained employment under this programme, all eligible persons had to register themselves with district

TABLE 1

Expenditure for major Employment Programmes

(Rs.crores)

	Wage Employment				Self-Employment			
	JRY[1]/ JGSY	MWS[2]	IAY[2]	EAS	IRDP/ SGSY	PMRY	KVIC[3]	Total (1) to (7)
(1)	(2)	(3)	(4)	(5)	(6)	(7)	(8)	(9)
1990-91	2588.52	279.74	213.07	—	809.49	44.51[1]	186	4121.33
1991-92	2663.23	495.18	263.01	—	773.09	50.00[1]	193	4437.51
1992-93	2709.59	534.05	233.84	—	693.08	45.00[1]	193	4408.56
1993-94	3878.71	639.74	481.00	183.75	956.65	137.00	208	6484.85
1994-95	4268.33	776.18	500.38	1235.45	1008.32	872.00	216	8876.66
1995-96	4466.91	559.07	1368.34	1720.61	1077.16	1378.00	337	10907.09
1996-97	2156.93	499.10	1383.90	2138.35	1126.90	114.94	309	7729.12
1997-98	2439.38	462.83	1591.48	2904.97	1109.54	1217.43	444.78	10170.41
1998-99	2518.92	474.34	1802.67	2819.77	1160.89	975.79	346.23	10098.61
1999-00	2205.60	*	2132.30	2432.10	1260.70	465.00	20.93	8697.63

Sources : Ninth Plan Document Vol. II, (ii) Annual Plans, and (iii) Basic Rural Stat istics.

Figures for 1999-2000 are based on Budget outlay and not expenditure.

The figures are for Self Employment Scheme for Educated Urban Youth (SEEUY).

Note 1 The Million Wells Scheme (MWS) which was originally a part of Jawahar Rozgar Yojana (JRY) had separate allocations between 1996-97 and 1998-99. But from 1999-2000 it was merged with Swarn Jayanti Gram Swarozgar Yojana (SGSY).

Note 2 With effect from 1992-93 names were attached to rural well construction and rural housing constructions under JRY. From 1992-93 rural well constructions were made under MWS and rural housing constructions under Indira Awas Yojana (IAY). IAY and MWS became separate schemes in 1992-93. MWS was merged to SGSY on 1.4.1999 but IAY continued to be a separate scheme.

Note 3 Expenditures of Khadi & Village Industries Commission (KVIC) are obtained from Department of Small Scale Industry and Agro & Rural Industry.

authorities and only registered beneficiaries were supposed to get employment. In 1997, the programme was extended to all blocks converting it to a geographically universal programme. The programme has been restructured with effect from 1st April 1999. Along with providing wage employment opportunities to rural poor during the period of acute shortage of employment, the secondary objective of the restructured programme is creation of durable community, social and economic assets for sustained development.

A comprehensive evaluation of the EAS by the Programme Evaluation Organisation (PEO) of the Planning Commission has revealed a number of flaws. The wage : material norm of 60 : 40 has not been observed. Genuine muster rolls have also not been maintained. Prescribed norms relating to the type of assets to be created (40% for watershed development and 20% each for minor irrigation link roads and buildings for schools and anganwadis) have not been followed. There has been a tendency to prefer assets such as school buildings and buildings for anganwadis which are not the most labour intensive. However, because of the requirement that employment can only be provided to registered beneficiaries the average employment per beneficiary was found to be 31 days per year, which is much higher than for the JRY (see below).

(b) Jawahar Gram Samriddhi Yojana

The JGSY was introduced on 1.4.99 as the restructured version of the erstwhile Jawahar Rozgar Yojana (JRY), which was itself initiated on 1.4.89 by merging two pre-existing separate wage employment programmes, the National Rural Employment Programme and the Rural Labour Employment Guarantee Programme. The total allocation for the JGSY in 2001-02 is Rs. 1650 crores (BE).

The JRY, like its predecessors the NREP and RLEGP was initially designed as a programme for direct employment generation through the construction of various types of durable assets in rural areas. Some of the infrastructure assets created *e.g.*, irrigation or water conservation works were also expected to contribute to farm productivity in rural areas and thus generate indirect employment, as for example, when irrigation increases cropping intensity and thereby the demand for labour increases. However, this type of indirect employment creation was not the main consideration in choosing the durable assets to be created in the short-term. For example, construction of school buildings may improve the quality of education and thus increase productivity and possibly also employment in the longer-term, but it has limited indirect employment effects in the short-term. Similarly, construction of rural houses or panchayat buildings helps develop rural areas in a broad sense, but does not generate indirect employment in the short-run.

Since the primary objective of the programme was the creation of direct employment, projects selected for implementation under JRY had to conform to the requirement that at least 60% of the expenditure had to be on the wage component. The insistence upon a high wage proportion often made it difficult to undertake work of a durable type that would add to the productive employment potential of rural areas. In other words, there was often a potential conflict between the objective of creating direct wage employment in the short-run and the objective of promoting broader based rural development, with indirect employment creation which is permanent.

An important feature of JRY was that, unlike the EAS, it was implemented at the panchayat level, with funds being devolved to village panchayats, intermediate bodies at tehsil level and district panchayats in the ratio of 70:15:15. Devolution of resources has brought about involvement of elected representatives in selection and implement at ion of the rural works which will in the longer-run ensure greater participation. However, a concurrent evaluation of JRY conducted in 1993-94 revealed several problems.

- Projects selected often bore little relationship to local

needs and conditions reflecting inadequate planning and design capability at the decentralised level.

- Resources were spread thinly to ensure wide coverage of area and as a result the quality of individual works has suffered. The duration of employment created in any area has also been relatively limited
- At the village level there was a strong preference for construction of durable assets. Since these could not be fitted within the prescribed norms for labour : material cost, muster rolls were fudged to get around these norms. The volume of employment reported as being created under the programme is, therefore, exaggerated.
- Fudging of muster rolls is also used for misappropriation of funds and has become a major source of corruption. This also implies that officially reported figures of employment created are exaggerated. According to one study, actual employment created may be only one-third of the reported amount.
- JRY was meant to be implemented by use of local labour but, in practice, works in many areas were carried out by contractors. As a result, employment was provided to labour from outside the area.
- The timing of work was often not consistent with seasonal periods of slack labour demand in agricultural activity. As a result, the employment generated may not have helped to supplement incomes of the poor in the local area.

These problems were sought to be addressed by the restructuring of JRY into JGSY. It was recognised that there is a strong preference at the village level for creation of durable assets which often required acceptance of a lower wage component than 60%, it was also recognised that a programme for construction of community assets must involve the community and, therefore, be "demand driven" with direct employment creation being a secondary objective. In consequence, wage : material norms have been abolished. This is likely to reduce the volume of direct employment creation under JGSY though it could increase the potential indirect employment created by the programme if the assets created are production enhancing. However, this depends upon the rural works being well designed and implemented. There is evidence of improvement as a result of these initiatives especially in the selection of projects based on local needs and also ensuring that local workers get work.

Since both JSGY and EAS are major programmes, which provide rural employment, it is useful to consider their contribution to rural employment creation by taking the two schemes together. The estimated total number of mandays generated under the two schemes based on official records is shown in table 2 along with the equivalent manyears (see footnote to the table for the basis of conversion). The total employment generated by these two programmes in 1998-99 (the last year for which full year information is available) is equivalent to 4.4 million manyears. Compared to the size of the total rural labour force of over 300 million this is only 1.5% and if adjustments are made for the likely over-reporting in official figures, the percentage is even lower. However, comparing the employment created under these schemes to the total labour force in rural areas is not appropriate since these schemes are aimed specifically at the rural poor. If we assume that this segment is about 30% of the rural labour force, the contribution of the employment schemes increases to about 4.5% of the labour force. This is still small but considering the scale of unemployment in rural areas (around 7%) it can be said to make a significant difference. One can, therefore, conclude that the schemes do help to contain the level of unemployment at the margin.

TABLE 2

Employment generated from Rural Wage Employment Programmes

	Mandays of Employment (Lakhs)			
	JRY/ JGSY	EAS	Total (1) + (2)	Manyears of Employment (millions)[1]
(1)	(2)	(3)	(4)	(5)
1990-91	8745.59		8745.59	4.9
1991-92	8092.01		8092.01	4.5
1992-93	7821.01		7821.01	4.3
1993-94	10258.40	494.74	10753.14	6.0
1994-95	9517.07	2739.56	12256.63	6.8
1995-96	8958.25	3465.27	12423.52	6.9
1996-97	7453.88	4030.02	11483.90	6.4
1997-98	3958.00	4717.74	8675.74	4.8
1998-99	3752.10	4165.31	7917.41	4.4
1999-00	1450.05(P)	1515.16(P)	2965.21	1.6(P)

Source : (i) Ninth Plan Document Vol.II, (ii) Annual Plans and (iii) Basic Rural Statistics.

(P) Data for 1999-00 are not for the full year. Data are as per report on physical progress prepared on 3.3.2000 by Ministry of Rural Development.

*Note*1 : While converting mandays into manyears, 180 days' work has been assumed as work for the whole year.

An important feature revealed in table 2 is that the total volume of employment generated by these schemes is not increasing over time. This is because rising material cost and wage rates, and also a shift in emphasis towards asset creation, has made it difficult to increase volume of employment provided by these schemes within budgetary resources available. Since budget constraints are likely to remain very severe, it is reasonable to assume that while special employment progrmmes play an important role in providing supplementary employment which will support income levels among the rural poor, they cannot be expected to generate significant additional employment to meet the needs of the growing labour force. We, therefore, recommend that these schemes should continue but their limitations in contributing to future growth in employment and, therefore, their role in the overall employment strategy should also be appreciated.

(c) Self-Employment for the Rural Poor : From IRDP to SGSY

Promotion of self-employment for the rural poor has long been an important element in the overall employment strategy and the Integrated Rural Development Programme (IRDP) started in 1980-81 has been a major instrument for this purpose. IRDP was designed to assist identified beneficiaries below the poverty line to take up some form of self-employment as a means of generating additional income which might take the households above the poverty line. Eligible beneficiaries below the poverty line were identified by the District Rural Development Agency (DRDA) and assisted through a combination of capital subsidy provided by the government plus credit provided by the commercial banks. The banks were supposed to ensure that credit is extended only to projects which are commercially viable.

Over the years a number of subsidiary and allied programmes evolved under the umbrella of IRDP such as the Training of Rural Youth for Self-Employment (TRYSEM), the Development of Women and Children in Rural Areas (DWCRA) and the Million Wells Scheme (MWS) all of which were introduced in the 7th Plan, the Ganga Kalyan Yojana (GKY) introduced in 1.2.1997, and the more recent the Supply of Improved Toolkits to Rural Artisans (SITRA) introduced in 1992.

On 1.4.99 all rural self-employment programmes were merged into the Swaranjayant Gram Swarozgar Yojana (SGSY) in order to ensure greater integration of the programmes at the implementing level. It is too early to evaluate the impact of the restructuring brought about by SGSY, but it is worth reviewing the limitations of the earlier IRDP, revealed by numerous independent evaluations. It should be noted that these assessments are based on studies of the working of IRDP prior to the recent restructuring of the programme, and some of these deficiencies may have been overcome.

- Beneficiaries were often not of the targeted group and subsidies and loans were appropriated by non-poor individuals through political connections. This vitiates the effectiveness of targeting though it does not by itself negate the employment generating effect.
- The average investment per family was often too low to generate additional income on the scale needed to take families out of poverty. This investment amounted to Rs. 7889 at the beginning of the Eighth Plan. It had risen to Rs. 16,753 at the beginning of the Ninth Plan, but because of inflation the increase in real terms was not very substantial. The inadequacy of the investment means that projects were unviable and, therefore, did not generate sustainable employment.
- The projects selected were often unviable because the beneficiaries were typically not in a position to choose viable projects and manage them. A variety of problems including access to raw materials or lack of markets for their production remain unresolved. The assessment of viability by commercial banks was generally perfunctory because banks typically regarded IRDP lending more as a social compulsion than as normal commercial banking activity.

- The target driven approach to IRDP lending meant that banks engaged in mechanical lending to meet targets. For some time, IRDP became a scheme for distributing milch animals without regard for whether feed or veterinary care would be available, or whether the milk offtake could be assured. The same animal was often sold over and over again to new IRDP loanees. Over time a variety of tertiary activities became eligible for financing but the quality of lending did not improve significantly. In UP, a bank branch gave 20 loans for setting up shops in a village of 143 households.
- There is evidence of massive leakage and corruption. Beneficiaries receiving loans often have to bribe officials of banks and the district administration and this situation is accepted by beneficiaries because there is in any case an impression that bank loans under IRDP do not have to be repaid. The recovery rate from IRDP loans was as low as 32% in 1999-2000 whereas other micro-credit programmes implemented through NGOs such as the Rashtriya Mahila Kosh have recovery rates of 90%.
- TRYSEM was designed as a training scheme linked to IRDP in the hope that the provision of training would help to ensure project viability. However, only 3% of IRDP beneficiaries actually received training under TRYSEM. What is more disturbing, only 23% of those trained under TRYSEM received assistance from IRDP. The training imparted was not related to the capacity or aptitude of the trainees nor to demand for the respective skills. Many TRYSEM beneficiaries viewed the programme simply as a means of receiving a stipend during the training period and not as a way of developing genuine skills which would help in self-employment.
- SITRA provides artisans with a kit of improved

handtools. The financial limit for the value of tools is Rs. 2000 of which the beneficiary pays 10%, the rest being covered by a subsidy. This scheme is reportedly well received by beneficiaries.

- DWCRA is a not her sub-component of IRDP which aims at improving the living condition of women. It encourages collective work in the form of group activities which are known to work better. The nature of the programme varies from state to state but it has worked very well in some states such as Andhra Pradesh, Kerala, Tripura and Gujarat. In Andhra Pradesh, DWCRA is essentially a programme implemented through Self-Help groups. The group approach creates more opportunities for better employment. Watershed development, which generates more employment, is also being encouraged in Andhra Pradesh.

The number of families assisted through IRDP has declined steadily from around 3.7 million per year in the Seventh Plan to 2.2 million in the Eighth Plan and further to 1.8 million per year in the first two years of the Ninth Plan. A large part of the explanation lies in the fact that the total size of the investment required for viable projects has increased whereas the total resources available under the programme have not increased commensurately.

From 1980-81, when the programme began, to 1989-90, the programme has assisted 53.5 million families which is almost equal to the total number of rural poor families in the country. If the programme were really able to achieve its objective of raising assisted families out of poverty it would have achieved nearly complete elimination of poverty in rural areas. It has clearly not been done so for all the reasons documented above. As noted above, some elements of IRDP *e.g.*, SITRA and DWCRA are working well, but the programme as a whole has suffered from serious deficiencies. The restructuring of IRDP into SGSY is definitely a step in the right direction and may lead to improve performance in future.

2. KHADI AND VILLAGE INDUSTRIES

An important element in the government's strategy to promote employment in rural areas is the support provided for khadi and for a number of traditional village industries including beekeeping, handmade paper, ghani oil, pickle masala, dalia, agarbathi, leather products, soap etc. There is no explicit linkage to poverty in the choice of beneficiaries and any entrepreneur willing to promote these industries in rural areas is eligible. The Khadi and Village Industries Commission (KVIC) estimates that in 1998-99 the khadi and village industries assisted sector provided full time employment for 2.6 million persons and part time employment for another 3.3 million. The promotion of Khadi and Village Industries is the responsibility of the KVIC at the apex level, with statutory KVI Boards in each State which assist various implementing agencies, including societies of producers. KVIC has a total budgetary allocation of about Rs. 400 crore in 1999-2000, which is used for the following activities :

- It provides grants and rebates to the implementing agencies to support Khadi and polyvastra. The grants are for interest subsidy, training, marketing.
- Marketing assistance for both khadi and village industries is provided by sales outlets managed departmentally by KVIC as well as by non-department outlets.
- KVIC also has a small training programmes for artisans and entrepreneurs through which a total of 11797 persons were trained in 1998-99.
- KVIC operates a Margin Money Scheme for village industries whereby 25% of the project cost up to Rs.10 lakhs and 10% for additional cost above Rs.10 lakhs is provided as a grant, which has a lock-in-period of 2 years. The scheme is implemented through

the nationalized commercial banks and regional rural banks.

The annual value of output from this sector is estimated at Rs.5000 crores and the net earnings from this activity is estimated at Rs.1500 crores.

The Rural Employment Generation Programme (REGP) of KVI was launched in Eighth Plan and was initially targeted to create 2 million jobs in the Eighth Plan period 1992-93 to 1996-97. The programme envisaged five types of employment generating activities : (i) Khadi; (ii) district level employment programmes; (iii) 125 blocks employment programme introduced in the Gandhi Jayanti year; (iv) national projects for production of hand-made paper, bee-keeping and leather production in rural areas and (v) the margin money scheme (MMS). Progress of REGP was not found very satisfactory and taking into account the slow pick up of the scheme, the target of 2 million jobs under REGP had to be scaled down to 1 million jobs by the end of Ninth Plan. The main emphasis under REGP also shifted mainly to the MMS component.

Under the Margin Money Scheme, 60 per cent of resources needed for a venture are provided by the commercial banks at a subsidised interest rate, about 25 per cent by Government through KVIC, and about 15 per cent by the beneficiary. Eligible agencies under the scheme are : (i) individuals (rural artisans/entrepreneurs) for projects upto Rs.10 lakhs and (ii) institutions, cooperative societies, trusts registered with KVIC/KVIB for projects up to Rs.25 lakhs. 25% of the project cost up to Rs.10 lakhs will be provided by KVIC as Margin Money by way of backend subsidy. For projects above Rs.10 lakhs and upto Rs. 25 lakhs, rate of margin money will be 25 per cent of Rs. 10 lakhs plus 10% of the remaining cost of the project.[1] The borrower is required to contribute 10% of the project cost (5% in case of weaker section). The margin money is deposited by KVIC with the banks initially in its name, and after the sanction of credit by banks, it is transferred as a term deposit of two years in the name of the borrower at the loan-sanctioning branch. This amount will be first available for adjustment by banks to the borrower's loan account after a period of two years from the date of disbursement of the loan.

One of the weaknesses of KVI activity revealed by data provided by KVIC is that the quality of employment opportunities generated from these activities is relatively modest. For example, KVIC data indicate an annual income of only Rs. 4000 for full time workers (*i.e.*, only Rs. 333 per month) and only about Rs.1500 (*i.e.*, Rs. 125 per month) for part time workers. These figures are very low even for rural areas. The khadi programme in particular suffers from some basic infirmities. Costs are high and the product at the lower end of the quality range is not able to compete with mill-produced fabric available in the market. This explains why the production of khadi is decreasing. It was 109 million sq. metres in 1990-91 and has declined to 98 million sq. metres in 1998-99. Employment in this sector has also fallen from 14.15 lakh persons in 1990-91 to 13.85 lakh persons in 1998-99.

The potential for generating employment opportunities in rural areas through establishment of rural enterprises definitely needs to be fully exploited. The scope for expansion of employment in the Khadi sector is very limited and it is likely that employment in this sector will continue to fall. However, employment in village industries could expand provided these units are provided appropriate support in term of credit or marketing assistance. The emphasis under the KVIC programme should, therefore, be given to setting up economically viable rural enterprises with financial assistance from banks, and close monitoring by the banks for the fulfillment of the terms of credit.

NOTE

1. For the weaker section beneficiaries, the margin money grant will be at the rate of 30% of the project cost upto Rs.10 lakh and plus 10% of the remaining cost of the project up to Rs. 25 lakh.

9

Bio-Mass Energy Resource Development in India : with Special Reference to Uttar Pradesh

*Awadhesh Kr. Singh**

Bio-mass resources are contributing substantially towards meeting the energy needs of the developing countries, especially in the domestic sector in the rural areas. Bio-mass, in all forms, supplies almost 14 per cent of the world's primary energy. In the developing world, fuelwood provides a source of energy for basic subsistence, *i.e.*, for cooking and in the developed world, fuelwood is used for power generation. It is presently the largest energy resource in the developing countries where it provides 35 per cent of the primary energy. Bio-mass energy is likely to remain an important global energy source in the future. The total amount of biomass produced, per annum, in India is about 1249 million tonnes. Assuming the energy equivalent of bio-mass as 4400 kilo calories per kg., the total energy comes to about 525 giga-kilo calories. This can be increased by improved photosynthesis and also by developing species which can thrive on saline soils and in favourable environment. Interestingly, about 40 per cent of the generated biomass (potential) can be used as bio-energy resource. This will be equivalent to 350 million tonnes

*Faculty Member, Institute of Development Studies, Lucknow University, Lucknow.

of wood or 175 million tonnes of kerosene in terms of energy. Moreover, the agricultural wastes in India covering crop residues and wastes from agro-industrial operations like rice milling, sugarcane (bagasse) manufacture and production of tea, groundnut coconut oil, etc., come to around 600 million tonnes/year.[1] Availability of animal wastes such as slaughter house waste, animal carcasses, fisheries wates and leather and wood waste is estimated around 45 million tonnes/year. These wastes could also be utilized as fertilizers and raw materials for production of glue and gelatin, liquid soaps, lubricants, etc. The quantity of industrial wastes available in India has been estimated to the tune of 85.5×10^6 tonnes/ year; fly ash (46.42 per cent), wastes from steel industry (40.79 per cent), lime sludge (5.59 per cent), chemicals (5.25 per cent) and red mud (1.75 per cent).[2] On the other hand, urban wastes contain about 46.5 per cent of organic matter, 3.2 per cent of rags, 1 per cent of plastics and about 43 per cent of moisture. The inorganic contents of refuse are relatively recovered and reused but emphasis needs to be placed on utilization of the organic position through combusting, incineration, pyrolysis and sanitary land fills with bio-gas recovery. It is to be noted that domestic waste water ($3650 \times 10^6 m^3$) can contribute 219×10^3 tonnes of potash and 1460×10^3 tonnes of organic matter with value at Rs. 2000 million per annum.[3]

A significant aspect of Indian energy scene is the important role and predominance of non-commercial forms of energy, providing more than 40 per cent of the total energy being consumed in the country. The contribution from the firewood, agricultural wastes and animal dung in the total non-commercial energy consumption in 65 per cent. The share of human and animal power is 15 percent. Industry sector alone consumes more than half of total energy while transport sector accounts for roughly one-fourth of total energy consumed. Source-wise energy consumption in rural household sector demonstrates firewood as the major source of fuel (68.5 per cent) followed by oil product (16.9 per cent), animal dung (8.3 per cent), coal (2.3 per cent), electricity (0.6 per cent) and others (3.4 per cent). It is significant to note that about one-third of the total power supply in India is consumed in the rural areas, even though they constitute three-fourths of the population, only 7 per cent of rural households are electrified, compared to 76 per cent in urban areas. Most of households in rural areas use kerosene for lighting while only 1.2 per cent and 1.3 per cent rural households use LPG and kerosene for cooking, the counterpart urban figures being 27 and 24 per cent.[4] It is also to be noted here that traditional wood stoves are still used in more than 112 million homes, which consume more than 133 million tonnes of fuelwood annually. Moreover, at present 166.85 million tonnes fuelwood is required annually but production of fuelwood is only 28.40 million tonnes per annum leading to 138.40 million tonnes of deficit.[5] It will be difficult to supply 16 million tonnes of LPG, 29 million tonnes of kerosene, 168 Kwh of electricity, 254 million tonnesof firewood to the households in 2010 A.D.[6] In this context, it may be noted that great expectations are placed today on non-conventional renewable energy resources in India provided that wider diffussion of appropriate technologies and sustained growth of renewable energy resources are assured through policy initiatives and environmental driven awareness.

Present paper examines the current profile of energy consumption pattern in rural areas, potential supply of biomass resources, important characteristics affecting the fuel mix in rural areas, potential for electricity generation and commercial use of bio-fuels. Moreover, forest resources in the state of Uttar Pradesh have been critically analysed, and potential for energy plantation in the state has been discussed in detail.

The Rural Economy and Energy Use

The land surface area of India covers nearly 3.3 million km^2 (about 329 million hectares) with three-fourths of total population living in more than 5,68,000 villages. More than half of the total land area is available for cultivation and that proportion is likely to increase in next decade. The land holdings are predominantly small and marginal with an average of slightly more than one hectare. Agriculture, forestry and fishing accounted for about 28 per cent of national gross domestic product while economy is predominantly agricultural one. More than 40 per cent of the rural population in India lives below poverty line. The poor in rural areas gather fuels often at a zero private cost, and it may be difficult for them to switch to commercial fuel, unless these are subsidized. Moreover, rural households are overwhelmingly dependent on traditional fuels, because there has been a very low penetration of commercial fuels and of such alternative technologies as biogas, improved chulhas, etc. The most important energy use in household sector is cooking, consuming 90 per cent of total energy in domestic sector.

Rural energy demand is closely associated to agriculture, and about 70 per cent of commercial energy supplied in the agriculture sector is in the form of fertilizers or pumped water, principally for irrigation, but also for domestic use.

Energy Demand

Interestingly, the bulk of the energy consumed in rural areas (almost 60 per cent) is used by households and more than 90 per cent of rural household energy is consumed for cooking and heating water. This high proportion of energy used for cooking and heating water in rural households is also attributable to the use of by-traditional fuels, dung and fuelwood, with a low efficiency of consumption in traditional devices.

The national aggregate average useful energy consumption from bio-fuels alone is over 725 K. Cal/pc/d (about 3 KJ/PC/d)but there are significant variations among the agro-climatic regions. The fuel mix in the different agro-climatic regions indicates variation, the national aggregate relative fuel mix indicated by REDB data, 59:18:23 for firewood, dung cake and agricultural residues is very close to the one used by the ESI committee and the WGEP (65:15:20) for firewood, dungcake and agricultural residues. There are, however, noticeable differences between the agro-climatic zones in the fuel mix. For example, Eastern plateau and hill have a very high per capita useful energy consumption (1264 K. Cal. or 5.29 MJ) with an overwhelming part coming from firewood (93:0:7) for firewood, dungcake and agricultural residuces. In the upper Gangetic plains, on the other hand, firewood accounts for less than 20 per cent of the useful energy consumption (19:79:3 for firewood, dungcake and agriculture residues). The estimated national aggregate demand in physical units, based on NCAER, IREP and the REDB estimates for firewood, dung cake and agricultural residues are seriously conflicting with each other, the most obvious feature of the different demand/requirement estimates is the wide variation in the estimates. The bio-fuel requirements for the recommended normative energy levels are in the range of 150-240 million tonnes/year of firewood, 40-65 million tonnes/year of animal dung and 47-76 million tonnes/year of agricultural residues. The consumption levels are in the range of 93-252 million tonnes/year of firewood, 54-107 million tonnes/year of animal waste/dung and 36-99 million tonnes/year of agricultural residues. The variation in the national aggregate stands out higher than 95 per cent confidence interval of the REDB estimates. Moreover, the national aggregates seem to give the impression that REDB estimates are constantly higher. In fact, the state-wise aggregates indicate that there is no such clear pattern. For example, the REDB estimates for firewood are higher largely due to higher consumption in the states of Andhra Pardesh, Madhya Pradesh, Orissa, Tamil Nadu and West Bengal. The IREP estimates for firewood, on the other hand, are substantially higher for the states of Gujarat, Kerala and Uttar Pradesh. Similarly, dung cake estiamtes of NCAER for Bihar and Madhya Pradesh are substantially higher than both the IREP and REDB estimates[7] (Table 1).

TABLE 1

Bio-Fuel Use in Rural Uttar Pradesh

(Million Tonnes/year)

Particular	Uttar Pradesh	All India
Firewood		
REDB Average	16.6	252.1
IREP	21.9	169.0
NCAER	15.56	93.30
Dung Cake		
REDB Average	37.2	106.9
IREP	17.2	54.2
NCAER	23.50	83.20
Agricultural Residues		
REDB Average	5.6	99.2
IREP	17.3	62.8
NCAER	6.98	36.70

Note : REDB = Rural Energy Data Base, by Joshi, *et.al.*, 1992

IREP = Integrated Rural Energy Planning, Planning Commission, New Delhi, 1992.

NCAER = National Council for Applied Economic Research New Delhi, 1985.

Natrajan has pointed out that towns and cities were witnessing a transition from bio-mass based fuels (like firewood and cow dung) to petroleum based fuels (like kerosene and LPG) resulting in a drastic decline in urban firewood consumptions from 16.5 million tonnes in 1978-79 to 9.5 million tonnes in 1983-84 even though the urban population had increased during that period, such a change was not discernible in the villages.[8] Natrajan went on to estimate the future demand of firewood for India for the years 1994-95 and 1999-2000 assuming a GDP growth rate of 6 per cent per annum from 1989-90 onwards. He also assumed that as the country's cattle population had not shown any growth in the recent past, cowdung availability would remain stagnant. He arrived at total firewood demand ranging from 146.2 MT to 164.6 MT for 1994-95 and between 183.6 MT to 216.4 MT for 1999-2000 depending on the availability of kerosene in urban areas.[9]

For the first time the Census of India collected data in 1991 on the type of fuel used by different households. The Census results also confirmed that out of the 151 million households in India in 1991 (39.5 million in urban areas and 111.5 million in rural areas), 92 per cent in rural areas and 39 per cent in urban areas were dependent on bio-fuels (Table 2). Besides industrial and timber use, about 62.27 per cent households depend upon wood and charcoal and 15.89 per cent on cowdung cake and bio-gas as their primary source of energy for cooking which put a heavy stress on biomass resouces.[10] However, NCAER data on biomass based fuels in 1992-93 present a different picture. It demonstrates that 55.8 per cent firewood logs, 62.9 per cent firewood twigs, 50.7 per cent crop residues and 63.2 per cent cow dung are used by rural households. More households are getting firewood from their own farms (83.9 per cent in case of firewood logs and 94.2 per cent in case of firewood twigs). It is interesting to note that changes in the percentage of rural households collecting firewood from different sources between 1978-79 and 1992-93 have been observed. More than 48 per cen rural households were reported collecting fuelwood from own farm while 29.8 per cen rural households were collecting fuelwood from roadside, bushes and trees, however, only 17 per cent households were reported to be collecting fuelwood from forests. There was more than 18 percentage points decline in rural households collecting fuelwood from forests during 1978-79 to 1992-93.

TABLE 2

Firewood Usage in India

Percentage of Rural Households Using Firewood	States
90-100 per cent	Tripura, Nagaland, Kerala, Assam, Arunachal Pradesh, Mehgalaya, Manipur, Andhra Pradesh, Himachal Pradesh, Tamil Nadu, Karnataka and Mizoram.
80-90 per cent	Madhya Pradesh, Rajasthan & Sikkim
70-80 per cent	Orissa, Gujarat Maharashtra & Goa
60-70 per cent	Haryana
50-60 per cent	Uttar Pradesh
40-50 per cent	Bihar, Punjab & West Bengal
Percentage of Urban Households Using Firewood	**States**
70-80 per cent	Nagaland and Kerala
60-70 per cent	Tripura and Manipur
50-60 per cent	Assam, Arunachal Pradesh, Orissa, Tamil Nadu and Mizoram
40-50 per cent	Madhya Pradesh, Rajasthan, Andhra Pradesh and Karnataka
30-40 per cent	Uttar Pradesh, Meghalaya and Goa
20-30 per cent	Haryana and Bihar
10-20 per cent	Himachal Pradehs, Punjab, Gujarat and Maharashtra
0-10 per cent	Sikkim and West Bengal

Source : *Census of India*, 1991.

After the second oil crisis hit the world in the late 1970s, the Planning Commission had set up a working group on

Energy Policy which had projected firewood consumption figures in its report submitted in 1979. The report had argued that nationwide firewood consumption would rise to 140 MT in 1983 but would slowly thereafter fall to 138 MT in 1991, 131 MT in 1993 and 97 MT in 2000 because of government programmes aimed at substituting fuelwood. Later, however, the Advisory Board on Energy, a Think Tank set up by the Government of India, in its report submitted in 1985 had projected firewood consumption of the order of 300-330 MT. The NCAER survey data revealed that total household energy consumption in rural areas in 1992-93 was 153.8 MTCR (Million Tonnes Coal Replacement). The average annual growth rate between 1978-79 and 1992-93 was around 4 per cent whereas the number of rural households increased by 2.5 per cent, as a result of which the average household energy consumption had increased from 1047 kilogram of coal replacement (kgcr) to 1329 kgcr. Firewood consumption in the meanwhile had increased from 78.85 MT to 131.37 MT at an average annual growth rate of 4.76 per cent. This level of firewood consumption is quite close to the projections made by the WGEP in 1979 though the reasons appear to be quite different. Not surprisingly, the NCAER 1992-93 survey data shows that though cowdung consumption increased from 66.76 MT in 1978-79 to 86.73 MT in 1992-93, its share fell from 22.51 per cent to 17 per cent. Crop residues consumption also increased slightly from 29.53 MT to 34.96 MT but its share fell from 17.41 per cent to 13.35 per cent (Table 3). In 1992-93 as compared to 1978-79, the NCAER survey reported that not only the share of firewood in the form of twigs had also gone down from 35.62 per cent to 29.11 per cent but also the share of firewood in the form of logs had gone up dramatically from 18.95 per cent to 32.49 per cent. The percentage of households using firewood logs also went up dramatically from 35 per cent to 58.8 per cent.

TABLE 3

Rural Household Energy Consumption in India

Particulars	1978-79			1992-93		
	Quantity	Tonnes of Coal Replacement (Mill.)	Per centage	Quantity	Tonnes of Coal Replacement (Mill.)	Per-centage
Coal/Soft Coke	1.143 MT	1.713	1.92	0.429 MT	0.584	0.38
Kerosene	414.00 M. Ltr.	2.279	2.55	1103 M. Ltr.	6.831	4.44
Cow Dung	66.76 MT	20.087	22.51	86.73 MT	26.151	17.00
Crop Residues	29.53 MT	15.531	17.41	34.955 MT	20.530	13.35
Firewood Logs	20.11 MT	16.905	18.95	57.96 MT	49.989	32.48
Firewood Twigs	58.74 MT	31.774	35.62	73.42 MT	44.785	29.11
Others		0.913	1.03		4.971	3.23
Total		89.202	100.00		153.841	100.00

Source : I. trajan, Trends in Firewood Consumption in Rural India, *Margin*, NCAER, Delhi, October-December, 1995.

Bio-Mass Production and Power Generation

Biomass is a major source and it is consumed globally at nearly the same rate as natural gas. Bio-mass may play an even larger role in the future if it is converted into modern energy carriers mainly fluid (gaseous and liquid) fuels and electricity. There are several reasons for considering bio-mass in this context[11] :

1. Bio-mass is far more widely available than fosil fuels and, with good management practices, can be produced renewably.
2. As development proceeds, consumers want modern energy carriers because they are cleaner and more convenient than traditional fuels.

3. The prospects are good that modern energy carriers can be produced from bio-mass at competitive costs under a wide range of circumstances.
4. If bio-mass is produced sustainably and then efficiently converted to modern energy carriers, biomass could emerge as a major player in the world's commercial energy economy.
5. Modernized bio-mass energy can provide a basis for rural development and employment in developing countries, thereby helping curb urban migration.
6. In developing countries, growing bio-mass for energy on deforested and otherwise degraded lands might provide a mechanism for financing the restoration of these lands.
7. In industrialized countries, growing bio-mass for energy on excess crop lands can provide a new livelihood for farmers who might otherwise abandon farming because of food crop over production.
8. If biomass is grown sustainably, its production and use leads to no net build up of carbon dioxide (CO_2) in the atmosphere, because the CO_2 released in combustion is offset by the CO_2 extracted from the atmosphere during photosynthesis.

Moreover, the material of plants and animals is called biomass. It is organic carbon based material that reacts with oxygen in combustion and natural metabolic processes to release heat. The initial material may be transformed by chemical and biological processes to produce intermediate bio-fuels such as methan gas, ethanol liquid or charcoal solid. The energy storage aspect okf biomass and bio-fuels is of fundamental importance. The net energy density available in combustion ranges from about 10 MJ Kg^{-1} (green wood) to about 40 MJ kg^{-1} (fats and oils), and 55 MJ kg^{-1} for methan. Biomass is, however, mostly carbon hydrate material with a heat of combustion of about 20 MJ kg^{-1} dry matter.[12] The success of bio-mass system is regulated by principles that are often not appreciated[13] :

1. Every bio-mass activity produces a wide range of products and services. For instance where sugar is made from cane, many commercial products can be obtained from otherwise moalsses and fiber. If the fibre is burnt, then any excess process heat can be used to generate electricity. Washings and ash can be returned to the soil as fertilizer.
2. Some fuel products may require more energy to manufacture than they produce, *e.g.*, ethanol from starch crops. However, such an energy deficiency need not be an economic handicap, since process energy can be available at very low cost by consuming otherwise waste material, *e.g.*, straw, crop fibre, forest trimmings.
3. The full economic benefit of agro-industries is likely to be widespread and difficult to assess. The terms of reference have to be carefully established. For example, distinctions have to be made between : (a) the national benefit of increased employment in the rural sector, self-sufficiency, reduced imports, etc. and (b) the projectability of local rural business having to operate for their own interests without national planning.
4. Bio-fuel production is only likely to be economic if the production process uses materials already concentrated, probably as a by-product and so available at low cost. Thus, there has to be a supply of bio-mass already passing near the proposed place of production, just as hydro-power depends on a natural flow of water already concentrated by a catchment. Examples are the wastes from animal enclosures, offcuts and trimmings from saw mills, municipal sewage, husks and shells from coconuts, and straw from cereal grains. It is extremely important to identify and quantify these flow of biomass in a national or local economy

before specifying likely biomass developments. If no such concentrated bio-mass already exists as a previously established system, then the most of biomass collection is usually too great and too complex economic development.

5. The main dangers of extensive biomass fuel use are deforestation, soil erosion and the displacement of good crops by fuel crops.
6. Biofuels are organic materials so there is always the alternative of using these materials as chemical feedstock or structural materials. For instance, palm oil is an important component of soaps; plastics and pharmaceutical goods can be made from natural products; and building board can be made from plant fibres constructed as composite materials.

The potential availability of biomass from crop residues which have energy potential has been estimated to be 1038.608 million tonnes. The crop residues include maize fob, maize stalks, rice husk, paddy stalks, sugarcane bagasse, groundnut shell, arhar sticks, jute sticks and cotton stalks. No doubt, most of these crop residues are being consumed by either agro-based industries or villages in the form of fodder and fuel for domestic purposes. Sugarcane begasse alone constitutes around 80 per cent of agro-residues biomass while paddy stalks accounted for 7 per cent in availability of agro-crop residues.[14] In a study by Pradeep Chaturvedi[15] surplus agro residues in India during 1991-92 is estimated to be 94.20 million tonnes in absolute quantity. This simply demonstrates that paddy stalks, cotton stalks, jute sticks, maize stalks are being consumed by industries and villagers. Thus, out of the total surplus agro-residues in the country, cotton stalks accounted for 28.50 per cent, rice stalk 22.78 per cent, bagasse 19.11 per cent, coir pitch and dust 13.25 per cent, and Jawar (sorghum)and maize stalks 11.96 per cent. Similarly in the state of Uttar Pradesh energy from crop residues can be harvested 20.83×10^{13} k.cal/kg. as a huge potential of biomass energy is available, if it is used in a proper way.[16] Since present calorific value has been estimated on the basis of total main production of crops, roughly 40 per cent can be termed as surplus, *i.e.*, 8.332 × 10^{13} k. cal/kg per annum which is sufficient to produce 7.40 × 10^{7} megawatt electricity per annum.[17] Moreover, potential energy from biomass crop residues, agro-industrial wastes and energy plantations can be harnessed to the tune of 17000 megawatt in Uttar Pradesh.[18]

Forest Resources

Forests play a vital role in the economy of developing countries. A large segment of India's population depends on forests for energy, housing, fodder and small timber. The demands for forest products and services is increasing with the growth in population and economy whereas the forest cover in the country is deteriorating. The increased demand of forest produce, land hunger by the increasing population and forestry are amongst the main causes of deterioration in forest cover.[19]

The recorded forest area of the country is 76.5 million ha. (about 23 per cent of total area of country). However, actual forest cover is 64 million hectare (19.5 per cent of total area) out of which 38.6 million hectare has good forest cover having crown density of more than 40 per cent, 25million hectare is degraded with crown density in between 10 per cent to 40 per cent. Some forest area is virtually blank, even bereft of any root stock. As per the state of Forest Report, 1995, there is a decrease in the forest cover of 507 sq. kms. in the country as compared with that in 1993. Even the density of good forests is decreasing, and the situation is getting worse with further degradation of degraded forests. State-wise forest cover is shown in table 4. The states of Punjab, Haryana and Rajasthan are now left with nominal forest area (below 5 per cent of total area). Another six states have between 5 to 15 per cent of total area under forest (Gujarat, Jammu & Kashmir, Maharashtra, Tamil Nadu, Uttar Pradesh and West Bengal). Seven states — Andhra

TABLE 4

Land Area, Forest Area, Population and Per Capita Area in Selected States in India

State	Land Area (in '000 ha.)	Forest Area (in '000 ha.)	Percentage of Forest Area to Total Land Area	Population (in '000)	Per Capita Forest Area (ha.)	Covered Forest Area ('000 ha.)	% of Covered Forest Area with respect to Land Area
Andhra Pradesh	27507	6376	23.2	66508	0.10	4711	17.1
Assam	7844	3071	39.1	22414	0.14	2406	30.7
Bihar	17388	2923	16.3	86374	0.03	2656	15.3
Himachal pradesh	5567	3759	67.7	5171	0.73	1250	22.4
Jammu & Kashmir	22224	2018	9.1	7719	0.26	2043	9.2
Kerala	3886	1122	28.9	29099	0.04	1034	26.6
Madhya Pradesh	44345	15450	34.8	66181	0.23	13516	30.5
Maharashtra	30769	6384	20.8	78937	0.08	4384	14.2
Gujarat	19602	1939	9.9	41310	0.05	1232	6.3
Sikkim	710	265	37.3	406	0.65	313	44.1
Tamil Nadu	13006	2263	17.4	55859	0.04	1777	13.7
West Bengal	8875	1188	13.4	68078	0.02	828	9.3
Rajasthan	34224	3170	9.3	44006	0.07	1328	3.9
Karnatka	19179	3872	20.2	44977	0.09	3238	16.9
Uttar Pradesh	29441	5166	17.5	139113	0.04	3399	11.5

Source : *State of Forest Report*, 1995 and *Forestry Statistics of India*, 1995.

Pradesh, Bihar, Himachal Pradesh, Karnataka, Kerala, Madhya Pradesh and Orissa — have between 15 and 33 per cent of area under forests. On the other hand, Arunachal Pradesh, Manipur, Mizoram, Nagaland and Andaman & Nicobar Islands have 80 per cent of area under forest cover. In the state of Uttar Pradesh, recorded forest area has been reported to be 51,669.52 sq. kms. and around 80 per cent forest cover is under control of Forest Department. Moreover, 67.2 per cent forest area has been reported in Hill region while eastern region comprises 9.5 per cent forest area and lowest forest area was reported in western region (4.9 per cent). Interestingly,

TABLE 5

Species-wise Plantation in Uttar Pradesh

(Hectare)

Species	Upto the end of 1986-87	1987-88	1988-89	1989-90	1990-91	1991-92	Upto the end of 1992-93	1994-95
Teak	59873	2814	2746	2150	1368	2021	72892	2054
Sal	10021	495	655	545	411	339	13042	69
Eucalyptus	103962	3440	3784	3422	2578	2208	122757	1192
Bamboo	82658	38	76	24	—	—	82802	—
Sissoo	38122	3231	2653	2571	1055	1231	51482	1666
Semal, Gutel Allanthus	11601	48	118	49	7	198	12124	68
Kanju	2332	126	113	65	48	52	2887	58
Khair	13924	322	540	281	321	297	16209	476
Mulberry/Paper Mulberry	2117	58	356	19	5	9	2572	—
Poplar	4678	685	616	411	330	364	7505	375
Deodar	18448	1243	1763	1252	1050	1060	26683	1558
Chir	25235	5233	4271	3523	4094	3938	50374	4795
Cypress/ Bluespine	1414	33	35	7	116	71	2011	618
Fir/Spruce	392	—	11	18	44	23	494	64
Oak	2409	621	1188	769	473	1682	8588	866
Miscellaneous and Mixed	691859	62672	67925	60709	49193	54542	1037500	43026
Total	1069045	81059	86850	75815	61083	68035	1509922	57785

Source : *U.P. Forest Statistics*, 1994 and 1997.

out of total forest area (33986 sq. kms.), 44.3 per cent has been reported in Hills while eastern region comprises just 6.7 per cent forest area. The plantation in Uttar Pradesh has been shown in table 5. Out of 1509922 hectares of plantation upto the end of 1992-93, the important species were reported to be cucalyptus, teak, bamboo, sal, sissoo, khair, deodar, chir and semal gutel allanthus. It is to be noted that the state has growing stock of 3386.33 lakh cubic metre with the volume of 99.71 per hectare. Annual increament of forest resources was reported at 58.18 cubic metre and it has been estimated that demand of raw materials and supply in the year 2000 has a wide gap which is not easy to be narrowed down (Table 6).

TABLE 6

Growing Stock, Volume Per Hectare and Annual Increment and Demand for Forest Produce

Particulars	Unit	Figures
Growing Stock	Lakh Cu. M.	3386.33
Volume	Per hectare	99.71
Annual Increment	Lakh (cu.m.)	58.18
Demand for Raw Materials in 2000 AD		
Raw Material for		
Saw Wood	000 Cu. M.	
Demand		3000
Supply		100
Pulp wood	000 cu.m.	
Demand		2500
Supply		300
Other Industrial Wood	000 cu.m.	
Demand		3500
Supply		200

India has a growing stock of 4.74 billion m^3 with an annual increment of around 87.62 million m^3. The current demand of timber is around 30 million m^3, out of which 8.3 million m^3 is needed for paper, pulp and panel products and 15.4 million m^3 for saw milling, *i.e.*, housing, packaging, furniture, etc. During 1994-95, nearly US $ 600 million worth of wood and wood products were imported. The total timber requirement is estimated to grow to a level of 60 million m^3 by the year 2010 — 20.5 million m^3 for paper and panel products and 27 million m^3 for saw milling. The present requirement of fuelwood in the country is around 280 million tonnes, which is likely to rise to 356 million tonnes by the year 2010.

Productivity of some important timber species in state of Uttar Pradesh is shown in table 7. Productivity cubic metre/ ha. per annum of important species has been reported at just 0.308 while average potential production m^3/ha. Per annum ranges between 8.1 and 12.7. During 1991-92, 520974 m^3 round forest produce was obtained from forest (Table 8). Moreover, during 1994-95, 337196 m^3 round of timber and 227468 m^3 round of firewood, with the value of Rs. 7806.10 lakh, and Rs. 509.53 lakh respectively, forest produces were obtained from forest (Table 9).

TABLE 7

Productivity of Some Important Timber Species in Uttar Pradesh

Species	Forest Area (hectare)	Productivity (cu.m./ha. (per annum)	Average Potentail Production (cu.m./ha./ p.a.)
Fir and spruce	96921	2.18	10.3
Deodar	24675	0.52	10.6
Kail	17534	0.37	12.7
Cypress	5242	1.23	11.5
Chir	412166	1.01	10.02
Sal	437223	0.69	8.1
Teak	69641	0.08	10.0+
Khair & Sissoo	73447	0.34	10.0+
Other/Miscellaneous	2076306	0.13	10.0+
Eucalyptus/Popular	—	3.4	10.0+
Total	4098676	0.308	

Source : *U.P. Forest Statistics*, 1997.

TABLE 8

Major Forest Produce in Uttar Pradesh

(M^3 Round)

Species	1988-89	1989-90	1990-91	1991-92
Sal	70475	82761	74141	86977
Teak	22925	16830	20628	18215
Sisso	18007	14902	12515	11550
Khair	16873	8515	12062	12563
Eucalyptus	280351	198145	159017	156895
Miscellaneous	153023	94147	117000	116396
Total	559654	415300	395363	402596
Chir	114724	55578	71306	62329
Deodar/Kail	20112	9852	11742	32789
Fur/Spruce/ Cypress	4357	5671	7639	23260
Total	139173	71101	90687	118378
Grand Total	698827	486401	486050	520974

Source : *U.P. Forest Statitsics*, 1994.

According to Harikant,[20] logging waste along on account of fuelwood belleting of axe is equivalent to 472200 wagons of soft coke or 7041 megawatt hours of electricity. Wood waste as chips in coniferous forests is equivalent to another 0.4 million m^3 of fuelwood. If requisite infrastructure is developed in potentially exploitable areas which have not been tapped so far, about 6.05 million m^3 of fuelwood can be made available.[21]

Energy Plantations

Energy crops are those planted mainly in order to obtain energy as substitute for petrochemical products. They are selected with primary objective of obtaining the greatest possible quality of energy under given geo-climatic conditions.

TABLE 9

Forest Produces in Uttar Pradesh

Species/Items	Unit of Quantity	Production			Value (Lakh Rs.)		
		1992-93	1993-94	1994-95	1992-93	1993-94	1994-95
Timber	M^3 Round	410330	469962	337196	7012.85	9234.75	7806.10
Firewood	M^3 Round	294123	359580	227468	523.54	769.50	509.53
Resin	Qtl.	79421	77767	67452	1362.07	1553.57	1463.71
Tendu Leaves	Qtl.	193940	141573	183667	2116.00	2113.68	2901.94
Bamboo	Score	312466	241555	208675	121.86	94.21	102.25
Khair Gilta	Qtl.	5154	27185	27082	54.61	271.85	297.90
Baib Grass	Qtl.	34741	30440	27510	42.03	36.95	37.14
Medicinal Herbs	Qtl.	16343	142020	19243	17.32	16.62	24.83
Hides & Horns	Qtl.	1252	1476	2351	1.25	1.62	2.84
Honey & Wax	Qtl.	515	304	519	11.10	7.30	13.71
Cash Crops	Qtl.	38570	34680	40810	343.16	339.17	439.09
Gum	Qtl.	1362	1281	6320	14.62	15.12	82.05
Fish	Qtl.	4050	1874	4576	45.00	29.98	80.53
Boulder &	M^3	146348	322418	320687	607.58	472.09	571.22
Bajari		2855091	2196991	2418418			
Lime/Livestock	M^3	603196	—	128665	301.60	227.99	237.17
		—	414521	346793			
Misc. Grass	Qtl.	28877	102133	—	4.90	18.38	—
Fodder Grass							
Grazing	Qtl.	106769	42140	15619	367.28	160.13	119.00
Canes	Bundles	2851	2977	1595	3.36	3.48	1.34
Miscellaneous	—	—	—	—	385.39	342.06	69.84
Total Values					13335.52	15688.45	14760.13

Source : *U.P. Forest Statistics*, 1997.

Such crops may use either plants traditionally used for food (sugarcane, grains, sorghum, beet, artichoke, cassava, etc.) or non-food plants (bamboo reed, mediterranean thistle, forest species) with a great capacity for producing biomass, often under marginal agro-climatic conditions. The main objective of energy forestry/plantation programme in India is to produce fuelwood rather than industrial wood. 'Therefore, selection of species for different agro-climatic conditions has assumed greater significance. The specific objectives for the selection of species are[22] (i) larger biomass field; (ii) high calorific value; (iii) fast growth; (iv) good capacity (regeneration of the harvest); (v) high adaptability; (vi) use of establishment; (vii) little after care; (viii) identification of plants for problem regions and (ix) species with nitrogen fixing ability.

There are many advantages of energy plantations in the Indian context, this system provides almost an inexhaustible and renewable source of energy which is essentially local and independent of the unreliable finite source of fuel. Establishment of these plantations can help to release quantities of cow dung at present being inefficiently utilized for direct use as organic manure or fermented anacrobically to yield methane and nutrient rich slurry for land application. Energy plantation also provides a number of additional products like fruits, seeds, oil, edible leaves and roots, and base for rearing of silk worm, tannins from bark, medicinal products and other useful products. Apart from this, energy plantation lessens the burden on forest resources.

Even if one-third of the estimated 80 million hectares of barren and waste land can be recovered by energy plantation programme, a generation capacity of about 48000 MW can be created, which is considerably more than the entire installed power capacity in the country today from all thermal, hydro-nuclear sources. Moreover, power from energy plantation could be available from a number of decentralised installations, thus minimising transmission and distribution cost. This would also provide fuelwood and charcoal to meet the cooking needs of the rural poor, provide green biomass cover in arid zones and raise rural income. The investment cost for such projects could be only about Rs. 12,000 per kw.[23] It is to be noted that energy plantation with a predicted crop yield of 15 tonnes of dry poplor per hectare per year can lead to electricity production of 10,000 to 12,000 kw/hectare/year. India generates a vast amount of bio-mass material which can be utilised for power generation.

The average yield of fuelwood for forest has been recorded at 0.5+ hectare/year. If all the 345.85 million tonnes of fuelwood equivalent energy requirement was to be met from fuelwood alone, then plantation of over 606 million hectare would be required. Different experiments and reserches conducted under projects, funded by the Government of India, have indicated through energy plantation demonstrations an achievable average productivity of cultivation of 20 tonnes per hectare per year. In that case total area required for meeting the fuelwood need would be only 15.15 million hectare. Yield recorded under 22 different bio-energy varieties/species in the research centres have shown productivity upto the 36.80 and minimum to 6.2 tonnes/hectare/year while the average yield computed so far is 17.25+ tonnes/hectare/year.

TABLE 10

Estimated Land Suitable for Plantations in U.P.

Plantable Sites	Unites	Area
Along Road Side	Km.	21,988
Along Canals	Km.	19,443
Along Railway lines	Km.	2,325
Community Land	hectare	199, 095
Degraded Forest Land	Hectare	434, 049
Private land of farmers not suitable for agriculture	Hectare	839,400*
Non-Forest degraded area	Lakh hectare	66.35
Forest degraded area	Lakh hectare	14.26

*Including 438000 hectares of alkaline/Saline land.

Source : *U.P. Forest Statistics*, 1997.

In India, saline and alkali soil land consists of about 7 million hectares of area in Uttar Pradesh, Gujarat, West Bengal, Rajasthan, Punjab, Maharashtra, Haryana, Orissa, Karnataka and Madhya Pradesh. Of these, around 1.05 million hectare is in Uttar Pradesh. Out of total waste land in India (1295.80 million hectare), 80.61 million hectare waste land was reported in Uttar Pradesh. Again, out of total waste land in Uttar Pradesh, 66.35 million hectare is non-forest degraded land while 14.26 million hectare is forest degraded land. Estimated land suitable for plantation in Uttar Pradesh has been shown in table 10. In India, large area can be exploited which is being left out without proper use *viz.*, side area of railway tracks, roads, canals, drainage and tributaries. It works out that if 5-6 rows of trees and plants at a distance of 2 metres are planted, strip plantation at 25 per cent survival rate basis would yield nearly 1200 million tonnes fuelwood yearly.

Constrains in Development of Bio-Energy

The energy planners and policy makers in India have generally supported conventional sources of energy for a variety of socio-political reasons. Although, subsidies and financial incentives were given liberally to Renewable Energy Technologies (RETs), these technologies remained marginalized in the overall energy scenario. The total investment in renewable was too small and mostly on an experimental basis for demonstration purposes without any long-term planning or commitment.

Financial Constraints

The viability of various technologies vary depending upon the location and context, which related to the technical input-output parametric reltionship. Extending those to financial results in using their opportunity cost poses a real challenge for energy planner. Because of difficulties in assessing realistic cost and benefits of renewable energy projects financial cost acts as critical barrier to the dissemination of RETs in country.

Technical Constraints

There is a number of technical barriers which inhibit the diffusion of renewable technologies in India *e.g.*, irregular availability of primary resource for many renewable technologies; follow-up, and the consequent need for back-up based on the conventional sources of energy. Moreover, lack of standardisation in system components resulting from the wide range of design features and technological standard and absence of long-term policy instruments have resulted in manufacturing services and maintenance difficulties.

Social Constraints

Intensitively on the part of policy makers and planners to take into various socio-cultural factors in renewable programmes proved a costly mistake in terms of failure in field trails. In most of cases social and cultural aspects have assumed equal importance with technological or financial factors.

Policy Measures[24]

The following are some of the priority areas to meet various criteria and constraints regarding utilization of renewable energy sources and particularly bio-mass energy resources :

1. Improving Efficiency of Traditional Use Pattern

The present use of fuelwood, burning of combustible materials in the open traditional chulhas is not viable. These traditional chulhas emit smoke, which is dangerous to health and environment. It uses a lot of fuel, which is collected by women and children. It is obvious that the less efficient chulhas, the greater is the need of fuel and resultant loss of valuable resources and time. It is hazardous as burns and scale can result from spark emitting from burning logs or from unstable pots. Development of efficient energy conservation devices such as furnaces, stoves (chulhasa), heat exchanges, and a host of others can not only provide clean fuel with minimum smoke but also produce adequate energy to meet all the needs of the household or processing units, small or large. Therefore, improved chulhas should be widely used for cooking purpose. It will involve popularity, mobilisation and priority action programme to conserve fuelwood.

2. More Stress on Bio-Gas Plants

The high cost of power generation, transmission and distribution especially in remote areas calls for the immediate need for popularising the traditional fuel wood as the major source of domestic fuel to save the forest resources as well as greenness. In view of high cost of commercial sources of energy such as kerosene oil, diesel, petrol and electricity and still insignificant development and popularity of solar devices, emphasis should be placed on bio-gas plants to provide not only gas for homes but also manure for land, consistent with sanitary conditions. Several studies suggest that full utilization of existing bio-gas plants is still a major constraint, besides large number of bio-gas plants are faulty. Therefore, appropriate rural technology development especially in case of bio-gas plant is called for.

3. Development of Multiple Use Pattern

The establishment of technological devices for generation of energy from bio-mass is viable and eco-friendly. These should be used to meet the energy needs for parboiling, mining, bran stabilization and oil extraction and setting up many new industries based on ash, gram oil and deoiled bran. Many chemical and agro-based industries can also be sustained through establishing technological devices for conversion of energy and use of by-products from crop residues and plants.

4. Need for National Bio-Resource Policy

Energy from bio-mass specially crop residues has been considered as viable and cost effective. Bio-mass resource also seems as an industrial raw material besides providing source to sustain agro and chemical industry. Therefore, a national Bio-Resource Policy is imperative for each country. Such policy should include bio-mass resource survey, bio-mass generation, mobilization of bio-mass through a resource management system and conversion technology. Such a policy should be integrated with other national policies, to focus resource management research and development and utilization of energy sources.

5. Bio-Energy Education

The success of bio-energy resources production and utilization is not possible unless we have a clear-cut policy regarding bio-energy education. Bio-energy programme is very vast in magnitude and has production, conservation and utilization aspects. Involvement of people at all levels, teaching and training apart from curriculum development for school and colleges is highly desirable.

6. Promotion of Energy Plantation

Several studies have suggested that there is a huge deficit in the availability and demand of fuelwood in the country. India has a wide area of waste land that can be easily used for plantation of fast growing plants that will serve the purpose of meeting our energy requirement and also have economic-environmental benefits.

7. Structural Changes in the Institutions

A fundamental change is required in institutional set-up. Structural modifications are required at the national, state and district level institutions to make the renewable energy programme more effective and meaningful. At each level, it is very important to integrate renewable energy planning within an overall energy planning process in India.

Although, energy is a recognized constraint for most sectors of the Indian economy. There is no integrated energy policy for the country as a whole. The energy sector itself is fragmented into various ministries and departments, *i.e.*, the Ministry of Power, the Ministry of Petroleum and Natural Gas, the Ministry of Coal and the MNES. The absence of coordination under one nodal ministry for energy could be an important reason for duplication, over-lapping and poor performance of energy sub-sectors in India. While there are a number of high-powered committees with representation from the concerned Ministries and Departments for coordination of energy projects and programmes, in reality, these committees mainly look after just the clearance of new power projects.

8. Networking of Institutions and Integration of Programmes

Networking of various institutions and private enterprises is a vital change required for the ultimate success of the renewable energy programme in India. The lab-to-land concept which connected agricultural universities with individual farmers during the green revolution in India should be used to transfer technology to entrepreneurs and industries. A networking approach would ensure participation of all concerned actors involved in the promotion of renewable energy programmes. In this process, government departments and agencies would essentially play a coordinating or facilitating role and would provide the overall framework of action, or an enabling environment for commercialization of renewables in India. The NGOs (Non-Governmental Organizations), private sector and research centres could play a pivotal role in the delivery process.

In the Indian context, this change in roles and networking appraoch would be a very difficult process initially, but would ultimately help in the successful implementation of renewable energy programmes. The government could also play another important role of facilitating the transfer of technology through lowering import barriers, removing distortions in fiscal policies (making a level playing field for renewables), laying down standards and promoting north-south co-operation in research and development.

9. Strengthening Linkages with NGOs and Voluntary Organizations

Given the size of the country and magnitude of the problem, participation of NGOs and VOs (Voluntary Organizations) is a pre-requisite for ensuring success in renewable energy programmes. The promotion of renewable energy resoruces require development of local level capacity of integrated systems within local economics and environment.

In this respect, NGOs and Vos can play an important role in providing the interface between the government and the people promoting field demonstration and helping in commercialization efforts.

10. Strengthening of Training Facilities and Information Dissemination

Many institutional barriers can be overcome by organizing proper training for the target groups and the trainers, and introducing a free flow of information for awareness, feedback and appreciation. The solar cooker programme could have had a greater impact in the rural areas if training target groups had been emphasized in the first place. Similarly, information dissemination can be very effective in informing the target groups of the environmental benefits of using RETs. Strengthening training facilities and promoting free flow of information on the technologies, their economic and social aspects could be an effective strategy to promote RETs in India.

11. Establishment of Power Project

On the basis of available bio-mass in a taluka/Tehsil installation of power project for generation of electric and energy sources is socially and economically viable. Developing of such a technological device would provide energy sources to nearby industries and households for various purposes. The most appropriate technological devices may be gasifire and stir ling engines.

REFERENCES

1. Moudal, *Jorunal of IAEM*, Vol. 22, 1995, pp. 203-208.
2. *Ibid.*
3. *Ibid.*
4. Das, Anjana and Dayal, Vikram, "An Energy Shortage Closer to Home," *Economic Times*, January 15, 1998.
5. Chaturvedi, P., *Bio-Energy Resources : Planning Production and Utilization*, Concept Publications, New Delhi, 1995, p. 31.
6. *Op.cit.*

7. Sinha, C.S. and Joshi, Vina, "Bio-fuel Demand Estiamtion in rural and Renewable Energy : Perspectives from Developing Countries," in Venkat Ramanna, P., (ed.) *TERI*, Delhi, p. 139.
8. Natrajan, I., "Trends in Firewood Consumption in Rural India," *Margin*, NCAER, Delhi, October-December, 1995.
9. Agrawal, "Myth About Forest Depletion : The False Predictions," *Down to Earth*, Vol. 7, No. 1, May 31, 1998, p. 31.
10. Jafri, S.S.A., *Misuse of Biomass as a Primary Source of Energy in India : A Serious Threat to Environment*, Working Paper 21, International Society of City and Regional Planners & Japan Association for Planning Administration, JAPA, OGAKI-Japan, 17-20 September, 1997.
11. Hall, David O' *et al.*, *Biomass for Energy : Supply Process, in Renewable Energy Sources for Fuels and Electricity* (ed.) Thomas, B., Johnson, *et al.*, Earthscan Pub. Ltd., London, 1993, p. 596.
12. Twidell, J.W., *Renewable Energy Resources*, University Press, Cambridge, U.K., 1987, p. 282.
13. *Ibid.*
14. Singh, A.K, *Assessment of Bio-mass Energy Resources in Uttar Pradesh, Project Report*, 1996, SRISHT, Lucknow.
15. Chaturvedi, Pradeep, *op. cit.*, p. 31.
16. Singh, A.K., 'Bio-Mass Energy Resources in India," *Kurukshetra*, August 1998.
17. Singh, A.K. and Singh, U.P., *Human Ecology and Development in India*, Ashish Publications Pvt. Ltd., Delhi
18. NEDA, Government of U.P., 1997.
19. Oberai, C.P., "Sustainable Afforestation : Key to Sustainable Development," *Yojana*, August 1997, p. 31.
20. Harikant, "Logging Waste : A Potential Source of Energy," *Indian Forest*, 107 : 818-22, 1981.
21. Vimal, O.P. and Tyagi, P.D., *Energy From Biomass,* Agricole Pub. Academy, New Delhi, 1994, p. 42.
22. *Ibid.*
23. Chaturvedi, P., *op. cit.,* p. 93.
24. Sing, A.K., "Rural Energy Scenario : An Approach to Non-Conventional Energy Resources," paper presented in National Seminar on "Emerging Trends in Indian Economy,' held at Yojana Bhawan, Lucknow, 28-29 April 1998.

10

Progress, Problems and Prospects of Floriculture : An Economic Analysis with special reference to West Bengal

*Subrata Kumar Ray**

INTRODUCTION

Accelerated growth in agricultural production and productivity is very urgent for overall stability of the Indian economy. The rapid commercialisation of agriculture through diversification in Indian agriculture is needed for the acceleration of agricultural growth. Diversification in favour of horticultural crops, say, flower crops is more rational because these crops are characterised by high productivity per unit of area, much higher returns, higher potential for employment generation and exports, comparatively lower requirement of water, etc. It is to note that floriculture has become much more commercialised in recent years following sweeping changes in the global markets. Development in recent times in terms of quantum jump in yields of flower crops and institutional thrust in exploiting the export potential clearly reveal the great future for the growth of flower crops in India. "Considering the powerful thrust that floriculture can give to the overall economy, the National Commission on

*Lecturer and Head, Department of Economics, Sabang S.K. Mahavidyalaya, Midnapur, West Bengal.

Agriculture (NCA) has recommended 5 lakh hectares of land under floriculture by 2000 A.D. to raise production".[1]

Therefore, the rapid expansion of cultivation of flower as a non-conventional commodity of modern commercial agriculture may be thought as an urgent need today for both the stability to the economy and improvement of economic well-being of Indian farmers, in particular, the resource — poor farmers. In this context, the questions that may arise are : what is the scenario of floriculture in the country? What are the factors influencing the growth of floriculture? What are the constraints limiting the growth of floriculture? What are the prospects of floriculture in India? The present study is a modest attempt to seek answers to these and other related questions.

The importance of such study arises out of two considerations :

(1) the importance of the floriculture in the national economy and

(2) the inadequacy of existing literature to give answers to some of the issues stated above.

Importance of Floriculture

Han's love for flower is as old as humanity itself. Asthetic sense of mankind is eternally connected with its existence with equal importance as that of food and subsistence. The famous saying testifies this — "If I had two pence, with one I would buy a loaf of bread, with the other a rose."[2] Flowers and ornamental plants are very important today from asthetic, economic and social point of view.[3] Development of floriculture has assumed considerable importance in recent times following both internal and external demand.[4] In European countries flower cultivation has become a commercial occupation providing livelihood to a good number of producers. India is also slowly but steadily moving towards that direction.[5] Floriculture has occupied a significant position in the agricultural sector of the economy as an important source of employment and income for the farming farming families, particularly, the small and marginal ones in the perspective of low and declining landman ratio and the consequent proliferation of marginal farmers. Flowers cultivation is highly labour-intensive and particularly suited to small holdings. All floriculture products having a high demand both in the internal market and abroad can be produced in some or the other parts of India because of agroclimatic varieties prevailing in different zones.[6] Though there were ups and downs over the years the export of cut flowers and flower buds from India has been registering a significant increase in recent years.[7] It is to note that the share of floriculture in total horticultural products exports from India has risen from 0.84% in 1991-92 to 1.91% in 1995-96 (DGCIS, 1996). Again the annual exponential growth rate of flower exports from India has increased from 6.92% during 1978-79 to 1979-80 to 15.56% during 1980-81 to 1995-96 (Sau, 1998). Again, the continued stagnation of exports emphasizes the development of floriculture (having strong export potentiality) as a device for maintaining the stability of Indian economy. Therefore, the good export potentiality, labour-intensive cultivation methods, lower cost of cultivation, etc., of flowers highlights the very importance of expansion of flower cultivation in the country for solving the problem of unemployment and poverty. The expansion of flower cultivation can improve the economic condition of the poorer of the poor. An acre under flower cultivation can help support a family consisting of five to six members. It can fetch an annual income of Rs. 30,000, if much valued flowers like orchids, carnation and gladiali are grown over the said area.[8]

Flowers have also enormous medicinal properties.[9]

Review of Existing Literature

The existing literature on floriculture may broadly be classified into the following categories :

(i) Studies related to the Horticultural Products

There exists a large number of studies related to the production, marketing and exports of horticultural produces *viz.*, Kaul (1997), Rao (1997), Dahiya and Singh (1997), Prakash and Srivastava (1997), Singh (1997), Jugale (1997), Krishnaiah (1997), Jairath (1997), Prasad and Yadav (1997), Kumar, Kushwaha, Singh and Singh (1997), Khodaskar (1997), Sharma (1997), Rao and Rao (1997), Arora, Saxena and Tewari (1997), etc.

(ii) Production and Marketing of Flowers

The studies on the production and marketing of flowers are not very large. For example, Alagumahi, Apjugam and Rajesh (1997) have studied the performance of flower crops *vis-à-vis* field crops in Madurai districts of Tamil Nadu. Singh, Prasad, Nigam and Saran (1997) have studied the economics of flower production in the district Farukhabad of Uttar Pradesh (U.P.). They concluded that the flower cultivation has a great potential for increasing income and employment of the farmers of the study area. Saini and Sharma (1997) have examined the economic sustainability and market potential of hi-tech floriculture in Himachal Pradesh (H.P.). Koranne and Naik (1997) have made an attempt to work out the cost and returns in the cultivation of rose and tuberose on a commercial basis and its economic viability for the sample cultivators in Akola and Buldhana districts of Maharashtra state. Samaddar (1995) has studied the prospect of floriculture in West Bengal (W.B.) and concluded that neither modern technologies nor organised marketing is being practised at present. There are also a few other studies related to the production and marketing of flowers *viz.*, Bhattacharya (1995), Laskar (1995), Saha and Mukherjee (1995), Saha (1994), Agarwal and Duhiyod (1997), Bal and Bal (1997), Rahim and Sarkar (1997), Dahiya, Goyal and Pandey (1997), Maiti (1995), Maitra (2000) etc.

(iii) Export of Floricultural Products

Ashokan and choski (1997) have examined the problems and the potential for exporting Indian floricultural products and the constraints faced by the Indian exporters. Sharma, Nadda and Sharma (1997) have studied the status and constraints of floriculture export trade and suggested that there is a need for a coherent strategy with major focus and speedy importation of hi-tech infrastructure, germplasm material etc. to strengthen the export-oriented floriculture in India. Sau (1998) has studied the trend and potentiality of flower exports from India.

Thus, the brief review of the existing literature on floriculture would indicate its inadequacy to give sufficient answers to our research questions. Our present study is an attempt to remedy some of the gaps that exist in the existing literature.

Scope and Objectives of the Study

From this brief review of existing literature it may be said that there is a need to examine (i) the current scenario of flower cultivation in India; (ii) the reasons behind the expansion of flower cultivation *i.e.*, the factors influencing the growth of floriculture in the country; (iii) the constraints limiting the growth of floriculture in the country and (iv) the prospects of floriculture in the country.

To fulfil the above mentioned gaps for research, the present study sets the following objectives :

(i) To examine the trend of area, production and yield of flowers in the country.

(ii) To analyse the economics of floriculture with special emphasis on the factors influencing the growth of floriculture in the state like West Bengal.

(iii) To examine the problems and prospects of floriculture in the country.

Outline of the Study

Section II discusses the hypothesis of the study. Section III provides the data base and methodology used in the study. Section IV examines the trend of area, production and yield of flowers in India by major states and West Bengal by major districts. Section V discusses the economics of flower cultivation with special reference to the force behind the development of floriculture. Section VI discusses the problems of floriculture in the country. Section VII discusses the prospects of floriculture in the country. Section VIII summarises the findings made earlier and makes some concluding observations.

II

HYPOTHESES

The hypotheses which are tested in this study are as follows :

(1) The area, production and yield for flowers have risen over years for the sample areas.

(2) The smaller the size of land holdings, the larger the percentage of area under floriculture.

(3) The larger the percentage of area under floriculture, the larger the employment of labour, particularly, female labour and child labour.

(4) The larger the percentage of area under flower cultivation, the larger the profit per unit of cultivated area.

(5) The larger the credit availability, the larger the percentage of area under floriculture and hence larger the profit per unit of cultivated area.

(6) The flower cultivators live above poverty line.

(7) Gross earnings from floriculture constitute a significant percentage of total family income.

(8) The lower the resource base of cultivator households, the larger the percentage of area under floriculture.

III

DATA BASE AND METHODLOGY

In this study both the primary and secondary data have been used. On account of various deficiencies of secondary data, primary data have been collected from 40 farm households of two villages *viz*., Bargachiya and Tahala in Midnapur (East).

Simple statistical techniques like, average, regression, corelation, etc., have been applied. Benefit-cost ratios have been calculated for different crops (where net returns include the contributions of family labour also).

The study area covers all India, selected 21 states namely, Andhra Pradesh (A.P.). Assam, Bihar, Delhi, Haryana Karnataka, Madhya Pradesh (M.P.), Maharashtra, Punjab, Tamil Nadu, Manipur, West Bengal (W.B.), Uttar Pradesh (U.P.), Jammu & Kashmir (J&K), Himachal Pradesh (H.P.), Rajasthan, etc., and selected five districts of West Bengal *e.g*., Midnapur, Nadia, Howrah, 24-Parganas (N & S) and Darjeeling, different blocks of Midnapur (East) district and two villages of Midnapur (East) District.

IV

TREND OF AREA, PRODUCTION AND YIELD OF FLOWERS

A. State Level Analysis

It is observed that the percentage of area under flowers to Gross Cropped Area (GCA) has increased over years during 1988-89 to 1997-98 for India and the sample states *viz*., Andhra Pradesh (A.P.), Delhi, Haryana, Himachal Pradesh (H.P.)., Jammu & Kashmir (J & K), Karnataka, Madhya Pradesh (M.P.), Orissa, Punjab, Tamil Nadu and Manipur. In other words, the Cropping Pattern (C.P.) has changed in favour of flower cultivation for India and those sample states (Table-1). In this context, we may examine the trend of area under flower cultivation in different states of India during the same period. It is observed that the area under flower cultivation in India has increased from 28809 hectores in 1988-89 to 73970.88 hectores in 1998-99 (this increase is 156.76%). The state level analysis reveals that the area under flower cultivation has increased over years during 1988-89 to 1998-99 for most of the sample states (Table-2). For example, the area under flower cultivation in West Bengal has increased from 3150 hectores in 1988-89 to 10,500 hectores in 1998-99 (this increase is 186.34%). The percentage change of area during 1988-89 to 1998-99 is the highest (3958.82%) for Delhi, but that during 1993-94 to 1998-99 is highest for Daman & Diu. On the other hand, the percentage share of area under flower cultivation in 1988-89 has been highest (29.10%) for Tamil Nadu. This percentage share in 1998-99 has become largest (28.09%) for the state of Karnataka. The states like Andhra Pradesh, Assam, Delhi, Haryana, Himachal Pradesh, Karnataka, Madhya Pradesh, Manipur, Orissa, Punjab, West Bengal, have increased their percentage share of area under flower cultivation to total area under flower cultivation of India during 1988-89 to 1998-99. For example, the percentage share of area under flower cultivation in West Bengal has increased from 10.93% in 1988-89 to 14.19% in 1998-99.

Let us concentrate on the trend of production of flowers in different states of India during 1993-94 to 1998-99. It is observed that the production of loose flowers in India has risen from 232536. 3 M.T. in 1993-94 to 459163.41 M.T. in 1998-99 (this increase is 97.46%). But the production of cut flowers in India has increased from 5122.8 lakhs in 1993-94 to 1155.13 lakhs in 1998-99 (Table-3 and diagram-1). An increasing trend of flower production is found for most of the states in India during 1993-94 to 1998-99. For example, the production of loose flowers in West Bengal has risen from 9020 M.T. in 1993-94 to 58,000 M.T. in 1998-99 (this increase is 543.01%). Karnataka has ranked first in the production of flowers (87998 MT) during 1993-94. Karnataka has taken a lead in production of rose, Carnation, Chrysanthemum, gladiolas, Ornamental foilage, plants, etc.

Kerala has started production of orchids, anthurian and foilage plants on commercial basis. In West Bengal also, roses, winter season flowers, "Rajanigandha" and foilage plants are grown on commercial basis.[10] Again, Tamil Nadu has produced largest amount of flowers (133, 125 MT) in 1998-99.

Let us now focus on the flowers crop-wise trend of area, production and productivity in different states of India during 1993-94 to 1995-96. It is observed that the area under most of the flower crops, *viz.*, rose, gladiolus, marigold, jasmine, chrysanthemum, carnation etc., has shown as increasing trend for most of the sample states during 1993-94 to 1995-96 (Table-4). Similar increasing trend is also observed for the production of these flower crops. It is to note that in case of West Bengal the area and production of different flower crops have declined over years during 1993-94 to 1995-96. For example, the area under rose has decreased from 1987 hectores in 1993-94 to 1080 hectares in 1995-96 (*i.e.*, by 64%). The area under Jasmine and gladiolus has also decreased during this time period.

The productivity of different flower crops show no definite trend for those sample states. In case of Uttar Pradesh, the percentage of area under gladiolus to total area under floriculture is highest (36.86% in 1994-95 and 36.31% in 1995-96). In case of West Bengal, marigold occupies the largest percentage area (15.86% in 1993-94 and 16.78% in 1995-96). Rose has a leading role in floriculture of Daman & Diu. In case of Pondichery the percentage of area under rose and Jasmine has increased over years during 1993-94 to 1995-96. Gladiolus plays a leading role in floriculture of Manipur (since the percentage area is highest during 1993-94 to 1995-96). In case of Orissa, the percentage area under gladiolus, marigold, chrysanthemum, tuberose has increased over years during 1993-94 to 1995-96. In case of Punjab, the percentage area under gladiolus and chrysanthemum has increased over years during the same period. Rose plays a leading role in floriculture of Rajasthan (since percentage area is 60.25% during 1994-95 to 1995-96). On the other hand, gladiolus occupies the largest percentage area (60%) in floriculture of Himachal Pradesh during 1993-94 to 1995-96. But the jasmine occupies the largest percentage area in floriculture of Karnataka during the same period. Marigold has a leading role in floriculture of Maharashtra, Assam, Bihar and Haryana during 1993-94 to 1995-96. In case of Delhi, the percentage area under chrysanthemum, tuberose has declined over years during 1993-94 to 1995-96.

B. District Level Analysis

Focussing on the district level scenario of West Bengal in 1987-88, it is observed that Midnapur has the largest contribution in the production of flowers in West Bengal (Table-5). Again, the yield rate and under cultivation of flowers are also higher in case of Midnapur as compared to other sample districts of the State. Therefore, Midnapore district (particularly, Midnapur (East)) has a leading role in the yield of floriculture production in the State. This needs a closer look on the floriculture of Midnapur (East) district. It is observed that though the total area, production and yield of flowers (as a whole) in Midnapur (East) has increased in 1997-98 as compared to 1986-87, but that is not so for different varieties viz., summer flower (only the area has declined over years) and winter flower (only the area remained constant) (Table-6). The percentage increase in production and yield in 1997-98 as compared to 1986-87 has been very impressive in case summer flower in Midnapur (East) district.

C. Block Level Analysis

Let us examine the trend of area, production and productivity of flowers in different blocks of Midnapur (East) District during 1986-87 to 1997-98. It is observed that the area, production and productivity of most of the flower crops viz., summer flowers, winter flowers and bhadoi flowers have shown as increasing trend for most of the blocks in Midnapore (East) district during 1986-87 to 1997-98 (Table-7, 8 & 9).

For example the area under summer flowers in Tamluck-II has risen from 20 hectares in 1986-87 to 50 hectares in 1997-98 (this increase is 150%). In case of Panskura-II only, the area under summer flowers has decreased from 1400 hectares in 1986-87 to 700 hectares in 1997-98. On the other hand, the area under both the winter and bhadoi flowers in Tamluk-II has increased by 150% during 1986-87 to 1997-98 (Table-8). Again, the area under winter flowers in Panskura-II has declined from 1400 hectares in 1986-87 to 750 hectares in 1997-98 (this decrease is 46.43%) (Table-8). On the other hand, the area under bhadoi flowers in Panskkura-II has decreased from 1200 hectares in 1986-87 to 1000 hectares in 1997-98 (this decrease is 16.67%) (Table-9). But an increasing trend of area under winter or bhadoi flowers is found for other blocks *viz*., Panskura-I, Daspur-I and II during 1986-87 to 1997-98.

The percentage share of area under summer flowers or winter flowers or bhadoi flowers in 1986-87 has been the highest for Panskura-II (for example, 80.23% for summer flowers, 77.13% for winter flowers and 81.53% for bhadoi flowers) (Table-7, 8 and 9). The production and productivity of all types of flowers in 1986-87 are also the highest for Panskura-II. That is Panskura-II has played a leading role in floriculture of Midnapur (East) during 1986-87. The analysis of percentage share of area under different types of flowers in 1997-98 reveals that Panskura-I plays a leading role in case of summer and wintor flowers, but Panskura-II occupies the highest percentage area (*i.e.*, 55.40%) in case of bhadoi flowers cultivation in Midnapore (East) district. The analysis of production and yield of all types of flowers in 1997-98 shows the dominating role of Panskura-I and II in the floriculture of Midnapore (East) District. As a whole, Panskura-I and II have played a leading role in the floriculture of Midnapur (East) district during 1986-87 to 1997-98.

From the above analysis it can be concluded that the hypothesis (1) is almost accepted.

V

ECONOMICS OF FLOWER CULTIVATION : A MICRO LEVEL STUDY

Let us examine the different economic aspects of flower cultivation in the sample villages of Midnapur (East) district. We shall test first the hypothesis 2,3,4,5 and 8 for the sample cultivators. The estimated regression equations are given in table-10.

The results in table-10 have the following implications :

First, the smaller size classes of land holdings have larger percentage of area under floriculture. It is found that the size of holdings explains 29% variation in area under floriculture.

Second, the larger expansion of floriculture can generate larger scope of employment of labour, particularly, females and child labour. The results show the statistically significant relationship between the area under floriculture and employment of labour, particularly, female and child labour.

Third, the profitability (*i.e.*, Gross Profit (G.P.) per unit of G.C.A.) of a farm is influenced positively by the increase in the share of area under floriculture. In other words, it can be said that the larger the percentage of area under floriculture, the larger the G.P. per unit of G.C.A. The result shows that the per cent area under floriculture explains 91% variation in G.P. per acre.

Fourth, the resource base of a farm influences significantly the percentage area under floriculture and the relationship between those two variables is inverse.

Fifth, the expansion of floriculture is significantly influenced by the availability of credit tot he cultivators.

On the other hand, the table-11 indicates that the availability of credit has changed largely the cropping pattern in favour of floriculture. So, the hypothesis (which states that the larger the availability of credit, the larger the percentage of area under floriculture) is accepted.

From the above observations it can be concluded that all the hypotheses 2, 3, 4, 5 and 8 are accepted for the sample cultivator households.

It is to note that the percentage of area under floriculture to G.C.A. ahs increased over years for all the sample cultivators. The sample cultivators have expanded floriculture by reducing the area under other crops, particularly, betelevine. Let us examine the reasons behind such increase in the percentage of area under floriculture. First, it is observed that the benefit-cost ratio employment opportunities, cash requirement, environmental or natural adversities, non-availability of skilled labour, etc., are the main factors responsible for the larger area shift in favour of floriculture. Table-12 shows that the benefit-cost ratio is higher for all kinds of flowers as compared to the different varieties of paddy and bangla betelvine (except Mitha betelvine). So this higher benefit-cost ratio of flower cultivation may be an important factor influencing the expansion of floriculture. Though the benefit-cost ratio of Mitha betelvine is higher that that of all other sample crops, the expansion of area under Mitha betelvine cultivation is inhibited by several other factors, *viz.*, the requirement of larger amount of capital for cultivation (which is often not possible for the poor cultivators in a small farm economy), natural calamities and other environmental adversities (which cause heavy loss in cultivation). Second, the floriculture has a strong potential to employ more female and child labour which increase the gross returns in a small farm economy having abundance of both family (and hired) female and child labour. This strong employment potentialities of female and child labour has increased the percentage of area under floriculture to G.C.A. Third, the lower capital requirement, larger use of less skilled and non-adult labour and less necessity of timely operation in different stages of production in case of floriculture as compared to betelvine cultivation have helped the large spread of floriculture (specially shifting the area from betelvine cultivation to the floriculture).

Fourth, the risk factors are higher in case of betelvine cultivation as compared to floriculture (due to higher capital investment, requirement of more skilled and adult labour, adverse effects of natural calamities and other environmental factors, etc., for betelvine cultivation). The higher risk factors have motivated sample cultivators to popularise the floriculture as main cash crop enterprise.

Fifth, the better price incentives and marketing facilities (than during earlier periods) have also made more spread of floriculture.

Our sample cultivator households are very much dependent on floriculture for their income. We observe that gross income from floriculture constitutes a significant percentage of total family income (50% to 60%). So the hypothesis (7) is accepted.

Floriculture absorbs largely the domestic labour and gives them adequate earnings. We observe that the sample marginal cultivators have managed to live above poverty line through floriculture (where the Per Capita Income Per Month (PCIPM) ranges from Rs. 330.00 to Rs. 800.00). So the hypothesis (6) is accepted.

VI
PROBLEMS OF FLORICULTURE

The constraints limiting the growth of floriculture can be seen as demand side problems and supply side problems (which may be presented schematically in the following way).

We shall discuss in detail about these constraints in the following manner :

Demand Side Problems

There is a need for the analysis of marketing channels for flowers of floricultural crops to highlight the demand side problems. Let us highlight the marketing channel for flowers or floral products in West Bengal. The marketing of flowers in the local market is done on the basis of open auction and direct negotiation. It is largely exported to other districts and states. Pattern of movement and involvement of intermediaries are dependent on scale and area of operations. The tree given below reflects the idea about the marketing channel of flowers (see schematic presentation of "Marketing channel of flowers/floral products).

In Calcutta wholesale trade there are brokers, itinerant merchants, traders and commission agents who have their usual role to play in assembling and distribution of flowers. The small cultivators sell flowers either through collectors or directly in the local market. But the big farmers may sell either in the local market or in the state level market directly. From the state level market flowers are exported to different countries, states and districts. Sometime, the big traders store their flowers in cold storage and sell later. In flower markets located in district headquarters or in villages transactions take place between producers and consumers, producers, wholesale traders retailers and consumers, etc. The brokers or commission agents have a catalytic role for selling flowers in different stages. In the local market, there exist aratdars, big traders, small traders or farias, retailers and decorators. Among them big traders and small traders bring flowers in the state level market where brokers/commission agents, small traders, itinerant merchants, big traders, permanent shopkeepers, etc. are found. Among them, the big traders only export floricultural products to other countries.

From the above discussion it is evident that the flower market becomes controlled and dominated by big merchants. The flower growers are even deprived of the low price on the plea that traders have not received the quantity of flowers shown at the time of auction and/or the said flowers have a damaged portion which was not known at the time of auction. Some enterprising flower growers have been in search of other markets outside the State.

Some flowers are sent to neighbouring states and some major cities in India. However the amount of despatch is negligible (Samaddar, 1995). Since the flower markets are

A Scematic Presentation of Problems of Floriculture

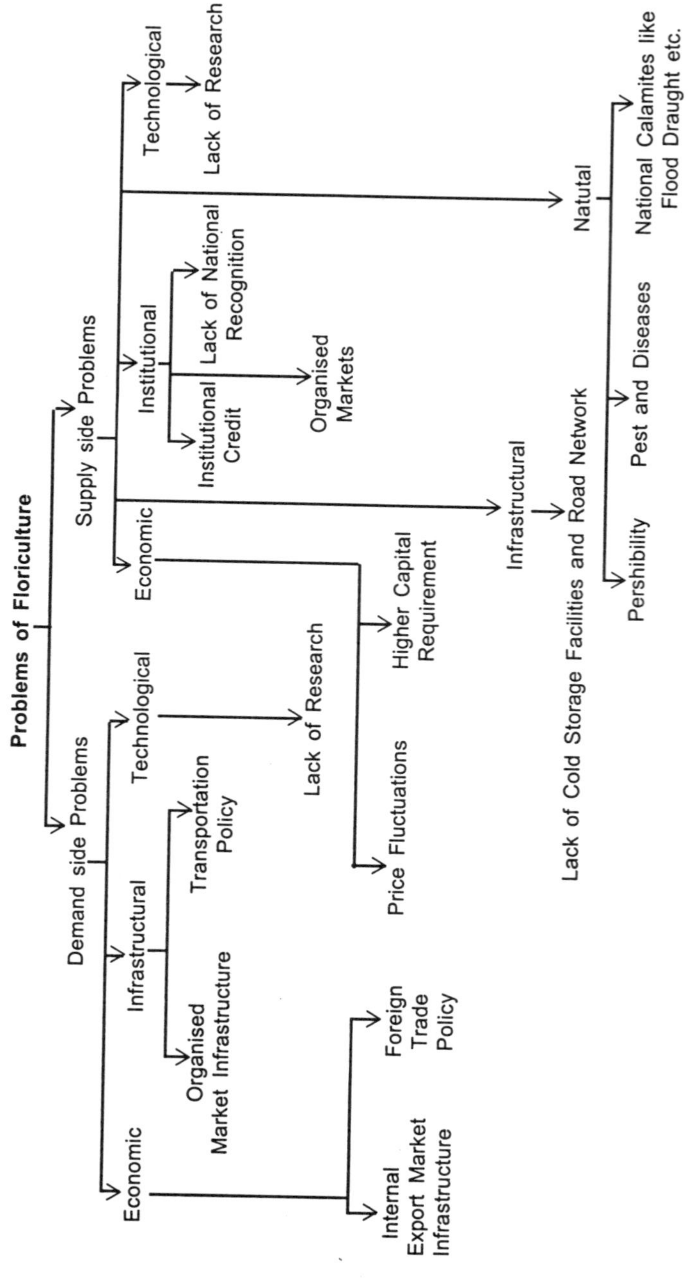

A Schematic Presentation of Marketing Channel of Flowers/Floral Products

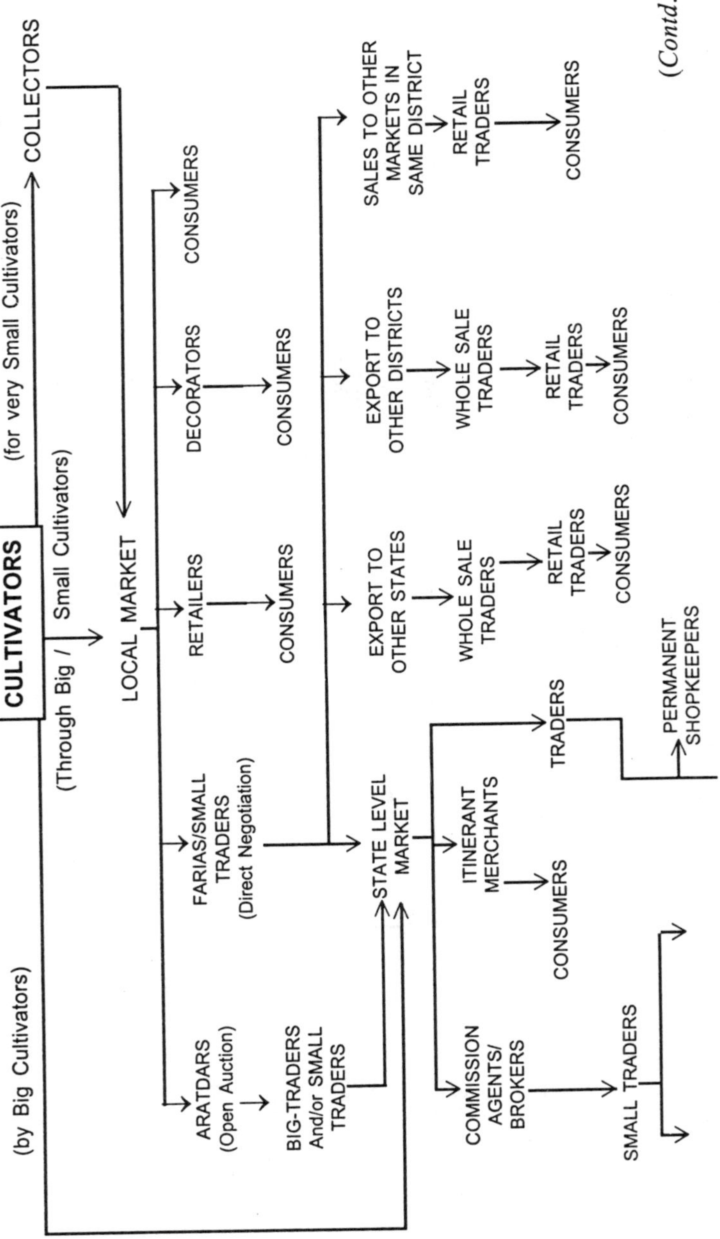

(Contd.)

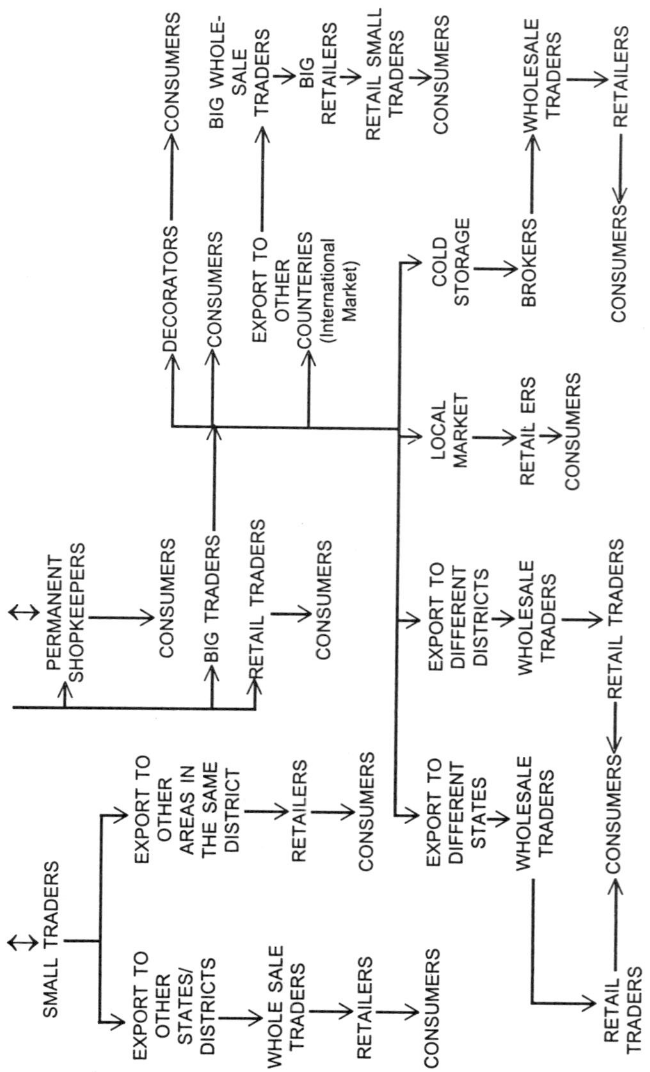
SMALL TRADERS
EXPORT TO OTHER STATES/ DISTRICTS
WHOLE SALE TRADERS
RETAILERS
CONSUMERS
EXPORT TO OTHER AREAS IN THE SAME DISTRICT
RETAILERS
CONSUMERS
PERMANENT SHOPKEEPERS
CONSUMERS
BIG TRADERS
RETAIL TRADERS
CONSUMERS
DECORATORS
CONSUMERS
CONSUMERS
EXPORT TO OTHER COUNTERIES (International Market)
BIG WHOLE-SALE TRADERS
BIG RETAILERS
RETAIL SMALL TRADERS
CONSUMERS
EXPORT TO DIFFERENT STATES
WHOLESALE TRADERS
RETAIL TRADERS
CONSUMERS
EXPORT TO DIFFERENT DISTRICTS
WHOLESALE TRADERS
RETAIL TRADERS
LOCAL MARKET
RETAIL ERS
CONSUMERS
COLD STORAGE
BROKERS
WHOLESALE TRADERS
RETAILERS
CONSUMERS

disorganised, the commission brokerage is exorbitant. Sellers are not getting prompt payments. Bringing out flowers markets under ambit of regulation would remedy many inherent problems in the system (Sau, 1998).

It is often reported by the challandars or big traders that sufficient space is not provided by the Railways, particularly during peak marketing seasons. Besides, there exists no arrangements for keeping the flower baskets within any shed at the railway station to save the tendered flowers from rain or sunlight. Transportation of flowers by Airways has been monopolised by a few big traders having an illegal understanding with the employees of airway (eliminating the small and medium flowers traders).

"Exploration of new markets, reduction of air freight charges and minimisation of 'Cess' will go a long way towards sales promotion from this country as well as from this state for ensuring economic benefit to the growers, traders and to nation at large" (Laskar, 1995).

"World trade in floriculture products is fast increasing. ... India's share in global floriculture trade is very meagre and insignificant. In spite of having almost all the inputs for being a leader in international flower market, India could not make any dent on it" (Mukherjee, 1995).

The demand for flowers is also limited by the lack of research for other multipurpose uses of flowers.

Market infrastructure of flowers is also not organised and developed. There is a lack of market centres for flowers in the country and this pehnomenon is inhibiting the demand for floricultural products.

Supply Side Problems

Post-harvest damage to flower crops is colossal. The price fluctuates tremdenously 5 to 8 times in the off season. There are not sufficient cold stores for storing flowers. As a result, the flower growers suffer seriously due to the unstable price in the market. The price fluctuates from hour to hour.

According to West Bengal Agricultural Marketing (Regulation) Act, 1972, flower is not still a notified commodity. Planning for its growth is thus neglected.

Higher capital requirement for the cultivation of some kinds of flowers often inhibits the growth of floriculture in the country (which is specially true for the resource poor farmers). In this case the Institutional Credit (I.C.) may play a catalytic role to increase the cultivation of floral products in the country. But unfortunately the I.C. is also not provided sufficiently and timely for the floriculture in the country.

Again organised market infrastructure for flowers is generally absent and market places are insufficient for the smooth supply of flowers (which may keep pace with the demand and provide growers right returns at right time).

The physical constraints like perishability of flowers crops, pest and diseases and natural calamities like floods, drought, etc., effects adversely the growth of floriculture.

"In order to accelerate the flower cultivation in the state it is necessary to take up planned schemes for providing technical know how to the farmers for cultivation of different seasonal flowers in a better way and marketing of the produce at a remunerative price so that the resource poor marginal and small farmers of the state involve themselves more in flower cultivation to be able to survive on their own" (Saha and Mukherjee, 1995).

There is also a need for research for meeting the diversified demand for floral products.

"Technology transfer holds the key with increasing accent on areas such as Research and Development (R&D), availability of finance and the creation of adequate infrastructural facilities. Our farmers need to be aware of the state of the art bio-technological application and information network to keep them up to date on recent developments in commercial floriculture. India has to strike a balance between meeting the domestic demand for relatively cheap flowers and producing high quality flowers for the much needed foreign exchange. It is urgent to make a detailed and careful appraisal of the characteristics and contours of the national and internal markets before we are able to compete on an equal footing with other business rivals in international markets like Netherlands, Columbia, Israel and Italy. It is also imperative to ensure drip irrigation, tissue-culture production, glass house breeding, improved air transport, good roads, power supply refrigeration of flowers and marketing outlets. The interest of the farmers in floriculture can be sustained with assured reasonable returns" (Mukherjee, 1995).

VII

PROSPECTS OF FLORICULTURE

Flowers have a good market in the USA, Germany, Notherland, the UK and also in the Persian Gulf countries and Hongkong. Cut flowers and flower buds are in good demand in foreign countries where flower is used in bouquets or for ornamental purposes. The demand for Indian orchids is increasing steadily. There is a tremendous potentiality for the development of flower exports from India. During the late 80's and early 90's there has been significant country-wise diversification of exports. In 1995-96, the U.S.A. was the leading flower importing country followed by the U.K., Germany, Saudi Arabia and Netherland in contrast to Saudi Arabia being the leading flower importing country from India (Table-13). It is revealed from this table that Saudi Arabia accounted for 46% of total exports, Kuwait 13% and U. Arab EMTE 10% of the total exports in 1982-83. But their shares declined drastically in 1995-96. On the other hand, the share of German FREP, Japan, Netherland, U.K. significantly increased during this period. In 1995-96, the USA accounted for about 34% of total exports from India, while Netherland 16%, German FREP 14% and the U.K. 9%. India exported cut flowers and foilage to only 9 countries of world during 1982-83. The number of importing countries increased significantly to 47 during 1995-96. This shows the significant country-wise diversification of India's flower exports.

It is to note that the export of floriculture from India in 1991-92 was Rs. 1480 lakhs which rose to Rs. 3083.80 lakhs in 1994-95 and to Rs. 9660.97 lakhs in 1998-99 (Table-14 and Diagram-II). The share of floriculture in total value of exports of agricultural and horticultural products has increased from 0.82% in 1996-97 to 1% in 1998-99. On the other hand, the share of floriculture in total value of exports of horticultural products has risen from 5.44% in 1996-97 to 6.88% in 1998-99. But the share of horticultural products in total value of exports of agriculture and horticulture products has decreased from 15.07% in 1996-97 to 14.5% in 1998-99.

From the above analysis it can be said that floral products (or flowers) have an important potentiality to earn foreign exchange. This may reduce the deficit in balance of payments of the country like India.

Again, the flower cultivation requires a large volume of employment of human labour (Table-15). For example, the labour employment per acre is 300, 250, 200, 200 and 400 respectively for nightqueen, bela, jui, rose and marigold. "Floriculture will become as an important source of employment generation in India characterised by chronic unemployment" (Maitra, 2000). This may solve the problem of chronic unemployment in a country like India. Side by side, the profitability of different varieties of flower cultivation is relatively good (Table-15). For example, the profit per acre is Rs. 24,000.00, Rs. 20,500.00, Rs. 15,000.00, Rs. 16,000.00 and Rs. 14,000.00 respectively for nightqueen, bela, jui, rose & Marigold. On the other hand, cost of cultivation is lower for different flower crops as compared to other crops. Hence, the benefit-cost ratio is higher for most of the flower crops (Table-12). From the micro level study it can be said that cultivator households with smaller size of land holdings, lower resource base allocate more land for floriculture. Again, the floriculture has a stronger potential for (i) employment of labour, particularly, female and child; (ii) gross profit per unit of land.

Therefore, the good export potential, strong employment opportunity, higher profitability, etc., justify the good prospect of floriculture in a country like India (characterised by chronic unemployment and massive poverty, serious balance of payments crisis, smaller size of land holdings, etc.).

VIII

SUMMARY AND CONCLUSIONS

Flower is an important cash-crop in India. Diversification in favour of horticultural crops, say, flower crops is more rational. Floriculture has occupied a significant position in the agricultural economy of the country as an important source of employment and income for the farming families, particularly, the small and marginal ones, in the perspective of low and declining land-man ratio and the consequent proliferation of marginal farmers. All floral products having a high demand both in the internal market and abroad can be produced in some or the other parts of India. The State level analysis reveals that the area under flower cultivation has increased over years during 1988-89 to 1998-99 for most of the sample states including all India. The C.P. has changed in favour of floriculture for India and most of the sample states. The percentage change of area is highest (3958.82%) for Delhi during 1988-89 to 1998-99. The percentage share of area of a sample state to total area under floriculture in India has risen for most of the states during 1988-89 to 1998-99. An increasing trend of production of flowers is found for India as a whole and most of the states. The flower crop-wise analysis reveals that both the area and production of most of the different flower crops have risen over years during 1993-94 to 1995-96. But the productivity of those flower crops shows no definite trend for those sample states.

Focusing on the district level scenario in West Bengal

in 1987-88, it is observed that Mdnapur has the largest contribution in the production of flowers in the State. The similar picture is found for area and yield rate of flower in Midnapur. A close look on the Midnapur (East) district shows that though the total area, production and yield of flowers has increased in 1997-98 as compared to 1986-87, but that is not so for different varieties of flowers.

The Block level analysis reveals that the area, production and productivity of most of the flower crops have shown an increasing trend for most of the blocks in Midnapore (East) district during 1986-87 to 1997-98. As a whole, Panskura-I and II have played a significant role in the floriculture of Midanpur (East) district during the same period.

The field level study reveals the following observations :

1. The smaller size classes of land holdings have larger percentage of area under floriculture.
2. The farms enjoying credit facilities have used larger share of their land for floriculture.
3. The larger expansion of flower cultivation has generated larger scope of employment of labour, particularly, female and child labour.
4. The larger share of area under floriculture can increase the profitability.
5. The farms with lower resource-base shift their land largely (say, from betelvine cultivation to flower cultivation) due to the higher benefit-cost ratio, higher employment opportunities of female and child labour.
6. The gross income from floriculture constitutes significant percentage of total family income.
7. The flower cultivators live above poverty line.

The marketing of floral products is done through different stages and a number of representatives. The marketing of flowers in local market is done on the basis of open auction and direct negotiation. In Calcutta wholesale trade, there are brokers, itinerant merchants, traders and commission agents who have their usual role to play in assembling and distribution of flower.

Both the demand side and supply side problems are limiting the growth of floriculture in the country. The good exports potential, higher employment opportunity, etc., justify the good prospect of floriculture in India.

The credit, particularly Institutional Credit (I.C.) needs to be provided to flower cultivators, in particular, smaller ones at the reasonable rate for the expansion of cultivation of flowers. Floriculture may be thought as an employment generation and poverty alleviation programme.

There is a tremendous potentiality of floriculture in India where land and labour are cheap relative to the European countries. In order to realise this fully the following policy prescriptions may be made :

First, emphasis must be given for expanding research on floriculture and popularising the results of research. Transfer of up-to-date technology from the developed nations also holds the key.

Second, foreign assistance may be taken to develop the skill of labour for better management of flower cultivation. And if this is done the country may produce quality flowers for international market. If necessary, the assistance programme may be done with foreign companies primarily on the basis of the condition of 100% repurchase.

Third, since the floriculture necessitates a larger amount of cheap credit, the Government must formulate a policy for the provision of adequate I.C. at reasonable rates to flower cultivators particularly, a resource poor ones.

Fourth, the infrastructural facilities such as air-conditioning, road and air-transport, supply of power, marketing outlets, refrigeration of flowers, drip irrigation should be improved and organised. Glass house breeding may also be developed.

Fifth, for the elimination of exploitation of the growers of flowers by the intermediaries, co-operatives societies must be organised so that flower growers and the co-operatives despatch the produce to the wholesellers or for exports. NAFED may participate in the export business of flowers.

Sixth, a crop insurance scheme must be introduced in the case of flower cultivation.

Seventh, there must be a proper market intelligence system covering the growing and the foreign consuming areas.

Eighth, the Government must take major responsibilities for developing appropriate infrastructure such as appropriate road network, developed air-transportation, continuous supply of electricity, marketing through the assimilation of flower products of small cultivators, understanding and creation of demand of floricultural products in the foreign markets.

Ninth, there is the requirement of fixation of export target well in advance.

Tenth, the market infrastructure should be organised and expanded for the better marketing facilities of floricultural products.

Lastly, the expansion of floriculture must be designed as a programme for the alleviation of poverty and unemployment, specially the female unemployment. That is, the growth of floriculture may be thought as a development programme for the weaker sections and/or classes of the societies say female and small marginal farmers.

To conclude, the present study has some limitations. There is a scope for further study considering the price, etc., factors of flower crops.

NOTES

1. Editoria, *Hata Bazare*, 1995, April-June, 2nd year, No. 4.
2. Bhattacharya, P.K. (1995) "Floriculture in Indian perspective," *Hata Bazare*, No. 4, April-June.
3. Samaddar, H.N. (1995), "Prospect of Floriculture in West Bengal," *Hata Bazare*, No. 4, April-June.
4. Laskar, A.K. (1995), "Outlook of Floriculture," *Hata Bazare*, No. 4, April-June.

5. Deb. A., "Floriculture : Accent on New Areas Crucial", *Hata Bazare*, No. 4, April-June.
6. Sau, S.N. (1998), "Trend and Potentiality of Flower Exports From India," *V.U. Journal of Economics*, Vol. V.
7. *Ibid.*
8. *Ibid.*
9. *Ibid.*
10. *Ibid.*

REFERENCES

1. Asokan, S.R. and Chokshi, S.N. (1997), "Export of Floricultural Products : Problem and Prospect," *I.J. A.E.*; Vol. 52; No. 3, July-September, 1997.
2. Alagurmahi, T., Alajugam, M. and Rejesh, R. (1997) (Summary), "Performance of Flower Crops *vis-à-vis* Field Crops in Madurai District, Tamil Nadu," *I.J.A.E. op. cit.*
3. Agarwal, K.G. and Duhijod, D.D (1997), (Summary), "An Economic Analysis of Winter floriculture Grown in vicinity, Nagpur City of Maharastra," *I.J.A.E., op. cit.*
4. Bhattacharya, P.K. (1995), "Floriculture to Indian Perspective," *Hate Bazare*, No. 4, April-June.
5. Bhattacharya, B. (1999), "Export Stagnation Causes and Corrective Action," *Yojana*, Vol. 43, No. 1, January.
6. Bal, H.K. and Bal, H.S. (1997), "Flower Power in Punjab," *I.J.A.E., op. cit.*
7. Deb. A. (1995), "Floriculture : Accent on New Areas Crucial," *Hata Bazare, op. cit.*
8. De Sarkar, M. (1995), "Qualities of Flowers" (in Bengali), *Hate Bazare, op. cit.*
9. Dahiya and Singh (1997), "Horticultural Development in Himachal Pradesh, Profitability, Policy and Prospects," *I.J.A.E. op. cit.*
10. Dahiya, P., Goyal, S.K., Pandey, R.N., "Comparative Economics of Floriculture in Sonepat District (Haryana)," *I.J.A.E., op. cit.*
11. Directorate of Agricultural Marketing, Government of West Bengal (1987), *Flower Cultivation and Marketing in West Bengal.*
12. Dahiya, P.S. and Singh, R. (1997), " Horticultural Development in Himachal Pradesh : Profitability, Policy and prospects," *I.J.A.E., op. cit.*
13. Editorial, *Hate Bazare,* 1995, April-June.
14. Ghosh, S. (1995), "Flower Cultivation and Marketing in West Bengal" (in Bengali), *Hate Bazare, op. cit.*
15. Jugale, V.B. (1997), "Production and Marketing of Horticultural Products in Maharashtra," *I.J.A.E., op. cit.*

16. Koranna, V.M. and Naik, N.K. (1997) "Floriculture : An Economically Viable Enterprise," *I.J.A.E. op. cit.*
17. Kaul, G.L. (1997), Horticulture in India : production, Marketing and processing," *I.J.A.E., op. cit.*
18. Krishnaiah, J. (1997) "Horticulture in Andhra Pradesh : Production and Export Potential," *I.J.A.E., op. cit.*
19. Kaul, V.K. (1997) "Export of Horticultural Products from West Bengal," presented in the orientation programmes on Exports of Fruits and vegetables from West Bengal organised by National Institute of Agricultural Marketing, *I.J.A.E., op. cit.*
20. Kumar, H. Kushwah, R.K.S., Singh G.N. and Singh, C.P. (1997), "Effect of Expansion of Horticulture on Livestock Sector in District Varanasi, Uttar Pradesh" (Summary), *I.J.A.E., op. cit.*
21. Khodaskar, R.D. (1997), "Co-operative Economic Performance of Horticultural Groups and Other Crops with Special Reference to Varhedarna Village (Nasik district)," *I.J.A.E., op. cit.*
22. Laksar, R. (1995), "The Export of flowers from India," *Hata Bazare, op. cit.*
23. Laskar, A.K. (1995), "Outlook for Floriculture," *Hate Bazare. op. cit.*
24. Maity, R.G. (1995), "Flower-Non-Conventional Commodity of Modern Commercial Agricutlrue," *Kurukshetra*, November.
25. Mukherjee, N.K. (1995), "Marketing of Cut-Flower in West Bengal." *Hate Bazare, op. cit.*
26. Mukhopadhya, A. (1995), "Export Oriental Flower Industry : A Prospect," (in Bengali) *Hate Bazare, op. cit.*
27. Maitra, S. (2000), "Flower Trade : A Prospect," *Yuba Manas*, May-June.
28. Raman, S.S. 1995), "West Bengal will have Place in Flower : Trade in the World," (in Bengali), *Hate Bazare, op. cit.*
29. Rahim, K.M.B. and sarkar, D. (1997), "Techno : Organisational Characteristics of Floriculture in West Bengal," *I.J.A.E., op. cit.*
30. Rao, A.N., "Higher Employment and Income Potential of Horticultural Crops," *I.J.A.E., op. cit.*
31. Shah, D. (1997), "Changing Structure of Horticultural Production in Maharashtra : Trends and Indicators," *I.J.A.E., op. cit.*
32. Singh, D.V. (1997), "Hopes : An Import Substituting Horticultural Crops," *I.J.A.E., op. cit.*
33. Singh, R.B., Prasad, R.N., Nigam, H.K., Saran, R. (1997), "Economics of Flower Production in District Farrukhabad, Uttar Pradesh," *I.J.A.E., op. cit.*
34. Singh, B., Prasad, V. and Yadase, S.R. (1997), "Cost Structure and Economic Potentials of Horticultural Crops in District Farrukhabad, Uttar Pradesh," *I.J.A.E., op. cit.*

35. Saha, N. (1994), "Organised Market for Flowers will Develop in Kolaghat," (in Bengali), *Hate Bazare*; 1st year, 1st No., January-March.

36. Sau, S.N. (1998) : "Trend and Potentiality of Flower Exports from India," *V.U. Journal of Economics*, Vol.-V.

37. Samaddar, H.N. (1995), "Prospect of Floriculture in West Bengal," *Hate Bazare, op. cit.*

38. Sahrma, L.R. Nadda, A.L. and Sharma, P. (1997), "Export Oriented Floriculture in India : Status, Constraints and Strategies," *I.J.A.E., op. cit.*

39. Saini, A.S. and Sharma, K.D. (1997), "Economic Sustainability and Market Potential of Hi-Tech Floriculture in Himachal Pradesh," *I.J.A.E., op. cit.*

TABLE 1

State-wise Percentage of Area Under Flowers to Gross Cropped Area During 1988-89 to 1997-98

States/UTs	1988-89	1993-94	1997-98
Andhra Pradesh	0.03	0.04	0.08
Assam	0.001	0.008	0.01
Bihar	—	0.009	0.001
Delhi	—	0.02	0.006
Haryana	0.009	0.02	0.03
Himachal Pradesh	0.003	0.003	0.01
Jammu & Kashmir	0.004	0.01	0.02
Karnataka	0.08	0.03	1.92
Madhya Pradesh	—	0.003	0.006
Orissa	—	0.002	0.003
Punjab	0.003	0.005	0.008
Rajasthan	0.02	0.007	0.01
Tamil Nadu	0.02	0.02	0.03
Manipur	—	0.03	0.04
Uttar Pradesh	0.003	—	0.001
West Bengal	0.04	0.02	0.02
Daman & Diu	—	0.02	0.02
Pondichery	—	0.01	0.01
All India	0.02	0.03	0.05

Source : (i) National Horticultural Board, Ministry of Agriculture, Government of India.

(ii) Area & Production of Principal Crops in India, Government of India.

TABLE 2

Area Under Flower Cultivation in India by States during 1988-89 to 1998-99 (in Hectare)

States/UTs	1988-89	1993-94	1995-96	1998-99	% Change in 1998-99 Over 1988-89	% Change in 1998-99 Over 1993-94
Andhra Pradesh	3055 (10.60)	5778 (10.84)	22012 (26.84)	8387 (11.29)	173.55	44.63
Assam	31 (0. 107)	280 (0.52)	442 (0.54)	—	—	—
Bihar	—	85 (0.15)	104 (0.137)	86 (0.116)	—	1.17
Delhi	85 (0.29)	801 (1.50)	1866 (2.88)	3450 (0.66)	3958.82	330.71
Haryana	425 (1.47)	1200 (2.25)	1460 (1.78)	2250 (3.04)	429.41	87.5
Himachal Pradesh	25 (0.08)	30 (0.05)	30 (.037)	133.3 (0.180)	433.2	344.3
Jammu & Kashmir	40 (0.138)	—	—	75 (0.10)	87.5	—
Karnataka	7870 (27.31)	15243 (28.60)	191961 (23.37)	20780 (2.09)	164.04	36.32
Madhya Pradesh	—	915 (1.71)	1334 (1.63)	1956 (2.64)	—	113.77
Maharashtra	2045 (7.09)	2275 (4.26)	5657 (6.99)	4979 (6.73)	143.32	118.85
Manipur	36 (0.124)	56 (0.105)	78 (0.09)	140.5 (0.189)	290.2	150.89
Orissa	—	100 (0.187)	112 (.136)	175 (0.23)	—	75.0
Punjab	158 (0.54)	332 (0.62)	600 (0.93)	560 (0.75)	254.4	68.67
Rajasthan	2500 (8.67)	1207 (2.26)	1985 (2.42)	2353 (3.18)	- 5.88	94.94
Tamil Nadu	8384 (29.10)	12340 (23.15)	14194 (17.32)	17750 (23.99)	278.14	43.84
Uttar Pradesh	600 (2.08)	—	329.39 (.402)	350.08 (0.47)	—	—
West Bengal	3150 (10.93)	12610 (23.65)	12508 (15.26)	105.00 (14.19)	186.34	16.73
Daman & Diu	—	5 (0.009)	5 (0.006)	5 - (0.007)	—	0
Pondichery	—	40 (0.075)	46 (.056)	46 (0.06)	—	15
Gujarat	405 (1.40)	—	—	—	—	—
All India	28809 (100%)	53297 (100%)	81923 (100%)	73970.88 (100%)	156.76	38.79

Note : Figures in brackets indicate % to total.

Source : National Horticultural Board, Ministry of Agriculture, Government of India.

TABLE 3

Production of Flowers in India by States (in MT) % Change from 1993-94 to 1998-99

States/ UTs	1993-94		1998-99			
	Loose	Cut	Loose	Cut	Loose	Cut
Andhra Pradesh	17334.0	—	32000	—	84.60	—
Assam	37.0	—	—	—	—	—
Bihar	1430.00	2	1850	—	—	—
Delhi	4056.0	—	21007	—	29.37	—
Haryana	22400.0	327	40500	760	80.80	132.41
Himachal Pradesh	109.8	429	976	181	788.88	0.57
Jammu & Kashmir	—	—	46	5.8	—	—
Karnataka	87998.0	—	124290	—	41.24	—
Madhya Pradesh	9000.0	—	11470	—	0.87	—
Maharashtra	18188.0	—	38582	—	112.12	—
Manipur	23.0	—	93.03	—	304.47	—
Orissa	460.0	—	8685	933	1788.04	—
Punjab	548.5	—	3435	—	526.25	—
Rajasthan	—	—	2389	—	—	—
Tamil Nadu	61704.0	—	133125	—	115.74	—
Uttar Pradesh	—	—	225.88	160	—	—
West Bengal	9020.0	4790	58.00	—	543.01	—
Daman & Diu	51.0	—	51	—	—	—
Pondicherry	177.0	—	427	—	141.24	—
All India	232536.3	5122.8	459163.41	1155.13	97.46	7.45

Note : Loose Production in M.T., Cut Production in Lakh Nos.

Source : *National Horticultural Board*, Ministry of Agriculture, Government of India.

TABLE 4

Area, Production and Productivity of Flowers in Different States during 1993-94 to 1995-96

(Area in Hactare, Production in M.T. and Productivity in MT/HA)

Crop	Area		Production		Productivity		% Change from 1993-94 to 1995-96		
	1993-94	1995-96	1993-94	1995-96	1993-94	1995-96	Area	Production	Productivity
(1)	(2)	(3)	(4)	(5)	(6)	(7)	(8)	(9)	(10)
MANIPUR									
Rose	20 (35.71)	25 (32.05)	8	10	0.40	0.40	25	25	0
Gladiolus	22 (39.28)	26 (33.33)	12	13	0.55	0.50	18.18	8.33	–9.09
Chrysanthemum	2 (3.57)	5 (6.41)	0	0	0.05	0.05	150	0	0
Marigold	12 (21.42)	22 (28.20)	3	6	0.25	0.27	83.33	100	8
Total	56 (100)	78 (100)	23	29	0.41	0.37	39.29	26.09	– 9.76
ORISSA									
Rose	17 (17)	18 (16.07)	85.85	94	5.05	5.22	5.88	9.49	3.36
Gladiolus	5 (5)	6.5 (5.80)	4 Lac Spikes	5.40 Lac Spikes	—	—	30	1250	—
Marigold	27 (27)	30 (27.27)	1.88	155	0.07	5.17	11.11	8144.68	7285.71
Jasmine	7 (7)	7 (6.25)	36	37	5.14	5.29	0	2.77	2.91
Chrysanthemum	7 (7)	8.5 (7.58)	35	43	5.00	5.06	21.42	22.85	1.2
Tuberose	10 (10)	13 (11.60)	50	64	5.00	4.92	30	28	-1.6
Others	27 (27)	29 (25.89)	141.75	153	5.25	5.28	7.40	7.93	0.57
Total	100 (100)	112 (100)	460	546	4.6	4.9	12	18.69	6.52

(*Contd.*)

TABLE 4 (*Contd.*)

(1)	(2)	(3)	(4)	(5)	(6)	(7)	(8)	(9)	(10)
				PUNJAB					
Rose	180 (54.21)	150 (25)	75	375	0.42	2.50	-16.66	400	495.23
Gladiolus	20 (6.02)	170 (28.33)	300	1000	15.00	5.88	750	233.33	6.08
Marigold	122 (36.74)	220 (36.66)	122	1760	1.00	8.00	80.32	1342.62	700
Jasmine	5 (1.50)	5 (0.83)	1.5	25	0.30	5.00	0	1566.66	1566.66
Chrysanthemum	5 (1.50)	50 (13.33)	50	250	10.00	5.00	900	400	– 50
Carnation	—	5 (0.83)	—	200	—	40.00	—	—	—
Total	332 (100)	600 (100)	548.5	3610	1.65	6.02	80.72	558.16	301.21
				RAJASTHAN					
	1994-95		1994-95		1994-95				
Rose	1196 (60.25)	1196 (60.25)	1201	1201	1.00	1.00	0	0	0
Gladiolus	— —	— —	—	—	—	—	—		
Marigold	397 (20)	397 (2)	490	490	1.23	1.23	0	0	0
Jasmine	53 (3.67)	53 (2.67)	103	103	1.94	1.94	0	0	0
Chrysanthemum	24 (1.20)	24 (1.20)	1	1	0.04	0.04	0	0	0
Carnation	—	—	—	—	—	—	—	—	—
Others	315 (15.86)	315 (15.86)	107	107	0.34	0.34	0	0	0
Total	1985 (100)	1985 (100)	1902	1902	0.96	0.96	0	0	0

(*Contd.*)

TABLE 4 (*Contd.*)

(1)	(2)		(3)		(4)	(5)	(6)	(7)	(8)	(9)	(10)
UTTAR PRADESH											
	1994-95				1994-95		1994-95				
Rose	9.06	(5.95)	9.12	(5.38)	9.32	10.85	1.09	1.19	0.66	16.41	15.53
Gladiolus	56.12	(36.86)	61.51	(36.31)	80.12	84.45	1.43	1.37	9.60	5.40	– 4.19
Marigold	32.69	(21.47)	39.98	(23.60)	36.32	45.02	1.11	1.13	22.30	23.95	1.80
Jasmine	0.82	(0.53)	0.6	(0.35)	0.71	0.6	0.87	1.00	–26.82	–15.49	–13
Chrysanthemum	1.92	(1.26)	2.01	(1.18)	2.41	2.65	1.26	1.32	4.16	9.95	4.76
Carnation	0.5	(0.32)	0.5	(0.29)	0.11	0.1	0.22	0.20	0	–9.09	–9.09
Others	51.12	(33.58)	55.67	(32.86)	43.62	51.12	0.85	0.92	8.90	17.19	8.23
Total	152.23	(100)	169.39	(100)	172.61	194.79	1.13	1.15	11.27	12.84	1.77
WEST BENGAL											
Rose	1087	(8.62)	1080	(8.63)	14.8 CR Flowers	14.10 CR (Florwers)	0.0136 CR Flowers/HA	0.013 CR/HA	–0.64	–4.72	–4.41
Gladiolus	600	(4.75)	308	(3.18)	8.1 CR Spikes	5.9 CR Spikes	0.0135 CR Flowers/HA	0.014 CR/HA	–33.66	–27.16	3.70
Marigold	1000	(7.93)	1000	(7.99)	7500 T	7400 T	7.5 CR ”	7.4 T/HA	0	–1.33	–1.33
Tube Rose	2000	(15.86)	2100	(16.78)	25 CR Spikes	25.60 Cr Spikes	0.0215 CR ”	0.012 CR/HA	5	2.4	–4
Jasmine	450	(3.56)	430	(3.43)	600 T	500 T	1.33 CR”	1.162 T/HA	–4.44	–16.66	–12.63
Chrysanthemum	300	(2.37)	300	(2.39)	400 T	380 T	1.23 ”	1.26 T/HA	0	–5	–3.07
Others	7173	(56.88)	7200	(57.56)	520 T	N.A.	0.072 ”	—	0.37		
Total	12610	(100)	12508	(100)	47.9 CR & 9020 T	8280 T & 45.6 CR	0.00379	0.661T/HA	–0.81		

(*Contd.*)

TABLE 4 (*Contd.*)

(1)	(2)	(3)	(4)	(5)	(6)	(7)	(8)	(9)	(10)
			DAMAN & DUE						
Rose	3 (60)	3 (60)	39	39	13.00	13.00	0	0	0
Lily (Baremasi)	2 (40)	2 (40)	12	12	6.00	6.00	0	0	0
Total	5 (100)	5 (100)	51	51	10.20	10.20	0	0	0
			PONDICHERRY						
Rose	6 (15)	8 (17.39)	38	50	6.33	6.25	33.33	31.57	–1.26
Chrysanthemum	4 (10)	4 (8.69)	29	30	7.25	7.50	0	3.44	25
Jasmine	5 (12.5)	9 (19.56)	35	80	7.00	8.89	80	128.57	27
Tube Rose	4 (10)	—	25	—	6.25	—			
Marigold	10 (25)	4 (8.69)	18	9	1.80	2.25	–60	–50	25
Crossanda	6 (5)	— 20	—	3.33	—				
Others	5 (12.5)	21 (45.65)	12	258	2.40	12.29	320	2050	412.08
Total	40(100)	46(100)	177	427	4.42	9.28	15	141.24	109.95
			HIMACHAL PRADESH						
Gladiolus	18 (60)	18 (60)	2925000 N	2925000 N	162500 N/HA	162500 N/HA	0	0	0
Carnation	3 (10)	3 (10)	937500 N	937500 N	312500 N/HA	312500 N/HA	0	0	0
Lilies	1 (3.33)	1 (3.33)	62500 N	62500 N	62500 N/HA	62500 N/HA	0	0	0

(*Contd.*)

TABLE 4 (*Contd.*)

(1)	(2)	(3)	(4)	(5)	(6)	(7)	(8)	(9)	(10)
Maricold	44 (13.33)	4 (13.33)	109375 Kg	109375 Kg	27343.75 N/HA	27343.75 N/HA	0	0	0
Seasonal	1 (3.33)	1 (3.33)	500000 N	500000 N	500000 N/HA	500000 N/HA	0	0	0
Chrysanthemum	1 (3.33)	1 (3.33)	62500 N	62500	62500 N/HA	62500 N/HA	0	0	0
Pot Plants	2 (6.66)	2 (6.66)	15000 N	15000 N	7500 N/HA	7500 N/HA	0	0	0
Others	2 (6.66)	2 (6.66)	445 Kg	445 Kg	222.5 N/HA	222.5 N/HA	0	0	0
Total	30(100)	30(100)	109.82 MT 429.25 SP	109 MT 429.25 Nos			0	0	0
				KARNATAKA					
Rose	13.71 (8.99)	1694 (8.84)	3565	4404	2.60	2.60	23.55	23.55	0
Mericold	1858 (12.18)	2914 (15.20)	15793	24769	8.50	8.50	56.83	56.83	0
Jasmine	3500 (22.96)	4010 (20.92)	8750	100025	2.50	2.50	14.57	14.57	0
Chrysanthemum	2941 (19.29)	3717 (19.39)	29410	37170	10.00	10.00	26.38	26.38	0
Tuberose	1337 (8.77)	1171 (6.11)	9894	8665	7.40	7.40	–12.42	–12.42	0
Aster	803 (5.26)	960 (5.01)	8833	10800	11.00	11.25	19.55	22.26	2.27
Crossanda	1508 (9.89)	1908 (9.95)	2262	2862	2.50	2.50	26.52	26.52	0
Champaka	587 (3.85)	702 (3.66)	2935	3510	5.00	5.00	19.59	19.59	0
Others	1338 (8.77)	2085 (10.88)	6556	10217	4.90	4.90	55.82	55.84	0
	15243(100)	19161(100)	87998	112422	5.77	5.87	25.70	27.76	1.73

(*Contd.*)

TABLE 4 (*Contd.*)

(1)	(2)	(3)	(4)	(5)	(6)	(7)	(8)	(9)	(10)
				MAHARASHTRA					
Rose	601 (26.41)	922 (16.25)	1940	3453	3.23	3.75	65.05	77.98	16.09
Gladiolus	83 (3.64)	336 (5.93)	384	1294	4.63	3.85	304.81	261.49	-16.84
Maricold	852 (37.45)	1885 (33.32)	4352	8820	5.11	4.68	121.24	102.66	-8.41
Jasmine	406 (17.84)	—	9823	—	24.19	—	—	—	—
Chrysanthemum	333 (14.63)	674 (11.91)	1689	3102	5.07	4.60	102.40	83.61	-9.27
Carnation		3 (0.053)	—	56		18.67	—	—	—
Mogra	—	531 (9.38)	—	1711	—	3.22	—	—	—
Kagada	—	334 (5.90)	—	914	—	2.74	—	—	—
Gallardia	—	215 (3.80)	—	838	—	3.90	—	—	—
Aster	—	166 (2.93)	—	352	—	2.12	—	—	—
Others	—	591 (10.44)	—	2329	—	3.94	—	—	—
	2275(100)	5657(100)	18188	22869	7.99	4.04	148.65	25.74	-49.44
				ASSAM					
Rose	75 (26.79)	107 (24.20)	8	12	0.11	0.11	42.66	50	0
Gladiolus	25 (8.92)	50 (11.31)	3	7	0.12	0.14	100	133.33	166.66
Merigold	105 (37.5)	180 (40.73)	21	50	0.20	0.28	71.42	138.09	8
Jasmine	45 (16.07)	55 (12.44)	2	4	0.04	0.07	22.22	100	3
Chrysanthemum	30 (10.72)	50 (11.31)	3	6	0.10	0.12	66.66	100	2
Total	280 (100)	442(100)	37	79	0.13	0.18	57.86	113.51	38.46

(*Contd.*)

TABLE 4 (*Contd.*)

(1)	(2)	(3)	(4)	(5)	(6)	(7)	(8)	(9)	(10)
				BIHAR					
Gladiolus	5 (5.89)	6 (5.76)	2 Lac	3 Lac	40,000	40,000	20	50	0
Merigold	50 (58.82)	62 (59.62)	1250	1500	25.00	24.19	24	20	–3.24
Jasmine	30 (35.26)	36 (34.62)	180	210	6.00	5.83	20	16.56	–2.83
Total	85 (1000)	104 (100)	2Lac Spikes 1430 MT	3Lacs pieces 1710 MT			22.35		
				DELHI					
Rose	192 (23.98)	205 (10.99)	498	698	2.59	3.40	6.78	40.16	31.27
Gladiolus	57 (7.11)	128 (6.86)	93	173	1.62	1.35	124.56	86.02	–16.66
Marigold	192 (23.98)	384 (20.58)	260	5729	1.35	14.92	1000	2103.46	1005.18
Jasmine	—	—	—	—	—	—	—	—	—
Chrysanthemum	73 (9.11)	369 (19.78)	1585	387	21.59	1.05	405.47	–75.58	–95.13
Carnation	17 (2.12)	39 (2.09)	36	190	2.12	4.87	129.41	427.77	129.71
Tuberose	24 (2.99)	309 (16.56)	36	371	1.50	1.20	1187.50	930.55	–20
Others	246 (30.71)	432 (23.15)	1550	2726	6.31	6.31	75.60	75.87	0
Total	801(100)	1866(100)	4056	10274	5.06	5.51	123.96	153.30	8.89

(*Contd.*)

TABLE 4 (*Contd.*)

(1)	(2)	(3)	(4)	(5)	(6)	(7)	(8)	(9)	(10)
			HARYANA						
Rose	80 (6.67)	150 (10.27)	70 Lacs	125 Lacs	–0.875 lacs/HA	0.83 Lacs/HA	87.5	78.57	–5.14
Gladiolus	100 (8.32)	150 (10.27)	200 "	320 "	–2 lacs/HA	2.13 Lacs/HA	50	60	6.5
Mericold	800 (66.67)	800 (54.79)	20,000	20,000	–25 lacs/HA	2.5 Lacs/HA	0	0	0
Jesmine	—	—	—	—	—	—	—	—	—
Chrysanthemum	100 (8.33)	150 (10.27)	800	1200	–8 lacs/HA	8 Lacs/HA	50	50	0
Carnation	10 (0.83)	10 (0.68)	30 Lacs	30 Lacs	–3 lacs/HA	3 Lacs/HA	0	0	0
Tuberose	80 (6.67)	—	1600	—	–20 lacs/HA	—	—	—	—
Others	30 (25)	200 (13.70)	26.75 Lacs	165 "	–0.89 lacs/HA	0.82 Lacs/HA	566.66	516.82	–7.86
Total	1200 (100)	1460 (100)	326.75 Lacs N & 22400 T	640 Lac N & 21200 T			21.67		

Notes : Figures in brackets indicate Percentage to total.

Source : *National Horticultural Board*, Ministry of Agriculture, Government of India.

TABLE 5

Area, Production and Yield of a Few Flowers in W.B. by Districts during 1987-88

(Area in HQ., Production in '000 QTL, Yield in QTL/Ha)

Districts	Area		Production		Yield	
	Summer/ Rainy	Winter	Summer/ Rainy	Winter	Summer/ Rainy	Winter
1. Midnapur	2400 (24%)	3600 (36%)	125.5	220	52.29	61.11
2. Nadia	1200 (12%)	1600 (16%)	7.0	10.5	5.83	6.56
3. Howrah	400 (4%)	600 (6%)	2.5	3.2	6.25	5.33
4. (N+S) 24-Parganas	200 (2%)	320 (3.2%)	3.1	2.3	15.5	7.19
5. Darjeeling	—	500 (5%)	—	—	—	—

Note : (i) The figures in brackets indicate the percentages of total.

(ii) Total area under floriculture in W.B. during 1987-88 is 10,000 hectares.

Source : Government of West Bengal.

TABLE 6

Area Production, Yield of Flowers in Midnapur (East) District during 1986-87 to 1997-98 (Area (A) in Ha., Production (P) in MT, Yield (Y) in MT/Ha)

Crops	1986-87			1997-98			Increase during 88-98			% Change		
Summer	A	P	Y	A	P	Y	A	P	Y	A	P	Y
Flower	1745	3425	19.63	1605	20330	126.66	–140	16905	107.03	–8.02	493.58	545.24
Winter	1815	5943	32.74	1815	8080	44.52	0	2137	11.78	0	35.96	35.98
Bhadoi Flower	1472	14673	132.42	1805	21465	118.92	333	6792	(-) 13.5	22.62	– 10.19	46.29
Total :	5032	24041	61.61	5225	49875	96.7	193	25834	35.09	3.84	107.46	56.95

Source : *Brochure* published by Agriculture, Marketing Directorate on Marketing of Flowers (Year 1988), Government of West Bengal.

TABLE 7

Area (A), production (P) and Yield (Y) of Summer Flowers in different Blocks of Midnapore (East) District during 1986-87 to 1997-98

Area in HA, Production in MT, Yield in MT/HA

	1986-87			1997-98			% Change from 1986-87 1997-98		
	A	P	Y	A	P	Y	A	P	Y
BLOCK									
Tamluk-II	20 (1.15)	40	2	50 (3.11)	500	10	150	1125	400
Panskure-I	325 (18.62)	585	1.8	800 (49.84)	10,400	13	146.15	1677.78	622.22
Panskura-II	1400 (80.23)	2800	2	700 (43.61)	9100	13	-500.00	225	550
Ghatal	—	—	—	—	—	—	—	—	—
Daspur-I	—	—	—	35 (2.18)	210	6	—	—	
Daspur-II	—	—	—	20 (1.25)	120	6	—	—	—
Total	1745 (100)	3425	1.96	1605 (100)	20330	14.46	-8.02	493.58	637.76

Notes : Figures in brackets indicates percentages to total.

Soure : P.A.O. Midnapore (East).

TABLE 8

Area (A), Production (P) and Yield (Y) of Winter Flowers in Different Blocks of Midnapore (East) District during 1986-87 to 1997-98

(Area in HA, Production in MT, Yield in MT/HA)

	1986-87			1997-98			% Change from 1986-87 1997-98		
	A	P	Y	A	P	Y	A	P	Y
BLOCK									
Tamluk-II	20 (1.10)	70	3.5	50 (2.76)	200	4	150	185.71	14.29
Panskura-I	325 (17.91)	812	2.49	900 (49.59)	3600	4	176.92	343.35	60.64
Panskura-II	1400 (77.13)	4900	3.5	750 (41.32)	3750	5	–46.43	–23.47	42.86
Ghatal	—			5 (0.28)	20	4	—	—	—
Daspur-I	25 (1.38)	50	2	40 (2.20)	160	4	60	220	100
Daspur-II	45 (2.48)	113	2.5	70 (3.86)	350	5	55.56	209.73	100
Total	1815 (100)	5943	3.27	1815 (100)	8080	4.45	0	35.96	1.18

Note : Figures in brackets indicate percentages to total.

Source : P.A.O., Midnapur (East).

TABLE 9

Area (A), Production (p), Yield (Y) of Bhadoi Flowers in Different Blocks of Midnapore (East) District during 1986-87 to 1997-98

(Area in H.A., Production in MT, Yield in MT/HA)

	1986-87			1997-98			% Change from 1986-87 to 1997-98		
	A	P	Y	A	P	Y	A	P	Y
BLOCK									
Tamluk-II	20 (1.36)	160	8	50 (2.77)	500	10	150	212.50	25
Panskura-I	200 (13.59)	2000	10	720 (39.89)	640	0.88	260	-68.00	9120
Panskura-II	1200 (81.53)	12000	10	1000 (55.40)	12000	12	-16.67	0	20
Ghatal	2 (0.14)	18	9	— —	—	—	—	—	
Daspur-I	5 (0.34)	45	9	15 (0.83)	75	5	200	66.67	–44.44
Daspur-II	45 (3.06)	450	10	50 (2.77)	250	5	11.11	–44.44	–50.00
Total	1472 (100)	14673	9.96	1805 (100)	21465	11.89	22.62	46.29	193

Note : Figures in brackets indicate percentages to total.

Source : P.A.O., Midnapore (East).

TABLE 10

Estimated Regressions Equations for the Cultivator Households

Set of Cultivators	Fit	R^2
Whole Set	FA = 55.94 – 5.47 L.H.*	
	(–2.31)**	0.29
Whole Set	GP = 3204.08 + 167.46 FA	0.91
	(11.75)	
Whole Set	EMP = 189.69 + 4.56 FA*	0.28
	(2.24)	
Whole Set	FCEMP = 291.16 + 4.58 FA*	0.29
	(2.34)**	
Whole Set	FEMP = 176.93 + 4.95 FA	0.38
	(2.54)	
Set with Credit	FA = 10.07 + 0.011 TCR**	0.65
	(4.95)	
Whole Set	FA = 58.03 – 5.2 RB*	0.22
	(–1.93)	

Note : (i) Figures in brackets indicate – ratios, * indicates significant at 5% level and ** indicates significant at 1% level.

(ii) FA — percenatge of area under floriculture to G.C.A.; L.H. — size of land holding, G.P. = Gross Profit per acre.

EMP = Employment per acre, FCEMP = Employment of female and child labour per acre. FEMP = Employment of female labour per acre.

(iii) TCR = Total Credit per Acre.

(iv) RB = Resource Base.

TABLE 11

Frequency Distribution of Sample Cultivator Households (with Credit and without Credit) by Percentage of Area Under Floriculture

% Area under Floriculture	Households with Credit				Households without Credit			
	Pre-loan		Post-loan		1994		1998	
	No.	%age	No.	%age	No.	%age	No.	%age
0	14	70	0	0	5	25	5	25
0 to 5	2	10	11	55	10	50	9	45
6 to 10	3	15	5	25	3	15	3	15
11 to 20	1/20	5	4/20	20	2/20	10	3/20	15

Source : Field Level Survey.

TABLE 12

Benefit Cost Ratio and Percentage Employment by Sex of Floriculture *vis-à-vis* Betelvine cultivation & Paddy

Crops	Benefit Cost Ratio	% of Female Child Labour	% of Female Labour
Night-Queen (Rajanigandha)	3.00	50	40
Bell	1.86	80	65
Jasmine	0.937	75	60
Rose	2.66	40	35
Marigold	2.80	78	55
Betelvine			
(a) Bangla	1.10	20	15
(b) Mitha	5.56	15	12
Paddy			
(a) Aman (HYV)	0.342	15	12
(b) Boro (HYV)	0.85	35	20

Source : Field level Survey.

TABLE 13

Exports of Cut Flowers and Foliage and Other Cut Flowers from India by Major Countries

	Countries	1982-83	1986-87	1990-91	1992-93	1994-95	1995-96
1.	Australia	—	3 (.04)	217 (.85)	1021 (1.21)	1851 (.82)	3658 (.78)
2.	German FREP	37 (5)	119 (1.83)	4953 (19.39)	13959 (16.53)	36983 (16.38)	65257 (14.03)
3.	Kuwait	99 (13)	340 (15.25)	73 (.28)	118 (.14)	5	456 (.10)
4.	Japan	—	92 (1.42)	56 (.22)	1402 (1.66)	12038 (5.33)	53053 (11.41)
5.	Netherland	19 (2.5)	—	445 (1.74)	2946 (3.48)	29043 (12.86)	76050 (16.36)
6.	Oman	—	19 (2.29)	242 (.94)	613 (.72)	65 (.03)	139 (.03)
7.	Saudi Arabia	340 (46)	1107 (17.10)	1183 (4.63)	5007 (5.93)	2783 (1.23)	4810 (1.03)
8.	Singapore	78 (10)	—	—	246 (2.29)	843 (.37)	1525 (.33)
9.	Sri Lanka	—	—	—	1651 (1.95)	4087 (1.81)	8152 (1.75)
10.	Arab EMTE	77 (10)	285 (4.40)	7 (.03)	1233 (1.46)	4216 (1.86)	11460 (2.46)
11.	U.K.	—	1 (.01)	6895 (26.99)	24829 (29.40)	22821 (10.10)	39557 (8.51)
12.	U.S.A.	—	4329 (66.88)	6114 (23.98)	2767 (3.27)	10269 (4.55)	157811 (33.94)
13.	Other Countries	95 (12)	177 (2.73)	5354 (20.96)	28645 (33.92)	100759 (44.63)	42958 (9.24)
	Total	745 (100)	6472 (100)	25539 (100)	84439 (100)	225763 (100)	464886 (100)

Source : Government of India.

TABLE 14

Value of Exports of Floriculture from India, 1991-92 to 1998-99

Year	Value of Exports (Rs. in Lakhs)
1991-92	1480.00
1992-93	1491.00
1993-94	1883.65
1994-95	3083.80
1995-96	6014.15
1996-97	6339.86
1997-98	8120.67
1998-99	9660.97

Source : APEDA, Government of India.

TABLE 15

Labour Employment & Profitability of Different Varieties of Flowers

Name of Flowers	Labour Employment Per Acre (No.)	Profit/Agre. (Rs.)
Nightqueen	300	24,000.00
Bela	250	20,500.00
Jui	200	15,000.00
Rose	200	16,000.00
Marigold	400	14,000.00

Source : Directorate of Agricultural Marketing, Government of West Bengal.

Diagram-I

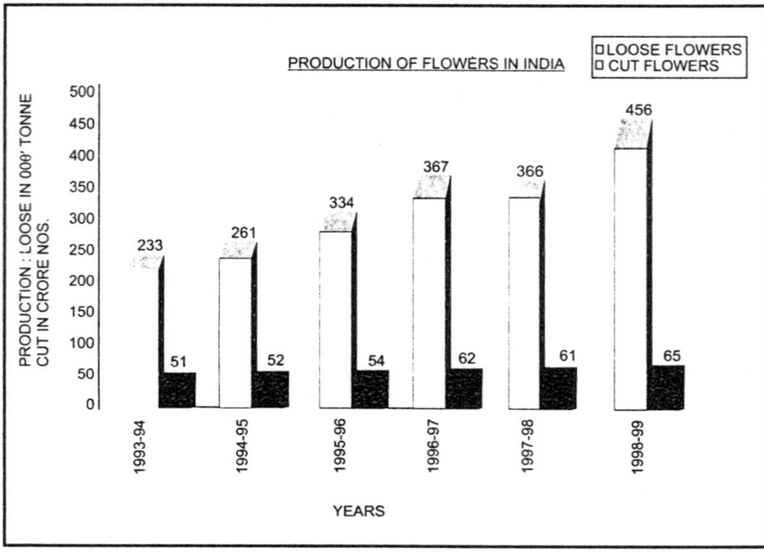

Diagram-II

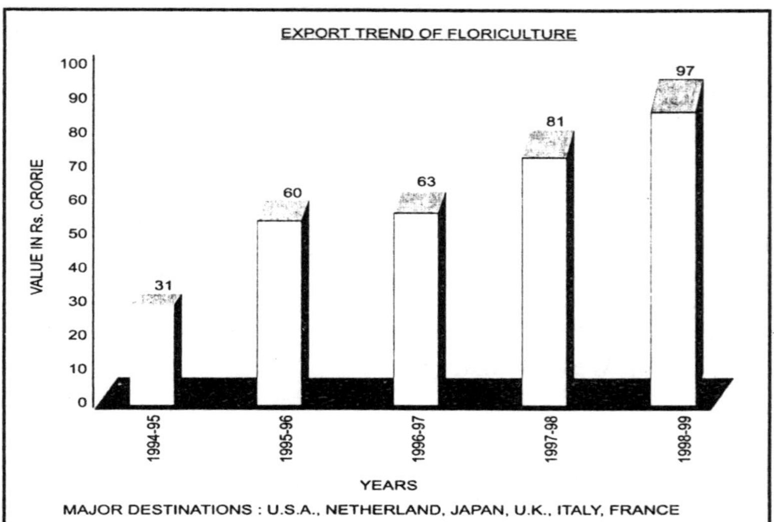

11

Rural Development Schemes

PANCHAYATI RAJ

April 24,1993 is a red-letter day in the history of Panchayati Raj in India as on this day the Constitution (73rd Amendment) Act, 1992 came into force to provide constitutional status to the Panchyati Raj institutions.

73rd Amendment Act, 1992

The salient features of the Act are :

- To provide 3-tier system of Panchayati Raj for all States having population of over 20 lakh.
- To hold Panchayat elections regularly every 5 years.
- To provide reservation of seats for Scheduled Castes, Scheduled Tribes and women (not less than 33%).
- To appoint State Finance Commission to make recommendations as regards the financial powers of the Panchayats.
- To constitute District Planning Committee to prepare draft development plan for the district as a whole.

Powers and Responsibilities

According to the Constitution, Panchayats shall be given powers and authority to function as institutions of self-government. The following powers and responsibilities are to be delegated to Panchayats at the appropriate level :

- Preparation of plan for economic development and social justice.
- Implementation of schemes for economic development and social justice in relation to 29 subjects given in Eleventh Schedule of the Constitution.
- To levy, collect and appropriate taxes, duties, tolls and fees.

Gram Sabha

In the Panchayati Raj set up, the Gram Sabha, the general assembly of villagers, has a key role for effective functioning of Panchayats. In the Gram Sabha meeting, the rural poor, the women and the marginalised people would now get an opportunity to join in decision making on matters affecting their lives. Active functioning of the Gram Sabha would ensure a participatory democracy with transparency, accountability and achievement.

- Gram Sabha should meet at least in each quarter preferably on Republic Day, Labour Day, Independence Day and Gandhi Jayanti.
- Decide developmental work to be undertaken by Panchayats based on needs assessment.
- Suggest remedial measures for economy and efficiency in the functioning of the Panchayats.
- Question and scrutinise the decisions of Panchayats in the meeting of Gram Sabha.
- Discuss the Annual Financial Statement of Gram Panchayats.

The Provisions of the Panchayats (Extension to the Scheduled Areas) Act, 1996

This Act extends Panchayats to the tribal areas of eight States, namely : Andhra Pradesh, Bihar, Gujarat, Himachal Pradesh, Maharashtra, Madhya Pradesh, Orissa and Rajasthan. This has come into force on 24th December 1996. Except

Rajasthan and Bihar all States have passed laws to give effect to the provisions contained in the Act, 40 of 1996.

Under the Act, Gram Sabha has been vested with powers for :

- Ownership of minor forest produce.
- Development plans approval.
- Selection of beneficiaries under various programmes.
- Consultation on land acquisition.
- Manage minor water bodies.
- Control mineral leases.
- Regulate/Prohibit sale of intoxicants.
- Prevent alienation of land and restore unlawfully alienated land of STs.
- Manage village markets.
- Control money lending to STs.
- Control institutions and functionaries in all social sector.

Training and Awareness Generation Programme

The Ministry of Rural Development extends limited financial assistance to the States in their effort to train and create awareness among the elected members of Panchayats and functionaries. The State Governments are being asked to conduct such training courses. The Ministry has also been providing financial assistance through the Council for Advancement of People's Action & Rural Technology (CAPART) to the non-governmental organisations for conducting training and awareness generation programmes on Panchayati Raj. This Ministry also commissions research and evaluation studies related to Panchayati Raj from voluntary organisations/institutions.

JAWAHAR GRAM SAMRIDHI YOJANA

Introduction

Jawahar Gram Samridhi Yojana (JGSY) is the restructured, streamlined and comprehensive version of the erstwhile Jawahar Rozgar Yojana (JRY). It has been launched on 1st April 1999. It has been designed to improve the quality of life of the rural poor by providing them additional gainful employment.

Objective

The primary objective of Jawahar Gram Samridhi Yojana is the creation of demand-driven village infrastructure including durable assets to enable the rural poor to increase the opportunities for sustained employment. The secondary objective is the generation of supplementary employment for the unemployed poor in the rural areas.

Target Group

People living in villages constitute the target group of JGSY. Preference is given to SCs/STs, families living below the poverty line and physically handicapped persons.

Salient Features

* The programme is being implemented entirely at the Village Panchayat level. District Rural Development Agencies (DRDAs)/ Zilla Parishads (ZPs) will release the funds including State matching share directly to Village Panchayats.

  - Village Panchayat is the sole authority for preparation of Annual Action Plan and its implementation with the approval of Gram Sabha.
  - 22.5 per cent of JGSY funds have been earmarked for individual beneficiary schemes for SCs/STs.
  - 3 per cent annual allocation would be utilised for creation of barrier free infrastructure for the disabled.
  - Wages under JGSY will either be the minimum

wages notified by the States or higher wages fixed by States through the procedure prescribed by the State Governments.

- The emphasis of JGSY will be on the creation of durable assets at the village level. Therefore, it has been decided to suitably relax the condition of maintenance of 60:40 wage-material ratio so as to enable the Panchayats to build up demand-driven rural infrastructure, simultaneously taking due care of need-based wage employment generation.
- Village Panchayats will have the power to execute works/schemes up to Rs. 50,000 with the approval of Gram Sabha. No other administrative or technical approval will be necessary. However, for works/schemes costing more than Rs. 50,000, after taking the approval of the Gram Sabha, the Village Panchayat shall seek the technical/administrative approval of appropriate authorities.
- In many States Village Panchayats are not sufficiently equipped with staff nor do they have sufficient funds to bear other administrative expenditure/contingency. Under JRY Village Panchayats were permitted to spend upto Rs. 1,000 per year for purchasing items of stationery, registers, etc. However, this is hardly adequate both due to escalation of costs and enhanced responsibilities of Gram Panchayats. It is, therefore, decided to allow Village Panchayats to incur expenditure upto Rs. 7500 or 7.5 per cent of funds, whichever is less, in a year on administrative expenditure/contingency and for employing technical consultancy.
- 15 per cent of funds can be spent on maintenance of assets.
- Under JRY, allocation of funds to the Village Panchayats were made on the basis of population.

The Village Panchayats having less than 1000 population were taken as of 1,000 population and more than 10,000 taken as 10,000 for the purpose of allocation of funds to the village panchayats. It has been decided to remove the present upper ceiling of 10,000 population for allocation of JGSY funds to the village panchayats. Now the funds to the village panchayats would be allocated on the basis of population without any ceiling of 10,000 as at present.

- DRDA/ZP/Intermediate Panchayats will be responsible for overall guidance, coordination, supervision, monitoring and periodical reporting.

Funding Pattern

The programme will be implemented as a Centrally sponsored scheme on cost sharing basis between the Centre and the States in the ratio of 75:25. DRDAs/Zila Parishads will release the funds including State matching share directly to Village Panchayats. In the case of Union Territories, entire funds under the scheme will be provided by the Centre.

Implementing Agency

The Programme is to be implemented by village panchayats with the approval of Gram Sabha. For seeking assistance, Village Pardhan, Panchayat members, Block Development Officer, District Collector or District Rural Development Agency may be contacted.

SWARNJAYANTI GRAM SWAROZGAR YOJANA

Introduction

Notwithstanding the impressive progress that has been made by the country on different fronts, poverty continues to be a matter of serious concern. The effect of large percentage of the poor on the country's development is obvious. The situation needs to be redressed quickly. It is in this context that the self-employment programmes acquire significance. Swarnjayanti Gram Swarozgar Yojana (SGSY) is the single self-employment programme for the rural poor. Launched on April 1, 1999 the programme replaces the earlier self-employment and allied programmes — IRDP, TRYSEM, DWCRA, SITRA, GKY and MWS, which are no longer in operation. SGSY is an innovative and carefully thought-out Yojana. It takes into account all the strengths and weaknesses of the earlier self-employment programmes. It offers the perfect balance of credit and subsidy.

Objectives

Swarnjayanti Gram Swarozgar Yojana aims at establishing a large number of micro-enterprises in the rural areas, building upon the potential of the rural poor. It is rooted in the belief that the rural poor in India have competencies and given the right support can be successful producers of valuable goods/services. Persons assisted under this programme will be known as Swarozgaris and not beneficiaries. A significant aspect of SGSY is that every family assisted under this programme will be brought above the poverty line in three years and, therefore, the programme aims at creating substantial additional incomes for the rural poor. Subject to availability of funds, it is proposed to cover 30 per cent of the rural poor in each block in the next five years.

Target Group

The programme has been designed to provide proper support and encouragement to tap the inherent talents and capabilities of the rural poor. It will target the most vulnerable among them. At least 50 per cent of the Swarozgaris will be SCs/STs, 20 per cent women and 3 per cent disabled.

Salient Features

- SGSY is conceived as a holistic programme of micro-enterprises covering all aspects of self-employment, *viz.*, organisation of the rural poor into self-help groups and their capacity building, planning of activity clusters, infrastructure build up, technology, credit and marketing.

- SGSY lays emphasis on activity clusters. 2-5 key activities will be identified for each block based on the resources, occupational skills of the people and availability of markets. Selection of key activities will be with the approval of the Panchayat Samitis at the block level and the District Rural Development Agency (DRDA)/Zila Parishad (ZP) at the district level. The activities will be taken up in suitable clusters to enable extension of appropriate facilities. Care would be taken to involve as many panchayats as possible in covering the key activities. The major share of SGSY assistance will be in activity clusters. SGSY will adopt a project approach for each key activity. The existing infrastructure for the cluster of activities will be reviewed and critical gaps will be filled under SGSY.
- SGSY focuses on Group approach. This would involve organisation of the poor into Self-Help Groups (SHGs) and their capacity building. Efforts would be made to involve women members in each SHG. Group activity will be given preference and progressively majority of the funding will be for self-help groups. In each Panchayat Samiti, at least half of the groups will be exclusively women groups.
- The Gram Sabha will authenticate the list of families below the poverty line identified in the BPL census. Identification of individual swarozgaris will be made through a participatory process.
- SGSY is a credit-cum-subsidy programme. Credit will be the critical component in SGSY, subsidy being only an enabling element. Accordingly, SGSY envisages a greater involvement of the banks, in the planning and preparation of projects, identification of activity clusters, infrastructure planning as well as capacity building and choice of activity of the SHGs, selection

of individual Swarozgaris, pre-credit activities and post-credit monitoring including loan recovery.

- SGSY seeks to promote multiple credit rather than a one-time credit 'injection'. The credit requirement of the Swarozgaris will be carefully assessed and they will be encouraged to increase their credit intake over the years.
- Subsidy under Swarnjayanti Gram Swarozgar Yojana would be uniform at 30 per cent of the project cost subject to a ceiling of Rs. 7,500 (for SCs/STs it would be 50 per cent and Rs. 10,000 respectively). For self-help groups, subsidy would be 50 per cent of the project cost subject to a ceiling of 1.25 lakh. There will be no limit on the subsidy for irrigation projects.
- Special emphasis will be laid on skill development of the Swarozgaris through well-designed training courses tailored to the activities selected and to the requirements of each Swarozgari.
- Closer attention to technology and marketing needs of the swarozgaris would be the hallmark of SGSY. Technology intervention will seek to add value to the local resources, including processing of the locally available material from natural and other resources for local and non-local market. SGSY will provide for promotion of marketing of the goods produced by the SGSY Swarozgaris. This would involve market intelligence, development of markets, consultancy services as well as institutional arrangements for marketing of the goods including exports.
- SGSY takes into account the role of every participant — the panchayats, gram sabhas, banks financial institutions, NGOs as well as the technical institutions in the district. Care has been taken to involve them right from the conceptualisation stage so that they work as a team for the success of the programme.

- In order to facilitate poverty reduction efforts requiring coordinated action by different departments, pioneering projects, etc., SGSY has a provision for special projects which will be sanctioned by the Ministry of Rural Development.

Funding Pattern

Funds under the SGSY will be shared by the Central and State Governments in the ratio of 75:25. The Central allocation earmarked for the States will be distributed in relation to the incidence of poverty in the States. However, additional parameters like absorption capacity and special requirement will also be taken into consideration during the course of the year.

Implementing Agency

The SGSY will be implemented by the DRDAs through the Panchayat Samitis. The process of planning, implementation and monitoring would integrate the banks and other financial institutions, the PRIs, NGOs as well as technical institutes in the districts.

EMPLOYMENT ASSURANCE SCHEME

Introduction

Employment Assurance Scheme was launched on 2nd October 1993 for implementation in 1778 identified backward blocks of different States. The blocks selected were in the drought prone areas, desert areas, tribal areas and hilly areas. Later, the scheme was extended to the remaining blocks of the country in phased manner. At present, the scheme is being implemented in all the rural blocks of the country. The programme has been restructured from 1.4.99.

Objective

As its name suggests, the primary objective of the EAS is to provide gainful employment during the lean agricultural season in manual work to all able bodied adults in rural areas who are in need and desirous of work, but cannot find it. The work may be either on farm or on other allied operations or on the normal plan/non-plan works during such a period. The secondary objective is the creation of community, social and economic assets for sustaining employment and development.

Target Group

The EAS would be open to all adult rural poor who are in need of wage employment. A maximum of two adults per family (generally expected number of adults in a family) would be provided wage employment, when there is demand during lean agricultural season subject to availability of funds.

Salient Features

- EAS will be the single wage employment programme to be implemented at the district/block levels throughout the country.
- The funds to the States will be allocated on the basis of proportion of rural population in a State to the total rural poor in the country or such other criteria as decided by the Central Government from time to time.
- 70 per cent of the funds flowing to the districts would be allocated to the blocks and 30 per cent reserved at the district level to be utilized in the areas of distress.
- The selection of works would be decided by Zilla Parishads after consultations with elected representative of the areas.
- In the absence of Elected Bodies, a committee comprising of local MPs and MLAs and other elected representatives would be constituted for selection of works.
- The expenditure will be in the ratio of 60:40 for wage/non-wage component.

- The Employment Assurance Scheme will operate at district/block levels throughout the country. However, priority would be given to the areas suffering from endemic labour exodus.
- Persons seeking wage employment under EAS would be engaged in the works included in the annual action plan prepared for this purpose by the ZP.
- The provisions of employment under this scheme should result in the creation of durable and productive assets.

Achievements

- The scheme had Central allocation of Rs. 1,990.00 crore during 1998-99. Complete Central share had been released to States/UTs. As per reports received upto March 1999 against total availability of Rs. 3,357.15 crore, the utilization reported is Rs. 2819.76 crore and the employment generated is 4165.31 lakh mandays. Since inception of the scheme, the total number of registered wage seekers is 4.29 crore.

Funding Pattern

- The resources under the scheme would be shared between Centre and States in the ratio of 75:25 respectively.

Implementing Agency

Zilla Parishads

Corrective Action taken

The restructured EAS programme will be implemented from the financial year 1999-2000.

RURAL HOUSING

Government announced, in 1998, a National Housing and Habitat Policy which aims at providing 'Housing for All' and facilitating the construction of 20 lakh additional housing units (13 lakh in Rural Areas and 7 lakh in Urban Areas) annually, with emphasis on extending benefits to the poor and the deprived. An Action Plan for Rural Housing has accordingly been prepared.

Under 'Rural Housing', an allocation of Rs. 1,710 crores had been made during 2000-2001 to implement the Action Plan, which has been approved with the objective of providing "Shelter for All" by ending shelterlessness by the end of the Ninth Plan period and conversion of all unserviceable kutcha houses to pucca/semi pucca by the end of the Tenth Plan period, through the construction of additional 13 lakh houses annually. The Action Plan consists of the following elements :

- Conversion of unserviceable kutcha houses in Indira Awaas Yojana (IAY).
- Pradhan Mantri Gramodaya Yojana-Gramin Awaas.
- Credit-cum-Subsidy Scheme for Rural Housing.
- Samagra Awaas Yojana
- Innovative Stream for Rural Housing & Habitat Development.
- Rural Building Centres.
- Enhancement of equity contribution by Ministry of Rural Development to HUDCO.
- National Mission for Rural Housing & Habitat.

1. Indira Awaas Yojana

The Government of India is implementing Indira Awaas Yojana since the year 1985-86 to provide assistance for construction of dwelling units to members of Scheduled Castes, Scheduled Tribes and freed bonded labourers and non-Scheduled Castes/Scheduled Tribes living below the poverty line in the rural areas which was a sub scheme of erstwhile JRY. From the year 1993-94, the scope of the scheme was extended to cover non-Scheduled Castes and Scheduled Tribes rural poor subject to the condition that the benefit to non

SC/ST would not be more than 40 per cent of the IAY allocation. The benefits of the Scheme have also been extended to the families of Ex-servicemen of the armed and paramilitary forces killed in action. Three per cent of the houses are reserved for the below the poverty line disabled persons living in the rural areas. IAY became an independent Scheme w.e.f. 1.1.96.

The funding pattern of IAY is on 75:25 basis between the Centre and the States. During 1999-2000, the allocation of funds under Indira Awaas Yojana to the States/UTs had been made, based on poverty ratios, as approved by the Planning Commission and rural housing shortage (Census 1991). Both parameters have been accorded equal weightage. Similarly, allocation from States to Districts have been made on the basis of proportion of SC/ST population and housing shortage. The ceiling on construction assistance under the Indira Awaas Yojana currently is Rs. 20,000 per unit for plain areas and Rs. 22,000 for hilly/difficult areas. These ceiling came into effect from 1.8.96.

District Rural Development Agencies (DRDAs)/Zilla Parishads on the basis of allocations made and targets fixed shall decide Panchayat-wise number of houses to be constructed under IAY, during a particular financial year and intimate the same to the Gram Panchayat. Thereafter, the Gram Sabha will select the beneficiaries restricting its number to the target allotted from the list of eligible households, according to the guidelines and as per priorities fixed. No approval of Panchayat Samiti will be required. The Panchayat Samiti should, however, be sent a list of selected beneficiaries for their information. This amendment in the IAY guidelines came into force with effect from 1.4.1998.

According to 1991 Census, the total rural housing shortage is 137.2 lakh in rural areas. There are about 103.1 lakh unserviceable kutcha houses which require upgradation in the rural areas. As the need for upgradation of unserviceable kutcha houses in the rural areas is acutely felt, therefore, with effect from 1.4.99, 20 per cent of the IAY allocation had been earmarked for conversion of unserviceable kutcha houses into pucca/semi pucca houses. A maximum assistance of Rs. 10,000 per unit is provided for conversion of unserviceable kutcha houses into pucca/semi pucca.

Further, the allotment of dwelling units should be in the name of a female member of the beneficiary household. Alternatively, it can be allotted in the name of both husband and wife. Sanitary latrine and smokeless chullah are integral parts of the I.A.Y. house. The construction of the house is the responsibility of the beneficiary. The I.A.Y. house is not to be constructed and delivered by any external agency such as government departments, NGOs, etc. No specific type design has been stipulated for an IAY house. Choice of design, technology and materials for construction of an IAY house is the sole discretion of the beneficiaries.

The Central allocation under IAY for 2000-2001 is Rs. 1,613.69 crore for construction of 1244320 houses. Out of this 20 per cent of the funds amounting to Rs. 322.78 crore have been earmarked for upgradation of unserviceable kutcha houses into pucca/semi pucca houses. The State-wise allocation and target for 2000-01 is at Annexure-I. First instalment of funds to the tune of Rs. 740.51 crores has been released during 2000-01 and Rs. 52.33 crores has been released as advance second instalment to Andhra Pradesh and Gujarat due to flood and drought affected regions respectively. An additional assistance of Rs. 100.75 crores was released to Rajasthan and Orissa.

About 64 lakh houses have been constructed under IAY since inception of the Scheme. Nearly Rs. 10662.55 crores expenditure have been incurred since inception of the Scheme under IAY. Financial and Physical progress under IAY (Plan/ Year-wise) since 1985-86 till 28th September 2000 is at Annexure-II.

Members of Parliament and members of Legislative Assemblies are members of the Governing Bodies of District

Rural Development Agencies (DRDAs). Instructions have been issued to the effect that member of Parliament belonging to Lok Sabha will have to be co-opted as the member of the Governing Body of more than one DRDA if his constituency spans over more than one district. Similarly Member of Rajya Sabha will also be a member of DRDA Governing Body of the concerned district if he hails from or in the Governing Body of a DRDA of his choice to be intimated to the Chairman in writing. Further there are guidelines to the effect that Governing Body meeting are to be held regularly and once in a quarter after giving sufficient notice to all the members, including the members of Parliament and members of Legislative Assemblies. It has also been suggested by this Ministry that the meetings of the DRDA Governing bodies should be convened, as far as possible, when Parliament would not be in Session. Besides, instructions have also been issued to constitute District and Block Level Vigilance and Monitoring Committees and District and Block Level EAS Committees wherever not done by including members of Parliament representing the Districts and ensuring that invitations for the meetings of these Committees are also sent in advance to them.

Indira Awaas Yojana has been evaluated by the Programme Evaluation Organisation of the Planning Commission which carried out a Quick Study of the IAY in 1992-93. According to the evaluation done by the Planning Commission, 86.4 per cent of the houses constructed under the Yojana were occupied and lived in. Again about 84 per cent of the households expressed satisfaction/partial satisfaction with the houses given to them. The main reasons for their satisfaction with the IAY houses were able to satisfy socio-cultural needs, suits life style, good construction, etc. Concurrent Evaluation on IAY is in progress.

2. Pradhan Mantri Gramodaya Yojana

PMGY has been launched only from 2000-01. Ministry of Rural Development is the nodal Ministry for the implementation and monitoring of the programme PMGY: Rural shelter. The guidelines have been circulated to all States/ UTs. The Scheme is based on Indira Awas Yojana. States/ UTs are required to send us project proposals for release under PMGY. Releases are to be made by the Ministry of Finance on recommendation of this Ministry. A minimum of Rs. 375 crores were available under PMGY and States/UTs can avail more funds for the purpose out of 25 per cent funds kept at their disposal for all components of PMG under discretionary quota. A few proposals have already been received and after the approval of the Committee constituted for the purpose have been referred to Ministry of Finance for releasing funds. However, Ministry of Finance have issued order for releasing Ist instalment of grant to all State Governments for meeting their requirements for first six months on *ad hoc* basis, as a special case. Total amount thus released is Rs. 185 crores. State-wise release of funds is at Annexure-III.

3. Credit-Cum-Subsidy Scheme for Rural Housing

The Credit-Cum-Subsidy Scheme for Rural Housing was launched w.e.f. 1st April 1999. The Scheme targets rural families having annual income upto Rs. 32,000 to enable/ facilitate construction of houses for all rural households who have some repayment capacity. The target group under the Scheme will be the rural households having an annual income of Rs. 32,000 only. However, preference will be given to rural household who are below poverty line. While subsidy is restricted to Rs. 10,000, the maximum loan amount that can be availed of is Rs. 40,000. The subsidy portion is shared by the Centre and the State in 75:25 ratio. The loan portion is to be disbursed by the commercial banks, housing finance institutions etc. During 1999-2000 an amount of Rs. 60.69 crores was released under the scheme. Rs. 150.00 crores were allocated under the Scheme for construction of 1.09 lakh houses during 2000-2001. State-wise allocations and targets under the Scheme are given at Annexure-IV.

During the current financial year, funds will be released after the receipt of utilization certificates from the States/ UTs.

4. Samagra Awaas Yojana

It was decided to take up the Samagra Awaas Yojana in 1999-2000, on pilot basis, in one Block each of 25 districts of 24 States and one Union Territory which have been identified for implementing a participatory approach under the Accelerated Rural Water Supply Programme. A special Central Assistance of Rs. 25 lakhs is being provided for each Block for undertaking overall habitat development and IEC work. Rs. 2.67 crores were released during 1999-2000. During 2000-01 an amount of Rs. 0.65 crores has been released so far.

5. Innovative Stream for Rural Housing and Habitat Development

To encourage innovative, cost effective and environment friendly solutions in building/housing sectors in rural areas, this Scheme has been launched with effect from 1-4-1999. The objective of the Innovative Stream for Rural Housing and Habitat Development is to promote/propagate innovate and proven housing technologies, designs and materials in the rural areas. The Innovative Stream for Rural Housing and Habitat Development is being implemented on Project basis. All recognized Governmental organizations/institutions and reputed NGO's well experienced in the technology promotion and propagation of cost effective and environmental friendly housing technologies, designs and material may apply for funding to the Ministry of Rural Development. So far an amount of Rs. 331.73 lakhs has been released under this Scheme since inception in 1999-2000.

6. Setting up of Rural Building Centres

The primary objectives of setting up of Rural Building Centres are : (a) Technology transfer and information dissemination, (b) Skill upgradation through training and

(c) Production of cost effective and environment friendly materials/components. For setting up of each Building Centre, a one time grant of Rs. 15 lakhs were provided. Rs. 54 lakhs was released under the scheme during 1999-2000. During 2000-2001, Rs. 3 crores have been allocated to implement the Scheme. So far Rs. 66 lakhs have been released under scheme during the year. Thus, a total amount of Rs. 120 lakhs has been released since its inception.

7. Equity Support to Housing and Urban Development Corporation Limited

To meet the requirement of EWS and LIG groups in rural areas and to improve the outreach of housing finance in rural areas, it has been decided to increase the equity support to HUDCO from Rs. 5 crores to Rs. 355 crores during the Ninth Five Year Plan period, in pursuance of which Rs. 50 crore was released during 1998-99 and Rs. 150 crores were released during 1999-2000. HUDCO proposes to finance the construction of additional 6 lakh houses during the current year. An MOU between Ministry of Rural Development, Ministry of Urban Development and HUDCO for 2000-2001 is under consideration. During 2000-2001, Rs. 100 crores have been earmarked as equity support to HUDCO.

8. National Mission for Rural Housing and Habitat

A National Mission for Rural Housing and Habitat has been set up by the Ministry of Rural Development to facilitate the induction of science and technology inputs, on a continuous basis, in the sector and to provide convergence to technology, habitat and energy-related issues in order to provide affordable shelter for all in the rural areas, within a specified time-frame, and through community participation. Towards this end, an Executive Council under the Chairmanship of the Minister of Rural Development and an Empowered Committee under the Chairmanship of Secretary (Rural Development) have been constituted. First meeting of the Empowered

Committee on National Mission for Rural Housing & Habitat was held on 13th March 2000 under the Chairmanship of the Secretary (RD).

NATIONAL SOCIAL ASSISTANCE PROGRAMME

Introduction

The National Social Assistance Programme (NSAP) comprises three separate Schemes, namely, National Old Age Pension Scheme (NOAPS), National Family Benefit Scheme (NFBS) and National Maternity Benefit Scheme (NMBS). The Programme introduces a national policy for social security assistance to the poor families and represents a significant step towards the fulfilment of the Directive Principles in Articles 21 and 22 of the Constitution recognising the concurrent responsibility of the Central and State Governments in the matter. The NSAP is a Centrally Sponsored Programme to extend 100 per cent Central assistance to the States/UTs to provide the benefits under it in accordance with the norms, guidelines and conditions laid down by the Central Government. The Programme has come into effect from August 15, 1995.

Objective

The objective of the Programme is to extend financial assistance to old persons having little or no regular means of subsistence, to households living below the poverty line in case of death of the primary breadwinner and to pregnant women of households below the poverty line upto the first two live births.

Target Groups

The assistance under the National Social Assistance Programme NSAP is available to the destitutes, the poorest of the poor and families below the poverty lines. The Scheme-wise target groups are as under :

- National Old Age Pension Scheme (NOAPS) :
- Old persons who are destitutes in the sense of having no regular means of subsistence from their own sources

of income or through financial support from family members or other sources.

- National Family Benefit Scheme (NFMS) :
- Households below the poverty line on the death of the primary breadwinner. The 'primary breadwinner' has been defined as the member of the family whose earnings contribute substantially to the total household income.
- National Maternity Benefit Scheme (NMBS) :
- Pregnant women of the households living below the poverty line upto the first two live births.

Salient Features

National Old Age Pension Scheme (NOAPS) :

- Age of the applicant (male or female) should be 65 years or above.
- The applicant must be a destitute in the sense of having little or no regular means of subsistence from his/her own sources of income or through financial support from family members or other sources.
- The amount of pension is Rs. 75 per month per beneficiary. The State Government may add to this amount from their own sources.
- Upper ceiling on the number of beneficiaries for a State/UT is prescribed by the Central Government.

National Family Benefit Scheme (NFBS) :

- Central assistance for a lumpsum family benefit is available for the households below the poverty line on the death of the primary breadwinner in the bereaved family.
- The amount of assistance is Rs. 10,000.
- The primary breadwinner is a member of the family whose earnings contribute substantially to the total household income.

- The death of the primary breadwinner due to natural or accidental causes should have occurred while he or she is in the age group of 18 to 64 *i.e.*, more than 18 years of age but less than 65 years of age.
- The maximum limit of the total number of beneficiaries of a State/UT is prescribed by the Central Government.
- The family benefit is paid to such surviving members of the households of the deceased who, after local enquiry, is determined to be the head of the household.

National Maternity Benefit Scheme (NMBS) :

- A lumpsum cash assistance of Rs. 500 to the pregnant woman of the household living below the poverty line is given provided she is 19 years of age or above.
- The benefit is available upto the first two live births.
- The benefit is disbursed several weeks prior to the delivery. In case of delay, the benefit may be given even after the birth of the child.

Achievement

The original budget provision for the National Social Assistance Programme during the year 1998-99 was Rs. 700 crores. However, the allocation was reduced to Rs. 620 crores at RE stage. The amount utilised against this RE is Rs. 620.20 crores during 1998-99.

The achievement made by the States/UTs through the financial assistance as above in extending benefits to the target groups during 1998-99 is being assessed. The provisional position in this regard is as follows :

- NOAPS : 60,61,762 Beneficiaries.

  NFBS : 19,62,238 Beneficiarie.

  NMBS : 11,52,558 Beneficiaries.

Funding Pattern

The National Social Assistance Programme (NSAP) is a

Centrally sponsored programme for which 100 per cent Central assistance is made available to the States/UTs to provide benefits for the three Schemes under it in accordance with the norms, guidelines and conditions laid down by the Central Government. The funds are released directly to the districts in two instalments during a year.

Implementing Agency

The programme is implemented by the district level implementing authorities headed by the District Collector/ Magistrate/Deputy Commissioner. It is implemented with the assistance of the Panchayats and Municipalities in the delivery of social assistance to make it more responsive and cost effective.

Evaluation Conducted

The State level and District level Committees constituted as per the provisions of the NSAP guidelines meet from time to time to monitor and evaluate the performance of the schemes in their respective States/Districts. The nodal Ministry at the Centre also monitors States' progress in implementing the schemes to evaluate performance of each one of them. An Evaluation Study on the Programme covering eight States has also been completed recently through a reputed Research Organisation. Another two such Studies are in progress in the States of Rajasthan and Uttar Pradesh.

Corrective Action taken

Various aspects emerging from the periodical review meetings at the Centre, States and districts are taken note of and appropriate actions are taken accordingly for ensuring improvement in the implementation of the schemes. The findings of the Research Organisation which has since submitted its Report are being studied.

TRAINING

National Institute of Rural Development

Introduction

The National Institute of Rural Development (NIRD) is an autonomous organization under the aegis of the Ministry of Rural Development with its Headquarter at Hyderabad. It has also a regional centre at Guwahati to cater the special needs of North Eastern Region.

Objectives

The National Institute of Rural Development (NIRD) conducts training programmes and organises conferences, seminars and workshops. The Institute also undertakes research, action research and consultancy in the field of rural development.

Target Group

Rural Development functionaries involved in the implementation of Rural Development Schemes include elected representatives of Panchayati Raj Institutions.

Salient Features

NIRD is the country's apex body for undertaking training, research, action research, consultancy and documentation functions in the rural development sector.

Achievements

During the year 1999-2000, the Institute conducted 152 training programmes. More than 4260 participants attended these training courses.

Funding Pattern

The scheme is funded 100 per cent by the Govt. of India. The allocation to this Institute for the year 2000-2001 is Rs. 5.00 crores for Plan and Rs. 7.75 crores for Non-Plan.

Strengthening/Establishment of State Institutes of Rural Development (SIRDs)

Introduction

There is a Centrally Sponsored Scheme for Strengthening/ Establishment of State Institutes of Rural Development (SIRDs) which was considered vital for Human Resource Development since the VIth Five-Year Plan. So far 25 SIRDs have been established in 25 States for intensifying training-related activities in the States.

The objective of the SIRD is to train Rural Development functionaries as well as elected representatives of Panchayati Raj Institutions in the concerned State. The SIRDs have linkage with NIRD as well as Extension Training Centres (ETCs).

Funding Pattern and Achievements

This is a demand driven-scheme and no State-wise/SIRD-wise allocation of funds is made. The funds released to the States are in the ratio of 50:50 in respect of recurring expenditure and 100 per cent in respect of non-recurring expenditure. The budget estimate for the scheme during 2000-2001 is Rs. 7.25 crores.

Every year a colloquium is held at NIRD to discuss the various aspects of training of Rural Development functionaries by SIRDs. The suggestions and recommendations made in the colloquium are implemented for betterment of functioning of these institutions.

Strengthening/Establishment of Extension Training Centres (ETCs)

The scheme of Strengthening/Establishment of Extension Training Centres (ETCs) for imparting training to district/block/village level rural development functionaries was taken up during the VII Five Year Plan. There are 87 ETCs in the country at present.

The objective of this scheme is to train district/block/

village rural development functionaries as well as elected representatives of Panchayati Raj Institutions.

Salient Features

The ETCs have the linkages with SIRDs in their State so as to serve the vital role of imparting training to the Rural Development functionaries. They also provide training to the grassroot level workers.

Funding Pattern and Achievements

Central assistance is 100 per cent for non-recurring expenditure and the recurring expenditure is provided to the maximum ceiling of Rs. 5.00 lakhs per annum per ETC. The scheme is demand-driven in nature. The budget allocation for the scheme during 2000-2001 is Rs. 3.00 crores.

Organisation of Training Courses, Seminars & Workshops (OTC)

A Central Sector Plan scheme for providing financial assistance for organizing training courses, seminars, workshops etc., on the subjects relevant to rural development, has been in operation since the VI Five Year Plan. The objective of the scheme is to train the rural development functionaries as well as elected representatives of PRIs.

The OTC is a demand-driven scheme and for an individual proposal, generally an amount of Rs. 2.00 lakhs for a seminar, workshop, training courses is provided. The training programmes, seminars, workshops are conducted through reputed institutes, State Institute of Rural Development, academic department of Universities etc.

The Plan outlay for the year 2000-2001 is Rs. 1.25 crores, out of which Rs. 1.15 crores are for the scheme of 'Organisation of Training Courses, Seminars and Workshops' and Rs. 0.10 crores for the "Career Management" activities of the employees of this Ministry.

COUNCIL FOR ADVANCEMENT OF PEOPLE'S ACTION & RURAL TECHNOLOGY (CAPART)

Recognising the need for an organisation that would coordinate and catalyse the development work of voluntary agencies in the country, particularly to ensure smooth flow of benefits to the underprivileged and socio-economically weaker sections of society, Government of India, in September 1986 set up the Council for Advancement of People's Action and Rural Technology (CAPART), a registered society under the aegis of the Department of Rural Development, by merging two autonomous bodies, namely, People's Action for Development of India (PADI) and Council for Advancement of Rural Technology (CAPART).

The main objectives of the CAPART are :

- To encourage, promote and assist voluntary action for the implementation of projects intending enhancement of rural prosperity.
- To Strengthen and promote voluntary efforts in rural development with focus on injecting new technological inputs;
- To act as a catalyst for the development of technology appropriate for rural areas.
- To promote, plan, undertake, develop, maintain and support projects/schemes aimed at all-round development, creation of employment opportunities, promotion of self-reliance, generation of awareness, organisation and improvement in the quality of life of the people in rural areas through voluntary action.

CAPART made useful contribution towards the implementation of the following programmes/schemes :

1. Jawahar Rozgar Yojana
   (Now renamed as Gram Samridhi Yojana (JGSY)
2. Development of Women & Children in Rural Areas (DWCRA)
   (The Schemes DWCRA, IRDP, MWS have been

merged in single scheme renamed as Swarnjayanti Gram Swarozgar Yojana [SGSY])

3. Integrated Rural Development Programme (IRDP)
4. Million Well Scheme (MWS)
5. Accelerated Rural Water Supply Programme (ARWSP)
6. Central Rural Sanitation Programme (CRSP)
7. Indira Awaas Yojana (IAY)
8. Panchayati Raj (PR)
9. Promotion of Voluntary Action in Rural Development (RD)
10. Organisation of Beneficiaries (OB) and Social Animators Training (SAT)
11. Advancement of Rural Technology Scheme (ARTS)
12. Watershed Development
13. Assistance to NGOs/V.A.S.

Regional Centres

With a view to bringing CAPART nearer to the people and to ensure closer interaction between CAPART and voluntary agencies at the grassroot level, functioning of CAPART has been decentralised by setting up of nine Regional Committees/Regional Centres at Jaipur, Lucknow, Ahmedabad, Bhubaneswar, Patna, Chandigarh, Hyderabad, Guwahati and Dharwad. The Regional Committee are empowered to sanction project proposals to voluntary agencies upto an outlay of Rs. 10.00 lakhs in their respective regions.

Funding Pattern

The quantum of assistance is normally decided on the basis of the nature of the project and the capability of the organisation to take up the project/to handle the funds requested. On acceptance of the terms and conditions, CAPART releases sanctioned funds in suitable instalments depending upon the nature of the project, quantum of assistance involved and the proportion of assistance to be mobilised from other sources including beneficiaries' contribution.

Implementing Agency

NGOs are provided financial assistance through CAPART.

Monitoring & Evaluation

CAPART has fairly well developed monitoring system. CAPART projects are monitored with the help of its own officers and external monitors. CAPART has a system of empaneling project Evaluators on different subjects. CAPART projects are monitored at three different stages :

(i) Pre-funding appraisal

(ii) Mid-term appraisal

(iii) Post-Evaluation

DRDA ADMINISTRATION

Objective

The objective of DRDA Administration is to strengthen the DRDAs and to make them more professional.

Scope

All the staff working in DRDAs and other are entrusted with implementing Rural Development programmes of the Ministry.

Funding

The funding pattern of the programme will be in the ratio of 75:25 between the Centre and the States.

MONITORING AND EVALUATION

Introduction

Monitoring is an important tool for ensuring proper implementation of a project or programme. This is the reason, the Ministry of Rural Development lays great emphasis on monitoring and evaluation of rural infrastructure development programmes in general and poverty alleviation and employment generation schemes in particular being implemented in various States. Effective monitoring of the programmes is considered to be essential particularly in the context of substantial step up in the allocation of funds for rural development programmes in the 8th and 9th Five Year Plans. It is well recognized that the success of the programmes largely depends on the effective delivery system and efficient implementation at the grassroot level so that the desired results could be achieved. In order to ensure this, the Ministry has evolved a comprehensive system of monitoring and evaluation for the poverty alleviation and the infrastructure development programmes. Various methods are used for monitoring and evaluation is conducted through professional agencies.

The Policy and Planning Section is a part of the Monitoring Division. This Section deals with the Annual Plans, Five Year Plans and perspective planning of employment generation and poverty reduction programmes. Similarly, inputs for formulation of policies for employment generation and poverty reduction programmes are also provided by this Section.

Objective

Regular monitoring of the programmes is done to assess the physical and financial progress in implementation of the Schemes and to disseminate the information regarding progress. Concurrent evaluation of the programmes is intended for periodic assessment of their impact and to know their strengths and weaknesses so that necessary steps are taken to streamline and improve the process of implementation. Evaluation studies also help to a great extent in devising proper policies and redesigning concerned programmes to ensure that the intended benefits reach the target groups. Transparency in implementation is a major objective of the monitoring and evaluation mechanism.

Target Groups

The policy makers, planners, programme implementing agencies, representatives of the people at various levels such as Village, Block, District, State and the Centre beneficiaries of the programmes etc. are the major target groups.

Salient Features

The comprehensive system of monitoring and evaluation employed by the Monitoring Division includes various mechanisms such as Progress Reports, Financial Returns/Audit Reports, Intensive Inspections by Officers of both Central Government and the State Governments, Areas Officers Scheme, Review by various Committees, namely, Parliament Committee as well as Standing Parliamentary Committee and Concurrent Evaluation Reports and impact research studies of the programmes of the Ministry. In the 50th year of Independence, the Monitoring Division introduced a high tech review system through the Video-Conference as an instrument to monitor the implementation of the programmes. To provide information which should be readily available to the users anywhere in India and abroad, a Home Page indicating all the detailed information regarding the programmes of the Ministry has been put on INTERNET to generate awareness among the masses and research world. Accordingly, high transparency is ensured through these programmes.

Achievements

Monthly progress reports on the programmes of the erstwhile Department of Rural Development and the Department of Rural Areas & Employment indicating physical achievements and financial performance are brought out every month. In addition quarterly, half yearly and annual progress reports are also being received from the State Governments and these reports are quite exhaustive with emphasis on quality and social targets as prescribed in the respective guidelines and manuals of the programmes/schemes. Concurrent Evaluation of JRY, IRDP & TRYSEM have already been conducted and reports published. A research study on the impact of the programmes in the Meerut district has also been completed. Concurrent Evaluation of both (IAY) and (MWS) have been taken up in October 1998.

The following five research studies have been completed and reports published :

Tribal system of Self Management included under V and VI Schedules —

(a) Rural Development Activities in Andhra Pradesh.

(b) Analysis of the expenditure pattern of JRY in Bihar.

(c) Multi-sectoral study of development scenario of selected backward districts.

(d) Development of Rural Infrastructure Indicators Literature Search.

In addition, a research study on "Feedback on Rural Development Programmes based on SE Studies Conducted by IAS Probationers" is ongoing.

Instructions have already been issued to various State Governments to constitute Vigilance and Monitoring Committees at the district, block and village levels to monitor the implementation of the programmes and bring more transparency to the programmes. A schedule of inspection which prescribes minimum number of field visits for each functionary at the supervisory level from the State Government to the block is drawn up and strictly adhered to. Review Committee at various levels *i.e.*, Central/State/District/Block and Village undertook detailed review of the overall performance of the rural development programmes.

The Area Officers Scheme is an important mechanism for monitoring various programmes of the Ministry with special reference to quality, time schedule and proper achievement of physical and financial targets. The Area Officers from the Ministry visited the respective States and submitted comprehensive reports of different aspects of implementation of various programmes. The procedure adopted for release of funds stipulates the receipt of utilisation certificate from the State Governments and audit of accounts and reports before release of second and subsequent instalments. Setting up of Monitoring and Vigilance Committee and their periodic meetings are also insisted upon for release of funds from the Ministry.

The new initiative taken by the Monitoring Division includes impact assessment studies of all the programmes being implemented in the same village/district/state. The Operation Research Group conducted an impact assessment study in Meerut district of U.P. recently and the report was circulated. Such studies are entrusted to various reputed institutions and professional agencies in other States namely, Manipur, Meghalaya, Bihar, Punjab, Gujarat, Kerala and Karnataka.

The Monitoring Division also provided necessary input for policy formulation and finalisation of the programmes for the 9th Five Year Plan and Annual Plan 1999-2000. During the current year, the Monitoring Division organised three Video Conferences in which problems and prospects of implementation of various programmes were discussed with the State Government officials.

Funding Pattern

100 per cent funded by the Ministry of Rural Development.

Implementing Agency

Concurrent Evaluation and research studies are conducted through reputed independent research institutions.

Evaluation Conducted

Jawahar Rozgar Yojana

1. First Round (Jan. 1992-Dec.1992)
2. Second Round (1993-94)

Integrated Rural Development Programme

(i) First Round (Oct. 1985-Sept. 1986)

(ii) Second Round (Jan. 1987-Dec. 1987)

(iii) Third Round (Jan. 1989- Dec. 1989)

(iv) Fourth Round (Sept. 1992-Aug. 1993)

(v) Fifth Round (July 1995-June 1996)

Training of Rural Youth for Self Employment

Quick Evaluation (Jan. 1993-Aug. 1993)

Corrective Action taken

Based on the findings of the Concurrent Evaluations, necessary corrective measures are taken by the Programme Divisions concerned and State Governments to improve the implementation of the Programmes. Issues raised by the Area Officers in the report were taken up with the State Governments for corrective action. Similarly, various shortcomings pointed out by the concurrent evaluation reports were communicated to the programme implementing agencies for taking corrective action.

RAJIV GANDHI NATIONAL DRINKING WATER MISSION

Accelerated Rural Water Supply Programme

Introduction

The Accelerated Rural Water Supply Programme (ARWSP) was introduced in 1972-73 by the Government of India to assist the States and Union Territories (UTs) to accelerate the pace of coverage of drinking water supply. The entire programme was given a Mission approach with the launch of the Technology Mission of Drinking Water and Related Water Management, also called the National Drinking Water Mission (NDWM), in 1986. It was one of the five Societal Missions launched by the Government of India. The NDWM was renamed as the Rajiv Gandhi National Drinking Water Mission (RGNDWM) in 1991.

Rural water supply is a State subject. The State Governments have been implementing the Rural Water Supply Programme under the State Sector Minimum Needs Programme (MNP). The Central Government, through the Rajiv Gandhi National Drinking Water Mission (RGNDWM) supplements the efforts of the State Governments by providing Central assistance under the Accelerated Rural Water Supply Programme (ARWSP).

Objective

The following are the objectives of the Mission :

- To cover the residual Not Covered (NC), Partially Covered (PC) and quality affected rural habitations.
- Evolve appropriate technology mix.
- Improve performance and cost effectiveness of ongoing programmes.
- Create awareness on the use of safe drinking water.
- Take conservation measures for sustained supply of drinking water.

Target Groups

Rural population, Not Covered (NC), Partially Covered (PC) and quality affected rural habitations.

Salient Features

The salient features of the revised policy for implementation of Accelerated Rural Water Supply Programme during the 9th Plan period are as under :

- The present allocation criteria of funds under ARWSP to the States based on normative criteria should be replaced with a need-based approach to achieve the objectives of coverage within the time frame set by the National Agenda for Governance of the Government. The States having large number of Not Covered and quality affected habitations and which are in drought prone, desert regions and hard rock areas would get more allocation than the States well endowed with water resources.
- Decentralisation of powers to States for implementation of Sub-Mission programmes.
- Enhance ceiling for Operation and Maintenance (O&M)

from the present level of 10 per cent to 15 per cent of the annual plan allocation.

- Providing 100 per cent funds for the nascent programmes such as Human Resource Development, Research & Development, Information Education & Communication and Management Information System.
- Institutionalising community based demand-driven rural water supply programme with cost sharing instruments by communities, gradually replacing the current supply-driven, centrally maintained non-people participating rural water supply programme.
- Institutionalising water quality monitoring and surveillance systems.

Achievements

- Out of total number of 12,30,663 rural habitations in the country, 13,87,670 habitations have now access to safe drinking water.
- Special efforts are being made for ensuring sustainability of the facilities provided under the Accelerated Rural Water Supply Programme by initiating action to institutionalise community based rural water supply programme.
- Special emphasis is being given to areas affected with quality problems due to excess fluoride, arsenic, iron and other pollutants.

Funding Pattern

The central assistance of ARWSP is normally released in two instalments subject to specific instructions from the Ministry of Finance. The first instalment is released in April without any condition except that the last instalment in the previous financial year was drawn by the State/UT Government. If the last instalment in the previous financial year was not drawn, the first instalment of funds in the new financial year will be released only after receipt of specific request along with the proforma prescribed for the release of funds.

The second instalment to cover the balance of the annual allocation will be released on fulfilment of the following conditions :

- Receipt of a specific proposal from the State/UT Government along with prescribed proforma progress reports and returns.
- Utilisation of 60 per cent of the available resources under ARWSP and MNP (unutilised opening balance, if any, from the previous years plus funds released in the first instalment) by the end of December in each year.
- Receipt of certificate of actual expenditure under MNP and ARWSP from the Accountant General upto the year preceding the previous financial year.
- Receipt of utilisation certificate under MNP and ARWSP signed by the Chief Engineer and countersigned by the Secretary for the previous financial year.
- Certificate that the unfinished works are given priority for completion.
- Certificate that no work started more than three years ago remains incomplete.
- Certificate that schemes technically cleared six months ago have been taken up for implementation.
- The receipt of the district-wise allocation of funds under ARWSP and MNP should be sent by 30th April.
- The allocated amount will be released in full only if the proposal for the release of second instalment, complete in all respects, satisfying all the above conditions is received latest by 31st December. Proposal received after 31st December will be subjected to progressive cuts on the allocation, even if the proposal

is complete in all respect, as per the details indicated below :

Month of receipt of proposal for the release of the 2nd instalment	Cuts on the allocated amount
December	Nil
January	10%
February	20%
March	30%

- In respect of proposals for the release of 2nd instalment received late, cuts will be affected on the total allocation and the 2nd instalment will be restricted to only the balance amount left after adjusting the cuts.

Any Other Condition That may be Prescribed from Time to Time

The utilisation of funds under ARWSP will be regularised in the following manners :

(a) 20 per cent of the annual outlay will be earmarked in accordance with ARWSP criteria to those State Governments which implement the following :

- adoption of a demand-driven approach based on empowerment of villagers to ensure their full participation in the project through a decision making role in the choice of scheme design and management arrangements.
- Focus on village level capacity building (Village Water and Sanitation Committees).
- Ensure an integrated service delivery mechanism by streamlining the functions of the agencies involved in project implementation.

- 10 per cent capital cost sharing and 100 per cent sharing of O&M cost by users.
- Taking up of conservation measures for sustained supply of water through rain water harvesting and groundwater recharge structures.

(b) The share of the States which do not introduce the reforms will be given to other States implementing the reforms measures for coverage of NC/PC quality affected habitations as an incentive.

(c) Earmark need-based funds for sub-mission projects with funding pattern of cost sharing by the Centre and State Government in the ratio of 75:25.

Implementing Agency

The Public Health Engineering Departments are the programme implementing agencies in the States except in the following four States. The details of implementing agencies in these States are as under :

Name of the State	Implementing Agencies
Gujarat	Gujarat Water Supply and Sewerage Board
Kerala	Kerala Water Authority
Maharshtra	Maharashtra Water Supply and Sewerage Board
Uttar Pradesh	U.P. Jal Nigam

Evaluation Conducted

The Programme Evaluation Organisation (PEO) of Planning Commission evaluated ARWSP in 1996.

In 1998 Mission commissioned Monitoring and Evaluation studies through survey methods in 13 States, *viz.*, Punjab, Haryana, Uttar Pradesh, Madhya Pradesh, Gujarat, Rajasthan, Maharashtra, Karnataka, Andhra Pradesh, Tamil Nadu, West Bengal, Orissa and Bihar. The evaluation was done by reputed research institutions like Indian Institute of Rural Management, Jaipur, All India Institute of Hygiene & Public Health, Calcutta, Media Research Group, New Delhi, WAPCOS Ltd., New Delhi, etc. The studies have now been completed.

Corrective Action Taken

The findings of the evaluation studies have been forwarded to the respective States for initiating necessary corrective measures.

CENTRALLY SPONSORED RURAL SANITATION PROGRAMME

Introduction

Rural sanitation is a State Subject. The state governments implement the rural sanitation programme under state sector Minimum Needs Programme (MNP). The Central Government Supplements the States efforts providing financial and technical assistance through the Centrally sponsored Rural Sanitation Programme (CRSOP).

The Centrally Sponsored Rural Sanitation Programme (CRSP) was launched in 1986 with the objective of improving the quality of life of the rural people and to provide privacy and dignity to women. The concept of sanitation was expanded in 1993 to include personal hygiene, home sanitation, safe water, garbage and excreta disposal and waste water disposal. The components of the programme include construction of individual sanitary latrines for households Below the Poverty Line (BPL), conversion of individual sanitary latrines, construction of village sanitary complexes for women, setting up of sanitary marts, intensive campaign for awareness creation and health education etc.

Objective

- Accelerate coverage of rural population, especially among households Below the Poverty Line (BPL) with sanitation facilities, complementing the efforts in rural water supply.

- Generate felt need through awareness creation and health education involving voluntary organisations and panchayati raj institutions.
- Eradicate manual scavenging by converting all existing dry latrines into low cost sanitary latrines.
- Encourage cost effective and appropriate technologies to support other objectives.

Target Group

The rural population below the poverty line.

Salient Features

The revised policy for implementation of the rural sanitation programme during the 9th Plan period has been approved by the Union Cabinet. The salient features of the policy are as under :

- Raise sanitation coverage to at least 50 per cent by 9th Plan.
- Total Sanitation Campaign (TSC) in select districts with 50 per cent allocation during first year.
- Balance 50 per cent for existing allocation-based programme.
- Switch over from allocation based-programme to a demand-driven one.
- Shift from high subsidy to low subsidy regime.
- Greater beneficiary participation and private sector involvement.
- Active participation of NGOs/Cooperative institutions etc.
- Emphasize school sanitation.
- Increased technological options and adoption of Vertical upgradation concept

Achievements

- The total latrines constructed under the programme

(CRSP+MNP) upto the end of the Eighth Plan period (1996-97) were 4,337,609 with a total expenditure of Rs. 757.62 crores.

- The central allocation for the year 1997-98 was Rs. 100.00 crores; the state MNP provision was Rs. 209.83 crores. The total latrines constructed in 1997-98 were 1,387,080.
- During 1998-99 the Central allocation was Rs. 67.00 crores as against the state MNP provision of Rs. 213.34 crores and 824,520 household latrines have been constructed up to January 1999.

Funding pattern

Under the revised programme the states are required to formulate Total Sanitation Campaigns (TSCs) in select districts. To allow time for the proper grounding of the new approach, the existing "allocation-based programme" will also be continued and would be phased out at the end of the 9th Plan period. While the first year will have 50 per cent of funds earmarked for the existing programme, only 30 per cent will be allotted in the next year followed by 10 per cent during the third year.

The state government should provide matching contribution under the Minimum Needs Programme (MNP) equivalent to the allocation under CRSP.

The extent of subsidy from Centre, State and Beneficiaries/ Panchayats for a few components of the programmes are in the following ratio :

Programme Total Sanitation Campaign (TSC) Normal

- Construction of household 60:20:20
- Sanitary latrines, women's Complexes etc. 60:20:20
- School sanitation 60:30:10
- Alternate delivery mechanism 60:30:10
- Rural Sanitary Marts/Production of annual Centre Allocation 80:20

Implementing Agency

The programme is being implemented through the state government Departments/ Boards (PHED/ Panchayati Raj/ Rural Development).

Evaluation Conducted

A very comprehensive baseline survey on Knowledge, Attitudes and Practices (KAP) in rural water supply and sanitation was conducted during 1996-97 covering 39000 respondents in 74 districts throughout the country. The study showed that 55 per cent of those with private latrines were self-motivated. Only 2 per cent of the respondents claimed the existence of subsidy as the major motivation factor, while 54 per cent claimed to have gone in for sanitary latrines due to convenience and privacy. The study also showed that 51 per cent of the beneficiaries were willing to spend upto Rs. 100 to acquire sanitary toilets.

Corrective Action taken

Taking into account the deficiencies of the programme which were mainly due to heavy reliance on subsidy, inadequate participation of beneficiaries, limited choice of models and inadequate involvement of NGOs, a comprehensive review of the rural sanitation programme has been done. The changes effected in the programme involve a major shift from a high-subsidy to a low-subsidy regime, adoption of "total sanitation Campaign" approach, choice of technology according to customer preferences and greater community participation. School sanitation is an important component of this programme.

DROUGHT PRONE AREAS PROGAMME

Introduction

The Drought Prone Areas Programme (DPAP) is one of the areas development programmes launched by the Government in 1972-73 to tackle the special problems faced by those fragile areas which are constantly affected by severe drought conditions. These areas are characterised by large human and cattle populations which are continuously putting heavy pressure on the already fragile natural resource base for food, fodder and fuel. This continuous biotic pressure is leading to fast and continuous depletion of vegetative cover, less and less rainfall, increasing soil erosion and fast receding ground water level due to continuous exploitation without any effort to recharge the underground acquires.

Objective

The basic objective of the programme is to minimise the adverse effects of drought on the production of crops and livestock and productivity of land, water and human resources thereby ultimately leading to the drought proofing of the affected areas. The programme also aims at promoting the overall economic development and improving the socio-economic condition of the resource poor and disadvantaged sections inhabiting the programme areas.

Target Area

Fragile areas which are constantly affected by severe drought conditions.

Salient Features

- The thrust of the programme is on capacity building and empowerment of village community, ensuring participation of Panchayati Raj Institutions and NGOs in the programme implementation at grassroot level and transfer of funds as well as decision-making power to the local people.
- Since 1995-96, a new approach based on watershed development has been adopted and so far 6252 watershed development projects have been sanctioned for implementation in 13 States through local communities during a four year period.
- The programme also aims at restoring of ecological balance by harnessing, conserving and developing natural

resources, *i.e.*, land, water, vegetative cover and raising land productivity.

Funding

The Programme allocation is to be shared equally by the Centre and State Governments on 50:50 basis. The cost norms adopted under DPAP for various eco-systems depending on the severity of the problem area are as below :

Eco-system Type	Per Hectare Average Cost (Rs.)	Watershed Project Cost (Rs. in lakhs)
Semi Arid Region	2,000	20.00
Dry Sub-Humid Region	3,000	15.00
Dry Sub-Humid (Hilly) Region	2,000	20.00

Achievements

Since inception in 1972-73 till 1992-95, as a part of core sector activities, 30 lakh hectares under land resources development, 926,000 hectares under water resources development and 1782,000 hectares under afforestation and pasture development have been successfully treated. Since 1 April 1995 this programme is being implemented on watershed projects basis and at present 5956 watershed projects out of 6265 are under implementation at various stages.

Implementing Agency

- DRDA/ZP are the nodal Government agencies at the district level to act as a facilitator and provider of finances and technical assistance to the people's organisations executing the watershed projects.

Elaborate institutional mechanism is clearly defined for effective participation of the local people and the Panchayati Raj Institutions at all stages of project management.

DESERT DEVELOPMENT PROGRAMME

Introduction

Over the years, the increase in human and livestock population in drought prone and desert areas has placed the natural resources of the region under great stress. The major problems are continuous depletion of vegetative cover, increase in soil erosion and fall in ground water table. All these factors account for diminishing productivity of land and loss of natural resources. The problems would have been worse but for introduction of some highly focussed specific area development programmes in such regions. On the recommendations of the National Commission on Agriculture in its Interim Report (1972) and the Final Report (1976), the Desert Development Programme (DDP) was started in the year 1977-78. The programme was started both in the hot desert areas of Rajasthan, Gujarat and Haryana, and the cold desert areas of Jammu & Kashmir and Himachal Pradesh.

Objective

- The objective of the programme has been to mitigate adverse effects of desertification and adverse climatic conditions on crops, human and livestock population, combating desertification.
- The programme also aims at restoring of ecological balance by harnessing, conserving and developing natural resources, *i.e.*, land, water, vegetative cover, and raising land productivity.

Target Area

- Hot desert areas of Rajasthan, Gujarat, Haryana, Karnataka and Andhra Pradesh and the cold deserts of Jammu & Kashmir and Himachal Pradesh.

Salient Features

- The thrust of the programme is on capacity building and empowerment of village community, ensuring participation of Panchayati Raj Institutions and NGOs in the programme implementation at grassroot level and transfer of funds as well as decision-making power to local people.

- Since 1995-96, a new approach based on watershed development has been adopted and so far 2202 watershed development projects have been sanctioned for implementation in seven States through local communities. A watershed project is required to be implemented in a four years period.

Funding

The DDP is a centrally Sponsored Programme and funds are released to DRDAs/ZPs for implementation of the programme.

Achievements

Since inception in 1977-78 till 1992-95, as a part of core sector activities, 185,000 hectares under land resource development, 83,000 hectares under water resources development and 285,000 hectares under afforestation and pasture development had been successfully treated. Since 1 April 1995 this programme is being implemented on watershed project basis and 2202 watershed projects sanctioned so far are at various stages of implementation.

Implementation Agency

- At the district level, the DRDA/ZP is in overall charge of implementation of the programme. The DRDA/ZP is advised in regard to selection of Project Implementation Agencies (PIAs), approval of Watershed Plans, training, publicity etc., by a district level Watershed Development Advisory Committee under the chairmanship of Project Director, DRDA/CEO, ZP.
- The DRDA/ZP selects the Project Implementation Agencies (PIAs) which could be besides DRDA/ZP itself, autonomous organisations, public sector

undertakings, voluntary organisations, cooperatives, banks etc. The PIA remains in-charge of implementation of the Watershed Projects. A multi-disciplinary team designated as Watershed Development Team (WDT) assists each PIA in implementation of these Watershed Projects.

- Planning and implementation of the Watershed Project is done with the technical support of the multi-disciplinary Watershed Development Team by the Watershed Association (WA) comprising all adult members of the villages in the watershed areas; 75 per cent amount of the project fund is spent directly by the Watershed Association on the development works of each project.
- The Watershed Committee comprising 10-12 nominated members by the Watershed Association from amongst the users groups, self-help groups, with representation from Gram Panchayat, Watershed Development Team, women, Scheduled Castes and Scheduled Tribes is the executive body of the Watershed Association.
- As regards the Panchayati Raj Institutions (PRIs), the Zila Parishad at the district level remains overall in-charge of implementation. The Panchayat Samiti and Gram Panchayat will have the right to monitor and review the implementation of the programme.

WASTELANDS DEVELOPMENT

Development of wastelands is an important programme which includes, among other things, checking land degradation, increasing bio-mass availability and putting wastelands to sustainable use. To attain this objective, the following Schemes/ Programmes are being implemented :

- Integrated Wastelands Development Project (IWDP) Scheme
- Technology Development, Extension and Training Scheme

- Support to NGOs/VAs (Grant-in-Aid) Scheme
- Investment Promotional Scheme (IPS)
- Wastelands Development Task Force (WDTF)

(i) Integrated Wastelands Development Project (IWDP)

This scheme has been under implementation since 1989-90, and has come to this Department along with the National Wastelands Development Board in July 1992. From 1 April 1995, the scheme is being implemented on watershed basis under the new guidelines for Watershed Development.

The Scheme also helps in generation of employment in rural areas besides enhancing people's participation in the wastelands development programmes at all stages. This leads to equitable sharing of benefits and sustainable development.

The major activities taken up under the Scheme are :

- Soil and moisture conservation measures like terracing, bunding, trenching, vegetative barriers, etc.
- Planting and sowing of multi-purpose trees, shrubs, grasses, legumes and pasture land development.
- Encouraging natural regeneration.
- Promotion of agro-forestry and horticulture.
- Wood subsitution and fuel-wood conservation measures.
- Measures needed to disseminate technology.
- Training, extension and creation of greater degree of awareness among the participants.
- Encouraging people's participation.
- Upto May 1999, 228 IWDP projects (128 under old guidelines and 120 under new guidelines) were sanctioned in 25 States with a total outlay of Rs. 778.12 crores to treat total project area of 15.98 lakhs hectare.

(ii) Technology Development, Extension and Training Scheme

Technology support is extremely vital for the success of a land based programme, especially in the development of wastelands. Realising this, it was decided to have a separate Technology Development, Extension and Training Scheme so as to develop suitable technologies for the reclamation of wastelands for sustained production of food, finel-wood, fodder etc.

The objectives of the Scheme are as under :

Development of data base for planning and sustainable development of wastelands.

Operationalisation of appropriate cost effective and proven technologies for development of various categories of wastelands specially problem of land affected by soil erosion, land degradation, salinity, alkalinity, waterlogging, etc.

Implementation of location specific pilot projects/ demonstration models including pisciculture, duckery, domesticated animals and birds, etc.

Dissemination of research findings and appropriate technologies for promoting wastelands development.

Evaluation of the impact, and replication of these models to larger areas.

Organising publicity, awareness campaign, seminars/ conferences, circulation and handouts/extension materials, etc.

The Scheme is being implemented through ICAR, State Agricultural Universities, Government and private institutions having adequate institutional framework and organisational back-up. Successful implementation of this Scheme is expected to bridge the gap between the existing technologies and the need relevant to the latest situation.

During the Eighth Five Year Plan, 66 projects with total investment of Rs. 828 lakhs have been sanctioned under the Scheme. During 1998-99 an amount of Rs. 802 lakhs has been spent for the project implementation. An amount of Rs. 800 lakhs has been allocated under the Scheme to cover

3000 hectares of area during 1999-2000. So far an amount of Rs. 10.531 lakhs has been released under the Scheme.

(iii) Support to NGOs/VAs (Grant-in-Aid) Scheme

Under this Scheme 100 per cent grant is provided to registered voluntary agencies, cooperatives, mahila mandals, yuva mandals and other similar organisations for undertaking work directly or indirectly, encouraging afforestation and wastelands development. Projects meant for creation of awareness, appropriate technology application, training, extension and publicity are also considered under this scheme.

During Eighth Five Year Plan, 232 projects were sanctioned in favour of voluntary agencies and a sum of Rs. 13.75 crores was released to VAs for development of about 20,000 hectares of wastelands.

All projects under the Scheme are now being sanctioned by CAPART. The Department has transferred all fresh applications and ongoing projects under the scheme to CAPART except 75 cases which are being implemented by cooperatives and trusts etc. During 1998-99, an amount of Rs. 2.03 crores has been kept for development of 2,650 hectares of wastelands. During 1999-2000, a provision of Rs. 2 crores has been made for implementation of the scheme.

(iv) Investment Promotional Scheme

The Scheme was launched in 1992-95 in order to stimulate involvement of the corporate sector/financial institutions etc., to pool in resources for development of non-forest wastelands. The principal objectives of the scheme include : (i) to facilitate/attract/chennalise/mobilise resources from financial institutions, banks, corporate bodies and individuals for development of wastelands in non-forest areas belonging to the Central and State Governments, Panchayats, Villages communities and private farmers, (ii) to facilitate production and flow of additional biomass including farm forestry products used as raw material for different types of industries and horticulture/commercial plantations.

Under this Scheme, central promotional grant/subsidy to the general category (individual/groups) is limited to Rs. 25 lakhs or 25 per cent of the project cost on farm development activities, whichever is less subject to the condition that the promoters' contribution in the project shall not be less than 25 per cent of the project cost. The quantum of subsidy in the case of small farmers is 30 per cent and in the case of marginal farmers and SC/ST farmers it is 50 per cent of the project cost on farm development activities. The promoters' contribution in the case of small farmers is 10 per cent of the project cost whereas it is 'nil' in the case of marginal and SC/ST farmers. The project promoted by Nationalised Banks, Regional Rural Banks, Land Development Banks and Cooperative Banks are eligible for promotional grants/subsidy under the Scheme.

Upto 1995-96, only four projects have been sanctioned under the Scheme during 1992-95 and 1995-96. The Scheme could not be implemented during 1996 and 1997-98 as the Scheme was being restructured on the advice of the Standing Committee of Parliament for Urban and Rural Development to make it more popular and broad-based for implementation during Ninth Five Year Plan. The scheme has since been restructured.

During 1998-99, three projects were sanctioned and an amount of Rs. 2.20 lakhs was released as subsidy under the scheme. During 1999-2000, a budget provision of Rs. 200 lakhs has been kept.

(v) Wastelands Development Task Force

This Scheme is being implemented through ex-servicemen for development of 1200 hectares of Wastelands in the ravines of Chambal in Morena district of Madhya Pradesh since 1992. The objective of the Scheme is to provide disciplined force of regeneration of wastelands through afforestation including : (i) soil and moisture conservation, (ii) plantation and its protection and (iii) employment of ex-servicemen.

The Force consists of 300 ex-servicemen under the command of the Territorial Army and Group of 15 Army/Territorial Army Personnel. The total area of 1200 hectares of ravenous land has been developed upto 31.3.99. A budget provision of Rs. 1 crore has been kept during 1999-2000 to meet up the left over liabilities of the project. The Department is also considering to extend the scheme to cover additional 800 hectares in next three years.

LAND REFORMS (LR)

Introduction

The Land Reforms Policy adopted since Independence aims at restructuring agrarian relations to achieve an egalitarian social structure; elimination of exploitation in land relations; realising the age-old goal of land to the tiller; increasing agricultural productivity and production and infusing equality in local institutions.

Objectives

The aim of Land Reforms (LR) in the successive Five Year Plans is the fulfilment of all the principles of the National Land Reforms Policy consisting of the following objectives :

- Abolition of intermediary tenures;
- Tenancy reforms;
- Ceiling on agricultural holdings and re-distribution of surplus land;
- Updating and maintenance of land records.

Target Group

Landless rural poor.

Achievements

- Intermediary tenures have been abolished. Consequently over 20 million cultivators have been brought into direct contact with the State to gain access to an estimated 6.07 million hectares of land vested in the State.

- Legislative provisions have been made providing for conferment of ownership rights on tenants or allowing cultivating tenants to acquire ownership rights on payment of a reasonable compensation to the landlords. An estimated 12.42 million cultivators have been conferred ownership rights on 6.32 million hectares of land.
- Under various ceiling laws, till September 1998, 3.04 million hectares of land has been declared surplus, 2.15 million hectares have been distributed to 5.54 million beneficiaries mostly belonging to weaker sections. In addition, about 0.88 million hectare of Bhoodan land and 5.97 million hectares of wasteland have also been distributed.
- Legislative provisions have been made for consolidation of holdings and 64.08 million hectares of land has been consolidated in the country so far.
- For preparation, maintenance and up-dating of land records the accent has been on induction of modern technology. With this objective, the Central government has allocated Rs. 1627.36 million to the States/UTs for purchase of equipment, strengthening of training infrastructure, etc. under the Centrally Sponsored Scheme for Strengthening of Revenue Administration & Updating of Land Records (SRA & ULR).
- One significant area of modernisation is the Government decision to initiate computerisation of land records. At present, the scheme is being implemented in all the districts of the country except those where land records are not maintained. The scheme provides land holders easy access to entries of the land records and enable them to have copies of land records quickly and at cheap rates. For this, an assistance of Rs. 1093.72 millions has been given to the concerned States/UTs.

- An outlay of Rs. 430.0 millions has been earmarked for Land Reform Schemes during the financial year 1999-2000
- Comprehensive amendments in Land Acquisition Act, 1894 have been proposed so as to make it more farmers friendly.
- A comprehensive policy document on the resettlement and rehabilitation of project affected persons is expected to be shortly finalised.
- Major initiative has been taken to ensure transparency in land records management.

CENTRALLY SPONSORED SCHEME FOR COMPUTERISATION OF LAND RECORDS

Introduction

1. The Centrally Sponsored Scheme on Computerisation of Land Records (CLR) was started in 1988-89 with 100% financial assistance as a pilot project in eight Districts/ States *viz,* Rangareddy (A.P.), Sonitpur (Assam), Singhbhum (Bihar), Gandhinagar (Gujarat), Morena (M.P.), Wardha (Maharashtra), Mayurbhanj (Orissa) and Dungarpur (Rajasthan) with a view to remove the problems inherent in the manual system of maintenance and updating of Land Records and to meet the requirements of various groups of users. It was decided that efforts should be made to computerise Core Data contained in land records so as to assist development planning and to make records accessible to people/ planners/ administrators.

Objectives

2. The main objectives of the Scheme are :

(i) Computerisation of ownership and plot-wise details for issue of timely and accurate copy of the record of rights to the land owners.

(ii) To achieve low cost, easily reproducible storage media for reliable preservation for long time.

(iii) To provide fast and efficient retrieval of information, both graphical and textual.

(iv) Creation of a Land Information System and database for Agricultural Census.

Progress during 8th Plan

3. During 8th five year Plan, the scheme was approved as a separate Centrally Sponsored Scheme on Computersation of Land Records. The total expenditure under the Scheme during 8th plan period was Rs 59.42 crores. The year-wise break-up of B.E., R.E. and actual expenditure during the 8th Plan period are given below :

(Rs. in crores)

S.No	Year	B.E	R.E	Expenditure
1.	1992-93	5.00	5.00	Funds were not released as EFC approval was awaited.
2.	1993-94	8.00	8.00	8.76
3.	1994-95	NIL	10.50	10.50
4.	1995-96	20.00	20.00	20.00
5.	1996-97	20.00	20.00	20.16

Total expenditure during 8th Plan period 59.42 crores.

Role of NIC

4. The scheme is being implemented in joint collaboration with the National Informatics Centre (NIC) which is responsible for supply, installation and maintenance of hardware, software and other peripherals. NIC is also responsible for providing training to the revenue officials and technical support for implementation of the scheme. The Ministry of Rural Development is providing funds to the State Governments for site preparation, data entry work and purchase of furniture and other miscellaneous expenditure.

Financial Progress

5. Since inception of the scheme, the Ministry has released Rs. 141.61 crores upto 31.3.2000. The utilisation of funds reported by the States/UTs is Rs. 87.73 crores which is approximately 62 per cent of the total funds released. At present the scheme is being implemented in 544 districts of the country leaving only those districts where there are no land records.

The State-wise progress of funds released and utilised by States/UTs may be seen in Annexure-I.

6. The year-wise break up of funds released and expenditure during the first three years of the 9th Plan Period are given below :

9th Plan Budget provision : Rs. 150 crores

(Rs. in Crores)

Year	B.E.	R.E	Expenditure
1997-98	20.00	20.00	20.19
1998-99	30.00	25.00	24.75
1999-2000	33.00	33.00	32.24
2000-2001	50.00	—	15.98
			(upto 19.9.2000)
Total	133.00	78.00	93.16

Operationalisation of the Scheme at Tehsil/Taluk Level

7. During 1997-98, a decision for operationalisation of the scheme at the Tehsil/Taluk level was taken for facilitating delivery of computerised land records to users and public at large. Under this programme, funds are released to State Government for purchase of hardware, software and other peripherals and upto 19.9.2000, 1857 Tehsils/Taluks have been covered under the programme.

Pilot Projects on Digitisation of Cadastral Maps

8. The Ministry had also requested all the State Governments to submit proposals for Pilot Projects for Digitisation of Cadastral Survey Maps in 2 or 3 tehsils of any district in their state. So far 32 Pilot Projects on Digitisation of Cadastral Survey Maps covering 21 states *viz.*, A.P., M.P., Maharashtra, Manipur, Meghalaya, Mizoram, Gujarat, Goa, Haryana, Jammu & Kashmir, Bihar, Kerala, Karnataka, Tamil Nadu, Tripura, Nagaland, Orissa, Punjab, U.P., West Bengal and Pondicherry have been sanctioned by the Ministry.

Physical Progress

9. In about 100 districts, data entry and data validation work has been completed and ROR are being issued to land owners.

The six best performing States are West Bengal, A.P., Karnataka, Tamil Nadu, Sikkim and Orissa.

Monitoring of the Scheme

10. The progress of implementation of the scheme is periodically reviewed at the level of Joint Secretary as well as through annual conferences of Revenue Secretaries and Revenue Ministers of the States/Uts. The officers of the Ministry also visit various States in order to assess the progress of the scheme and to have a first-hand information regarding bottlenecks in the implementation of the scheme.

11. Recently, it was decided to go in for Campaign mode for data entry in specified dates of each Quarter in various States. Accordingly, Data-entry schedule for various States was chalked out and intimated to them for necessary action. It has also been decided to review and monitor the progress of the scheme through Video Conferencing interaction. The last Video Conference with the State Governments was held in August-September 2000.

Evaluation Studies

12. Since the feedback from the States regarding implementation of the scheme has not been forthcoming and progress of utilisation of funds has also been very low, it was decided in 1998 to conduct comprehensive Evaluation Studies in eight districts of different states *viz.*, Andhra Pradesh (Rangareddy), Madhya Pradesh (Hoshangabad), Maharashtra (Amravati), Karnataka (Mysore), Orissa (Mayurbhanj), Rajasthan (Jaipur), Uttar Pradesh (Aligarh) and West Bengal (Haora).

These studies have since been completed and the main findings of these studies are :

(i) The monitoring machanisem need to be strengthen as this is a crucial component for the success of the scheme.

(ii) There is a need to develop more awareness about the implementation of the scheme.

(iii) Training under the programme is inadequate, it should be conducted at different levels *viz.*, District, Tehsil and Village.

(iv) Computerisation of Land Records and setting up a Land Information System (LIS) is incomplete without a vectorised data base of land holdings through Digitisation of Cadastral Survey Maps.

(v) There is a need of Networking of the scheme at different levels so that data move from District to State and then to Centre through NICNET Network of the NIC.

13. There are some bottlenecks in implementation of the scheme by the State Governments. The Bottlenecks and the Remedial measures required to be taken for effective implementation of the scheme are indicated in Annexure-II.

ANNEX - I

Statement Showing the Breakup of Amount Released and Utilised under Computerisation of Land Records Programme as on 31-8-2000, (Since Inception in 1989)

COMPUTERISATION OF LAND RECORDS

(Rs in lakhs)

Sl. No.	Name of the State U.T.	Funds Released								Funds Released so far	Funds Used so far	% of Utilisation
		Between 1989-93	During 1993-94	During 1994-95	During 1995-96	During 1996-97	During 1997-98	During 1998-99	During 1999-2000			
1.	A.P.	25.00	78.00	105.00	210.00	15.00	0.00	829.90	174.05	1436.95	1177.18	82%
2.	ASSAM	25.00	33.00	50.00	50.00	80.00	97.50	0.00	0.00	335.50	67.56	20%
3.	BIHAR	20.00	30.00	100.00	0.00	0.00	367.50	30.50	0.00	548.00	35.30	6%
4.	GUJRAT	25.00	10.00	10.00	120.00	0.00	75.00	24.61	79.68	344.29	210.93	61%
5.	GOA	0.00	15.00	5.00	0.00	20.00	0.00	0.00	63.50	103.50	55.00	53%
6.	HARYANA	21.00	19.00	55.00	180.00	0.00	19.00	15.00	56.00	365.00	153.82	42%
7.	H.P.	25.00	15.00	50.00	55.00	60.00	0.00	6.60	28.60	240.20	45.00	19%
8.	J & K	25.00	4.00	20.00	0.00	0.00	30.00	189.00	18.00	286.00	186.34	65%
9.	KARNA.	25.00	43.00	28.00	120.00	95.00	69.20	342.50	501.88	1224.58	1107.27	90%
10.	KERALA	25.00	40.00	30.00	200.00	30.00	69.00	79.50	102.75	576.25	383.00	66%
11.	M.P.	33.00	45.00	90.00	75.00	45.00	485.50	237.82	668.38	1679.70	987.32	59%
12.	MAHA.	25.00	60.00	95.00	195.00	241.00	197.50	108.59	791.17	1713.26	873.60	51%

(Contd.)

ANNEX - I (*Contd.*)

Sl. No.	Name of the State U.T.	Funds Released								Funds Released so far	Funds Used so far	% of Utilisation
		Between 1989-93	During 1993-94	During 1994-95	During 1995-96	During 1996-97	During 1997-98	During 1998-99	During 1999-2000			
13.	MANIPUR	25.00	0.00	0.00	0.00	124.88	0.00	0.00	38.35	188.23	25.00	13%
14.	MEGHA	0.00	0.00	0.00	0.00	0.00	0.00	0.00	14.00	14.00	0.00	0%
15.	MIZORAM	0.00	15.00	10.00	0.00	60.00	0.00	50.00	37.78	172.78	85.00	49%
16.	NAGA.	0.00	0.00	0.00	0.00	0.00	0.00	0.00	25.15	25.15	0.00	0%
17.	ORISSA	32.50	55.00	30.00	135.00	270.00	0.00	20.50	171.12	714.12	586.55	82%
18.	PUNJAB	25.00	53.62	45.00	0.00	75.00	52.50	0.00	31.50	282.62	32.67	12%
19.	RAJA.	25.00	50.00	68.00	150.00	210.00	0.00	43.60	0.00	546.60	411.00	75%
20.	SIKKIM	12.00	0.00	0.00	20.00	0.00	0.00	22.40	12.80	67.20	32.00	48%
21.	T.N.	25.00	83.00	45.00	90.00	210.00	60.00	30.98	237.29	781.27	541.02	69%
22.	TRIPURA	25.00	40.00	20.00	0.00	15.00	75.80	0.00	38.00	213.80	144.62	68%
23.	U.P.	25.00	75.00	129.00	165.00	270.00	247.50	142.50	0.00	1054.00	450.00	43%
24.	W.B.	25.00	85.00	65.00	235.00	180.00	173.00	300.78	110.00	1173.78	1159.00	99%
25.	D & N. H.	0.00	12.38	0.00	0.00	0.00	0.00	0.00	0.00	12.38	0.00	0%
26.	DELHI	8.03	0.00	0.00	0.00	0.00	0.00	0.00	0.00	8.03	0.00	0%
27.	PONDI.	0.00	15.00	0.00	0.00	0.00	0.00	0.00	23.55	38.55	23.55	61%
28.	CHANDI.	0.00	0.00	0.00	0.00	15.00	0.00	0.00	0.00	15.00	0.00	0%
	TOTAL	501.53	876.00	1050.00	2000.00	2015.88	2019.00	2474.78	3223.55	14160.74	8772.73	62%

ANNEXURE II

Computerisation of Land Records

1. Bottlenecks in Implementation of the Scheme by the State Governments

- Delay in transfer of funds to implementing authority by the State Governments.
- Delay in construction of room with A.C. etc. for installation of computers and other equipments.
- Delay in development of appropriate software as per the requirement of the State Government.
- Delay in supply and installation of the hardware by the NIC.
- Lack of adequate training facilities to revenue staff to handle computers.
- Non-availability of private vendors for taking up the job of data-entry work.

2. Ways and Means to make the Scheme more Effective

- To gear up monitoring mechanism for review of implementation of the scheme as the physical and financial progress reports are not being received regularly from the State Governments.
- Direct release of funds to the State level implementing authorities.
- Organisation of regular training programme for revenue staff.
- The Evaluation of the scheme should be entrusted to reputed research organisations by the State Government.

CENTRALLY SPONSORED SCHEME FOR STRENGTHENING OF REVENUE ADMINISTRATION AND UPDATING OF LAND RECORDS (SRA & ULR)

1. Updating of Land Records is vital for increasing productivity of land, implementing various Rural Development

Programmes and also for effective enforcement of Land Reforms. Properly maintained land records minimise land disputes and create social harmony in villages.

2. Although the importance of a proper Land Record System has been emphasised right from the First Five Year Plan, this work did not receive the importance it deserves. For a variety of reasons, land records in most parts of the country are not in a good shape. States have attributed this condition of land records to constraint of resources. This is because Record of Rights, since British period, are prepared by carrying out cadastral surveys followed by settlement operations which is time consuming, staff-oriented and involves high cost. The equipments used in these operations are also outmoded. Even where there is a system of periodical updating of land records, lack of adequate revenue machinery, proper infrastructural facilities, absence of training are factors responsible for badly maintained land records. States have not been able to strengthen their revenue machinery and survey and settlement organisations because of paucity of resources. The work of revenue department in the State Governments gets very low priority in the allocation of funds as it is considered a non-plan activity. That is why, over the years the work has remained neglected even though some plan funds are also allocated for updating of land records in some States. In various fora such as the Revenue Ministers' Conference there has been a unanimous demand for allocation of substantial financial assistance to State Governments for expeditious completion of this work.

3. With a view to assisting the States/UTs in the task of updating of land records, a Centrally Sponsored Scheme for Strengthening of Revenue Administration and Updating of Land Records (SRA & ULR) was started in 1987. The main objectives of the scheme are :

- Strengthening of Survey and Settlement organisation for early completion and preparation of land records in areas where this work still remains to be done.

- Setting up of survey and settlement organisations especially in the North-Eastern Region, where no land records exist.
- Imparting pre-service and in-service training to revenue, survey and settlement staff and strengthening of training infrastructure for this purpose.
- Providing facilities for modernisation of survey and settlement operations, printing of survey maps, reports/documents, storage, copying and updating of land and crop records using, among other things, latest science and technology inputs.
- Strengthening of revenue machinery at village and immediate supervisory levels on a selective basis to make the workload of these functionaries manageable.

4. Initially, the scheme was approved for the States of Bihar and Orissa in 1987-88 and extended to other States/UTs during 1989-90. The scheme is being implemented by the State Governments through their Revenue/Land Reforms Departments. It is financed by the Centre and the State on 50 : 50 sharing basis. However, Union Territories are provided full Central assistance.

5. For providing Central assistance under the scheme, States and UTs are required to prepare schemes covering one or more of the above objectives. These proposals are considered by the Technical Committee constituted under the scheme. The Committee considers the proposals on the basis of the requirement projected by the concerned State/UT, utilisation of funds released during the previous years and the progress made under the scheme. On the basis of the recommendations made by the Technical Committee the cases are sent to Finance Division for its concurrence.

6. Under this scheme States/UTs have been given assistance for purchase of modern survey equipments like Global Positioning System (GPS), EDM, total stations, theodolites, work stations, aerial surveys, office equipments like photocopiers,

laminating machines, binding machines and basic facilities to improve work efficiency at the lower levels of revenue administration, construction of record rooms for proper storage of land records, construction of office-cum-residence of Patwaries, construction/repair/renovation of Training Institutes and equipments for training, etc. An illustrative list of items for which financial assistance is provided is placed at Annexure-I.

7. The expenditure under the scheme during 7th Plan was Rs. 13.95 crores against an allocation of Rs. 20.81 crores. The year-wise position of release of funds under the scheme is given below :

(Rs. in Crores)

Year	Funds Released
Total 7th Plan	13.95
1990-91	13.62
1991-92	9.05
Eighth Plan 1992-93	18.95
1993-94	24.26
1994-95	17.07
1995-96	18.80
1996-97	19.15
Total Eighth Plan	98.23
Ninth Plan	18.83
1997-98	9.05
1998-99	10.25
1999-2000	
Grand Total	172.98

B.E. 2000-2001, 25.00 crores

Funds released : 3.30 crores (upto 31-8-2000)

Upto 31.3.2000 financial assistance to the tune of Rs. 172.98 crores has been provided to the State Governments/ UTs towards Central share under the scheme. A statement showing the State-wise position of release of funds and its utilisation as on 31.8.2000 is given in Annexure-II (a) & II (b).

Monitoring of the Scheme

8. For monitoring of the Scheme, States/UTs are required to submit Quarterly Progress Report (QPR) in the prescribed proforma on the progress of the Scheme. The monitoring of the scheme includes proper utilisation of funds by the States on items approved by the Technical Committee and does not include any monitoring of actual updating of revenue records, issuance of updated record of rights, land holders passbook, printing of revenue settlement maps etc.

9. The Committee on Revitalization of Land Revenue Administration known as 'Appu Committee', constituted by the Government of India, has, inter-alia, made the following recommendations relating to this scheme :

(a) High priority should be accorded to the introduction of modern technology and techniques in the following three areas :

- day-to-day functioning of the Land Administration Department.
- The Maintenance of Land Records and continuous updating of land related information, including mutations.
- Survey and Settlement.

(b) The Committee has strongly recommended that Centrally Sponsored Scheme for Strengthening of Revenue Administration and Updating of Land Records (SRA & ULR) should continue during Ninth Five

Year Plan and outlays under the scheme substantially stepped up to bring about the desired improvements. The Committee also recommended that Centre's share under the scheme may be increased appropriately in order to make this programme successful in various States.

10. With the limited budget provision, Government of India has not been able to increase the percentage towards Central share from the existing 50 per cent. Keeping in view the overall position of Revenue Administration and Land Records in various States, there is strong need to enhance the budget provision under the Scheme.

11. There are many bottlenecks in implementing the Scheme by the State Governments. Some of the bottlenecks and remedial measures needed have been given Annexure III.

ANNEXURE I

Illustrative List of Activities for which Central Assistance is being provided to the States/UTs under the Centrally Sponsored Scheme for SRA & ULR

Construction of Buildings :

This includes construction/extension of Training Institutes, Hostels for these institutes, Patwarghars and Records Rooms.

Transport :

This includes purchase of vehicles for Training Institutes and for movement of survey-equipments.

Furniture :

Purchase of furniture for newly opened offices of Revenue Inspectors, furniture for Committee Rooms and Library Halls, for training institutes, for dormitories and mess.

Modern Survey Equipments :

This includes purchase of modern survey instruments like Global Positioning System (GPS), Total Stations, EDM, theodolite, work station, etc., for survey operations as well as for Training Institutions for training the survey and settlement staff.

Maps/Storage facilities :

This includes equipments for preparation of maps, steel almirahs for protection of maps and records, containers for records such as map-filing cabinets, racks, bags, etc.

Digitisation :

This includes equipments for digitisation of survey-records and land holdings.

Miscellaneous items :

These include micro-filming of records/maps, photo-copiers, laminating machines, binding machines, risographs, fax machines and setting up of computer cells.

ANNEX II(A)

Release of Funds Towards Central Share under the Centrally Sponsored Scheme for Strengthening of Revenue Administration & Updation of Land Records (SRA & ULR) As on 31-8-2000

(Rs. In Lakhs)

Sl.No.	States/Uts.	1987-88	1988-89	1989-90	1990-91	1991-92	1992-93	1993-94	1994-95	1995-96	1996-97	1997-98	1998-99	1999-2000	Total
1.	Andhra Pradesh			100.000					35.500		37.300				172.800
2.	Arunachal Pradesh				1.000				150.000					22.750	173.750
3.	Assam			100.000	50.000		40.000	42.125	150.000			15.074			397.199
4.	Bihar	100.000			150.000			45.850		782.000					1077.850
5.	Gujarat				100.000		248.700							73.500	422.200
6.	Goa				30.000	4.000		15.690	20.000		6.250				75.940
7.	Haryana			50.000	50.000	25.000		78.000	50.000					19.285	272.285
8.	Himachal Pradesh				110.000			36.000	50.000		148.925	100.100	99.845	150.000	694.870
9.	J & K			100.000			120.000	97.000	266.500		193.000	294.500	90.000	35.000	1196.000
10.	Karnataka				7.500	100.000		108.000	22.250		166.620	344.595			748.965
11.	Kerala			100.000	75.000		54.680	106.200	22.225	273.130	123.680	25.000	127.750	83.500	991.165
12.	Madhya Pradesh		296.640		12.450	143.975	351.890	235.320	306.700	41.450	332.275	97.750	70.650	119.450	2008.550
13.	Maharashtra				189.840	10.750	87.660			285.000	234.000	202.500		60.000	1069.750
14.	Manipur			15.000				45.175							60.175
15.	Meghalaya				50.000										50.000

(Contd.)

Annex II(A) (*Contd.*)

S.No.	States/Uts.	1987-88	1988-89	1989-90	1990-91	1991-92	1992-93	1993-94	1994-95	1995-96	1996-97	1997-98	1998-99	1999-2000	Total
16.	Mizoram			15.000		29.500	22.100	29.650	220.000		26.500		48.300	165.735	556.785
17.	Nagaland				17.500	6.500	7.700	37.950						68.550	138.200
18.	Orissa	100.000				55.215	90.000	110.400							355.615
19.	Punjab				162.500	165.870	206.450	580.255			53.900		96.370		1265.345
20.	Rajasthan			100.000	70.000	43.480	189.150	105.805	40.750	284.590	63.785	74.635	150.550	49.730	1172.475
21.	Sikkim				16.000						33.600	21.700	75.160		146.460
22.	Tamil Nadu			100.000	10.000	74.000	62.880	75.350		38.800					361.030
23.	Tripura			15.000				10.625	18.450		25.500	40.000			109.575
24.	Uttar Pradesh			100.000			281.890	530.040	238.155		232.120	372.426	146.380	57.500	1958.511
25.	West Bengal			103.310	200.000	173.750	110.900	92.500	86.500	150.000	200.000	275.250		120.000	1512.210
26.	A & N Islands				10.680		20.850			11.500					43.030
27.	Chandigarh				15.000	17.000									32.000
28.	D & N Haveli							25.000							25.000
29.	Delhi				25.000	17.000			10.000		10.000				62.000
30.	Daman & Diu					6.500									6.500
31.	Lakshdweep									13.500	12.210				25.710
32.	Pondicherry				10.000	32.880		18.880	20.400		14.910	19.550			116.620
															0.000
	Total	200.000	296.640	898.310	1362.470	905.420	1894.850	2425.815	1707.430	1879.970	1914.575	1883.080	905.005	1025.000	17298.565

ANNEX II(B)

Actual Expenditure Reported by States/Uts. under the Centrally Sponsored Scheme for Strengthening of Revenue Administration & Updating of Land Records (SRA & ULR) As on 31-8-2000

(Rs. in Lakhs)

Sl. No.	States/UTs	Funds utilised										Total	%age Utili-sation
		upto 1990-91	1991-92	1992-93	1993-94	1994-95	1995-96	1996-97	1997-98	1998-99	1999-2000		
1.	Andhra Pradesh	22.730		6.750	13.000	52.000			13.030			107.510	62.216
2.	Arunachal Pradesh	1.000					16.640	73.640	59.690			150.970	99.980
3.	Assam	100.000		50.000				52.000				202.000	50.856
4.	Bihar	89.250	10.000	100.000			616.375					815.625	75.671
5.	Gujarat		45.895	1.280	3.460	73.830	14.735	10.535	80.480	66.045	126.140	422.400	100.000
6.	Goa	14.490	10.700	11.000	13.500	16.565	14.485	1.220	1.400			83.360	109.771
7.	Haryana	14.300		24.995	25.000	38.000	25.000	25.000	50.000	33.430	19.720	255.445	93.815
8.	Himachal Pradesh		49.235	36.500	11.000	49.265	50.000	126.000	123.025	99.845		544.870	78.413
9.	J & K	5.020	35.000	31.110	54.940	56.730	176.995	228.055	277.465	255.330		1120.645	93.699
10.	Karnataka	7.500	25.000				100.500	171.510	118.500		55.650	478.660	63.909
11.	Kerala	83.645	19.995	37.990	32.480	85.255	120.115	243.270	100.000	127.250		850.000	85.757
12.	Madhya Pradesh	309.090	143.975	350.405	230.850	119.975	56.325	136.355	374.270	164.385		1885.630	93.880
13.	Maharashtra				99.065	188.995		403.055	43.400	50.345	255.970	1040.830	97.297

(Contd.)

ANNEX II(B) (*Contd.*)

Sl. No.	States/UTs	Funds utilised upto 1990-91	1991-92	1992-93	1993-94	1994-95	1995-96	1996-97	1997-98	1998-99	1999-2000	Total	%age Utili-sation
14.	Manipur	0.150										0.150	0.249
15.	Meghalaya											0.000	0.000
16.	Mizoram	15.000		29.500	22.100	29.650	220.000		26.500	8.150		350.900	71.520
17.	Nagaland	5.500	15.250		7.700	18.975			8.245	3.250		58.920	84.594
18.	Orissa	72.025			32.195	71.415				26.400	15.740	217.775	61.239
19.	Punjab		9.450	227.764	276.272	0.880	5.480	170.355	408.050			1098.251	86.795
20.	Rajasthan	125.530	15.320	103.260	84.870	46.035	64.815	163.170	114.505	143.545	30.950	892.000	76.078
21.	Sikkim				4.970	1.035		13.195	22.550			41.750	28.506
22.	Tamil Nadu	5.765	39.580	34.505	29.320	94.290	70.000	46.345	3.385			323.190	89.519
23.	Tripura	5.910	5.415		1.288	5.200	5.363	21.620	5.505	22.244		72.545	66.206
24.	Uttar Pradesh	99.250		231.890	528.015	64.945	194.200	162.770	145.965	135.960	65.010	1628.005	83.125
25.	West Bengal	103.310	75.220	50.000	69.995	45.975	136.265	83.500	134.000	244.000	190.740	1133.005	74.924
26.	A & N Islands			5.800	3.820	5.810	2.950	1.320	8.480			28.180	66.489
27.	Chandigarh	0.000	0.000	0.000	9.470	0.000	0.000	0.000	28.080			37.550	117.344
28.	D & N Haveli											0.000	0.000
29.	Delhi	20.420		7.480	8.110	5.050	3.200					44.260	71.387
30.	Daman & Diu			6.500								6.500	100.000
31.	Lakshdweep						13.500	12.210				25.710	100.000
32.	Pondicherry		9.990	31.340		15.400	16.940					73.670	63.171
Total		1099.885	510.025	1378.069	1561.420	1085.275	1923.883	2145.125	2146.525	1380.179	759.920	13990.306	80.876

ANNEXURE - III

SRA & ULR

1. Bottlenecks in implementing the Scheme by the State Governments.

(a) Delay in release of matching State share by State Governments.

(b) Delay in undertaking construction works such as construction of buildings for Training Institute, Record Rooms, Patwarghars, Circle Inspector's office-cum-residences etc. by PWD of the State Government.

(c) Delay in selection/identification of latest technical equipments and training of Revenue Staff for operation of the scheme.

(d) Delay in purchase of modern office equipments etc. due to prevailing system of centralised purchase prevailing in some States.

(e) Delay in collecting information from Village, Tehsil, District level and compilation of the same at the State level and remitting the same at the National level.

(f) Delay in release of funds by Central Govt. due to late receipt of proposals and utilisation certificates from the States.

(g) Delay in getting the Schemes approved by the Technical Committee.

2. Ways and means to make the Scheme more effective

(a) Increase the Central share from 50% to 80% for all States except North Eastern States for which Central share may be raised to 100%.

(b) The budget provisions, scope and area of financing under the Scheme to be substantially increased.

(c) Proposals for adoption of latest technology in survey,

settlement, map preparation and preservation of documents need to be given 'top priority'.

(d) Monitoring mechanism to review the implementation of the Scheme needs to be strengthened by the State Governments as the prescribed QPRs are not being received regularly.

Annexures

ANNEXURE-I

List of Subjects Allocated and Programmes Implemented by the Ministry of Rural Development

I. Department of Rural Development (*Gramin Vikas Vibhag*)

Under the sub-heading "A. DEPARTMENT OF RURAL DEVELOPMENT (GRAMIN VIKAS VIBHAG)", for the existing entries, the following entries shall be substituted, namely :

1. All matters relating to panchayati raj and panchayati raj institutions.
2. Nodal responsibility for all matters relating to the Minimum Needs Programme in rural areas in the field of elementary education, adult education, rural health, rural electrification and the nutrition programmes.
3. Public cooperation, including all matters relating to voluntary agencies for rural development. Council of Advancement of People's Action and Rural Technology (CAPART) and National Fund for Rural Development, other than aspects which fall within the purview of Department of Drinking Water Supply.
4. Cooperatives relatable to the items in this list.
5. All attached or subordinate offices or other organisations concerned with any of the subjects specified in this list.
6. All matters relating to rural roads including those under the Minimum Needs Programme in the rural areas.

7. Road works financed in whole or in part by the Central Government in tribal areas of Assam specified in Part I and Part II of the Table appended to paragraph 20 of the Sixth Schedule to the Constitution.
8. All matters relating to cooperation with the Centre for Integrated Rural Development for Asia and Pacific (CIRDAP) and the Afro-Asian Rural Reconstruction Organisation (AARRO).
9. (a) All matters pertaining to rural employment or unemployment such as working out of strategies and programmes for rural employment including special works, wage or income generation and training related thereof.
   (b) Implementation of the specific programmes of rural employment evolved from time to time.
   (c) Micro level planning related to rural employment or unemployment and administrative infrastructure thereof.
10. Integrated rural development including small farmers development agency, marginal farmers and agricultural labourers, etc.
11. Rural housing including Rural Housing Policy and all matters germane and incidental thereto under country or rural planning, in so far as it relates to rural areas.

II. Department of Land Resources (*Bhomi Sansadhan Vibhag*)

1. Land reforms, land tenures, land records, consolidation of holding and other related matters.
2. Administration of the Land Acquisition Act, 1894 (1 of 1894) and matters relating to acquisition of land for purposes of the Union.
3. Recovery of claims in a State in respect of taxes and other public demands, including arrears of land revenue

and sums recoverable as such arrears, arising outside that State.

4. Land, that is to say, collection of rents, transfer and alienation of iand, land improvement and agricultural loans excluding acquisition of non-agricultural land or buildings, town planning improvements.
5. Land revenue, including the assessment and collection of revenue, survey of revenue purposes, alienation of revenues.
6. Duties in respect of succession to agricultural land.
7. National Wastelands Development Board.
8. National Land Use and Wasteland Development Council.
9. Promotion of rural employment through Wastelands Development.
10. Promotion of production of fuel wood, fodder and timber on non-forest lands, including private wastelands.
11. Research and development of appropriate low cost technologies for increasing productivity of wastelands in sustainable ways.
12. Inter-departmental and interdisciplinary coordination in programme planning and implementation of the Wastelands Development Programme including straining.
13. Promotion of people's participation and public cooperation and coordination of efforts of Panchayats and voluntary and non-Government agencies for Wastelands Development.
14. Drought Prone Area Programmes.
15. Desert Development Programmes.

III. Department of Drinking Water Supply (*Peya Jal Poorti Vibhag*)

1. Rural Water Supply (subject to overall national perspective of water planning and coordination assigned to the Ministry of Water Resources), sewage, drainage and sanitation relating to rural areas; International cooperation and technical assistance in the field.

2. Public cooperation, including matters relating to voluntary agencies in so far as they relate to rural water supply, sewage, drainage and sanitation in rural areas.
3. Co-operatives relatable to the items in this list.
4. Cooperation with respect to matters relating to drinking water supply projects and issues, which cover both urban and rural areas.

ANNEXURE-II

Approved Outlays in Respect of Plan Schemes of the Department of Rural Development

(Rs. in crores)

Sl. No.	Name of the Schemes	Approved Outlay 1999-2000	2000-2001	2001-2002
1	2	3	4	5
1.	Jawahar Gram Samridhi Yojana	2095.00	1650.00	1650.00
2.	Employment Assurance Scheme	1700.00	1300.00	1600.00*
3.	Swarnjayaṇti Gram Swarozgar Yojana*	1215.00	1000.00	500.00
4.	DRDA Administration	—	220.00	220.00
5.	Indira Awaas Yojana	1710.00	1710.00	1527.00
6.	National Social Assistance Programme	725.00	715.00	835.00
7.	Annapurna	—	100.00	300.00
8.	Grants to National Institute of Rural Development	5.00	5.00	5.00
9.	Strengthening of State Training Centres	4.25	7.25	8.75
10.	Strengthening of Ext. Training Centres	3.00	3.00	3.00
11.	Training Courses, Seminars & Workshops	1.25	1.25	1.25
12.	Communication Cell	10.00	10.00	10.00
13.	Assistance to CAPART	13.00	13.00	30.00#
14.	Promotion of Voluntary Schemes	26.00	13.00	0.00
15.	Organisation of Beneficiaries	4.00	4.00	0.00
16.	Roads in Special Problem Areas	0.50	0.50	0.00
17.	Panchayat Development & Training	3.00	3.00	5.00
18.	Monitoring Mechanism	2.00	5.00	10.00
19.	Prime Minister's Gramodaya Yojana Rural Roads (New Schemes)	0.00	0.00	2500.00
	Total	7517.00	6760.00	9205.00

* Including Food for Work Programme.

\# The Scheme of Promotion of Voluntary Scheme & Organisation of Beneficiaries merged with the Scheme Assistance of CAPART.

ANNEXURE-III

Financial Progress under Jawahar Gram Samridhi Yojana during 1999-2000 upto March

(Rs. in lakhs)

Sl. No.	State/UTs	Balance as on 1-4-99	Allocation			Releases			Total Funds Available	Expenditure			Percentage Utilisation		
			Centre	State	Total	Centre (March)	State	Total		Total	Individual SC/STs	Disabled	Total	Individual SC/STs	Disabled
1	2	3	4	5	6	7	8	9	10	11	12	13	14	15	16
1.	Andhra Pradesh	1954.74	9319.52	3106.51	12426.03	9617.32	3205.45	12822.77	14777.51	9954.72	2618.77	9.31	67.36	26.31	0.09
2.	Arunachal Pradesh	381.09	204.90	68.30	273.20	142.71	47.57	190.28	571.37	461.48	102.5	0.35	80.77	22.21	0.08
3.	Assam	4466.90	5324.02	1774.67	7098.69	3787.01	1262.21	5049.22	9516.12	7800.48	2426.85	72.43	81.97	31.11	0.93
4.	Bihar	11666.61	30529.68	10176.56	40706.24	28484.06	9493.74	37977.80	49644.41	35324.14	10288.87	252.20	71.15	29.13	0.71
5.	Goa	3.16	137.12	45.71	182.82	124.11	41.37	165.48	168.64	114.34			67.80	0.00	0.00
6.	Gujarat	794.44	3508.04	1169.35	4677.39	3508.03	1169.23	4677.26	5471.70	4774.39	2896.68	29.39	87.26	60.67	0.62
7.	Haryana	425.85	2063.84	687.95	2751.79	2063.87	343.94	2407.81	2833.66	2666.87	914.99	0.00	94.11	34.31	0.00
8.	Himachal Pradesh	237.44	869.16	289.72	1158.88	1752.41	584.08	2336.49	2573.93	1163.94	366.01	0.85	45.22	31.45	0.07
9.	Jammu & Kashmir	159.84	1075.71	358.57	1434.28	897.74	299.22	1196.96	1356.80	805.55			59.37	0.00	0.00
10.	Karnataka	3919.71	7037.56	2345.85	9383.41	7037.56	2345.62	9383.18	13302.89	10191.73	2120.62	114.19	76.61	20.81	1.12
11.	Kerala	1129.91	3157.73	1052.58	4210.30	3157.72	1052.47	4210.19	5340.10	3652.85	964.06	4.54	68.40	26.39	0.12
12.	Madhya Pradesh	4119.90	15474.69	5158.23	20632.92	16926.38	5641.56	22567.94	26687.84	20841.39	7383.56	125.94	78.09	35.43	0.60
13.	Maharashtra	3049.74	13911.52	4637.17	18548.70	13911.47	4636.69	18548.16	21597.90	18748.46	5596.63	28.97	86.81	29.85	0.15

(Contd.)

ANNEXURE-III (*Contd.*)

1	2	3	4	5	6	7	8	9	10	11	12	13	14	15	16
14.	Manipur	66.24	356.92	118.97	475.89	115.54	38.51	154.05	220.29	93.87	58.37	0.45	42.61	62.18	0.48
15.	Meghalaya	280.64	399.88	133.29	533.17	132.18	44.06	176.24	456.88	180.98			39.61	0.00	0.00
16.	Mizoram	14.38	92.53	30.84	123.38	92.37	30.79	123.16	137.54	187.19	187.19	0.00	136.10	100.00	0.00
17.	Nagaland	86.09	274.30	91.43	365.73	223.90	74.63	298.53	384.62	291.76			75.86	0.00	0.00
18.	Orissa	2286.64	10659.61	3553.20	14212.82	15974.14	5324.18	21298.32	23584.96	13751.03	4815.17	62.87	58.30	35.02	0.46
19.	Punjab	214.15	1003.01	334.34	1337.34	975.08	324.99	1300.07	1514.22	1014.24	424.47	0.23	66.98	41.85	0.02
20.	Rajasthan	7037.70	5343.85	1781.28	7125.14	5343.85	1781.11	7124.96	14162.66	8149.69	2358.51	10.63	57.54	28.94	0.13
21.	Sikkim	20.24	102.45	34.15	136.60	102.45	34.15	136.60	156.84	206.97	39.29	85.52	131.97	18.98	41.32
22.	Tamil Nadu	263.93	8240.50	2746.83	10987.33	9163.14	3054.07	12217.21	12481.14	13391.37	4128.43	38.20	107.29	30.83	0.29
23.	Tripura	322.22	644.43	214.81	859.24	487.95	162.63	650.58	972.80	812.95	472.44	0.07	83.57	58.11	0.01
24.	Uttar Pradesh	5471.85	33598.18	11199.39	44797.57	33593.14	11196.59	44789.73	50261.58	35804.80	11819.36	200.84	71.24	33.01	0.56
25.	West Bengal	6840.43	11846.03	3948.68	15794.71	10800.26	3599.73	14399.99	21240.42	13074.47	3562.82	147.49	61.55	27.25	1.13
26.	A&N Islands	48.49	93.87	0.00	93.87	13.00	0.00	13.00	61.49	14.29	5.09		23.24	35.62	0.00
27.	D&N Haveli	0.00	61.96	0.00	61.96	30.98	0.00	30.98	30.98	0.85			2.74	0.00	0.00
28.	Daman & Diu	0.61	30.02	0.00	30.02	0.00	0.00	0.00	0.61	0.00			0.00	#DIV/0!	#DIV/0!
29.	Lakshdweep	8.26	47.06	0.00	47.06	23.53	0.00	23.53	31.79	10.43	10.43	0	32.81	100.00	
30.	Pondicherry	0.00	91.91	0.00	91.91	45.96	0.00	45.96	45.96	41.90	1.24	0	91.17	2.96	0.00
	Total	55271.20	165500.00	55058.39	220558.40	168527.86	55788.57	224316.43	279587.63	203527.13	63562.35	1184.47	72.80	31.23	0.58

ANNEXURE-III (*Contd.*)

Physical Performance under JGSY during 1999-2000 (Provisional)

Sl. No.	States/UTs	Month Code	Status of Works (in numbers) Works completed	Works under progress	Total Works	Works exclusively for SC/STs	Works Disabled	Total Mandays Generated (in lakh)
1	2	3	4	5	6	7	8	9
1.	Andhra Pradesh	3	40762	22763	63525	9773	39	133.89
2.	Arunachal Pradesh	3	525	81	606	120	3	5.92
3.	Assam	3	12456	5728	18184	5488	97	132.86
4.	Bihar	3	65784	48034	113818	15819	574	424.90
5.	Goa	3	45	146	191			1.26
6.	Gujarat	3	20370	4611	24981	11422	131	44.75
7.	Haryana	3	12469	2217	14686	4742	37	18.84
8.	Himachal Pradesh	3	6731	1117	7848	2320	5	14.43
9.	Jammu & Kashmir	3	2910		2910			9.74
10.	Karnataka	3	50697	25392	76089	16285	879	175.49
11.	Kerala	3	16068	15280	31348	8251	27	37.17
12.	Madhya Pradesh	3	54635	8304	62939	17162	479	265.27
13.	Maharashtra	3	68937	38347	107284	37822	150	341.55
14.	Manipur	2	980	463	1443	826	0	1.11
15.	Meghalaya	8	0	0	0	0	0	2.76
16.	Mizoram	3	1028	22	1050	1028	0	2.23
17.	Nagaland	3	2954	0	2954	0	0	6.96
18.	Orissa	3	50358	14096	64454	17756	316	211.51
19.	Punjab	3	10913	5448	16361	4721	150	6.62
20.	Rajasthan	3	15863	5623	21486	5235	23	105.06
21.	Sikkim	3	636	161	797	0	0	2.89
22.	Tamil Nadu	3	40953	1349	42302	19190	423	170.27
23.	Tripura	3	3114	125	3239	2292	0	14.49
24.	Uttar Pradesh	3	153536	39964	193500	51524	1674	438.89
25.	West Bengal	3	65664	23087	88751	24620	2746	113.86
26.	A & N Islands	2	40	3	43			0.21
27.	D & N Haveli	7						0.01
28.	Daman & Diu	7						0.00
29.	Lakshdweep	12	8	1	9	8		0.11
30.	Pondicherry	3	12	47	59	1	0	0.03
	Total		698448	262409	960857	256405	7753	2683.08

Note: Physical Progress is now monitored in terms of number of works completed and taken up in place of Mandays generation as JGSY has now become an infrastructure development programme as compared to generation of wage employment earlier.

ANNEXURE-IV

Financial and Physical Progress under Jawahar Gram Samridhi Yojana during 2000-01 upto the month of September

Sl. No.	State/UTs	Month Code	Balance as on 1-4-2000	Allocation			Releases			Total Funds Available	Funds Utilised			Percentage Utilisation		
				Centre	State	Total	Centre (September)	State	Total		Total	Individual SC/STs	Disabled	Total	Individual SC/STs	Disabled
1	2	3	4	5	6	7	8	9	10	11	12	13	14	15	16	17
1.	Andhra Pradesh	6	2145.44	8727.55	2908.89	11636.45	8044.52	2681.24	10725.76	12737.85	2466.09	647.28	0.00	19.36	5.08	0.00
2.	Arunachal Pradesh	9	121.82	456.91	152.29	609.19	0.00	0.00	0.00	121.82	32.74	7.53	0.00	26.88	6.18	0.00
3.	Assam	9	982.75	11872.04	3956.95	15828.99	0.00	0.00	0.00	982.75	781.46	208.73	33.60	79.52	21.24	3.42
4.	Bihar	9	15852.17	28590.47	9529.20	38119.67	13040.11	4346.27	17386.38	33238.55	14340.35	4272.69	95.44	43.14	12.85	0.29
5.	Goa	9	0.09	128.41	42.80	171.21	64.21	21.40	85.61	85.70	146.62			171.08	0.00	0.00
6.	Gujarat	9	545.03	3285.21	1094.96	4380.17	2644.20	881.31	3525.51	4070.54	3518.07	1901.79	87.73	86.43	46.72	2.16
7.	Haryana	9	295.61	1932.75	644.18	2576.93	966.38	322.09	1288.47	1584.08	1695.11	570.70	2.00	107.01	36.03	0.13
8.	Himachal Pradesh	9	303.71	813.95	271.29	1085.24	392.85	130.94	523.79	827.50	570.94	278.38	0.30	69.00	33.64	0.04
9.	Jammu & Kashmir	8	113.02	1007.38	335.76	1343.14	383.14	127.70	510.84	623.86	163.37			26.19	0.00	0.00
10.	Karnataka	9	3420.34	6590.54	2196.63	8787.17	3295.27	1098.31	4393.58	7813.92	3778.22	795.33	32.90	48.35	10.18	0.42
11.	Kerala	9	1547.48	2957.15	985.62	3942.77	395.26	131.74	527.00	2074.48	582.85	146.54	0.00	28.10	7.06	0.00
12.	Madhya Pradesh	8	4140.13	14491.75	4830.10	19321.86	8881.26	2960.12	11841.38	15981.51	9285.07	3186.67	59.57	58.10	19.94	0.37

13. Maharashtra	9	3917.70	13027.87	4342.19	17370.07	6513.90	2171.08	8684.98	12602.68	6668.09	1794.20	5.05	52.91	14.24	0.04
14. Manipur			795.90	265.27	1061.17	264.23	88.07	352.30	352.30				0.00	0.00	0.00
15. Meghalaya			891.69	297.20	1188.89	402.71	134.22	536.93	536.93				0.00	0.00	0.00
16. Mizoram	9	5.20	206.33	68.77	275.10	103.17	34.39	137.56	142.76	117.18	117.18	0.00	82.08	82.08	0.00
17. Nagaland	6	78.11	611.66	203.87	815.53	305.83	101.93	407.76	485.87	204.75			42.14	0.00	0.00
18. Orissa	9	3979.97	9982.52	3327.17	13309.70	4531.99	1510.51	6042.50	10022.47	7214.75	2489.47	27.70	71.99	24.84	0.28
19. Punjab	8	128.64	939.30	313.07	1252.37	493.36	164.44	657.80	786.44	609.43	285.84	0.00	77.49	36.35	0.00
20. Rajasthan	9	5077.01	5004.41	1667.97	6672.39	4779.17	1592.90	6372.07	11449.08	6422.20	1635.94	5.99	56.09	14.29	0.05
21. Sikkim	9	0.08	228.45	76.14	304.60	114.23	38.07	152.30	152.38	114.23	63.99		74.96	41.99	0.00
22. Tamil Nadu	9	406.35	7717.07	2572.10	10289.17	3858.54	1286.05	5144.59	5550.94	5523.45	1715.95	15.16	99.50	30.91	0.27
23. Tripura	8	0.00	1437.02	478.96	1915.97	718.51	239.48	957.99	957.99	53.87	31.17	0.00	5.62	3.25	0.00
24. Uttar Pradesh	9	14347.39	31464.06	10486.97	41951.03	15621.92	5206.79	20828.71	35176.10	2103.09	669.45	6.19	5.98	1.90	0.02
25. West Bengal	8	4946.38	11093.58	3697.49	14791.07	5080.77	1693.42	6774.19	11720.57	4698.73	1029.95	101.73	40.09	8.79	0.87
26. A & N Islands	9	32.23	84.64		84.64	11.72	0.00	11.72	43.95	2.40	0.44	0.00	5.46	1.00	0.00
27. D & N Haveli			55.87		55.87	27.94	0.00	27.94	27.94				0.00	0.00	0.00
28. Daman & Diu	9	3.03	27.07		27.07	0.00	0.00	0.00	3.03	0.00	0.00	0.00	0.00	0.00	0.00
29. Lakshdweep	9	30.21	42.43		42.43	0.00	0.00	0.00	30.21	8.48	0.00	0.00	28.07	0.00	0.00
30. Pondicherry	9	6.33	86.00		86.00	43.00	0.00	43.00	49.33	33.89	8.77	0.00	68.70	17.78	0.00
Total		62426.22	164550.00	54745.86	219295.86	80978.19	26962.48	107940.67	170366.89	71135.43	21857.99	473.36	41.75	12.83	0.28

Note: The blank column denote non-reporting of figures by the State/UTs.

ANNEXURE-IV (*Contd.*)

Physical Performance under JGSY during 2000-01 upto September

Sl. No.	States/UTs	Month Code	Status of Works (in numbers)					Total Mandays Generated (in lakh)
			Works completed	Works under progress	Total Works	Works exclusively for SC/STs	Works Disabled	
1	2	3	4	5	6	7	8	9
1.	Andhra Pradesh	6	10278	30844	41122	1882	0	30.27
2.	Arunachal Pradesh	9	88	77	165	26	0	0.57
3.	Assam	9	2436	3433	5869	897	27	11.80
4.	Bihar	9	35447	49395	84842	10201	326	152.19
5.	Goa	9	0	146	146	0	0	1.63
6.	Gujarat	9	14352	5640	19992	7343	197	32.37
7.	Haryana	9	5694	1114	6808	2000	10	10.33
8.	Himachal Pradesh	9	2991	1961	4952	1165	0	6.34
9.	Jammu & Kashmir	8						1.60
10.	Karnataka	9	20678	35753	56431	5514	405	50.50
11.	Kerala	9	2500	16251	18751	1111	0	6.34
12.	Madhya Pradesh	8	25814	14605	40419	8639	371	147.49
13.	Maharashtra	9	21611	43525	65136	10698	52	112.98
14.	Manipur							
15.	Meghalaya							
16.	Mizoram	9	416	0	416	416	0	1.23
17.	Nagaland	6						8.60
18.	Orissa	9	23571	19855	43426	8398	291	104.17
19.	Punjab	8	7176	6138	13314	3662	97	4.66
20.	Rajasthan	9	14584	9424	24008	5158	39	62.56
21.	Sikkim	9	247	371	618			1.74
22.	Tamil Nadu	9	10448	22168	32616	4226	95	69.51
23.	Tripura	8	18	207	225	9	0	0.75
24.	Uttar Pradesh	9	4910	33034	37944	1950	122	29.11
25.	West Bengal	8	40759	35466	76225	17449	2510	38.21
26.	A & N Islands	9	10	1	11	0	0	0.00
27.	D & N Haveli							
28.	Daman & Diu	9	0	0	0	0	0	0.00
29.	Lakshdweep	9	4	14	18	4	0	0.10
30.	Pondicherry	9	37	57	94	5	0	0.07
	Total		244069	329479	573548	90753	4542	885.12

Note: Physical Progress is now monitored in terms of number of works completed and taken up in place of Mandays generation as JGSY has now become an infrastructure development programme as compared to generation of wage employment earlier.

ANNEXURE-V

Gist of Recommendations of the National Rural Roads Development Committee (May, 2000)

Mission

In order to free each and every village in the country from the handicaps and deprivation of lack of access and to provide all the facilities like health care, education, etc. To the entire rural population, the Government should take up on priority the task of providing good All-weather roads to each and every village in the country. A time bound programme should be drawn up for the task. Such roads should be very durable and should need no maintenance for several years after construction.

Phasing

Considering the huge magnitude of the task, the programme should be taken up in two phases. In Phase-I, all the villages with a population of 500 or more should be tackled. In Phase-II, the remaining villages may be taken up. During Phase-I, if any smaller villages are found to lie close to a road being constructed in that Phase, such smaller villages may also be tackled in Phase-I for ease of construction and economy. If it is found during detailed planning that any area or pocket with smaller villages is especially deprived, the culverts and small bridges on the proposed alignments for approach roads to such villages may be taken up in Phase-I. The work should be started by tackling about 40 to 50 districts at the outset, each State to have 7 district with larger States getting an additional district.

Specifications

These roads should have a black top surface in view of the fast moving, pneumatic-tyred and heavy vehicles, which are plying even in rural areas today. The width of the carriage way should be 3.75 metres and the width of formation should be 7.5 metres. All the necessary cross drainage works and minor bridges should be constructed. The objective should be to ensure that in no case should the traffic be held up for more than 24 hours at a time and not more than six times a year even on the village roads. In some special cases, even major bridges may be constructed to ensure proper connectivity.

Authority

In order to ensure speedy and systematic execution of the programme, the Union Government should set up "National Rural Road Development Authority". Its Chairman should be of the status of a Cabinet Minister of the Union Cabinet, considering the onerous task entrusted to it.

Finances

The Authority should be authorised to raise finances for the programme by borrowings from suitable sources. The Union Government should guarantee the *release* of such loans. The Authority may also be given full freedom to tap any other sources of fund, which it may find suitable.

The earmarked portion of special cess on petrol and diesel collected every year should be made available for this Scheme. The Rural Development Department should also make available to the Authority Rs. 2,500 crores each year from its outlays. This should be non-lapsable.

The Central Government should also raise Rs. 5,000 crores by issuing tax-free bonds @ maximum 8% for the first 5 years. Interest on these bonds as well as guarantee for repayment should be given by the Central Government. However, principal repayment would be arranged by the Authority from its funds.

Execution

In order to ensure full accountability of the Authority to the lenders regarding the quality and proper standards of these works, the Authority should itself execute the programme with full cooperation from the State Government/Zilla

Parishads. The Authority should not be only a machinery for reimbursement of expenditure on road works over which it has no control.

Full cooperation of the State Government and the Zilla Parishads should be secured for the programme. Fixing the alignment of the road, should be done in consultation with Zilla Parishads and the State Government. The land acquisition will have to be done by the State Government. The State Government should also provide experienced personnel on deputation to the Authority whenever asked by it.

The Authority should carry out the works under this Programme in the districts where the local Zilla Parishads and the State Government permit the Authority to carry out these works. Where such permission is not forthcoming, the Authority should not carry out any work.

For managing the actual construction of these roads in the districts, the corporation may set up its cells in each district. This cell should have bare minimum staff. For detailed field working, services of suitable qualified consultants may be used freely.

In special difficult areas, the construction work could be entrusted to the BRO.

The Authority must carry out these works to a high standard of workmanship using modern machinery and latest methods. It should also strive to achieve all possible economy by using suitable technologies and materials.

The Authority should have full freedom to decide the methodology of carrying out the survey and execution of the works.

It should be made mandatory for the owner of the land required for these road works, to hand over the land without demur or protest. He should have no right to contest the need for alignment. He shall have full freedom to contest the amount of compensation. Project estimate shall provide for cost of acquiring land for the project.

Environmental and forest clearances should be made automatic wherever they are required as per the law. Project Implementation Authority shall be bound to take the mitigation measures.

Quarry permission as well as explosive permits and blasting permissions must be issued very expeditiously.

Online Management and Monitoring

The Authority should set up a computer based and internet based, detailed online management and monitoring system.

The responsibility for coordinating the design, development and delivery of the entire Online Management and Monitoring System for the programme should be allocated to Centre for Development of Advanced Computing (C-DAC), Ministry of Information Technology, Government of India, in view of their general expertise and experience in handling Electronic Governance projects and more specifically, the project for Statewide Computerisation of Public Works Department, Government of Maharashtra. Keeping in view the time-critical nature of the project, C-DAC may in turn involve their Authorised Training Centres across the country to provide support at the district locations through the availability of highly trained manpower.

Monitoring and Quality Audit

There should be a separate organisation for quality audit and monitoring of the road works of this Authority in each district. This organisation could draw experienced and retired persons from the Army and the BRO.

In each District, an Advisory Committee may be set up to review the progress once a month, occasionally visit the works, take note of the grievances of the local people and suggest suitable actions for redressal.

Maintenance

After completion of the works, the completed roads should be handed over to the State Governments/Zilla Parishads for further maintenance. It should be ensured that adequate provision is made for the maintenance.

Iron-Tyred Carts

The Government should encourage the development and use of pneumatic-tyred carts instead of the iron-tyred ones, presently in use by way of subsidies towards conversion and tax-exemption on tyres.

ANNEXURE-VI

State/Union Teritorry-wise Allocations for Rural Roads for the Year 2000-2001

(Rs. in crores)

Sl. No.	States/UTs	Amount
1	2	3
1.	Andhra Pradesh	190
2.	Bihar	150
3.	Chhattisgarh	87
4.	Goa	5
5.	Gujarat	50
6.	Haryana	20
7.	Himachal Pradesh	60
8.	Jammu & Kashmir	20
9.	Jharkhand	110
10.	Karnataka	95
11.	Kerala	20
12.	Madhya Pradesh	213
13.	Maharashtra	130

(Contd.)

ANNEXURE-VI (*Contd.*)

1	2	3
14.	Orissa	175
15.	Punjab	25
16.	Rajasthan	130
17.	Tamil Nadu	80
18.	Uttar Pradesh	315
19.	Uttaranchal	60
20.	West Bengal	135
21.	A&N Islands	10
22.	Dadra & Nagar Haveli	5
23.	Daman & Diu	5
24.	Lakshdweep	5
25.	Pondicherry	5
	North Eastern States	
26.	Arunachal Pradesh	35
27.	Assam	75
28.	Manipur	40
29.	Meghalaya	35
30.	Mizoram	20
31.	Nagaland	20
32.	Sikkim	20
33.	Tripura	25
	Total	2370

An amount of Rs. 130 crores has been earmarked for Rural Roads in Special Problem Areas.

ANNEXURE-VII

Financial Progress under Swarnjayanti Gram Swarozgar Yojana during 1999-2000 (Upto March, 2000) — As on 22-12-2000 — Provisional

(Rs. in Lakhs)

Sl. No.	Sates/UTs	Till Month	Opening Balance 1-4-99	Central Allocation	State Allocation	Total Allocation	Central Releases	State Releases	Total Funds Available	Utilisation	% of Uti. to funds Avail.	% of Uti. to Allocation	Total Credit Target	Total Credit Mobilised	% of Credit Mobilised
1	2	3	4	5	6	7	8	9	10	11	12	13	14	15	16
1.	Andhra Pradesh	3	2733.98	6219.55	2073.18	8292.73	6219.57	2061.77	11015.32	10044.08	91.18	121.12	21600.00	9379.59	43.42
2.	Arunachal Pradesh	3	512.87	136.74	45.58	182.32	92.14	21.23	626.24	240.22	38.36	131.76	880.00	13.20	1.50
3.	Assam	3	4459.11	3553.09	1184.36	4737.45	3062.36	221.87	7743.34	4509.16	58.23	95.18	7000.00	895.89	12.80
4.	Bihar	3	16277.55	20374.56	6791.52	27166.08	11918.05	3617.78	31813.38	10068.16	31.65	37.06	51000.00	10839.06	21.25
5.	Goa	3	67.33	59.78	19.93	79.71	59.78	11.58	138.69	11.22	8.09	14.08	170.00	0.00	0.00
6.	Gujarat	3	1512.76	2341.15	780.38	3121.53	2340.56	616.51	4469.83	2448.03	54.77	78.42	7500.00	2213.59	29.51
7.	Haryana	3	274.81	1377.36	459.12	1836.48	1784.18	459.68	2518.67	1963.41	77.95	106.91	4200.00	3000.13	71.43
8.	Himachal Pradesh	3	425.74	580.06	193.35	773.41	475.99	96.68	998.41	667.38	66.84	86.29	2000.00	2223.11	111.16
9.	Jammu & Kashmir	3	466.48	717.90	239.30	957.20	411.69	235.55	1113.72	787.32	70.69	82.25	1800.00	695.44	38.64
10.	Karanataka	3	4809.40	4696.65	1565.55	6262.20	2348.33	782.78	7940.51	3969.52	49.99	63.39	14000.00	3364.84	24.03
11.	Kerala	3	1537.63	2107.37	702.46	2809.83	2083.35	694.46	4315.44	2506.81	58.09	89.22	7000.00	5006.72	71.52
12.	Madhya Pradesh	3	4181.78	10327.33	3442.44	13769.77	10013.58	2979.65	17175.01	9918.36	57.75	72.03	31500.00	10859.11	34.47
13.	Maharashtra	3	4017.58	9284.11	3094.70	12378.81	9284.11	2517.34	15819.03	10257.28	64.84	82.86	28500.00	15404.06	54.05
14.	Manipur	4	R A	238.19	79.40	317.59	119.097	0.00	119.10	0.00	0.00	0.00	500.00	0.00	0.00

(Contd.)

ANNEXURE-VII (*Contd.*)

1	2	3	4	5	6	7	8	9	10	11	12	13	14	15	16
15.	Meghalaya	8	R A	266.87	88.96	355.83	131.52	58.05	189.57	75.02	39.57	21.08	600.00	69.43	11.57
16.	Mizoram	3	9.98	61.75	20.58	82.33	58.15	20.56	88.69	9.98	11.25	12.12	200.00	0.00	0.00
17.	Nagaland	3	134.58	183.06	61.02	244.08	102.087	0.00	236.67	228.94	96.74	93.80	400.00	94.16	23.54
18.	Orissa	3	2780.08	7113.90	2371.30	9485.20	7222.67	3377.06	13379.81	7457.65	55.74	78.62	20700.00	9417.58	45.50
19.	Punjab	3	352.97	669.38	223.13	892.51	664.98	270.17	1288.12	987.57	76.67	110.65	2000.00	227.96	11.40
20.	Rajasthan	3	4244.01	3566.34	1188.78	4755.12	3566.34	1188.78	8999.13	6270.68	69.68	131.87	14000.00	6116.18	43.69
21.	Sikkim	3	36.48	68.38	22.79	91.17	68.38	22.80	127.66	81.62	63.94	89.52	230.00	119.07	51.77
22.	Tamil Nadu	3	1155.38	5499.44	1833.15	7332.59	6999.46	2002.72	10157.55	10234.93	100.76	139.58	18000.00	7374.61	40.97
23.	Tripura	3	323.30	430.08	143.36	573.44	488.12	119.10	930.52	836.58	89.90	145.89	1100.00	920.17	83.65
24.	Uttar Pradesh	3	16001.62	22422.38	7474.13	29896.51	13337.96	4197.12	33536.70	6628.31	19.76	22.17	65000.00	10207.32	15.70
25.	West Bengal	3	11167.21	7905.68	2635.23	10540.91	3952.84	573.74	15693.79	5652.12	36.01	53.62	20000.00	7166.14	35.83
26.	A & N Islands	3	60.29	59.78		59.78	29.90		90.19	40.23	44.61	67.30	125.00	6.41	5.13
27.	D & N Haveli	8	14.63	59.78		59.78	29.89		44.52	2.34	5.25	3.91	125.00	0.00	0.00
28.	Daman & Diu	12	15.52	59.78		59.78	29.89		45.41	7.50	16.52	12.55	120.00	1.03	0.86
29.	Lakshdweep	3	17.52	59.78		59.78	29.89		47.41	0.25	0.53	0.42	125.00	0.40	0.32
30.	Pondicherry	3	74.41	59.78		59.78	29.89		104.30	81.77	78.40	136.78	125.00	31.07	24.86
	Total		77665.00	110500.00	36733.70	147233.70	86954.73	26146.98	190766.71	95986.43	50.32	65.19	320500.00	105646.27	32.96

NR — Not Reported.

Notes: 1. The opening balance comprising opening balances under erstwhile IRDP, TRYSEM, DWCRA, SITRA and GKY schemes.

2. The total Central releases were Rs. 93223.31 lakhs including Rs. 6268.58 lakhs released for Special Projects.

ANNEXURE-VII (*Contd.*)

Per Family Investment under SGSY during 1999-2000 (March, 2000) — Provisional

Sl. No.	States/UTs	Till Month	Total Subsidy Disbursed	Total Credit Disbursed	Total Investment	Per Family Investment (in Rupees)	Credit Subsidy Ratio
1	2	3	4	5	6	7	8
1.	Andhra Pradesh	3	6332.18	9379.59	15711.77	9511	1.48
2.	Arunachal Pradesh	3	216.94	13.20	230.14	7521	0.00
3.	Assam	3	496.60	895.89	1392.49	7747	1.80
4.	Bihar	3	5794.22	10839.06	16633.28	15634	1.87
5.	Goa	3	0.00	0.00	0.00	N.A.	N.A.
6.	Gujarat	3	1347.90	2213.59	3561.49	18414	1.64
7.	Haryana	3	1150.28	3000.13	4150.41	23924	2.61
8.	Himachal Pradesh	3	564.81	2223.11	2787.92	32275	3.94
9.	Jammu & Kashmir	3	419.71	695.44	1115.16	19111	1.66
10.	Karnataka	3	2214.73	3364.84	5579.57	29084	1.52
11.	Kerala	3	2168.70	5006.72	7175.42	24336	2.31
12.	Madhya Pradesh	3	5889.34	10859.11	16748.45	14938	1.84
13.	Maharashtra	3	6476.65	15404.06	21880.71	24866	2.38
14.	Manipur	4	0.00	0.00	0.00	N.A.	N.A.
15.	Meghalaya	8	35.22	69.43	104.65	14123	1.97
16.	Mizoram	3	0.00	0.00	0.00	N.A.	N.A.
17.	Nagaland	3	197.14	94.16	291.30	6134	0.00
18.	Orissa	3	5038.59	9417.58	14456.17	19370	1.87
19.	Punjab	3	99.66	227.96	327.62	19340	2.29
20.	Rajasthan	3	2603.50	6116.18	8719.68	25556	2.35
21.	Sikkim	3	49.21	119.07	168.28	24530	2.42
22.	Tamil Nadu	3	4467.04	7374.61	11841.65	18099	1.65
23.	Tripura	3	446.66	920.17	1366.83	16176	2.06
24.	Uttar Pradesh	3	4659.89	10207.32	14867.21	24514	2.19
25.	West Bengal	3	3466.73	7166.14	10632.87	11970	2.07
26.	A & N Islands	3	17.86	6.41	24.27	3053	0.36
27.	D & N Haveli	8	0.00	0.00	0.00	N.A.	N.A.
28.	Daman & Diu	12	0.48	1.03	1.51	25167	2.15
29.	Lakshdweep	3	0.20	0.40	0.60	20000	2.00
30.	Pondicherry	3	15.19	31.07	46.26	8712	2.05
	Total		54169.43	105646.27	159815.70	17113	1.95

N.A. — Not Available.

ANNEXURE-VII (*Contd.*)

Details of Swarozgaris Assisted under Swarnjayanti Gram Swarozgar Yojana (SGSY) 1999-2000 (Upto March, 2000) — As on 22-12-2000 (Provisional)

(No. of Swarozgaris)

Sl. No.	States/UTs	Till Month	Self-Help Groups: Group Formed	Self-Help Groups: Activity Taken-up	Members Covered under SHGs(*)	Individual Swarozgaris Assisted	Total Swarozgaris Assisted	Coverage of Disadvantaged Groups — Numbers: Scheduled Castes	Scheduled Tribes	Women	Handicap.	Percentage: Sheduled Castes	Scheduled Tribes	Women	Handicap.	Average Member of Col. 5
1	2	3	4	5	6	7	8	9	10	11	12	13	14	15	16	17
1.	Andhra Pradesh	3	167529	10423	135498	29692	165190	63491	15929	114262	3990	38.44	9.64	69.17	2.42	13.00
2.	Arunachal Pradesh	3	54	1	5	3055	3060	0	3060	1169	0	0.00	100.00	38.20	0.00	5.00
3.	Assam	3	4818	1152	12472	5502	17974	2216	3886	5850	129	12.33	21.62	32.55	0.72	10.83
4.	Bihar	3	9860	3128	35485	70908	106393	29876	16684	35727	331	28.08	15.68	33.58	0.31	11.34
5.	Goa	3	0	0	0	0	0	0	0	0	0	0.00	0.00	0.00	0.00	0.00
6.	Gujarat	3	4206	287	2731	16610	19341	2616	8054	6618	206	13.53	41.64	34.22	1.07	9.52
7.	Haryana	3	712	260	2730	14618	17348	8263	0	9527	136	47.63	0.00	54.92	0.78	10.50
8.	Himachal Pradesh	3	1222	180	1975	6663	8638	3163	994	3610	14	36.62	11.51	41.79	0.00	10.97
9.	Jammu & Kashmir	3	NR	NR	NR	5835	5835	NR	NR	NR	NR	0.00	0.00	0.00	0.00	N.A.
10.	Karnataka	3	7632	895	10638	8546	19184	5818	2126	10946	235	30.33	11.08	57.06	1.22	11.89
11.	Kerala	3	6761	440	4689	24796	29485	8133	456	15443	345	27.58	1.55	52.38	0.00	10.66
12.	Madhya Pradesh	3	19195	5562	56554	55564	112118	23573	30695	29435	530	21.03	27.38	26.25	0.47	10.17
13.	Maharashtra	3	19470	957	8747	79247	87994	21329	12869	36268	981	24.24	14.62	41.22	1.11	9.14

14. Manipur	4	NR	NR	NR	NR	NR					0.00	0.00	0.00	0.00	N.A.
15. Meghalaya	8	NR	NR	NR	741	741		741	403	0	0.00	100.00	54.39	0.00	N.A.
16. Mizoram	3	0	0	0	0	0	0	0	0	0	0.00	0.00	0.00	0.00	N.A.
17. Nagaland	3	367	184	2648	2101	4749	0	4749	2454	0	0.00	100.00	51.67	0.00	14.39
18. Orissa	3	10334	1011	9913	64720	74633	15017	18402	21713	194	20.12	24.66	29.09	0.26	9.81
19. Punjab	3	561	72	825	869	1694	1046	0	1040	5	61.75	0.00	61.39	0.30	11.46
20. Rajasthan	3	635	67	573	33547	34120	9804	5507	13847	145	28.73	16.14	40.58	0.42	8.55
21. Sikkim	3	17	5	5	681	686	61	288	270		8.89	41.98	39.36	0.00	1.00
22. Tamil Nadu	3	18661	3198	47264	18163	65427	30203	1309	52139	547	46.16	2.00	79.69	0.84	14.78
23. Tripura	3	419	17	290	8160	8450	1549	2934	2757	70	0.00	0.00	32.63	0.00	17.06
24. Uttar Pradesh	3	17389	173	1213	59434	60647	26130	782	15642	227	43.09	1.29	25.79	0.37	7.01
25. West Bengal	3	2481	1002	12925	75901	88826	26485	5008	36974	444	29.82	5.64	41.63	0.50	12.90
26. A & N Islands	3	74	0	703	92	795	18	78	223	0	0.00	0.00	0.00	0.00	N.A.
27. D & N Haveli	8	NR	NR	NR	NR	NR	0	0	0	0	0.00	0.00	0.00	0.00	N.A.
28. Daman & Diu	12	NR	NR	NR	6	6	0	6	4	0	0.00	100.00	66.67	0.00	N.A.
29. Lakshdweep	3	0	0	0	3	3	0	3	0	0	0.00	100.00	0.00	0.00	N.A.
30. Pondicherry	3	29	3	29	502	531	147	384	369	0	0.00	0.00	0.00	0.00	9.67
Total		292426	29017	347912	585956	933868	278938	134944	416690	8529	29.87	14.45	44.62	0.91	11.99

NR — Not Reported.

N.A. — Not Available.

(*) — This information with ref erence to Col. 4.

ANNEXURE-VIII

A. Financial Progress — Allocation, O.B., Total Funds Available and Funds Utilised under Swarnjayanti Gram Swarozgar Yojana (SGSY) during 2000-2001 upto December, 2000 (As on 12-2-2001)

(Rs. in Lakhs)

Sl. No.	States/UTs	Till Month	Opening Balance As on 1-4-2000	Central Alloca-tion	State Alloca-tion	Total Alloca-tion	Central Releases (upto date)	% of Central Releases	State Releases	Total Funds Available	Utilisation of Funds	% of Utilisation to Total Funds	% of Utilisation to Total Allocation
1	2	3	4	5	6	7	8	9	10	11	12	13	14
1.	Andhra Pradesh	12	516.65	5303.03	1767.68	7070.71	4104.75	77.40	569.97	5191.37	2928.67	56.41	41.42
2.	Arunachal Pradesh	11	229.45	276.91	92.30	369.21	49.46	17.86	9.47	288.38	52.74	18.29	14.28
3.	Assam	11	2334.42	7195.18	2398.39	9593.57	0.00	0.00	0.00	2334.42	323.28	13.85	3.37
4.	Bihar	12	12110.52	12616.76	4205.59	16822.35	471.13	3.73	2135.11	14716.76	5827.84	39.60	34.64
5.	Chattisgarh	9	2359.28	2800.88	933.63	3734.51	1027.97	36.70	277.97	3665.22	760.97	20.76	20.38
6.	Goa	12	9.44	50.00	16.67	66.67	25.00	50.00	16.67	51.11	1.48	2.90	2.22
7.	Gujarat	12	1520.01	1996.15	665.38	2661.53	1088.47	54.53	207.29	2815.77	1785.88	63.42	67.10
8.	Haryana	12	228.52	1174.37	391.46	1565.83	952.83	81.14	517.43	1698.78	1193.74	70.27	76.24
9.	Himachal Pradesh	12	328.14	494.67	164.89	659.56	230.06	46.51	183.36	741.56	506.57	68.31	76.80
10.	Jammu & Kashmir	10	620.41	612.10	204.03	816.13	89.23	14.58	0.00	709.64	330.68	46.60	40.52
11.	Jharkhand	12	3511.54	4755.33	1585.11	6340.44	300.16	6.31	811.30	4623.00	2398.40	51.88	37.83
12.	Karnataka	11	4539.44	4004.53	1334.84	5339.37	1370.96	34.24	165.19	6075.59	2056.60	33.85	38.52
13.	Kerala	12	2092.94	1796.82	598.94	2395.76	879.11	48.93	156.06	1466.81	1044.13	71.18	43.58

14. Madhya Pradesh	12	3957.99	6004.58	2001.53	8006.11	2499.03	41.62	495.97	6952.99	4454.54	64.07	55.64
15. Maharashtra	12	6040.78	7915.98	2638.66	10554.64	3445.84	43.53	4274.11	13760.73	4046.70	29.41	38.34
16. Manipur		N.R.	482.36	160.79	643.15	0.00	0.00	N.R.	0.00	N.R.	#VALUE!	#VALUE!
17. Meghalaya	11	300.07	540.42	180.14	720.56	0.00	0.00	24.49	324.56	39.87	12.28	5.53
18. Mizoram	11	79.47	125.06	41.69	166.75	0.00	0.00	0.00	79.47	45.53	57.29	27.31
19. Nagaland	7	74.93	370.70	123.57	494.27	0.00	0.00	60.00	134.93	53.86	39.92	10.90
20. Orissa	12	4335.02	6065.56	2021.85	8087.41	3479.02	57.36	880.70	8694.74	4325.66	49.75	53.49
21. Punjab	12	226.58	570.73	190.24	760.97	417.17	73.09	152.06	795.81	616.24	77.44	80.98
22. Rajasthan	12	2314.70	3040.77	1013.59	4054.36	1943.87	63.93	319.90	4578.47	2669.44	58.30	65.84
23. Sikkim	12	20.44	138.45	46.15	184.60	69.23	50.00	50.00	139.67	72.64	52.01	39.35
24. Tamil Nadu	12	789.36	4689.03	1563.01	6252.04	2739.05	58.41	1033.56	4561.97	3657.45	80.17	58.50
25. Tripura	12	79.71	870.92	290.31	1161.23	648.37	74.45	182.66	910.74	428.66	47.07	36.91
26. Uttar Pradesh	12	24026.11	18163.60	6054.53	24218.13	1366.89	7.53	124.57	25517.57	9789.77	38.36	40.42
27. Uttaranchal	10	1201.44	954.45	318.15	1272.60	209.33	21.93	196.94	1607.71	58.14	3.62	4.57
28. West Bengal	11	10288.94	6740.66	2246.89	8987.55	0.00	0.00	814.28	11103.22	448.84	4.04	4.99
29. A & N Islands	12	35.01	50.00		50.00	0.00	0.00		35.01	6.23	17.80	12.46
30. Daman & Diu	12	35.90	50.00		50.00	0.00	0.00		35.90	0.00	0.00	0.00
31. D & N Haveli	10	35.90	50.00		50.00	0.00	0.00		35.90	0.00	0.00	0.00
32. Lakshdweep	11	35.01	50.00		50.00	0.00	0.00		35.01	6.23	17.80	12.46
33. Pondicherry	12	28.59	50.00		50.00	25.00	50.00		53.59	7.12	13.29	14.24
Total		84306.71	100000.00	33250.00	133250.00	27431.93	27.43	13659.06	123736.39	49937.90	40.36	37.48

N.R.= Not Reported.

ANNEXURE-VIII (*Contd.*)

B. Financial Progress — Credit and Subsidy Disbursed, Total Investment and Per Swarozgari Investment under SGSY during 2000-2001 upto December, 2000 (As on 12-2-2001)

(Rs. in Lakhs)

Sl. No.	States/UTs	Total Credit Target	Credit Disbursed to SHGs	Credit Disbursed to Individual Swarozgaris	Total Credit Disbursed	% of Credit Disbursed	Subsidy Disbursed to SHGs	Subsidy Disbursed to Individual Swarozgaris	Total Subsidy Disbursed	Total Investment Column 6+10	Per Family Investment (In Rupees)	Credit Subsidy Ratio
1	2	3	4	5	6	7	8	9	10	11	12	13
1.	Andhra Pradesh	21600.00	1594.79	1987.90	3582.69	16.59	1172.06	886.31	2058.37	5641.06	12465	1.74
2.	Arunachal Pradesh	880.00	20.60	30.09	50.69	5.76	16.30	16.04	32.34	83.03	23389	1.57
3.	Assam	7000.00	71.31	143.92	215.23	3.07	34.41	61.61	96.02	311.25	9736	2.24
4.	Bihar	37040.00	503.48	6916.22	7419.70	20.03	418.79	3519.71	3938.50	11358.20	15055	1.88
5.	Chattisgarh	10020.00	34.63	293.73	328.36	3.28	23.33	126.03	149.36	477.72	3130	2.20
6.	Goa	170.00	4.02	4.02	8.04	4.73	1.45	1.45	2.90	10.94	36467	2.77
7.	Gujarat	7500.00	419.98	1752.33	2172.31	28.96	280.41	967.26	1247.67	3419.98	19320	1.74
8.	Haryana	4200.00	72.96	2829.31	2902.27	69.10	51.49	940.76	992.25	3894.52	29504	2.92
9.	Himachal Pradesh	2000.00	525.31	207.43	732.74	36.64	785.34	191.74	977.08	1709.83	19548	0.75
10.	Jammu & Kashmir	1800.00	N.R.	432.81	#VALUE!	#VALUE!	N.R.	130.41	#VALUE!	#VALUE!	#VALUE!	#VALUE!
11.	Jharkhand	13960.00	80.58	2379.88	2460.46	17.63	57.05	1358.85	1415.90	3876.36	12873	1.74
12.	Karnataka	14000.00	453.54	688.54	1142.08	8.16	412.05	327.74	739.79	1881.87	11084	1.54
13.	Kerala	7000.00	321.75	1752.24	2073.99	29.63	222.44	787.81	1010.25	3084.24	23741	2.05

14. Madhya Pradesh	21480.00	900.01	3536.81	4436.82	20.66	429.29	1590.85	2020.14	6456.96	23698	2.20
15. Maharashtra	28500.00	484.05	5827.85	6311.90	22.15	271.20	2144.95	2416.15	8728.05	29878	2.61
16. Manipur	500.00	N.R.	N.R.	0.00	0.00	N.R.	N.R.	#VALUE!	#VALUE!	#VALUE!	#VALUE!
17. Meghalaya	600.00	0.00	0.00	0.00	0.00	0.00	0.00	0.00	0.00	0	#DIV/0!
18. Mizoram	200.00	3.56	0.20	3.76	1.88	13.88	0.10	13.98	17.74	8696	0.27
19. Nagaland	400.00	8.88	6.55	15.43	3.86	13.50	14.70	28.20	43.63	3171	0.55
20. Orissa	20700.00	579.96	3536.01	4115.97	19.88	373.35	2005.33	2378.68	6494.65	20126	1.73
21. Punjab	2000.00	124.68	1203.58	1328.26	66.41	69.70	466.96	536.66	1864.92	30221	2.48
22. Rajasthan	14000.00	22.27	6309.23	6331.50	45.23	11.06	1859.80	1870.86	8202.36	35776	3.38
23. Sikkim	230.00	0.00	0.00	0.00	0.00	4.71	70.43	75.14	75.14	6400	0.00
24. Tamil Nadu	18000.00	2817.84	820.28	3638.12	20.21	1977.63	446.04	2423.67	6061.79	16007	1.50
25. Tripura	1100.00	9.90	141.97	151.87	13.81	4.15	82.40	86.55	238.42	10982	1.75
26. Uttar Pradesh	61755.00	334.19	5386.13	5720.32	9.26	208.74	3471.74	3680.48	9400.80	27924	1.55
27. Uttaranchal	3245.00	0.00	16.73	16.73		0.00	5.73	5.73	22.46	32551	2.92
28. West Bengal	20000.00	4.14	246.20	250.34	1.25	3.16	127.16	130.32	380.66	4024	1.92
29. A & N Islands	125.00	0.00	0.00	0.00	0.00	1.36	0.00	1.36	1.36	375	0.00
30. Daman & Diu	125.00	0.00	0.00	0.00	0.00	0.00	0.00	0.00	0.00	#DIV/0!	#DIV/0!
31. D & N Haveli	120.00	0.00	0.00	0.00	0.00	0.00	0.00	0.00	0.00	N.R.	N.R.
32. Lakshdweep	125.00	0.00	0.50	0.50	0.40	1.36	0.00	1.36	1.86	9300	N.R.
33. Pondicherry	125.00	0.80	2.02	2.82	2.26	0.40	0.96	1.36	4.18	12294	2.07
Total	320500.00	9393.23	46452.48	55845.71	17.42	6858.61	21602.87	28461.48	84307.19	18895	1.96

N.R. = Not Reported.

ANNEXURE-VIII (*Contd.*)

C. Physical Progress — No. of SHGs Formed, Economic Activities Taken up, No. of Swarozgaris Assisted ETC under SGSY during 2000-2001 upto December, 2000 (As on 12-2-2001)

(No. of Swarozgaris)

Sl. No.	States/UTs	Self-Help Groups			No. of SHGs Taken-up Economic Activities	Members Covered under SHGs	Individual Swarozgaris Assisted	Total Swarozgaris Assisted (Col. 7+8)	Coverage of Disadvantaged Groups (Numbers)				Percentage				Average Member of Col. 6
		Group Formed	No. of SHGs Passed Grade-I	No. of SHGs Passed Grade-II					Scheduled Castes	Scheduled Tribes	Women	Handicap.	Scheduled Castes	Scheduled Tribes	Women	Handicap.	
1	2	3	4	5	6	7	8	9	10	11	12	13	14	15	16	17	18
1.	Andhra Pradesh	197617	123016	74601	2189	30656	14598	45254	16652	4251	29220	1223	36.80	9.39	64.57	2.70	14.00
2.	Arunachal Pradesh	18	12	0	17	152	203	355	0	355	156	0	0.00	100.00	43.94	0.00	8.94
3.	Assam	4895	486	435	189	2277	920	3197	461	940	1528	19	14.42	29.40	47.79	0.59	12.05
4.	Bihar	8356	1386	579	4382	33589	41857	75446	24656	881	23426	283	32.68	1.17	31.05	0.38	7.67
5.	Chattisgarh	11528			1624	13741	1521	15262	1287	7614	5909	12	8.43	49.89	38.72	0.08	8.46
6.	Goa	0	0	0	0	30	0	30	1	0	11	0	3.33	0.00	36.67	0.00	N.R.
7.	Gujarat	3800	1740	481	380	2966	14736	17702	2818	6252	5776	211	15.92	35.32	32.63	1.19	7.81
8.	Haryana	1694	341	136	54	580	12620	13200	5711	0	6459	68	43.27	0.00	48.93	0.52	10.74
9.	Himachal Pradesh	1639	717	313	565	6290	2457	8747	3244	1032	4480	54	37.09	11.80	51.22	0.62	11.13
10.	Jammu & Kashmir	0	0	0	0	0	2214	2214	0	0	0	0	0.00	0.00	0.00	0.00	N.R.
11.	Jharkhand	3962	890	248	814	11418	18695	30113	5556	11595	10353	366	18.45	38.50	34.38	1.22	14.03
12.	Karnataka	4505	729	812	1072	14023	2955	16978	5611	1349	10577	188	33.05	7.95	62.30	1.11	13.08

13. Kerala	12276	3390	1121	375	3366	9625	12991	3872	233	7310	63	29.81	1.79	56.27	0.48	8.98
14. Madhya Pradesh	27330	4662	1365	1192	10601	16646	27247	7695	6918	8184	102	28.24	25.39	30.04	0.37	8.89
15. Maharashtra	13615	6182	1921	222	2235	26977	29212	5666	4610	9682	152	19.40	15.78	33.14	0.52	10.07
16. Manipur	N.R.	N.R.	N.R.	N.R.	N.R.	N.R.	0	N.R.	N.R.	N.R.	N.R.	0.00	0.00	0.00	0.00	N.R.
17. Meghalaya	336	12	13	21	468	0	468	0	468	432	0	0.00	100.00	92.31	0.00	22.29
18. Mizoram	64	48	0	16	203	1	204	0	204	115	0	0.00	100.00	56.37	0.00	12.69
19. Nagaland	86	N.R.	12	86	1269	107	1376	0	1376	464	0	0.00	100.00	33.72	0.00	14.76
20. Orissa	16116	3206	1632	740	4404	27866	32270	7252	7850	7469	85	22.47	24.33	23.15	0.26	5.95
21. Punjab	1035	83	23	67	731	5440	6171	3608	0	2072	27	58.47	0.00	33.58	0.44	10.91
22. Rajasthan	1179	47	32	14	121	22806	22927	6068	3843	8758	105	26.47	16.76	38.20	0.46	8.64
23. Sikkim	73	5	5	0	57	1117	1174	63	495	420	0	5.37	42.16	35.78	0.00	N.R.
24. Tamil Nadu	36010	8253	2992	2123	31218	6652	37870	18143	314	32304	169	47.91	0.83	85.30	0.45	14.70
25. Tripura	175	52	5	73	983	1188	2171	368	662	1397	0	16.95	30.49	64.35	0.00	13.47
26. Uttar Pradesh	31706	7864	732	140	2142	31524	33666	15570	108	8950	126	46.25	0.32	26.58	0.37	15.30
27. Uttaranchal	2004			0	0	69	69	28	10	4	0	40.58	14.49	5.80	0.00	#DIV/0!
28. West Bengal	5158	596	178	569	6799	2660	9459	3376	729	7327	8	35.69	7.71	77.46	0.08	11.95
29. A & N Islands	29	0	0	29	363	0	363	0	20	97	0	0.00	5.51	26.72	0.00	N.R.
30. Daman & Diu	0	0	0	0	0	0	0	0	0	0	0	#DIV/0!	#DIV/0!	#DIV/0!	#DIV/0!	N.R.
31. D & N Haveli	0	0	0	0	0	0	0	0	0	0	0	0.00	0.00	0.00	0.00	N.R.
32. Lakshdweep	2	0	0	2	20	0	20	0	20	0	0	0.00	100.00	0.00	0.00	N.R.
33. Pondicherry	235	68	3	1	10	24	34	0	34	24	0	0.00	100.00	70.59	0.00	10.00
Total	385443	163785	87639	16956	180712	265478	446190	137706	62163	192904	3261	30.86	13.93	43.23	0.73	10.66

N.R. = Not Reported.

ANNEXURE-IX

List of Special Projects Approved under the SGSY during 1999-2000 & 2000-2001

(Rs. in lakhs)

Sl. No.	Title of the Project	State/Org. from whom received	Share of Project cost for the Ministry	Amount Released as Ist Instalment	Amount Released as Balance Amount of Ist Instalment	Amount Released as 2nd Instalment	Total Released
1	2	3	4	5	6	7	8
Special Project Approved during 1999-2000							
1.	Dissemination and transfer of Appropriate Technology Govt. of Gujarat	Gujarat	225.000	113.000			113.000
2.	Gujarat Gram Haat Comprehensive Marketing Intervention and Support for the rural poor in Gujarat	Gujarat	900.000	450.000			450.000
3.	Setting up to Technology and training development centres Govt. of A.P.	A.P.	1125.000	563.000			563.000
4.	Setting up of Permanent Marketing Centres A.P.	A.P.	975.000	488.000			488.000
5.	Infrastructure Development (Instalation of Hydrams) in the State of Himachal Pradesh	H.P.	487.500	243.750			243.750
6.	Vandhan (Forest Wealth Baster District, M.P.)	M.P.	562.500	281.250			281.250
7.	Development of Muga Silk in Assam	Assam	510.990	255.495			255.495
8.	Development of Eri Silk in Assam	Assam	218.370	109.185			109.185
9.	Employment Generation through Mushroom Cultivation	Institute Rural Dev. SIRD (An Org. of State Govt.)	359.550	179.775			179.775
10.	Strengthening the Marketing Infrastructure and Establishment of Nodal Centre of Rural Technology in T.N.	T.N.	1098.000	549.000			549.000
11.	Economic Generation through Coir Production by Women SHGs in East Godavari dist.	A.P.	1081.500	544.500			544.500

ANNEXURE-IX (*Contd.*)

1	2	3	4	5	6	7	8
12.	Poverty Alleviation through use of Improved Agricultural Technology (Expansion of Israel Technology of Agri.) Special Project under SGSY for Chittoor Distt. (A.P.)	A.P.	1125.000	562.500			562.500
13.	Khankhedi Lift Irrigation Scheme District Neemuch	M.P.	1125.000	562.500			562.500
14.	Establishment of SARAS Marketing Centres and Tech. & Training Centres in UP	U.P.	712.500	356.250			356.250
15.	Mushroom Projection, UP	U.P.	768.750	384.375			384.375
16.	Green Banana Plantation, UP	U.P.	862.500	431.250			431.250
17.	Nehru Yuvak Kendra Sangathan (Project I for MP & Orissa)	NYKS*	1500.000	100.000			100.000
18.	Nehru Yuvak Kendra Sangathan (Project II for Assam & Orissa)	NYKS*	1338.000	100.000			100.000
	Sub-Total 1999-2000		14975.160	6273.830	0.000	0.000	6273.830
Special Project Approved during 2000-01							
19.	Setting up of Handlooms in Bhatinda District of Punjab	Punjab	363.000	181.500			181.500
20.	Project Gold Mines—Mushroom Cultivation, Floriculture and Sericulture in Bilaspur District of Himachal Pradesh	H.P.	245.820	122.910			122.910
21.	Sp. Project for construction of Water Harvesting Structures (Anicuts) in Dholpur District of Rajasthan	Rajasthan	369.525	184.762			184.762
22.	Employment Generation through Mushroom Cultivation	Institute Rural Dev. SIRD (An org. of State Govt.)	359.550			161.790	161.790
23.	Khankhedi Lift Irrigation Scheme District Neemuch	M.P.	1125.000			562.500	562.500
24.	Nehru Yuvak Kendra Sangathan (Project I for MP & Orissa)	NYKS*	1500.000		650.000		650.000
25.	Nehru Yuvak Kendra Sangathan (Project II for Assam & Orissa)	NYKS*	1338.000		569.000		569.000
	Sub-Total 2000-01		5300.895	489.172	1219.000	724.290	2432.462

*Initially Rs. 100.00 lakhs have been released to NYKS for each project for initital preparatory works and capacity building etc.

ANNEXURE-X

National Social Assistance Programme (Provisional) — As on 22-12-2000

Name of Scheme : National Old Age Pension Scheme (NOAPS)

Year : 2000-2001

(Rs. in Lakhs)

Sl. No.	States/UTs	Financial: O.B. 1-4-00	Allocation	Release: 1st Instal.	Release: 2nd Instal.	Release: Total	Additional funds (99-2000)	1% Adm. Charges	Total Release	Total Availability of funds	Exp. Reported	% Achievement	Reporting Month	Physical: State Target	No. of Benf. Reported: SC	ST	Others	Total	Women	Handicapped
1	2	3	4	5	6	7	8	9	10	11	12	13	14	15	16	17	18	19	20	21
1.	Andhra Pradesh	423.93	4361.76	2180.88	2059.24	4240.12	0.00		4240.12	4664.05	2308.56	49.50	8/2000	466000	202566	45475	165363	498102	139717	13108
2.	Arunachal Pradesh*	3.67	181.26	53.07	0.00	53.07	0.00		53.07	56.74	0.00	0.00	0	19365	0	0	0	0	0	0
3.	Assam	178.14	2624.343	1270.50	644.14	1914.64	19.65	26.24	1960.53	2138.67	735.83	34.41	9/2000	280379	3951	6473	28033	126170	14780	451
4.	Bihar	2475.00	5144.855	2518.79	0.00	2518.79	373.78		2892.57	5367.57	2073	38.62	9/2000	549664	137907	5817	165775	427860	149141	5437
5.	Chhattisgarh**	125.99	1243.22	621.60	247.47	869.07	0		869.07	995.06	520.65	52.32	9/2000	162400	13712	25674	71151	131395	44749	1033
6.	Goa	23.45	27.94	13.98	0.00	13.98	0		13.98	37.43	12.74	34.04	10/2000	2985	39	0	2156	2195	1155	0
7.	Gujarat	328.96	561.5997	256.32	24.51	280.83	0		280.83	609.79	322.85	52.94	11/2000	60000	1378	8	3601	7682	3234	80
8.	Haryana*	80.61	535.80	209.70	97.20	306.90	11.02		317.92	398.53	110.46	27.72	8/2000	57244	648	516	1413	16388	1030	0
9.	Himachal Pradesh	37.51	236.55	118.31	39.67	157.98	0.00		157.98	195.49	136.78	69.97	8/2000	25272	7660	719	13830	24370	8908	0
10.	J & K*	38.34	317.26	123.535	65.39	188.93	0.00		188.93	227.27	0.31	0.14	9/2000	33895	348	1112	1174	2634	1080	0
11.	Jharkhand**	825.65	1732.389	866.21	0.00	866.21	64.29		930.50	1756.15	282.34	16.08	9/2000	185084	25353	23904	41672	136991	52645	2109
12.	Karnataka*	598.35	2959.63	1479.89	1243.69	2723.58	0.00		2723.58	3321.93	1462.74	44.03	9/2000	316200	11518	6368	25544	242126	21985	0
13.	Kerala*	834.34	1396.31	685.19	73.05	758.24	0.00		758.24	1592.58	397.69	24.97	8/2000	149178	286	797	797	54266	0	0
14.	Madhya Pradesh	509.01	3342.24	1671.13	928.66	2599.79	0.00		2599.79	3108.80	1748.63	56.25	8/2000	436600	101929	81057	164036	412964	163092	16452

15. Maharashtra	1738.22	4158.509	1891.03	318.75	2209.78	96.69		2306.47	4044.69	1832.45	45.31	4/2000	444285	74144	56536	111103	283942	133996	1508
16. Manipur*	42.79	327.0641	163.56	0.00	163.56	0.00		163.56	206.35	9.26	4.49	6/2000	27449	14	26	982	1022	355	0
17. Meghalaya*	57.84	352.67	150.42	21.01	171.43	8.17		179.60	237.44	58.85	24.79	9/2000	37678	0	0	0	7146	1058	0
18. Mizoram	0.00	98.51	42.36	7.88	50.24	0.00		50.24	50.24	41.33	82.27	9/2000	10525	0	7366	0	8581	5000	0
19. Nagaland*	13.98	256.13	110.95	38.38	149.33	6.05		155.38	169.36	44.28	26.15	6/2000	27364	0	4100	0	8076	2000	110
20. Orissa	1329.88	3682.214	1545.93	258.02	1803.95	468		2271.95	3601.83	1646.62	45.72	9/2000	343400	97940	76446	134738	347470	142066	101
21. Punjab	65.16	386.79	193.44	0.00	193.44	42.38		235.82	300.98	222.56	73.95	10/2000	41324	17537	538	20400	38475	15830	334
22. Rajasthan	-114.90	1474.54	729.88	284.70	1014.58	60.82		1075.40	960.50	890.50	92.71	12/2000	157536	13165	3291	5486	90070	14506	0
23. Sikkim	0.00	94.57	47.30	47.27	94.57	0.00		94.57	94.57	47.28	49.99	11/2000	10104	3049	6552	10104	4904	0	0
24. Tamil Nadu	954.41	3276.00	1593	1246.13	2839.13	0.00		2839.13	3793.54	1921.93	50.66	8/2000	350000	389278	38492	1080561	1959876	95994	0
25. Tripura	18.41	565.46	282.73	0.00	282.73	0.00		282.73	301.14	146.91	48.78	10/2000	60412	7045	11752	11029	29826	12396	0
26. Uttar Pradesh	2452.05	7861.756	3896.32	586.72	4483.04	507.32		4990.36	7442.41	3234.67	43.46	11/2000	839931	110793	339	129063	293435	76674	0
27. Uttaranchal**	158.92	403.0738	201.54	84.31	285.85	0		285.85	444.77	209.89	47.19	9/2000	43063	8243	576	14658	32429	14055	733
28. West Bengal	1602.73	3312.50	1656.25	174.98	1831.23	0		1831.23	3433.96	1830.65	53.31	9/2000	353900	72203	14391	132287	352635	60070	96
29. A & N Islands*	0.00	17.38	0.00	0.00	0.00	0		0.00	0.00	0.00	#DIV/0!	0	1857	0	0	0	0	0	0
30. Chandigarh	6.88	13.66	6.83	0.00	6.83	0		6.83	13.71	0.00	0.00	0	1459	0	0	0	0	0	0
31. D & N Haveli	0.02	11.80	5.90	0.00	5.90	0		5.90	5.92	0.00	0.00	0	1260	0	0	0	0	0	0
32. Daman & Diu	0.88	2.48	1.24	0.00	1.24	0		1.24	2.12	0.76	35.85	7/2000	265	13	88	158	259	193	0
33. NCT Delhi	23.50	249.58	0.00	0.00	0.00	0		0.00	23.50	0.00	0.00	0	26665	0	0	0	0	0	0
34. Lakshdweep*	0.80	1.86	0.00	0.00	0.00	0		0.00	0.80	0.05	6.25	8/2000	199	0	23	0	23	16	0
35. Pondicherry	33.02	49.05	24.53	0.00	24.53	0		24.53	57.55	28.38	49.31	8/2000	5240	0	0	0	4102	0	0
Total	14867.54	51260.75	24612.32	8491.17	33103.49	1658.17	26.24	34787.90	49655.44	22278.95	44.87		5528183	1300719	418436	2335114	5545414	1175725	41552

* O.B. is provisional and based on latest expenditure report (1999-2000).

** New State.

@ Difference to BE is to be met with additional grants.

ANNEXURE-XI

National Social Assistance Programme (Provisional) — As on 22-12-2000

National Family Benefit Scheme (NFBS)

Year : 2000-01

(Rs. in Lakhs)

Sl. No.	States/UTs	O.B. 1-4-00	Alloca-tion	Release			1% Adm. Charges	Total Rele-ase	Total Avail-ability of funds	Exp. Repor-ted	% Achie-vement	Repor-ting Month	State Target	No. of Benf. Reported				Women	Handi-capped
				1st Instal.	2nd Instal.	Total								SC	ST	Others	Total		
1	2	3	4	5	6	7	8	9	10	11	12	13	14	15	16	17	18	19	20
1.	Andhra Pradesh	228.81	3035.50	1517.76	1495.51	3013.27		3013.27	3242.08	1594.44	49.18	9/2000	29188	2134	421	1730	22310	1285	129
2.	Arunachal Pradesh*	1.31	57.78	12.49	0	12.49		12.49	13.80	0.00	0.00	0	556	0	0	0	0	0	0
3.	Assam	137.33	1552.78	589.61	208.89	798.50	15.53	814.03	951.36	334.74	35.19	10/2000	14931	215	279	1390	3511	1126	1
4.	Bihar	649.76	1234.38	589.69	66.28	655.97		655.97	1305.73	693.94	53.15	9/2000	11869	905	103	2053	5848	2341	9
5.	Chhattisgarh**	55.37	1053.35	526.68	322.43	849.11		849.11	904.48	630.30	69.69	9/2000	15970	346	745	2295	4740	1240	0
6.	Goa	6.68	12.22	6.12	3.05	9.17		9.17	15.85	6.64	41.89	10/2000	118	0	0	81	81	79	0
7.	Gujarat	57.93	158.75	78.32	12.00	90.32		90.32	148.25	124.85	84.22	11/2000	1526	12	2	70	84	79	0
8.	Haryana*	12.57	54.21	23.19	7.24	30.43		30.43	43.00	14.99	34.86	8/2000	521	58	10	48	214	23	0
9.	Hmachal Pradesh	5.9	30.72	14.01	6.08	20.09		20.09	25.99	20.85	80.22	10/2000	295	75	4	107	204	66	0
10.	J & K*	9.87	57.38	23.75	11.97	35.72		35.72	45.59	1.95	4.28	9/2000	552	5	4	13	22	22	0
11.	Jharkhand**	172.79	465.63	229.72	4.17	233.89		233.89	406.68	190.52	46.85	10/2000	4477	150	281	370	1409	460	0
12.	Karnataka*	117.66	649.22	309.73	283.84	593.57		593.57	71 1.23	315.29	44.33	9/2000	6242	185	38	528	3962	0	0
13.	Kerala*	113.22	382.10	191.08	18.73	209.81		209.81	323.03	159.70	49.44	9/2000	3674	15	30	90	1663	129	0

14. Madhya Pradesh	372.55	2904.11	1452.05	376.96	1829.01		1829.01	2201.56	1317.82	59.86	8/2000	27924	2636	2732	4524	13292	4638	22
15. Maharashtra	256.35	1026.74	502.71	140.58	643.29		643.29	899.64	512.21	56.93	9/2000	9872	1449	1061	2827	6231	3497	146
16. Manipur*	11.61	5.00	32.51	0	32.51		32.51	44.12	2.84	6.44	6/2000	497	1	2	11	27	5	0
17. Meghalaya*	5.82	72.22	36.11	8.59	44.70		44.70	50.32	12.30	24.35	8/2000	694	0	0	0	58	0	0
18. Mizoram*	1.08	21.67	9.33	1.73	11.06		11.06	12.14	10.05	82.78	9/2000	208	0	0	0	90	10	0
19. Nagaland*	1.48	36.11	18.08	5.11	23.19		23.19	24.67	4.09	16.58	0	347	0	0	0	25	0	0
20. Orissa	311.71	1346.69	646.32	141.56	787.88		787.88	1099.59	798.87	72.65	9/2000	12949	1147	1055	2313	6563	2125	11
21. Punjab*	40.09	134.16	65.14	0	65.14		65.14	105.23	96.94	92.12	10/2000	1290	463	0	488	951	0	0
22. Rajasthan	35.67	468.16	226.87	47.35	274.22		274.22	309.89	127.05	41.00	8/2000	4502	83	7	100	659	169	0
23. Sikkim	0.10	21.67	6.52	0	6.52		6.52	6.62	0.00	0.00		208	0	0	0	0	0	0
24. Tamil Nadu	568.24	1904.76	978.82	661.38	1640.20		1640.20	2208.44	1336.64	60.52	9/2000	18315	2566	337	6522	13581	5969	5
25. Tripura	9.88	122.78	51.35	0	51.35		51.35	61.23	33.20	54.22	10/2000	1181	59	83	107	249	176	0
26. Uttar Pradesh	816.67	2775.42	1349.56	296.77	1646.33		1646.33	2463.00	1230.02	49.94	10/2000	26687	2784	0	5184	9651	4605	0
27. Uttaranchal**	46.02	246.48	123.25	44.51	167.76		167.76	213.78	144.44	6756	9/2000	2370	299	38	945	1482	725	0
28. West Bengal	440.06	975.73	487.95	19.72	507.67		507.67	947.73	377.27	39.81	9/2000	9382	418	199	1096	3494	359	0
29. A&N Islands*	1.43	2.86	0	0	0		0	1.43	0.00	0.00		27	0	0	0	0	0	0
30. Chandigarh	1.52	2.86	1.43	0	1.43		1.43	2.95	0.00	0.00	0	27	0	0	0	0	0	0
31. D&N Haveli	0.43	2.86	1.43	0	1.43		1.43	1.86	0.00	0.00		27	0	0	0	0	0	0
32. Daman & Diu	1.04	2.86	0.28	0	0.28		0.28	1.32	0.30	22.73	7/2000	27	2	1	3	2	2	0
33. NCT Delhi	5.90	31.46	0	0	0		0	5.90	0.00	0.00		303	0	0	0	0	0	0
34. Lakshdweep	1.40	2.86	0	0	0		0	1.40	0.00	0.00		27	0	0	0	0	0	0
35. Pondicherry	0.26	2.86	0	0	0		0	0.26	0.00	0.00	0	27	0	0	0	0	0	0
Total	4498.51	20914.34	10101.86	4184.45	14286.31	15.53	14301.84	18800.35	10092.25	53.68		206810	16007	7432	32895	100403	29130	323

* O.B. is provisional and based on latest expenditure report (1999-2000).

** New State.

@ The difference to BE is to be met with additional grants.

ANNEXURE-XII

National Social Assistance Programme (Provisional) — As on 22-12-2000

National Maternity Benefit Scheme (NMBS)

Year : 2000-01

(Rs. in Lakhs)

Sl. No.	States/UTs	O.B. 1-4-00	Alloca-tion	Release			1% Adm. Charges	Total Rele-ase	Total Avail-ability of funds	Exp. Repor-ted	% Achie-vement	Repor-ting Month	State Target	No. of Benf. Reported				Handi-capped
				1st Instal.	2nd Instal.	Total								SC	ST	Others	Total	
1	2	3	4	5	6	7	8	9	10	11	12	13	14	15	16	17	18	19
1.	Andhra Pradesh	128.81	1590.19	795.10	738.39	1533.49		1533.49	1662.30	862.14	51.86	9/2000	305806	42796	7803	35162	201610	2573
2.	Arunachal Pradesh*	2.33	27.11	1.17	0.00	1.17		1.17	3.50	0.02	0.57	4/2000	5213	0	4	0	4	0
3.	Assam	68.09	419.43	157.35	20.06	177.41	4.19	181.60	249.69	73.21	29.32	10/2000	80660	1629	1361	6497	11771	1
4.	Bihar	451.05	618.14	282.08	17.64	299.72		299.72	750.77	326.31	43.46	9/2000	118873	11013	524	12875	45128	20
5.	Chhattisgarh**	156.49	304.52	162.86	33.45	196.31		196.31	352.80	84.88	24.06	9/2000	58562	1047	1187	2174	12787	0
6.	Goa	2.51	2.58	0.00	0.00	0.00		0.00	2.51	0.08	3.19	10/2000	496	0	0	14	14	0
7.	Gujarat*	-10.44	104.00	44.14	1.92	46.06		46.06	35.62	40.60	113.98	10/2000	20000	2120	1059	3595	6958	0
8.	Haryana	22.76	64.69	25.57	1.59	27.16		27.16	49.92	17.21	34.47	10/2000	12440	1613	0	1633	3380	0
9.	Himachal Pradesh	12.46	19.11	6.26	0.07	6.33		6.33	18.79	13.02	69.29	10/2000	3675	815	50	1237	2222	0
10.	J & K*	16.66	49.27	12.64	7.14	19.78		19.78	36.44	0.00	0.00	0.00	9475	0	0	0	0	0
11.	Jharkhand**	71.52	205.45	94.16	5.84	100.00		100.00	171.52	82.05	47.84	10/2000	39509	1446	1883	2427	13061	0
12.	Karnataka*	59.06	402.66	190.12	73.99	264.11		264.11	323.17	173.95	53.83	9/2000	77435	1335	378	3308	23946	0
13.	Kerala*	46.07	136.58	52.85	15.02	67.87		67.87	113.94	33.35	29.27	8/2000	26265	29	78	288	4604	0

14. Madhya Pradesh*	160.93	600.20	278.39	27.24	305.63		305.63	466.56	194.88	41.77	9/2000	115423	292	624	504	26209	0
15. Maharashtra	151.40	453.49	209.83	44.22	254.05		254.05	405.45	214.99	53.03	4/2000	87210	9488	6331	15546	34265	0
16. Manipur*	7.63	48.80	24.42	0.00	24.42		24.42	32.05	3.95	12.32	6/2000	7374	14	12	358	758	0
17. Meghalaya*	10.22	52.81	12.20	6.09	18.29		18.29	28.51	11.36	39.85	9/2000	10156	0	0	0	600	0
18. Mizoram*	1.11	14.85	6.39	1.19	7.58		7.58	8.69	7.66	88.15	10/2000	2856	0	0	0	1472	0
19. Nagaland*	2.23	38.43	19.22	5.43	24.65		24.65	26.88	5.66	21.06	11/2000	7390	0	0	0	35	0
20. Orissa	174.25	624.24	280.99	3.74	284.73		284.73	458.98	366.21	79.79	4/2000	120046	9197	8469	16900	44932	159
21. Punjab	3.28	46.98	23.54	0.00	23.54		23.54	26.82	18.48	68.90	10/2000	9035	1672	1166	2638	5476	0
22. Rajasthan	176.17	325.34	55.54	0.00	55.54		55.54	231.71	29.03	12.53	8/2000	62565	179	13	218	3143	0
23. Sikkim	0.12	14.15	7.08	0.00	7.08		7.08	7.20	0	0.00		2721	0	0	0	0	0
24. Tamil Nadu	251.07	906.36	433.69	260.61	694.30		694.30	945.37	654.98	69.28	8/2000	174300	5556	49	15574	59131	0
25. Tripura	3.01	84.41	42.21	0.00	42.21		42.21	45.22	11.08	24.50	10/2000	16232	565	508	809	1882	0
26. Uttar Pradesh	584.51	1627.32	729.57	89.28	818.85		818.85	1403.36	687.31	48.98	7/2000	312945	29411	548	42783	99471	0
27. Uttaranchal**	29.07	86.60	39.63	8.16	47.79		47.79	76.86	33.72	43.87	9/2000	16655	270	10	919	3847	0
28. West Bengal	300.80	541.17	220.83	8.36	229.19		229.19	529.99	201.56	38.03	9/2000	104071	4132	1834	10088	38644	0
29. A & N Islands*	0.00	1.09	0.00	0.00	0.00		0.00	0.00	0	#DIV/0!		209	0	0	0	0	0
30. Chandigarh*	0.02	2.65	0.00	0.00	0.00		0.00	0.02	0	0.00		509	0	0	0	0	0
31. D & N Haveli	0.89	0.47	0.00	0.00	0.00		0.00	0.89	0	0.00		90	0	0	0	0	0
32. Daman & Diu	0.11	0.31	0.00	0.00	0.00		0.00	0.11	0	0.00	0.00	60	0	0	0	0	0
33. NCT Delhi*	0.00	36.97	0.00	0.00	0.00		0.00	0.00	0	#DIV/0!		7098	0	0	0	0	0
34. Lakshdweep	0.05	0.16	0.00	0.00	0.00		0.00	0.05	0	0.00		31	0	0	0	0	0
35. Pondicherry*	0.72	5.25	2.63	0.00	2.63		2.63	3.35	0.9	26.87	8/2000	1008	0	0	0	179	0
Total	2884.96	9455.78	4210.46	1369.43	5579.89	4.19	5584.08	8469.04	4148.59	48.99		1816394	124619	33891	175547	645529	2753

* O.B. is Provisional and based on latest expenditure report (1999-2000).

** New State. @ The difference to BE is to be met with additional grants.

ANNEXURE-XIII

State-wise Release Position for DRDA Administration Year 1999-2000

(Rs. in lakhs)

Sl. No.	States/UTs	Central Allocation	Central Release
1.	Andhra Pradesh	489.30	489.30
2.	Arunachal Pradesh	211.55	211.55
3.	Assam	463.03	463.03
4.	Bihar	1177.19	1177.19
5.	Goa	22.18	22.18
6.	Gujarat	491.02	491.02
7.	Haryana	332.00	332.00
8.	Himachal Pradesh	209.85	209.85
9.	Jammu & Kashmir	271.95	271.95
10.	Karnataka	489.30	489.30
11.	Kerala	290.03	290.03
12.	Madhya Pradesh	898.42	898.42
13.	Maharashtra	675.95	675.95
14.	Manipur	148.77	148.77
15.	Meghalaya	117.38	117.38
16.	Mizoram	129.32	129.32
17.	Nagaland	134.10	134.10
18.	Orissa	606.00	606.00
19.	Punjab	318.70	318.70
20.	Rajasthan	597.47	597.47
21.	Sikkim	19.45	19.45
22.	Tamil Nadu	606.34	606.34
23.	Tripura	76.77	76.77
24.	Uttar Pradesh	1701.98	1701.98
25.	West Bengal	391.37	391.37
26.	A. & N. Islands	41.86	41.86
27.	Daman & Diu	20.93	20.93
28.	D. & N. Haveli	20.93	20.93
29.	Lakshdweep	20.93	20.93
30.	Pondicherry	25.93	25.93
	Total	11000.00	11000.00

ANNEXURE-XIV

State-wise Allocation & Central Release for 2000-2001 under DRDA Administration Scheme

Sl. No.	States/UTs	No. of DRDAs	No. of Blocks	Central Allocation (Rs. in lakhs)	Central Release (1st Instt.) (Rs. in lakhs)
1.	Andhra Pradesh	22	330	1129.28	564.58
2.	Arunachal Pradesh	13	54	488.25	244.09
3.	Assam	23	214	1068.64	534.24
4.	Bihar	55	754	2716.88	1358.29
5.	Goa	2	11	81.11	40.55
6.	Gujarat	25	230	1133.21	566.52
7.	Haryana	19	114	766.24	383.06
8.	Himachal Pradesh	12	72	484.31	242.12
9.	Jammu & Kashmir	14	119	627.64	313.77
10.	Karnataka	27	175	1129.28	564.55
11.	Kerala	14	152	669.38	334.64
12.	Madhya Pradesh	61	459	2657.81	1328.70
13.	Maharashtra	33	320	1560.04	779.90
14.	Manipur	9	34	343.35	171.65
15.	Meghalaya	7	32	270.90	135.43
16.	Mizoram	8	30	298.46	149.21
17.	Nagaland	7	52	309.49	154.72
18.	Orissa	30	314	1398.60	699.20
19.	Punjab	17	138	735.53	367.71
20.	Rajasthan	32	237	1378.91	689.35
21.	Sikkim	1	8	44.89	22.44
22.	Tamil Nadu	28	385	1399.39	699.61
23.	Tripura	4	38	177.19	88.58
24.	Uttar Pradesh	83	904	3928.05	1963.76
25.	West Bengal	18	341	903.26	451.59
26.	A & N Islands	2	5	96.6	48.30
27.	D & N Haveli	1	1	48.30	24.15
28.	Daman & Diu	1	2	48.30	24.15
29.	Lakshdweep	1	5	48.30	24.15
30.	Pondicherry	1	6	59.85	29.93
	Total	570	5536	26001.4125	12998.94

ANNEXURE-XV

Scheme-wise Number of Projects Sanctioned by CAPART (since inception till 30-11-2000)

Year	JRY**	Housing	CRSP	OB/SAT	DWCRA	ARWSP*	ARTS	PC	IRDP	PR	SF	WSD	DA	Media	Total
Since inception upto 1987	35	—	—	229	48	30	151	128	—	—	—	—	—	—	621
1987-88	86	—	48	160	97	89	27	40	2	—	—	—	—	—	549
1988-89	150	—	260	230	194	89	35	50	64	—	—	—	—	—	1072
1989-90	144	—	123	202	145	362	42	99	51	—	—	—	—	—	1168
1990-91	103	—	—	224	111	541	46	99	22	—	—	—	—	—	1146
1991-92	237	—	325	278	177	1122	122	217	62	—	—	—	—	—	2540
1992-93	207	—	302	390	147	934	99	192	70	—	—	—	—	—	2341
1993-94	176	—	484	498	300	433	107	244	85	—	—	—	—	—	2327
1994-95	144	—	374	247	125	514	80	227	103	—	—	—	—	—	1814
1995-96	496	—	277	142	89	104	73	135	50	4	—	—	—	—	1370
1996-97	140	289	412	339	89	51	69	165	44	7	—	—	—	—	1605
1997-98	45	1	436	241	62	118	59	136	22	4	—	—	—	—	1124
1998-99	—	—	122	55	62	125	56	109	12	3	6	80	28	17	675
1999-2000	—	—	2	71	16	12	80	186	2	2	—	65	15	—	451
2000-2001	—	—	—	92	—	—	70	255	—	—	—	36	9	—	462
Total	1963	290	3165	3398	1662	4524	1116	2282	589	20	6	181	52	17	19265

Note: *ARWSP also include Drinking Water & Awareness Camp projects.

**JRY include Housing & other than Housing upto 1995-96. 1996-97 includes Social Forestry & Watershed Development.

ANNEXURE-XVI

Scheme-wise Amount Sanctioned by CAPART (since inception till 30-11-2000)

(Rs. in Crores)

Year	JRY*	Housing	CRSP	OB/SAT	DWCRA	ARWSP	ARTS	PC	IRDP	PR	SF	WSD	DA	Media	Total
Since inception upto 1987	131	—	—	1.09	1.44	1.37	8.89	3.48	—	—	—	—	—	—	17.58
1987-88	3.16	—	1.37	0.58	1.89	3.57	0.91	1.16	0.04	—	—	—	—	—	12.68
1988-89	7.04	—	5.62	0.64	3.23	3.41	1.96	5.19	0.92	—	—	—	—	—	28.01
1989-90	5.52	—	1.85	0.89	1.91	3.83	0.66	7.92	0.70	—	—	—	—	—	23.28
1990-91	4.60	—	—	1.07	1.51	5.90	0.87	2.66	0.66	—	—	—	—	—	17.27
1991-92	10.46	—	8.24	0.93	2.46	10.11	3.24	10.64	1.21	—	—	—	—	—	47.29
1992-93	8.60	—	8.35	2.58	2.01	13.16	3.20	6.34	1.25	—	—	—	—	—	45.49
1993-94	8.87	—	10.45	2.38	5.55	15.32	2.49	10.82	1.95	—	—	—	—	—	57.83
1994-95	9.70	—	8.09	1.85	2.84	18.02	2.54	9.54	2.38	—	—	—	—	—	54.96
1995-96	50.97	—	7.50	0.72	2.24	3.37	3.13	5.50	1.08	0.15	—	—	—	—	74.66
1996-97	5.98	25.26	12.37	1.34	2.27	1.95	5.09	6.45	1.08	0.19	—	—	—	—	61.98
1997-98	5.71	—	9.76	1.06	1.47	4.88	4.04	6.50	0.49	0.10	—	—	—	—	34.01
1998-99	—	—	3.15	0.47	1.62	5.70	4.62	5.79	0.31	0.03	0.16	9.16	1.47	0.65	33.13
1999-2000	—	—	0.12	0.57	0.51	0.41	3.98	8.63	0.07	0.09	—	4.00	0.35	—	18.73
2000-2001	—	—	—	1.08	—		4.81	13.60	—	—	—	5.04	0.48	—	25.01
Total	121.92	25.26	76.87	17.25	30.95	91.00	50.43	104.22	12.14	0.56	0.16	18.20	2.30	0.65	551.91

ANNEXURE-XVII

Scheme-wise Funds Released by CAPART to Sanctioned Projects (since inception till 30-11-2000)

(Rs. in Crores)

Year	JRY*	Housing	CRSP	OB/SAT	DWCRA	ARWSP	ARTS	PC	IRDP	PR	SF	WSD	DA	Media	IITF	Total
Since inception upto 1987	0.23	—	0.29	1.02	0.10	0.32	1.44	0.45	—	—	—	—	—	—	—	3.85
1987-88	1.03	—	0.39	0.31	0.73	1.80	1.60	0.70	—	—	—	—	—	—	—	6.56
1988-89	3.74	—	3.22	0.53	2.36	2.89	2.02	1.20	0.31	—	—	—	—	—	—	16.27
1989-90	4.05	—	2.58	0.52	1.26	3.72	1.44	1.80	0.46	—	—	—	—	—	—	15.83
1990-91	4.34	—	1.62	0.72	1.01	4.39	1.04	2.80	0.24	—	—	—	—	—	—	16.16
1991-92	7.47	—	2.60	0.93	1.98	8.04	1.73	5.04	0.68	—	—	—	—	—	—	28.47
1992-93	8.30	—	4.52	1.77	2.24	9.72	2.79	5.94	0.76	—	—	—	—	—	—	36.04
1993-94	10.76	—	9.54	2.44	4.32	12.58	2.56	11.32	1.23	—	—	—	—	—	—	54.75
1994-95	7.49	—	6.65	1.81	2.33	13.84	2.26	7.78	1.74	—	—	—	—	—	—	43.90
1995-96	27.59	—	6.17	0.82	1.70	6.23	2.55	4.89	0.98	0.22	—	—	—	—	—	51.15
1996-97	2.97	8.79	8.27	2.36	2.80	3.27	2.63	5.63	0.86	0.15	—	—	—	—	—	37.73
1997-98	3.87	10.37	7.56	1.51	2.72	3.42	3.53	5.43	0.55	0.08	—	—	—	—	—	39.04
1998-99	—	1.13	3.42	1.34	1.98	3.67	2.17	3.16	0.40	0.09	0.91	3.43	1.00	0.43	—	23.13
1999-2000	—	0.80	3.50	2.20	1.92	3.93	4.68	10.05	0.13	0.09	0.41	1.06	—	—	—	28.77
2000-2000 (till Nov. 2000)	—	0.45	—	1.80		0.65	4.76	11.19	0.04	0.05	0.31	1.29	0.23	—	0.86	21.63
Total	81.84	21.54	60.33	20.08	27.45	78.47	37.20	77.38	8.38	0.68	1.63	5.78	1.23	0.43	0.86	423.28

*JRY includes Social Forestry projects also.

ANNEXURE-XVIII

State-wise Number of Elected Panchayat Representatives in the three tiers showing breakup into SC/ST & Women

Sl. No.	States/UTs	Gram Panchayat				Panchayat Samiti				Zilla Parishad			
		SC	ST	Women	Total	SC	ST	Women	Total	SC	ST	Women	Total
1	2	3	4	5	6	7	8	9	10	11	12	13	14
1.	Andhra Pradesh	38674	15304	78000	230529	789	803	5420	14644	128	66	363	1093
2.	Arunachal Pradesh	Arunachal Pradesh Panchayati Raj Act not yet passed.											
3.	Assam			5469	30360			669	2564				845
		Figures not current. Fresh Elections due since October 1997											
4.	Bihar	Post 73rd Amendment elections not held in the State. Election issue *sub judice*. Figures not available.											
5.	Goa			468	1281				—				35
6.	Gujarat	4739	9550	21351	123470	279	561	1275	3814	57	114	254	761
7.	Haryana	12128	0	16704	54346	536	0	858	2430	66	0	182	226
8.	Himachal Pradesh	3824	672	6015	18264	280	74	558	1661	46	14	84	252
9.	J & K	73rd Amendment not applicable in the State. State proposes adopting 73rd Amendment.											
10.	Karnataka	17918	7575	35305	80627	601	169	1343	3340	165	47	335	919
11.	Kerala				10270				1547				300
12.	Madhya Pradesh	64997	132638	156181	474351	1345	2780	3169	9097	143	267	31	1036
		Fresh elections held but latest data not available.											
13.	Maharashtra	40766	35150	101182	303545	409	453	1174	3524	206	232	587	1762

(*Contd.*)

ANNEXURE-XVIII (*Contd.*)

1	2	3	4	5	6	7	8	9	10	11	12	13	14
14.	Manipur	35	44	555	1556	0	0	0	0	1	2	22	61
15.	Meghalaya												
16.	Mizoram	Traditional Councils perform duties of local government. 73rd Amendment not applicable in these States.											
17.	Nagaland												
18.	Orissa	7394	11823	27036	81077	478	809	1754	5260	85	131	284	854
19.	Punjab	23814	0	26939	75473Elections due								
20.	Rajasthan	17902	15616	33566	112897	943	804	1740	5494	177	154	33	1028
21.	Sikkim	40	298	326	873	0	0	0	0	6	40	28	92
22.	Tamil Nadu	18886	686	31548	125852	1358	41	2295	6499	137	3	22	648
23.	Tripura	1237	704	1809	5421	48	26	67	196	15	7	24	70
24.	Uttar Pradesh	101939	867	120591	799780	9126	135	13865	59991	389	7	634	2687
25.	West Bengal	13644	3319	17883	49225	2354	582	2997	8520	200	50	243	716
26.	A & N Islands	—	—	229	667	—	—	25	—	—	—	10	30
27.	Chandigarh	Current figures not available.											
28.	D & N Haveli	3	103	46	135				—	—	11	4	16
29.	Daman & Diu	1	17	25	63				—	1	3	5	15
30.	NCT Delhi	NCT government propose conduct of Panchayat elections.											
31.	Lakshdweep	0	79	30	79	0	0	0	0	0	22	8	22
32.	Pondicherry				120				—				16
		Current figures not available. Post 73rd Amendment elections not held in the State.											
	Total	367941	235445	681258	2580261	18546	7237	37109	128581	1822	1170	3153	13484

ANNEXURE-XIX

Financial Progress under Jawahar Gram Samridhi Yojana during 2000-01 upto the month of September in NE States

Allocation & Releases

(Rs. in lakhs)

Sl. No.	States/UTs	Month Code	Balance as on 1-4-2000	Allocation			Releases			Total Funds Available	Funds Utilised			Percentage Utilisation		
				Centre	State	Total	Centre	State	Total		Total	Individual SC/STs	Disabled	Total	Individual SC/STs	Disabled
1.	Arunachal Pradesh	9	121.82	456.91	152.29	609.19	0.00	0.00	0.00	121.82	32.74	7.53	0.00	26.88	6.18	0.00
2.	Assam	9	982.75	11872.04	3956.95	15828.99	0.00	0.00	0.00	982.75	781.46	208.73	33.60	79.52	21.24	3.42
3.	Manipur			795.90	265.27	1061.17	264.23	88.07	352.30	352.30				0.00	0.00	0.00
4.	Meghalaya			891.69	297.20	1188.89	402.71	134.22	536.93	536.93				0.00	0.00	0.00
5.	Mizoram	9	5.20	206.33	68.77	275.10	103.17	34.39	137.56	142.76	117.18	117.18	0.00	82.08	82.08	0.00
6.	Nagaland	6	78.11	611.66	203.87	815.53	305.83	101.93	407.76	485.87	204.75			42.14	0.00	0.00
7.	Sikkim	9	0.08	228.45	76.14	304.60	114.23	38.07	152.30	152.38	114.23	63.99		74.96	41.99	0.00
8.	Tripura	8	0.00	1437.02	478.96	1915.97	718.51	239.48	957.99	957.99	53.87	31.17	0.00	5.62	3.25	0.00
	Total		1187.96	16500.00	5499.45	21999.45	1908.68	636.16	2544.84	3732.81	1304.23	428.60	33.60	34.94	11.48	0.90

Note: The blank column denote non-reporting of figures by the States/UTs.

ANNEXURE-XX

Physical Performance under JGSY — (North-Eastern States) during 2000-01 upto September

Sl. No.	States/UTs	Month Code	Status of Works (in numbers)					Total Mandays Generated (in lakh)
			Works complete	Works under progress	Total Works	Works exclusively for SC/STs	Works Disabled	
1.	Arunachal Pradesh	9	88	77	165	26	0	0.57
2.	Assam	9	2436	3433	5869	897	27	11.80
3.	Manipur							
4.	Meghalaya							
5.	Mizoram	9	416	0	416	416	0	1.23
6.	Nagaland	6						8.60
7.	Sikkim	9	247	371	618			1.74
8.	Tripura	8	18	207	225	9	0	0.75
	Total		3205	4088	7293	1348	27	24.69

Note: Physical Progress is now monitored in terms of number of works completed and taken up in place of Mandays generation as JGSY has now become an infrastructure development programme as compared to generation of wage employment earlier.

ANNEXURE-XXI

Financial & Physical Progress Under IAY in Respect of NE States (2000-01)

(Rs. in lakhs) (In Nos.)

States	O.B. As on 1-4-2000	Allocation			Releases			Total Availability of Funds	Expenditure	%age Expen. to Avalability of Funds	Target*	Achievement	%age Achievement	Reporting Month
		Central	State	Total	Central	State Matching Share	Total							
Arunachal Pradesh	245.99	726.86	242.26	969.12	361.99	120.65	482.64	728.63	415.58	57.04	4246	1852	43.62	Oct. 2000
Assam	2876.36	16354.79	5451.05	21805.84	8177.40	2725.53	10902.93	13779.29	5952.93	43.20	98856	32512	32.89	Nov. 2000
Manipur	55.54	866.65	288.85	1155.50	194.40	64.79	259.19	314.73	102.65	32.61	5062	565	11.16	Oct. 2000
Meghalaya	900.83	1151.46	383.78	1535.24	398.65	132.87	531.52	1432.35	0.00	0.00	6726	0	0.00	NR
Mizoram	71.96	276.42	92.13	368.55	224.94	74.97	299.91	371.87	216.68	58.27	1615	1184	73.31	Oct. 2000
Nagaland	110.42	743.31	247.75	991.06	371.66	123.87	495.53	605.95	676.80	111.69	4342	4859	111.91	Nov. 2000
Tripura	22.28	1681.23	560.35	2241.58	840.62	280.18	1120.80	1143.08	1029.25	90.04	9821	0	0.00	Nov. 2000
Sikkim	21.52	199.28	66.42	265.70	99.64	33.21	132.85	154.37	23.95	15.51	916	337	36.79	Aug. 2000
Total	4304.90	22000.00	7332.60	29332.60	10669.30	3556.08	14225.38	18530.28	8417.84	45.43	131584	41309	31.39	

ANNEXURE-XXII

Financial & Physical Performance under Employment Assurance Scheme (EAS) during 2000-01 in N.E. States

(Rs. in Lakhs) (Lakh Mandays)

Sl. No.	States	Month Reporting Code	Opening Balance (as on 01-04-2000)	Central Allocation	State's Allocation	Total Allooca-tion	Centre Funds Released	State Share to be Released	Actual State Share Released	Total (Central-Plus State)	Total Available Funds (Col. 4+11)	Expenditure	%age Exp. to Total Avail.	Wage Employment to be Generated	Wage Employment Genera- (Achievement	%age Achievement to Target
1	2	3	4	5	6	7	8	9	10	11	12	13	14	15	16	17
1.	Arunachal Pradesh*	10	201.63	324.40	108.12	432.52	662.20	220.73	3.21	665.41	867.04	552.46	63.72	10.72	10.16	94.78
2.	Assam	10	1771.29	8432.00	2810.39	11242.39	3372.80	1124.27	0.00	3372.80	5144.09	2794.81	54.33	194.19	45.92	23.65
3.	Manipur	7	107.48	565.00	188.31	753.31	302.89	100.96	0.00	302.89	410.37	126.38	30.80	9.30	2.31	24.84
4.	Meghalaya	NR		634.00	211.31	845.31	204.81	68.27		204.81	204.81		0.00	13.77		
5.	Mizoram	10	307.81	148.00	49.33	197.33	130.89	43.63	19.73	150.62	458.43	377.01	82.24	2.50	4.14	165.60
6.	Nagaland	7	4.42	434.26	144.74	579.00	103.19	34.40	279.00	382.19	386.61	225.18	58.24	13.20	7.31	
7.	Sikkim	NR		162.20	54.06	216.26	81.10	27.03		81.10	81.10		0.00	3.08		
8.	Tripura	11	0.00	1020.26	340.05	1360.31	510.13	170.04	170.02	680.15	680.15	447.88	65.85	24.23	7.55	31.16
	Total		2392.63	11720.12	3906.32	15626.44	5368.01	1789.16	471.96	5839.97	8232.60	4523.72	54.95	270.99	77.39	28.56

Note: *Rs. 500 lakh released as Additional Central Funds in 1999-2000 but received by respective Districts during 2000-01, as reported by Arunachal Pradesh.

NR — Not Reported.

ANNEXURE-XXIII

National Social Assistance Programme

Allocation, Release, Reported Expenditure and No. of Beneficiaries pertaining to the North Eastern States Scheme : NOAPS, Year : 2000-01

(Rs. in Lakhs)

Sl. No.	States	O.B. 1-4-00	Alloca-tion	Release			Addi-tional Funds (99-2000)	Total Rele-ase	Total Avail-ability of funds	Exp. Repor-ted	Repor-ting Month	Target	No. of Benf. Reported				Women	Handi-capped
				1st Instal.	2nd Instal.	Total							SC	ST	Others	Total		
1.	Arunachal Pradesh	3.67	181.26	53.07	0.00	53.07	0.00	53.07	56.74	0.00	0	19365	0	0	0	0	0	0
2.	Assam	178.15	2624.34	1270.50	748.46	2018.96	19.65	2064.85	2243.00	959.85	10/2000	280379	17351	28273	70284	167943	61070	1308
3.	Manipur	42.79	327.06	163.56	0.00	163.56	0.00	163.56	206.35	55.66	6/2000	27449	14	26	982	1022	355	0
4.	Meghalaya	59.49	352.67	150.42	21.01	171.43	8.17	179.60	239.09	97.34	9/2000	37678	0	0	0	11008	1058	0
5.	Mizoram	0.00	98.51	42.36	7.88	50.24	0.00	50.24	50.24	41.33	11/2000	10525	0	7366	0	8581	5000	0
6.	Nagaland	13.96	256.13	110.95	38.38	149.33	6.05	155.38	169.34	79.77	6/2000	27364	0	6150	0	10126	2000	110
7.	Sikkim	0.00	94.57	47.30	47.27	94.57	0.00	94.57	94.57	47.28	11/2000	10104	3049	6552	10104	4904	0	0
8.	Tripura	18.41	565.46	282.73	0.00	282.73	0.00	282.73	301.14	153.92	10/2000	60412	6172	9759	8455	32094	9021	0
	Total	316.47	4500.01	2120.89	863.00	2983.89	33.87	3044.00	3360.47	1435.15	0.00	473276	26586	58126	89825	235678	78504	1418

ANNEXURE-XXIV

National Social Assistance Programme

Allocation, Releases, Reported Expenditure and No. of Beneficiaries pertaining to the North Eastern States Scheme : NMBS, Year : 2000-01

(Rs. in Lakhs)

Sl. No.	States	O.B. 1-4-00	Allocation	Release			Additional Funds (1999-2000)	1% Adm. Charges	Total Release	Total Availability of Funds	Exp. Reported	Month Code	Target	No. of Benf. Reported				Handicapped
				1st Instal.	2nd Instal.	Total								SC	ST	Others	Total	
1.	Arunachal Pradesh*	2.31	27.11	1.17	0.00	1.17	0.00	0.00	1.17	3.48	0.02	4/2000	5213	0	4	0	4	0
2.	Assam	67.87	419.43	157.35	20.06	177.41	0.00	4.19	181.6	249.47	80.30	10/2000	80660	1629	1361	6497	15032	1
3.	Manipur*	7.63	48.80	24.42	0.00	24.42	0.00	0.00	24.42	32.05	8.31	6/2000	7374	14	12	358	758	0
4.	Meghalaya*	6.95	52.81	12.20	6.09	18.29	00.0	0.00	18.29	25.24	18.28	11/2000	10156	0	0	0	2835	0
5.	Mizoram*	1.11	14.85	6.39	1.19	7.58	0.00	0.00	7.58	8.69	7.66	10/2000	2856	0	0	0	1472	0
6.	Nagaland*	2.23	38.43	19.22	5.43	24.65	0.00	0.00	24.65	26.88	11.09	11/2000	7390	0	0	0	955	0
7.	Sikkim	0.12	14.15	7.08	0.00	7.08	0.00	0.00	7.08	7.20	0.00	0	2721	0	0	0	0	0
8.	Tripura	3.01	84.41	42.21	1.13	43.34	0.00	0.00	43.34	46.35	11.08	10/2000	16232	565	508	809	1882	0
	Total	91.23	699.99	270.04	33.90	303.94	0.00	4.19	308.13	399.36	136.74		132603	2208	1885	7664	22938	1

*O.B. is Provisional and based on latest expenditure report (1999-2000).

ANNEXURE-XXV

National Social Assistance Programme (NSAP)

Releases, Reported Expenditure and No. of Beneficiaries pertaining to the North Eastern States Scheme : NFBS, Year : 2000-01

(Rs. in Lakhs)

Sl. No.	States	O.B. 1-4-00	Allocation	Release			Additional funds (1999-2000)	1% Adm. Charges	Total Release	Total Availability of Funds	Exp. Reported	Reporting month	Target	No. of Benf. Reported				Handicapped
				1st Instal.	2nd Instal.	Total								SC	ST	Total	Women	
1.	Arunachal Pradesh*	1.31	57.78	12.49	0.00	12.49	0.00	0.00	12.49	13.80	0.00	0.00	556	0	0	0	0	0
2.	Assam	137.28	1552.78	610.09	267.20	877.29	0.00	15.53	892.82	1030.10	371.51	10/2000	14931	225	301	3954	1300	1
3.	Manipur*	11.61	65.00	32.51	0.00	32.51	0.00	0.00	32.51	44.12	12.53	6/2000	497	1	2	27	5	0
4.	Meghalaya*	5.88	72.22	36.11	8.59	44.70	0.00	0.00	44.70	50.58	24.95	8/2000	694	0	0	225	45	0
5.	Mizoram*	1.08	21.67	9.33	1.73	11.06	0.00	0.00	11.06	12.14	10.05	11/2000	208	0	0	90	10	0
6.	Nagaland*	1.49	36.11	18.08	5.11	23.19	0.00	0.00	23.19	24.68	11.78	12/2000	347	0	52	77	43	0
7.	Sikkim	0.10	21.67	6.52	0.00	6.52	0.00	0.00	6.52	6.62	0.00	0.00	208	0	0	0	0	0
8.	Tripura	9.88	122.78	61.39	11.68	73.07	0.00	0.00	73.07	82.95	33.20	10/2000	1181	59	83	249	176	0
	Total	168.63	1950.01	786.52	202.70	938.71	0.00	15.53	954.24	1117.92	350.74		18622	285	438	4622	1579	1

*O.B. is Provisional and based on latest expenditure report (1999-2000).

ANNEXURE-XXVI

Rural Water Supply Programme
List of Sanctioned Sector Reform Projects

(Rs. in lakh)

Sl. No.	Name of the Districts	State	Amount Sanctioned	GOI Share
1	2	3	4	5
1.	Chittoor	Andhra Pradesh	4000.000	3740.000
2.	Khammam	Andhra Pradesh	3753.000	3509.000
3.	Nalgonda	Andhra Pradesh	4000.000	3740.000
4.	Prakasam	Andhra Pradesh	4000.000	3740.000
5.	Lohit	Arunachal Pradesh	900.000	841.500
6.	West Siang	Arunachal Pradesh	700.000	654.500
7.	Jorhat	Assam	1275.000	1188.600
8.	Kamrup	Assam	1000.000	935.000
9.	Sonitpur	Assam	1181.000	1103.489
10.	Dhanbad	Bihar	4000.000	3740.000
11.	Vaishali	Bihar	4000.000	3740.000
12.	Mehsana	Gujarat	4000.000	3740.000
13.	Rajkot	Gujarat	4000.000	3740.000
14.	Surat	Gujarat	4000.000	3740.000
15.	Karnal	Haryana	1507.000	1409.045
16.	Yamuna Nagar	Haryana	986.180	922.078
17.	Sirmour	Himachal Pradesh	2005.000	1857.500
18.	Srinagar	J&K	2511.000	2347.785
19.	Udhampur	J&K	2500.000	2250.000
20.	Bellary	Karnataka	4000.000	3740.000
21.	Mangalore	Karnataka	4000.000	3740.000
22.	Mysore	Karnataka	4000.000	3740.000
23.	Kasaragod	Kerala	4000.000	3740.000
24.	Kollam	Kerala	4000.000	3740.000
25.	Gwalior	Madhya Pradesh	2927.940	2737.620
26.	Hoshangabad	Madhya Pradesh	4000.000	3740.000

(Contd.)

ANNEXURE-XXVI (*Contd.*)

1	2	3	4	5
27.	Narsinghpur	Madhya Pradesh	4000.000	3740.000
28.	Raisen	Madhya Pradesh	4000.000	3740.000
29.	Sehore	Madhya Pradesh	1795.000	1678.150
30.	Amravati	Maharashtra	2126.000	1973.500
31.	Dhule	Maharashtra	3952.780	3692.958
32.	Nanded	Maharashtra	4000.000	3740.000
33.	Raigad	Maharashtra	3793.000	3473.800
34.	Serchhip	Mizoram	268.980	248.172
35.	Dimapur	Nagaland	594.000	555.390
36.	Balasore	Orissa	4000.000	3740.000
37.	Sundergarh	Orissa	4000.000	3740.000
38.	Bhatinda	Punjab	752.190	700.954
39.	Moga	Punjab	344.000	321.440
40.	Muktsar	Punjab	3992.800	3733.268
41.	Alwar	Rajasthan	4000.000	3740.000
42.	Jaipur	Rajasthan	4000.000	3740.000
43.	Sikkar	Rajasthan	2171.000	1986.050
44.	Sikkim South	Sikkim	1322.480	1210.069
45.	Sikkim West	Sikkim	892.350	816.500
46.	Coimbatore	Tamil Nadu	4000.000	3740.000
47.	Cuddalore	Tamil Nadu	4000.000	3740.000
48.	Perambalur	Tamil Nadu	4000.000	3740.000
49.	Vellore	Tamil Nadu	4000.000	3740.000
50.	West Tripura	Tripura	2819.400	2566.900
51.	Agra	Uttar Pradesh	3000.000	2805.000
52.	Chandauli	Uttar Pradesh	2500.000	2337.500
53.	Lucknow	Uttar Pradesh	4000.000	3740.000
54.	Mirzapur	Uttar Pradesh	3000.000	2805.000
55.	Sonebhadra	Uttar Pradesh	2500.000	2337.500
56.	Midnapur	West Bengal	4000.000	3740.000
57.	North 24 Parganas	West Bengal	4000.000	3740.000
	Total		169070.100	157718.268

ANNEXURE-XXVII

Financial Progress under Rural Water Supply Programme (ARWSP) during 2000-2001

(Rs. in lakhs)

Sl. No.	States/UTs	Month Code	Opening balance as on 1-4-2000	CENTRAL SECTOR (ACCELERATED RURAL WATER SUPPLY PROGRAMME) Allocation	Releases ARWSP	Total Availability of funds (4+6)	Expenditure incurred Total	SC	ST	Exp. on SC/ST as %age of total exp.	Exp. as %age of Avail-ability of funds	Exp.as %age of Alloca-tion
1	2	3	4	5	6	7	8	9	10	11	12	13
1.	Andhra Pradesh	11	0.00	11600.00	11600.00	11600.00	9124.00	2281.00	912.40	35.00	78.66	78.66
2.	Arunachal Pradesh	10	0.00	4365.00	1746.00	1746.00	1232.08	0.00	1232.08	100.00	70.57	28.23
3.	Assam	10	1906.89	7372.00	2949.00	4855.89	3620.68	0.00	0.00	0.00	74.56	49.11
4.	Bihar (Incl. Jharkhand)	8	5089.51	9380.00	2359.50	7449.01	74.75	26.16	0.00	35.00	1.00	0.80
5.	Goa	9	0.00	1404.00	702.00	702.00	18.68	0.60	0.00	3.21	2.66	1.33
6.	Gujarat	9	0.00	7085.00	7085.00	7085.00	6258.75	438.12	876.24	21.00	88.34	88.34
7.	Haryana	11	354.27	1943.00	1880.18	2234.45	1566.69	360.34	0.00	23.00	70.12	80.63
8.	Himachal Pradesh	9	0.00	5091.00	5091.00	5091.00	1716.27	570.13	0.00	33.22	33.71	33.71
9.	Jammu & Kashmir	6	6011.33	8788.00	3694.00	9705.33	0.00	0.00	0.00	#DIV/0!	0.00	0.00
10.	Karnataka	9	3397.34	10350.00	5175.00	8572.34	3568.72	474.20	39.76	14.40	41.63	34.48
11.	Kerala	9	1453.48	5746.00	2873.00	4326.48	766.24	103.25	7.36	14.44	17.71	13.34
12.	M.P. (Incl. Chattisgarh)	8	998.87	11109.00	7134.50	8133.37	4134.53	578.83	950.94	37.00	50.83	37.22
13.	Maharashtra	11	0.00	16934.00	6187.00	6187.00	6318.91	0.00	0.00	0.00	102.13	37.31

(Contd.)

ANNEXURE-XXVII (*Contd.*)

1	2	3	4	5	6	7	8	9	10	11	12	13
14.	Manipur	10	376.19	1475.00	0.00	376.19	17.07	0.00	0.00	0.00	4.54	1.16
15.	Meghalaya	10	325.78	1716.00	686.50	1012.28	268.60	0.00	268.60	100.00	26.53	15.65
16.	Mizoram	9	154.75	1226.00	490.50	645.25	111.85	0.00	111.85	100.00	17.33	9.12
17.	Nagaland	12	501.72	1275.00	182.20	683.92	375.93	·0.00	375.93	100.00	54.97	29.48
18.	Orissa	10	4256.02	6213.00	3106.50	7362.52	1596.03	263.35	254.70	32.46	21.68	25.69
19.	Punjab	11	2424.87	2383.00	1191.50	3616.37	1082.53	419.83	0.00	38.78	29.93	45.43
20.	Rajasthan	10	3864.94	16361.00	16361.00	20225.94	6144.14	1536.04	614.42	35.00	30.38	37.55
21.	Sikkim	10	1302.77	650.00	325.00	1627.77	149.31	37.33	14.93	35.00	9.17	22.97
22.	Tamil Nadu	10	0.00	7308.00	3654.00	3654.00	6532.67	1645.10	0.00	25.18	178.78	89.39
23.	Tripura	9	0.00	1521.00	608.00	608.00	560.00	80.00	160.00	42.86	92.11	36.82
24.	U.P. (Incl. Uttaranchal)	10	0.00	14776.00	9691.50	9691.50	4965.01	432.95	30.20	9.33	51.23	33.60
25.	West Bengal	11	10.12	7895.00	7837.31	7847.43	2601.62	650.40	260.16	35.00	33.15	32.95
26.	A & N Islands	9	4.40	13.00	0.00	4.40	0.00	0.00	0.00	0.00	0.00	0.00
27.	D & N Haveli	9	58.00	7.00	0.00	58.00	0.00	0.00	0.00	0.00	0.00	0.00
28.	Daman & Diu	0	0.00	0.00	0.00	0.00	0.00	0.00	0.00	0.00	0.00	#DIV/0!
29.	Delhi	0	0.00	5.00	0.00	0.00	0.00	0.00	0.00	0.00	0.00	0.00
30.	Lakshdweep	7	0.00	0.00	0.00	0.00	0.00	0.00	0.00	0.00	0.00	#DIV/0!
31.	Pondicherry	10	14.07	5.00	0.00	14.07	0.00	0.00	0.00	0.00	0.00	0.00
32.	Chandigarh			0.00	0.00	0.00						
	Total		32505.32	163996.00	102610.19	135115.51	62805.06	9897.63	6109.57	25.49	46.48	38.30

ANNEXURE-XXVII (*Contd.*)

Summary — Rural Water Supply — 2000-2001

(Rs. in lakh)

Item	O.B.	B.E.	R.E.	Releases	Availability	Expenditure	%age
1	2	3	4	5	6	7	8
ARWSP (Sector Reform)				14832.01	14832.01		0.00
ARWSP (Normal+DDP)	36482.11	192378.00		109387.19	145869.30	66224.50	45.40
Monitoring & Evaluation		100.00			0.00		#DIV/0!
ARWSP (M&I Units)	0.00	250.00		31.18	31.18		0
DPAP Areas		1.00			0.00		0
Sub-Missions (ARWSP)*		1.00		7530.20	7530.20	229.44	3.05
Professional Services		500.00		165.09	165.09		0
Research		150.00		29.26	29.26		0
CAPART	870.65	0.00			870.65		0
HRD/Training		500.00		574.99	574.99		0
IEC		550.00		29.07	29.07		0
MIS		1500.00		21.25	21.25		0
Exhibition		10.00			0.00		0
Seminar/Conference		25.00		6.42	6.42		0
Assistance from UNICEF		25.00		11.39	11.39		0
Other Charges		10.00		0.91	0.91		0
Grand Total	37352.76	196000.00	0.00	132618.96	169971.72	66453.94	39.10

* Releases made under ARWSP head.

Plan

DDP States	O.B.	Allocation	Release	Total Availability of Funds	Expenditure			%age Total Expenditure
					Total	SC	ST	
1	2	3	4	5	6	7	8	9
Andhra Pradesh	0.00	1659.00	1659.00	1659.00	0.00	0.00	0.00	0.00
Gujarat	0.00	400.00	400.00	400.00	1893.28	132.53	0.00	473.32
Haryana	632.43	19.00	19.00	651.43	617.35	141.99	0.00	94.77
H.P.	36.49	587.00	293.50	329.99	0.05	0.00	0.05	0.02
J&K	66.00	282.00	0.00	66.00	0.00	0.00	0.00	0.00
Karnataka	478.79	509.00	254.50	733.29	0.00	0.00	0.00	0.00
Rajasthan	2763.08	4151.00	4151.00	6914.08	908.76	227.19	90.88	13.14
Total	3976.79	7607.00	6777.00	10753.79	3419.44	501.71	90.93	31.80

Releases under Submission

Andhra Pradesh	1613.45
Gujarat	1775.68
Meghalaya	141.07
West Bengal	2000.00
Rajasthan	2000.00
Total	7530.20

ANNEXURE-XXVIII

Financial Progress under Rural Water Supply Programme (MNP) during 2000-2001

(Rs. in lakhs)

Sl. No.	States/UTs	Month Code	STATE SECTOR (MINIMUM NEEDS PROGRAMME)					Exp. on SC/ST as %age of total exp.	Exp. as %age of prov.
			Provision	Amount released to Impltg. Agency	Expenditure incurred				
					Total	SC	ST		
1	2	3	4	5	6	7	8	9	10
1.	Andhra Pradesh	11	10285.33	7265.00	7265.00	1816.25	726.50	35.00	70.63
2.	Arunachal Pradesh	10	2211.00	910.77	910.77	0.00	910.77	100.00	41.19
3.	Assam	10	6315.00	3986.20	3655.80	376.80	444.00	22.45	57.89
4.	Bihar	8	1532.00	290.48	60.00	22.20	0.00	37.00	3.92
5.	Goa	9	439.38	96.29	322.29	11.40	3.30	4.56	73.35
6.	Gujarat	9	21610.00	9955.00	5708.26	566.11	384.27	16.65	26.41
7.	Haryana	11	3820.00	2898.11	3234.97	744.04	0.00	23.00	84.69
8.	Himachal Pradesh	9	5963.25	5963.25	3711.02	864.87	355.38	32.88	62.23
9.	Jammu & Kashmir	6	5132.03	0.00	0.00	0.00	0.00	#DIV/0!	0.00
10.	Karnataka	9	10285.97	1716.46	3090.46	237.91	37.41	8.91	30.05
11.	Kerala	9	5005.00	977.30	977.30	9.47	0.00	0.97	19.53
12.	Madhya Pradesh	8	11109.00	7277.25	2933.65	1502.70	700.75	75.11	26.41

(Contd.)

ANNEXURE-XXVIII (*Contd.*)

1	2	3	4	5	6	7	8	9	10
13.	Maharashtra	11	27731.69	27731.69	27731.69	3624.68	2099.66	20.64	100.00
14.	Manipur	10	1616.45	676.35	676.35	0.00	0.00	0.00	41.84
15.	Meghalaya	10	1850.00	1850.00	239.79	0.00	239.79	100.00	12.96
16.	Mizoram	9	795.00	165.08	165.08	0.00	165.08	100.00	20.76
17.	Nagaland	12	1530.00	0.00	0.00	0.00	0.00	0.00	0.00
18.	Orissa	10	4692.08	1889.67	1889.67	311.79	510.98	43.54	40.27
19.	Punjab	11	3100.00	959.02	959.02	306.89	0.00	32.00	30.94
20.	Rajasthan	10	18000.00	18000.00	7769.29	1686.38	834.90	32.45	43.16
21.	Sikkim	10	550.00	0.00	321.24	191.15	76.46	83.31	58.41
22.	Tamil Nadu	10	41100.00	16174.27	13209.96	4515.65	0.00	34.18	32.14
23.	Tripura	9	2800.00	806.00	739.00	115.00	210.00	43.98	26.39
24.	Uttar Pradesh	10	24775.91	9613.44	9613.44	1667.41	111.62	18.51	38.80
25.	West Bengal	11	7000.00	3799.88	3040.56	760.14	304.06	35.00	43.44
26.	A & N Islands	9	1191.00	319.76	319.76	0.00	48.36	15.12	26.85
27.	D & N Haveli	9	275.00	275.00	90.77	1.81	88.96	100.00	33.01
28.	Daman & Diu	0	206.00	0.00	0.00	0.00	0.00	#DIV/0!	0.00
29.	Delhi	0	384.00	0.00	0.00	0.00	0.00	#DIV/0!	0.00
30.	Lakshdweep	7	93.97	43.22	43.22	0.00	43.22	100.00	45.99
31.	Pondicherry	10	257.15	144.76	144.76	88.70	0.00	61.27	56.29
32.	Chandigarh		0.00						
	Total		221656.21	125160.26	98823.12	19421.35	8295.47	28.05	44.58

ANNEXURE-XXIX

Approved Outlays of the Department of Land Resources

(Rs. in crores)

Sl. No.	Name of the Schemes	Approved Outlay		
		1999-2000	2000-2001	2001-2002
1	2	3	4	5
1.	Integrated Wastelands Development Projects	82.00	480.00	430.00
2.	Drought Prone Areas Programme (DPAP)	95.00	190.00	210.00
3.	Desert Development Programme (DDP)	85.00	135.00	160.00
4.	Computerisation of Land Records	33.00	50.00	45.00
5.	Strengthening of Revenue Machinery & Updating of Land Records	10.00	25.00	30.00
6.	Others	19.00	20.00	25.00
	Total — Land Resources	324.00	900.00	900.00

ANNEXURE-XXX

Approved Outlays of the Department of Drinking Water Supply

(Rs. in crores)

Sl. No.	Name of the Scheme	Approved Outlay		
		1999-2000	2000-2001	2001-2002
1	2	3	4	5
1.	Rural Water Supply Programme	1800.00	1960.00	2010.00
2.	Rural Sanitation	110.00	140.00	150.00
	Total	1910.00	2100.00	2160.00

ANNEXURE-XXXI

Release of Funds during 2000-2001
(As on 31-01-2001)

(Rs. in lakhs)

Sl. No.	States	IWDP	EAS (Watershed)	DPAP	DDP	Total
1	2	3	4	5	6	7
1.	Andhra Pradesh	1686.02	5686.94	3986.00	363.00	11721.96
2.	Arunachal Pradesh	0.00	NA	NA	NA	0.00
3.	Assam	218.36	NA	NA	NA	218.36
4.	Bihar/Jharkhand	0.00	NA	219.00	NA	219.00
5.	Gujarat	758.14	2003.95	944.00	1974.00	5680.09
6.	Haryana	0.00	407.03	NA	486.00	893.03
7.	Himachal Pradesh	665.46	140.25	126.00	451.00	1382.71
8.	Jammu & Kashmir	167.86	NA	0.00	784.00	951.86
9.	Karnataka	190.79	1325.35	818.00	256.00	2590.14
10.	Kerala	80.39	354.56	NA	NA	434.95
11.	Madhya Pradesh/Chhatisgarh	636.47	4681.55	2070.00	NA	7388.02
12.	Maharashtra	330.45	1958.35	1039.00	NA	3327.80
13.	Manipur	290.37	0.00	NA	NA	290.37
14.	Meghalaya	0.00	0.00	NA	NA	0.00
15.	Mizoram	230.42	0.00	NA	NA	230.42
16.	Nagaland	694.48	NA	NA	NA	694.48
17.	Orissa	253.38	1101.52	122.00	NA	1476.90
18.	Punjab	74.61	NA	NA	NA	74.61
19.	Rajasthan	589.13	2046.12	904.00	5644.00	9183.25
20.	Sikkim	140.00	NA	NA	NA	140.00
21.	Tamil Nadu	731.20	268.07	697.00	NA	1696.27
22.	Tripura	0.00	NA	NA	NA	0.00
23.	Uttar Pradesh/Uttaranchal	1235.17	2362.96	1724.00	NA	5322.13
24.	West Bengal	0.00	0.00	77.00	0.00	77.00
	Total	8972.70	22336.65	12726.00	9958.00	53956.35

NA—indicates that the scheme is not implemented in these States.

ANNEXURE-XXXII

State-wise details of Implementation of Ceiling Laws (September, 2000)

(In Acres)

Sl. No.	States/UTs	Declared surplus	Taken posse-ssion	Distributed to indv. benef.	Total No. of benef.
1	2	3	4	5	6
1.	Andhra Pradesh	792762	640180	581568	534603
2.	Assam	612500	575337	483951	444997
3.	Bihar	415447	390752	306964	379528
4.	Gujarat	227404	160190	139748	32174
5.	Haryana	107517	102534	102027	29203
6.	Himachal Pradesh	316556	304895	4374	6365
7.	Jammu & Kashmir	455575	450000	450000	450000
8.	Karnataka	268478	161834	121070	32880
9.	Kerala	139548	96253	66669	156568
10.	Madhya Pradesh	298763	260323	186942	74705
11.	Maharashtra	739206	670237	642002	140462
12.	Manipur	1830	1685	1682	1258
13.	Orissa	178503	167143	156494	138599
14.	Punjab	223115	105801	104199	28570
15.	Rajasthan	610676	568331	460879	81129
16.	Tamil Nadu	199729	190237	178801	141680
17.	Tripura	1995	1944	1598	1424
18.	Uttar Pradesh	374125	341464	258698	294062
19.	West Bengal	1372074	1283059	1042716	2536317
20.	D&N Haveli	9406	9305	6851	3353
21.	Delhi	1132	394	394	654
22.	Pondicherry	2326	1185	1046	1427
	Total	7348667	6483713	5298673	5509958

ANNEXURE-XXXIII

Distribution of Bhoodan Land (upto September, 2000)

(Area in lakh acres)

Sl. No.	States	Area		
		Donated	Distributed	Balance
1	2	3	4	5
1.	Andhra Pradesh	2.52	1.10	1.42
2.	Assam	0.01	0.01	Nil
3.	Bihar	21.18	7.23	13.95
4.	Gujarat	0.34	0.27	0.07
5.	Haryana	0.02	0.02	Nil
6.	Himachal Pradesh	Neg.	Neg.	Neg.
7.	J & K	Neg.	Neg.	Neg.
8.	Karnataka	0.11	0.05	0.06
9.	Kerala	0.02	0.02	Nil
10.	Madhya Pradesh	1.72	1.41	0.31
11.	Maharashtra	1.04	0.27	0.77
12.	Orissa	6.39	5.80	0.59
13.	Punjab	0.05	0.01	0.04@
14.	Rajasthan	1.15	1.14	0.01
15.	Tamil Nadu	0.24	0.21	0.03
16.	Uttar Pradesh	4.37	4.21	0.16
17.	West Bengal	Neg.	Neg.	Neg.
	Total	39.16	21.75	17.41

@ Area not taken possession.

ANNEXURE-XXXIV

Distribution of Government Wastelands as on September, 2000

Sl. No.	Name of States/UTs	Area Distributed (in Lakh Acres)
1	2	3
1.	Andhra Pradesh	42.02
2.	Assam	5.89
3.	Bihar	13.21
4.	Gujarat	13.81
5.	Haryana	0.00
6.	Himachal Pradesh	0.17
7.	Karnataka	13.72
8.	Kerala	4.57
9.	Madhya Pradesh	0.79
10.	Maharashtra	10.23
11.	Manipur	0.32
12.	Punjab	1.10
13.	Orissa	7.26
14.	Tamil Nadu	2.07
15.	Tripura	1.32
16.	Uttar Pradesh	24.89
17.	West Bengal	4.32
18.	Goa	0.05
19.	Mizoram	0.74
20.	Rajasthan	0.93
21.	Delhi	0.06
	Total	147.47

ANNEXURE-XXXV

Number of Tenants Conferred Ownership Rights (or Rights Protected) and Area Accrued to them as on September 2000

Sl. No.	States	No. of Tenants (In lakhs)	Area Accrued (lakh acres)
1	2	3	4
1.	Andhra Pradesh	1.07	5.95
2.	Arunachal Pradesh	System not prevalent	
3.	Assam	29.08	31.75
4.	Bihar	NR	NR
5.	Gujarat	12.76	25.92
6.	Goa	NR	NR
7.	Haryana	Tenancy not prevalent	
8.	Himachal Pradesh	4.01	NR
9.	Jammu and Kashmir	6.10	NR
10.	Kanataka	6.05	26.32
11.	Kerala	28.42	14.50
12.	Madhya Pradesh	Tenancy not prevalent	
13.	Maharashtra	14.92	42.90
14.	Manipur	NR	NR
15	Meghalaya	Nil	Nil
16.	Mizoram	Nil	Nil
17.	Nagaland	NR	NR
18.	Orissa	1.65	0.98
19.	Punjab	NR	NR
20.	Rajasthan	0.18	NR
21.	Sikkim	NR	NR
22.	Tamil Nadu	4.98	6.95
23.	Tripura	0.14	0.39
24.	Uttar Pradesh	NR	NR
25.	West Bengal	14.60	NR
	Union Territories		
26.	A.N. Islands	Nil	Nil
27.	Chandigarh	NR	NR
28.	D&N Haveli	0.26	0.64
29.	Delhi	NR	NR
30.	Daman and Diu	NR	NR
31.	Lakshadweep	Neg	Neg
32.	Pondicherry	Neg	Neg
	All India	124.22	156.30

NR — Not reported.

ANNEXURE-XXXVI

Consolidation of Landholdings — Statewise Information as on September, 2000

(Area in lakh acres)

Sl. No.	States/UTs	Area Consolidated
1	2	3
1.	Andhra Pradesh	8.18*
2.	Bihar	96.05*
3.	Gujarat	69.88
4.	Haryana	104.38
5.	Himachal Pradesh	29.91
6.	Jammu & Kashmir	1.37*
7.	Karnataka	26.76#
8.	Madhya Pradesh	95.53
9.	Maharashtra	526.50$
10.	Orissa	26.74
11.	Punjab	121.81
12.	Rajasthan	42.30@
13.	Uttar Pradesh	481.63
14.	Delhi	2.33
	Total	1633.47

* Scheme has been discontined (w.e.f. July, 1992 in Bihar).

Consolidation of Holding Act, 1966 has been repealed in 1991.

@ Scheme discontinued from 1965.

$ Implementation of the scheme stopped w.e.f. 1-4-93.

ANNEXURE-XXXVII

State-wise Information on Alienation and Restoration of Tribal Lands (As on September, 2000)

(Area in acres)

Sl. No.	States	No. of cases filed in the Court	Area	Cases Disposed of by the Court	Area	Cases Rejected	Area	Cases Decided in favour of Tribals	Area	Cases in which land was restored to Tribals	Area	Cases Pending in Court	Area
1	2	3	4	5	6	7	8	9	10	11	12	13	14
			(7+9)	(8+10)								(3-5)	(4-6)
1.	Andhra Pradesh	65875	287776	58212	256452	31737	150227	26475	106225	23383	94312	7663	31324
2.	Assam	2042	4211	50	19	—	—	50	19	50	19	1992	4192
3.	Bihar	86291	104893	76518	95151	31884	49730	44634	45421	44634	45421	9773	9742
4.	Gujarat	47926	140324	40400	120691	119	497	40281	120194	39503	118259	7526	19633
5.	Himachal Pradesh					Negligible							
6.	Karnataka	42582	130373	38521	115021	16687	47159	21834	67862	21834	67862	4061	15352
7.	Madhya Pradesh	53806	158398	29596	97123	29596	97123	NR	NR	NR	NR	24210	61275
8.	Maharashtra	45634	NR	44624	99486	24681	NR	19943	99486	19943	99486	1010	NR
9.	Orissa	1431	1712	594	816	152	204	442	612	212	455	837	896
10.	Rajasthan	651	2300	240	774	53	187	187	587	187	587	411	1526
11.	Tripura	28926	25295	28888	25274	20084	18366	8804	6908	8551	6732	38	21
	Total	375164	855282	317643	810807	154993	363493	162650	447314	158297	433133	57521	143961

ANNEXURE-XXXVIII

State-wise Break-up of Amount Released under the Scheme of Computerisation of Land Records (CLR) and Strengthening of Revenue Administration & Updating of Land Records (SRA & ULR)

(Rs. in lakh)

Sl. No.	States/UTs	CLR Total funds released since inception	SRA & ULR Total funds released since inception as Central Share
1.	Andhra Pradesh	1436.95	172.80
2.	Arunachal Pradesh	75.30	173.75
3.	Assam	335.50	397.20
4.	Bihar	548.00	1077.85
5.	Gujarat	344.29	422.20
6.	Goa	115.80	75.94
7.	Haryana	365.00	301.53
8.	Himachal Pradesh	240.20	694.87
9.	Jammu & Kashmir	286.00	1196.00
10.	Karnataka	1815.03	748.96
11.	Kerala	576.25	1086.17
12.	Madhya Pradesh	2193.58	2008.55
13.	Maharashtra	2168.26	1345.60
14.	Manipur	188.23	60.17
15.	Meghalaya	14.00	50.00
16.	Mizoram	252.78	776.79
17.	Nagaland	25.15	138.20
18.	Orissa	1101.82	355.61
19.	Punjab	282.62	1265.35
20.	Rajasthan	1229.87	1172.47
21.	Sikkim	67.20	146.46
22.	Tamil Nadu	1228.29	421.03
23.	Tripura	213.80	109.58
24.	Uttar Pradesh	1084.00	1958.51
25.	West Bengal	1631.18	1512.21
26.	A&N Islands	—	43.03
27.	Chandigarh	15.00	32.00
28.	D&N Haveli	12.38	25.00
29.	Delhi	8.03	62.00
30.	Daman & Diu	—	6.50
31.	Lakshadweep	—	50.71
32.	Pondicherry	62.10	116.62
	Total	17916.61	18003.66

ANNEXURE-XXXIX

The Breakup of Amount Released and Utilised by Various States/UTs under Computerisation of Land Records Programme Since Inception (As on 7-12-2000)

(Rs in lakhs)

Sl. No.	Name of the States/UTs	Funds Released									Funds Released so far	Funds used so far	% of utilisation	Unspent balances
		Between 1989-93	During 1993-94	During 1994-95	During 1995-96	During 1996-97	During 1997-98	During 1998-99	During 1999-00	During 2000-01				
1	2	3	4	5	6	7	8	9	10	11	12	13	14	15
1.	Andhra Pradesh	25.00	78.00	105.00	210.00	15.00	0.00	829.90	174.05	0.00	1436.95	1177.18	82%	259.77
2.	Arunachal Pradesh	0.00	0.00	0.00	0.00	0.00	0.00	0.00	0.00	75.30	75.30	0.00	0%	75.30
3.	Assam	25.00	33.00	50.00	50.00	80.00	97.50	0.00	0.00	0.00	335.50	67.56	20%	267.94
4.	Bihar	20.00	30.00	100.00	0.00	0.00	367.50	30.50	0.00	0.00	548.00	35.30	6%	512.70
5.	Gujarat	25.00	10.00	10.00	120.00	0.00	75.00	24.61	79.68	0.00	344.29	210.93	61%	133.36
6.	Goa	0.00	15.00	5.00	0.00	20.00	0.00	0.00	63.50	12.30	115.80	55.00	47%	60.80
7.	Haryana	21.00	19.00	55.00	180.00	0.00	19.00	15.00	56.00	0.00	365.00	153.82	42%	211.18
8.	Himachal Pradesh	25.00	15.00	50.00	55.00	60.00	0.00	6.60	28.60	0.00	240.20	45.00	19%	195.20
9.	Jammu & Kashmir	25.00	4.00	20.00	0.00	0.00	30.00	189.00	18.00	0.00	286.00	186.34	65%	99.66
10.	Karnataka	25.00	43.00	28.00	120.00	95.00	69.20	342.50	501.88	590.45	1815.03	1107.27	61%	707.76
11.	Kerala	25.00	40.00	30.00	200.00	30.00	69.00	79.50	102.75	0.00	576.25	383.00	66%	193.25
12.	Madhya Pradesh	33.00	45.00	90.00	75.00	45.00	485.50	237.82	668.38	513.88	2193.58	987.32	45%	1206.26

(Contd.)

ANNEXURE-XXXIX (*Contd.*)

1	2	3	4	5	6	7	8	9	10	11	12	13	14	15
13.	Maharashtra	25.00	60.00	95.00	195.00	241.00	197.50	108.59	791.17	455.00	2168.26	873.60	40%	1294.66
14.	Manipur	25.00	0.00	0.00	0.00	124.88	0.00	0.00	38.35	0.00	188.23	25.00	13%	163.23
15.	Meghalaya	0.00	0.00	0.00	0.00	0.00	0.00	0.00	14.00	0.00	14.00	0.00	0%	14.00
16.	Mizoram	0.00	15.00	10.00	0.00	60.00	0.00	50.00	37.78	80.00	252.78	85.00	34%	167.78
17.	Nagaland	0.00	0.00	0.00	0.00	0.00	0.00	0.00	25.15	0.00	25.15	0.00	0%	25.15
18.	Orissa	32.50	55.00	30.00	135.00	270.00	0.00	20.50	171.12	387.70	1101.82	586.55	53%	515.27
19.	Punjab	25.00	53.62	45.00	0.00	75.00	52.50	0.00	31.50	0.00	282.62	32.67	12%	249.95
20.	Rajasthan	25.00	50.00	68.00	150.00	210.00	0.00	43.60	0.00	683.27	1229.87	411.00	33%	818.87
21.	Sikkim	12.00	0.00	0.00	20.00	0.00	0.00	22.40	12.80	0.00	67.20	32.00	48%	35.20
22.	Tamil Nadu	25.00	83.00	45.00	90.00	210.00	60.00	30.98	237.29	447.02	1228.29	541.02	44%	687.27
23.	Tripura	25.00	40.00	20.00	0.00	15.00	75.80	0.00	38.00	0.00	213.80	144.62	68%	69.18
24.	Uttar Pradesh	25.00	75.00	129.00	165.00	270.00	247.50	142.50	0.00	30.00	1084.00	450.00	42%	634.00
25.	West Bengal	25.00	85.00	65.00	235.00	180.00	173.00	300.78	110.00	457.40	1631.18	1159.00	71%	472.18
26.	D & N Haveli	0.00	12.38	0.00	0.00	0.00	0.00	0.00	0.00	0.00	12.38	0.00	0%	12.38
27.	Delhi	8.03	0.00	0.00	0.00	0.00	0.00	0.00	0.00	0.00	8.03	0.00	0%	8.03
28.	Pondicherry	0.00	15.00	0.00	0.00	0.00	0.00	0.00	23.55	23.55	62.10	23.55	38%	38.55
29.	Chandigarh	0.00	0.00	0.00	0.00	15.00	0.00	0.00	0.00	0.00	15.00	0.00	0%	15.00
	Total	501.53	876.00	1050.00	2000.00	2015.88	2019.00	2474.78	3223.55	3755.87	17916.61	8772.73	49%	9143.88

ANNEXURE-XL

Release of Funds Towards Central Share under the Centrally Sponsored Scheme for Strengthening of Revenue Administration & Updation of Land Records (SRA & ULR)

(As on 7-12-2000)

(Rs. In Lakhs)

Sl.No.	States/UTs	1987-90	1990-91	1991-92	1992-93	1993-94	1994-95	1995-96	1996-97	1997-98	1998-99	1999-00	2000-01	Total
1	2	3	4	5	6	7	8	9	10	11	12	13	14	15
1.	Andhra Pradesh	100.00					35.50		37.30					172.80
2.	Arunachal Pradesh		1.00				150.00					22.75		173.75
3.	Assam	100.00	50.00		40.00	42.13	150.00			15.07				397.20
4.	Bihar	100.00	150.00			45.85		782.00						1077.85
5.	Gujarat		100.00		248.70							73.50		422.20
6.	Goa		30.00	4.00		15.69	20.00		6.25					75.94
7.	Haryana	50.00	50.00	25.00		78.00	50.00					19.29	29.25	301.54
8.	Himachal Pradesh		110.00			36.00	50.00		148.93	100.10	99.85	150.00		694.87
9.	J & K	100.00			120.00	97.00	266.50		193.00	294.50	90.00	35.00		1196.00
10.	Karnataka		7.50	100.00		108.00	22.25		166.62	344.60				748.97
11.	Kerala	100.00	75.00		54.68	106.20	22.23	273.13	123.68	25.00	127.75	83.50	95.00	1086.17
12.	Madhya Pradesh	296.64	12.45	143.98	351.89	235.32	306.70	41.45	332.28	97.75	70.65	119.45		2008.55
13.	Maharashtra		189.84	10.75	87.66			285.00	234.00	202.50		60.00	275.85	1345.60

(Contd.)

ANNEXURE-XL (*Contd.*)

1	2	3	4	5	6	7	8	9	10	11	12	13	14	15
14.	Manipur	15.00				45.18								60.18
15.	Meghalaya		50.00											50.00
16.	Mizoram	15.00		29.50	22.10	29.65	220.00		26.50		48.30	165.74	220.00	776.79
17.	Nagaland		17.50	6.50	7.70	37.95						68.55		138.20
18.	Orissa	100.00		55.22	90.00	110.40								355.62
19.	Punjab		162.50	165.87	206.45	580.26			53.90		96.37			1265.35
20.	Rajasthan	100.00	70.00	43.48	189.15	105.81	40.75	284.59	63.79	74.64	150.55	49.73		1172.48
21.	Sikkim		16.00						33.60	21.70	75.16			146.46
22.	Tamil Nadu	100.00	10.00	74.00	62.88	75.35		38.80					60.00	421.03
23.	Tripura	15.00				10.63	18.45		25.50	40.00				109.58
24.	Uttar Pradesh	100.00			281.89	530.04	238.16		232.12	372.43	146.38	57.50		1958.51
25.	West Bengal	103.31	200.00	173.75	110.90	92.50	86.50	150.00	200.00	275.25		120.00		1512.21
26.	A & N Islands		10.68		20.85			11.50						43.03
27.	Chandigarh		15.00	17.00										32.00
28.	D & N Haveli					25.00								25.00
29.	Delhi		25.00	17.00			10.00		10.00					62.00
30.	Daman & Diu			6.50										6.50
31.	Lakshdweep							13.50	12.21				25.00	50.71
32.	Pondicherry		10.00	32.88		18.88	20.40		14.91	19.55				116.62
	Total	1394.95	1362.47	905.42	1894.85	2425.82	1707.43	1879.97	1914.58	1883.08	905.01	1025.00	705.10	18003.67

ANNEXURE-XLI

Actual Expenditure reported by States/UTs under the Centrally Sponsored Scheme for Strenthening of Revenue Administration & Updation of Land Records (SRA & ULR) As on 7-12-2000

(Rs. In Lakhs)

Sl. No.	States/UTs	Funds utilised										Total	%age Utilisation
		upto 1990-91	1991-92	1992-93	1993-94	1994-95	1995-96	1996-97	1997-98	1998-99	1999-00		
1	2	3	4	5	6	7	8	9	10	11	12	13	14
1.	Andhra Pradesh	22.73		6.75	13.00	52.00			13.03			107.51	62.22
2.	Arunachal Pradesh	1.00					16.64	73.64	59.69			150.97	99.98
3.	Assam	100.00		50.00				52.00				202.00	50.86
4.	Bihar	89.25	10.00	100.00			616.38					815.63	75.67
5.	Gujarat		45.90	1.28	3.46	73.83	14.74	10.54	80.48	66.05	126.14	422.40	100.00
6.	Goa	14.49	10.70	11.00	13.50	16.57	14.49	1.22	1.40			83.36	109.77
7.	Haryana	14.30		25.00	25.00	38.00	25.00	25.00	50.00	33.43	19.72	255.45	93.82
8.	Himachal Pradesh		49.24	36.50	11.00	49.27	50.00	126.00	123.03	99.85		544.87	78.41
9.	J & K	5.02	35.00	31.11	54.94	56.73	177.00	228.06	277.47	255.33		1120.65	93.70
10.	Karnataka	7.50	25.00				100.50	171.51	118.50		55.65	478.66	63.91
11.	Kerala	83.65	20.00	37.99	32.48	85.26	120.12	243.27	100.00	127.25		850.00	85.76
12.	Madhya Pradesh	309.09	143.98	350.41	230.85	119.98	56.33	136.36	374.27	164.39	119.45	2005.08	99.83

(Contd.)

ANNEXURE-XLI (*Contd.*)

1	2	3	4	5	6	7	8	9	10	11	12	13	14
13.	Maharashtra				99.07	189.00		403.06	43.40	50.35	255.97	1040.83	97.30
14.	Manipur	0.15										0.15	0.25
15.	Meghalaya											0.00	0.00
16.	Mizoram	15.00		29.50	22.10	29.65	220.00		26.50	8.15		350.90	71.52
17.	Nagaland	5.50	15.25		7.70	18.98			8.25	3.25		58.92	84.59
18.	Orissa	72.03			32.20	71.42				26.40	15.74	217.78	61.24
19.	Punjab		9.45	227.76	276.27	0.88	5.48	170.36	408.05			1098.25	86.79
20.	Rajasthan	125.53	15.32	103.26	84.87	46.04	64.82	163.17	114.51	143.55	30.95	892.00	76.08
21.	Sikkim				4.97	1.04		13.20	22.55			41.75	28.51
22.	Tamil Nadu	5.77	39.58	34.51	29.32	94.29	70.00	46.35	3.39			323.19	89.52
23.	Tripura	5.91	5.42		1.29	5.20	5.36	21.62	5.51	22.24		72.55	86.20
24.	Uttar Pradesh	99.25		231.89	528.02	64.95	194.20	162.77	145.97	135.96	65.01	1628.01	83.12
25.	West Bengal	103.31	75.22	50.00	70.00	45.98	136.27	83.50	134.00	244.00	190.74	1133.01	74.92
26.	A & N Islands			5.80	3.82	5.81	2.95	1.32	8.48			28.18	65.49
27.	Chandigarh	0.00	0.00	0.00	9.47	0.00	0.00	0.00	28.08			37.55	117.34
28.	D & N Haveli											0.00	0.00
29.	Delhi	20.42		7.48	8.11	5.05	3.20					44.26	71.39
30.	Daman & Diu			6.50								6.50	100.00
31.	Lakshdweep						13.50	12.21				25.71	100.00
32.	Pondicherry		9.99	31.34		15.40	16.94					73.67	63.17
	Total	1099.89	510.03	1378.07	1561.42	1085.28	1923.88	2145.13	2146.53	1380.18	879.37	14109.76	78.37

ANNEXURE-XLII

Details of Drought Prone Areas Programme (DPAP) Projects

Sl. No.	States	Number of Projects (Batch No.)						Total
		1st 1995-96	2nd 1996-97	3rd 1997-98	4th 1998-99	5th 1999-2000	6th 2000-01	
1	2	3	4	5	6	7	8	9
1.	Andhra Pradesh	527	60	321	700	587	177	2372
2.	Bihar*	364	0	0	0	19	35	418
3.	Gujarat	275	100	19	55	230	179	858
4.	Himachal Pradesh	33	21	0	0	17	23	94
5.	Jammu & Kashmir@	0	0	0	0	0	0	0
6.	Karnataka	406	0	0	0	248	65	719
7.	Madhya Pradesh**	895	0	0	0	265	518	1678
8.	Maharashtra	818	0	0	0	219	278	1315
9.	Orissa	192	0	0	0	0	6	198
10.	Rajasthan	182	0	0	0	18	271	471
11.	Tamil Nadu	297	0	0	103	299	0	699
12.	Uttar Pradesh***	399	99	56	0	376	99	1029
13.	West Bengal	135	0	0	0	0	34	169
	Total	4523	280	396	858	2278	1685	10020

@ In Jammu & Kashmir, the programme is under implementation in two districts, namely, Doda and Udhampur under old guidelines.

* Includes information in r/o Jharkhand also.

** Includes information in r/o Chhattisgarh also.

*** Includes information in r/o Uttranchal also.

Note : A project under DPAP generally covers an area of 500 hectares.

ANNEXURE-XLIII

Central Releases under Drought Prone Areas Programme (DPAP)

(Rs. in crore)

States DPAP	1995-96	1996-97	1997-98	1998-99	1999-2000	Total
1	2	3	4	5	6	7
Andhra Pradesh	21.07	26.20	22.93	22.91	26.71	119.80
Bihar	7.25	0.34	1.15	2.38	2.30	13.42
Gujarat	10.14	7.31	5.28	7.77	8.79	39.29
Himachal Pradesh	0.67	1.94	0.70	0.52	0.90	4.72
Jammu & Kashmir	2.60	1.98	1.13	0.40	2.20	8.30
Karnataka	11.59	4.94	7.86	9.08	8.02	41.49
Madhya Pradesh	19.39	21.19	8.93	8.83	14.02	72.34
Maharashtra	17.21	12.61	19.86	5.52	6.45	61.65
Orissa	4.04	2.95	0.64	2.75	0.46	10.83
Rajasthan	6.44	1.52	4.19	1.74	3.86	17.74
Tamil Nadu	5.32	12.24	7.07	2.73	8.27	35.63
Uttar Pradesh	10.93	16.50	8.42	8.39	10.93	55.17
West Bengal	2.30	0.28	2.60	0.00	2.09	7.28
Total	118.95	109.98	90.75	73.00	94.99	487.67

ANNEXURE-XLIV

Details of Desert Development Programme (DDP) Projects

Sl. No.	States	Number of Projects (Batch No.) 1st 1995-96	2nd 1996-97	3rd 1997-98	4th 1998-99	5th 1999-2000	6th 2000-01	Total
1	2	3	4	5	6	7	8	9
1.	Andhra Pradesh	96	10	0	100	96	10	312
2.	Gujarat	345	0	0	100	250	150	845
3.	Haryana	107	6	0	100	76	66	355
4.	Karnataka	130	0	0	100	51	101	382
5.	Rajasthan	841	0	0	0	883	411	2135
6.	Jammu & Kashmir	94	49	36	0	96	73	348
7.	Himachal Pradesh	80	—	—	—	48	75	203
	Total	1693	65	36	400	1500	886	4580

Note : A project under DDP generally covers an area of 500 hectares.

ANNEXURE-XLV

Central Releases under Desert Development Programme (DDP)

(Rs. in crores)

States	1995-96	1996-97	1997-98	1998-99	1999-2000	Total
Andhra Pradesh	4.05	6.74	4.22	4.83	4.37	24.21
Gujarat	18.61	10.27	11.01	8.60	27.51	76.00
Haryana	4.50	6.34	7.97	6.08	4.54	29.43
Himachal Pradesh	6.36	8.00	1.50	0.30	2.55	18.71
Jammu & Kashmir	10.00	13.30	2.25	5.85	4.86	36.26
Karnataka	3.90	4.32	8.42	3.50	2.15	22.29
Rajasthan	53.58	16.40	34.64	50.64	39.01	194.27
Total	101.00	65.37	70.01	79.80	84.99	401.17

ANNEXURE-XLVI

Total Area Sanctioned under IWDP during the Period 1995-96 to 2000-2001 (Under New Guidelines as on 31-01-2001)

Sl. No.	States	1995-96 Area (in lakh ha)	1996-97 Area (in lakh ha)	1997-98 Area (in lakh ha)	1998-99 Area (in lakh ha)	1999-2000 Area (in lakh ha)	2000-2001 Area (in lakh ha)	Total Area (in lakh ha)
1.	Andhra Pradesh	0.08	0.16	0.61	0.75	0.50	0.75	2.85
2.	Arunachal Pradesh	0.00	0.00	0.00	0.02	0.00	0.00	0.02
3.	Assam	0.00	0.00	0.06	0.00	0.28	0.33	0.67
4.	Bihar	0.01	0.00	0.00	0.00	0.06	0.00	0.07
5.	Chhattisgarh	0.11	0.00	0.00	0.00	0.00	0.12	0.23
6.	Gujarat	0.00	0.01	0.12	0.70	0.62	0.73	2.18
7.	Haryana	0.05	0.00	0.12	0.00	0.00	0.00	0.17
8.	Himachal Pradesh	0.00	0.00	0.25	0.25	0.50	0.59	1.59
9.	Jammu & Kashmir	0.00	0.00	0.13	0.14	0.00	0.00	0.27
10.	Karnataka	0.00	0.00	0.49	0.62	0.61	0.00	1.72
11.	Kerala	0.10	0.00	0.00	0.00	0.00	0.00	0.1
12.	Maharashtra	0.00	0.00	0.10	0.34	0.58	0.47	1.49
13.	Manipur	0.00	0.00	0.18	0.36	0.13	0.00	0.67
14.	Madhya Pradesh	0.00	0.01	0.36	0.23	0.93	0.36	1.89
15.	Meghalaya	0.00	0.00	0.00	0.00	0.11	0.00	0.11
16.	Mizoram	0.00	0.00	0.00	0.00	0.00	0.38	0.38
17.	Nagaland	0.03	0.12	0.12	0.25	0.25	0.36	1.13
18.	Orissa	0.00	0.02	0.63	0.36	0.07	0.06	1.14
19.	Punjab	0.00	0.01	0.00	0.00	0.00	0.00	0.01
20.	Rajasthan	0.01	0.01	0.14	0.11	0.65	0.86	1.78
21.	Sikkim	0.00	0.05	0.18	0.12	0.20	0.00	0.55
22.	Tamil Nadu	0.00	0.01	0.05	0.09	0.53	0.74	1.42
23.	Uttar Pradesh	0.00	0.78	0.93	0.84	1.01	0.25	3.81
24.	Uttaranchal	0.00	0.00	0.00	0.00	0.00	0.12	0.12
	Total	0.39	1.18	4.47	5.18	7.03	6.12	24.37

ANNEXURE-XLVII

Release of Funds under IWDP Scheme during the Period 1995-96 to 1999-2000 (As on 31-01-01)

(Rs. in crores)

Sl. No.	States	1995-96	1996-97	1997-98	1998-99	1999-2000	2000-01	Total Releases
1	2	3	4	5	6	7	8	9
1.	Andhra Pradesh	7.47	9.76	10.75	9.81	9.49	16.86	64.14
2.	Arunachal Pradesh				0.09			0.09
3.	Assam			0.37	0.25	1.98	2.18	4.78
4.	Bihar	1.66	2.50					4.16
5.	Chhattisgarh	0.24	1.76		0.48	0.80	2.15	5.43
6.	Delhi			2.50				2.50
7.	Gujarat	4.46	6.81	3.07	5.46	4.92	7.58	32.30
8.	Himachal Pradesh	3.46	2.31	3.12	1.88	6.84	6.66	24.27
9.	Haryana	0.27	0.35	1.12	0.91	0.44		3.09
10.	Jammu & Kashmir	0.40		1.00	1.36	1.00	1.68	5.44
11.	Jharkhand	1.85	0.50			0.38		2.73
12.	Karnataka	2.15	0.68	4.34	5.13	7.07	1.91	21.28
13.	Kerala	2.82	0.70	0.40	0.79		0.80	5.51
14.	Maharashtra	0.16	0.13	0.70	2.43	3.48	3.31	10.21
15.	Meghalaya		0.37			0.65		1.02
16.	Manipur	0.30	0.14	1.35	2.85	1.68	2.90	9.22
17.	Madhya Pradesh	1.90	0.20	2.14	2.10	9.31	4.22	19.87
18.	Mizoram	0.30	0.20				2.30	2.80
19.	Nagaland	3.98	3.34	1.20	4.66	2.63	6.95	22.76
20.	Orissa	1.88	2.74	3.54	2.63	5.36	2.53	18.68
21.	Punjab	0.90	0.61		0.07	0.08	0.75	2.41
22.	Rajasthan	5.31	3.93	4.16	2.93	4.87	5.89	27.09
23.	Sikkim	2.16	1.96	1.94	1.76	2.62	1.40	11.84
24.	Tamil Nadu		3.22	2.82	1.76	4.85	7.31	19.96
25.	Tripura		0.30	0.70				1.00
26.	Uttar Pradesh	6.21	7.54	7.91	14.65	14.62	11.14	62.07
27.	Uttaranchal			0.73			1.21	1.94
28.	West Bengal	3.12	0.75					3.87
	Grand Total	51.00	50.80	53.86	62.00	83.07	89.73	390.46

ANNEXURE-XLVIII

Status of Coverage of habitations as reported by the States/UTs till November, 2000

Sl. No.	States/UTs	Status of Coverage (Provisional) NC	PC	FC	Total
1	2	3	4	5	6
1.	Andhra Pradesh	0	20186	49546	69732
2.	Arunachal Pradesh	429	1079	2790	4298
3.	Assam	1200	23979	45490	70669
4.	Bihar (including Jharkhand)	625	144	204667	205436
5.	Goa	16	41	339	396
6.	Gujarat	273	2895	27101	30269
7.	Haryana	8	155	6582	6745
8.	Himachal Pradesh	2250	12374	30743	45367
9.	Jammu & Kashmir	2348	3726	5110	11184
10.	Karnataka	39	22700	33943	56682
11.	Kerala	841	6928	1994	9763
12.	Madhya Pradesh (including Chhattisgarh)	1411	4564	153893	159868
13.	Maharashtra	2490	28088	55352	85930
14.	Manipur	74	469	2248	2791
15.	Meghalaya	603	1127	6909	8639
16.	Mizoram	0	564	347	911
17.	Nagaland	417	670	438	1525
18.	Orissa	271	1136	112692	114099
19.	Punjab	2012	3123	8314	13449
20.	Rajasthan	7541	26834	59571	93946
21.	Sikkim	0	624	1055	1679
22.	Tamil Nadu	0	8101	58530	66631
23.	Tripura	541	1147	5724	7412
24.	Uttar Pradesh (including Uttaranchal)	432	3792	270417	274641
25.	West Bengal	0	20475	58561	79036
26.	A & N Islands	0	155	349	504
27.	Dadra & Nagar Haveli	54	255	207	516
28.	Daman & Diu	0	1	31	32
29.	Delhi	0	0	219	219
30.	Lakshdweep	0	10	0	10
31.	Pondicherry	40	84	143	267
32.	Chandigarh	0	0	18	18
	Total	23915	195426	1203323	1422664

NC=Not Covered; PC=Partially Covered; FC=Fully Covered.

ANNEXURE-XLIX

Physical Progress under Rural Sanitation Programme during 2000-2001

Sl. No.	States/UTs	Month Code	Construction of sanitary latrines						Achievement as %age of annual target
			CRSP		MNP		Total		
			Target	Achievement	Target	Achievement	Target*	Achievement	
1	2	3	4	5	6	7	8	9	10
1.	Andhra Pradesh	0	32587	0	32588	0	65175	0	0.00
2.	Arunachal Pradesh	10	1840	0	1840	0	3680	0	0.00
3.	Assam	06	48632	0	48632	224	97264	224	0.23
4.	Bihar	09	90496	0	90496	0	180992	0	0.00
5.	Goa	10	369	0	370	4159	739	4159	562.79
6.	Gujarat	0	20286	0	20287	0	40573	0	0.00
7.	Haryana	0	10219	0	10219	0	20438	0	0.00
8.	Himachal Pradesh	10	4027	333	4027	127	8054	460	5.71
9.	Jammu & Kashmir	0	5014	0	5015	0	10029	0	0.00
10.	Karnataka	09	26321	13179	26322	22006	52643	35185	66.84
11.	Kerala	10	17025	9908	17026	0	34051	9908	29.10
12.	Madhya Pradesh	09	50006	130	50007	129	100013	259	0.26
13.	Maharashtra	0	45937	0	45938	0	91875	0	0.00
14.	Manipur	0	3249	0	3250	0	6499	0	0.00

(Contd.)

ANNEXURE-XLIX (*Contd.*)

1	2	3	4	5	6	7	8	9	10
15.	Meghalaya	09	3526	0	3527	389	7053	389	5.52
16.	Mizoram	0	907	0	907	0	1814	0	0.00
17.	Nagaland	0	2443	0	2443	0	4886	0	0.00
18.	Orissa	0	30129	0	30130	0	60259	0	0.00
19.	Punjab	0	8857	0	8858	0	17715	0	0.00
20.	Rajasthan	0	27297	0	27298	0	54595	0	0.00
21.	Sikkim	10	902	50	903	200	1805	250	13.85
22.	Tamil Nadu	10	32373	19293	32373	13358	64746	32651	50.43
23.	Tripura	0	5701	0	5701	0	11402	0	0.00
24.	Uttar Pradesh	06	111990	0	111991	0	223981	0	0.00
25.	West Bengal	09	48659	23129	48659	28901	97318	52030	53.46
26.	A & N Islands	0	781	0	781	0	1562	0	0.00
27.	Chandigarh	0	0	0	0	0	0	0	
28.	D & N Haveli	10	621	4	621	0	1242	4	0.32
29.	Daman & Diu	10	123	0	123	0	246	0	0.00
30.	Delhi	0	369	0	370	0	739	0	
31.	Lakshdweep	0	77	0	77	0	154	0	0.00
32.	Pondicherry	10	429	5	429	60	858	650	#DN/017.58
	Total		631192	66031	631208	69553	1262400	135584	10.74

* Tentative.

ANNEXURE-L

Physical Progress under Rural Sanitation Programme (CRSP (ab) + MNP) during 2000-2001

Sl. No.	States/UTs	Month Code	Annual target*	No. of sanitary latrines constd.			Achievement as %age of annual target	No. of Schools covered under sanitation
				SC	ST	Total		
1	2	3	4	5	6	7	8	9
1.	Andhra Pradesh	0	65175	0	0	0	0.00	0
2.	Arunachal Pradesh	10	3680	0	0	0	0.00	0
3.	Assam	06	97264	6	15	224	0.23	0
4.	Bihar	09	180992	0	0	0	0.00	0
5.	Goa	10	739	0	0	4159	562.79	0
6.	Gujarat	0	40573	0	0	0	0.00	0
7.	Haryana	0	20438	0	0	0	0.00	0
8.	Himachal Pradesh	10	8054	22	47	460	5.71	0
9.	Jammu & Kashmir	0	10029	0	0	0	0.00	0
10.	Karnataka	09	52643	7697	3244	35185	66.84	0
11.	Kerala	10	34051	1888	74	9908	29.10	0
12.	Madhya Pradesh	09	100013	0	3	259	0.26	0
13.	Maharashtra	0	91875	0	0	0	0.00	0
14.	Manipur	0	6499	0	0	0	0.00	0
15.	Meghalaya	09	7053	0	389	389	5.52	50
16.	Mizoram	0	1814	0	0	0	0.00	0
17.	Nagaland	0	4886	0	0	0	0.00	0
18.	Orissa	0	60259	0	0	0	0.00	0
19.	Punjab	0	17715	0	0	0	0.00	0
20.	Rajasthan	0	54595	0	0	0	0.00	0
21.	Sikkim	10	1805	0	0	250	13.85	0
22.	Tamil Nadu	10	64746	6951	0	32651	50.43	41
23.	Tripura	0	11402	0	0	0	0.00	0
24.	Uttar Pradesh	06	223981	0	0	0	0.00	0
25.	West Bengal	09	97318	18604	3034	52030	53.46	0
26.	A & N Islands	0	1562	0	0	0	0.00	0
27.	Chandigarh	0	0	0	0	0	#DIV/0!	0
28.	D & N Haveli	10	1242	1	3	4	0.32	0
29.	Daman & Diu	10	246	0	0	0	0.00	0
30.	Delhi	0	739	0	0	0	0.00	0
31.	Lakshdweep	0	154	0	0	0	0.00	0
32.	Pondicherry	10	858	12	0	65	7.58	0
	Total		1262400	35181	6809	135584	10.74	91

* Tentative.

ANNEXURE-LI

Financial Progress under Rural Sanitation Programme (CRSP and MNP) during 2000-2001

Sl. No.	States/UTs	Month Code	Opening balance as on 1-4-2000	Allocation	CRSP		MNP	
					Release	Expend.	Provision	Expend.
1	2	3	4	5	6	7	8	9
1.	Andhra Pradesh	0	340.86	203.67	583.48	0.00	642.12	0.00
2.	Arunachal Pradesh	10	33.68	11.50	0.00	0.00	5.00	0.00
3.	Assam	06	280.04	303.95	0.00	0.00	305.00	5.00
4.	Bihar (Incldg. Jharkhand)	09	918.41	565.60	0.00	0.00	300.00	0.00
5.	Goa	10	8.75	2.31	0.00	0.00	750.00	582.16
6.	Gujarat	0	471.89	126.79	0.00	0.00	1000.00	0.00
7.	Haryana	0	0.00	63.87	0.00	0.00	650.00	0.00
8.	Himachal Pradesh	10	0.76	25.17	12.58	36.45	325.00	10.95
9.	Jammu & Kashmir	0	16.04	31.34	0.00	0.00	523.76	0.00
10.	Karnataka	09	418.96	164.51	82.25	284.61	1500.00	284.62
11.	Kerala	10	469.21	106.41	152.89	179.22	930.00	104.25
12.	M.P. (Incldg. Chhattisgarh)	09	246.57	312.54	156.27	10.66	410.49	10.66
13.	Maharashtra	0	81.05	287.11	143.55	0.00	8448.79	0.00
14.	Manipur	0	48.48	20.31	0.00	0.00	90.08	0.00
15.	Meghalaya	09	6.76	22.04	9.09	4.89	70.00	6.97
16.	Mizoram	0	2.11	5.67	0.00	0.00	10.00	0.00
17.	Nagaland	0	21.00	15.27	0.00	0.00	15.00	0.00
18.	Orissa	0	1343.96	188.31	0.00	0.00	241.00	0.00
19.	Punjab	0	111.43	55.36	0.00	0.00	100.00	0.00
20.	Rajasthan	0	689.12	170.61	0.00	0.00	387.50	0.00
21.	Sikkim	10	23.43	5.64	2.82	7.50	25.00	8.75
22.	Tamil Nadu	10	1070.93	202.33	101.16	379.10	144.53	166.44
23.	Tripura	0	0.00	35.63	0.00	0.00	43.00	0.00
24.	Uttar Pradesh (Incldg. Uttaranchal)	06	787.01	699.94	0.00	0.00	1588.00	0.00
25.	West Bengal	09	147.94	304.12	0.00	50.15	400.00	61.94
26.	A & N Islands	0	0.00	4.88	0.00	0.00	496.83	0.00
27.	Chandigarh	0	0.00	0.00	0.00	0.00	0.00	0.00
28.	D & N Haveli	10	0.64	3.88	0.00	0.05	0.00	0.00
29.	Daman & Diu	10	5.87	0.77	0.00	0.00	5.00	0.00
30.	Delhi	0	0.00	2.31	0.00	0.00	25.00	0.00
31.	Lakshdweep	0	3.50	0.48	0.00	0.00	2.00	0.00
32.	Pondicherry	10	0.35	2.68	0.00	0.14	18.18	2.55
	Total		7548.75	3945.00	1244.09	952.77	19451.28	1244.29

ANNEXURE-LII

Financial Progress under Rural Sanitation Programme (MNP) during 2000-2001

(Rs. in lakhs)

Sl. No.	States/UTs	CENTRAL SECTOR (CENTRAL RURAL SANITATION PROGRAMME)													Exp. on SC/ST as %age of Total expenditure	Exp. as %age of Available	Exp. as %age of Allocation
		Month Code	Opening balance as on 1-4-2000			Allocation	Releases			Total Availability of Funds (6+10)	Expenditure incurred						
			Normal	Model villages	Total		CRSP Normal	Model villages	Total (8+9)		Total	Model Villages	SC	ST			
1	2	3	4	5	6	7	8	9	10	11	12	13	14	15	16	17	18
1.	Andhra Pradesh	0	0.00	340.86	340.86	203.67	101.83	481.65	583.48	924.34	0.00	0.00	0.00	0.00	#DIV/0!	0.00	0.00
2.	Arunachal Pradesh	10	33.68		33.68	11.50	0.00		0.00	33.68	0.00	0.00	0.00	0.00	#DIV/0!	0.00	0.00
3.	Assam	06	260.37	19.67	280.04	303.95	0.00		0.00	280.04	0.00	0.00	0.00	0.00	#DIV/0!	0.00	0.00
4.	Bihar (Incldg. Jharkhand)	09	885.24	33.17	918.41	565.60	0.00		0.00	918.41	0.00	0.00	0.00	0.00	#DIV/0!	0.00	0.00
5.	Goa	10	8.75		8.75	2.31	0.00		0.00	8.75	0.00	0.00	0.00	0.00	#DIV/0!	0.00	0.00
6.	Gujarat	0	471.89		471.89	126.79	0.00		0.00	471.89	0.00	0.00	0.00	0.00	#DIV/0!	0.00	0.00
7.	Haryana	0	0.00		0.00	63.87	0.00		0.00	0.00	0.00	0.00	0.00	0.00	#DIV/0!	#DIV/0!	0.00
8.	Himachal Pradesh	10	0.00	0.76	0.76	25.17	12.58		12.58	13.34	36.45	0.00	0.99	0.15	3.13	273.24	144.82
9.	Jammu & Kashmir	0	16.04		16.04	31.34	0.00		0.00	16.04	0.00	0.00	0.00	0.00	#DIV/0!	0.00	0.00
10.	Karnataka	09	404.89	14.07	418.96	164.51	82.25		82.25	501.21	284.61	0.00	59.96	16.92	27.01	56.78	173.00
11.	Kerala	10	181.56	287.65	469.21	106.41	53.20	99.69	152.89	622.10	179.22	0.00	24.17	0.81	13.94	28.81	168.42
12.	Madhya Pradesh (Incldg. Chhattisgarh)	09	239.25	7.32	246.57	312.54	156.27		156.27	402.84	10.66	0.00	0.00	3.30	30.96	2.65	3.41

(Contd.)

ANNEXURE-LII (*Contd.*)

1	2	3	4	5	6	7	8	9	10	11	12	13	14	15	16	17	18
13.	Maharashtra	0	0.00	81.05	81.05	287.11	143.55		143.55	224.60	0.00	0.00	0.00	0.00	#DIV/0!	0.00	0.00
14.	Manipur	0	48.48		48.48	20.31	0.00		0.00	48.48	0.00	0.00	0.00	0.00	#DIV/0!	0.00	0.00
15.	Meghalaya	09	6.76		6.76	22.04	9.09		9.09	15.85	4.89	0.00	0.00	4.89	100.00	30.85	22.19
16.	Mizoram	0	2.11		2.11	5.67	0.00		0.00	2.11	0.00	0.00	0.00	0.00	#DIV/0!	0.00	0.00
17.	Nagaland	0	21.00		21.00	15.27	0.00		0.00	21.00	0.00	0.00	0.00	0.00	#DIV/0!	0.00	0.00
18.	Orissa	0	1330.00	13.96	1343.96	188.31	0.00		0.00	1343.96	0.00	0.00	0.00	0.00	#DIV/0!	0.00	0.00
19.	Punjab	0	111.43		111.43	55.36	0.00		0.00	111.43	0.00	0.00	0.00	0.00	#DIV/0!	0.00	0.00
20.	Rajasthan	0	633.21	55.91	689.12	170.61	0.00		0.00	689.12	0.00	0.00	0.00	0.00	#DIV/0!	0.00	0.00
21.	Sikkim	10	23.43		23.43	5.64	2.82		2.82	26.25	7.50	0.00	0.75	1.87	34.93	28.57	132.98
22.	Tamil Nadu	10	1045.85	25.08	1070.93	202.33	101.16		101.16	1172.09	379.10	0.00	25.15	0.00	6.63	32.34	187.37
23.	Tripura	0	0.00		0.00	35.63	0.00		0.00	0.00	0.00	0.00	0.00	0.00	#DIV/0!	#DIV/0!	0.00
24.	Uttar Pradesh (Incldg. Uttaranchal)	06	739.52	47.49	787.01	699.94	0.00		0.00	787.01	0.00	0.00	0.00	0.00	#DIV/0!	0.00	0.00
25.	West Bengal	09	147.94		147.94	304.12	0.00		0.00	147.94	50.15	0.00	1.40	0.47	3.73	33.90	16.49
26.	A & N Islands	0	0.00		0.00	4.88	0.00		0.00	0.00	0.00	0.00	0.00	0.00	#DIV/0!	#DIV/0!	0.00
27.	Chandigarh	0	0.00		0.00	0.00	0.00		0.00	0.00	0.00	0.00	0.00	0.00	#DIV/0!	#DIV/0!	#DIV/0!
28.	D & N Haveli	10	0.64		0.64	3.88	0.00		0.00	0.64	0.05	0.00	0.02	0.03	100.00	7.81	1.29
29.	Daman & Diu	10	5.87		5.87	0.77	0.00		0.00	5.87	0.00	0.00	0.00	0.00	#DIV/0!	0.00	0.00
30.	Delhi	0	0.00		0.00	2.31	0.00		0.00	0.00	0.00	0.00	0.00	0.00	#DIV/0!	#DIV/0!	0.00
31.	Lakshdweep	0	3.50		3.50	0.48	0.00		0.00	3.50	0.00	0.00	0.00	0.00	#DIV/0!	0.00	0.00
32.	Pondicherry	10	0.35		0.35	2.68	0.00		0.00	0.35	0.14	0.00	0.09	0.00	64.29	40.00	5.22
	Total		6621.76	926.99	7548.75	3945.00	662.75	581.34	1244.09	8792.84	952.77	0.00	112.53	28.44	14.80	10.84	24.15

ANNEXURE-LIII

Financial Progress under Rural Sanitation Programme (MNP) during 2000-2001

(Rs. in lakhs)

Sl. No.	States/UTs	Month Code	STATE SECTOR (MINIMUM NEEDS PROGRAMME)					
			Provision	Expenditure incurred			Exp. on SC/ST as %age of total exp.	Exp. as %age of provi-sion
				Total	SC	ST		
1	2	3	4	5	6	7	8	9
1.	Andhra Pradesh	0	642.12	0.00	0.00	0.00	#DIV/0!	0.00
2.	Arunachal Pradesh	10	5.00	0.00	0.00	0.00	#DIV/0!	0.00
3.	Assam	06	305.00	5.00	0.00	0.00	0.00	1.64
4.	Bihar	09	300.00	0.00	0.00	0.00	#DIV/0!	0.00
5.	Goa	10	750.00	582.16	0.00	0.00	0.00	77.62
6.	Gujarat	0	1000.00	0.00	0.00	0.00	#DIV/0!	0.00
7.	Haryana	0	650.00	0.00	0.00	0.00	#DIV/0!	0.00
8.	Himachal Pradesh	10	325.00	10.95	1.99	0.22	20.18	3.37
9.	Jammu & Kashmir	0	523.76	0.00	0.00	0.00	#DIV/0!	0.00
10.	Karnataka	09	1500.00	284.62	59.97	16.92	27.01	18.97
11.	Kerala	10	930.00	104.25	2.89	0.00	2.77	11.21
12.	Madhya Pradesh	09	410.49	10.66	0.00	3.29	30.86	2.60

(*Contd.*)

ANNEXURE-LIII (*Contd.*)

1	2	3	4	5	6	7	8	9
13.	Maharashtra	0	8448.79	0.00	0.00	0.00	#DIV/0!	0.00
14.	Manipur	0	90.08	0.00	0.00	0.00	#DIV/0!	0.00
15.	Meghalaya	09	70.00	6.97	0.00	6.97	100.00	9.96
16.	Mizoram	0	10.00	0.00	0.00	0.00	#DIV/0!	0.00
17.	Nagaland	0	15.00	0.00	0.00	0.00	#DIV/0!	0.00
18.	Orissa	0	241.00	0.00	0.00	0.00	#DIV/0!	0.00
19.	Punjab	0	100.00	0.00	0.00	0.00	#DIV/0!	0.00
20.	Rajasthan	0	387.50	0.00	0.00	0.00	#DIV/0!	0.00
21.	Sikkim	10	25.00	8.75	0.88	2.19	35.09	35.00
22.	Tamil Nadu	10	144.53	166.44	18.34	0.00	11.02	115.16
23.	Tripura	0	43.00	0.00	0.00	0.00	#DIV/0!	0.00
24.	Uttar Pradesh	06	1588.00	0.00	0.00	0.00	#DIV/0!	0.00
25.	West Bengal	09	400.00	61.94	2.68	0.59	5.28	15.48
26.	A & N Islands	0	496.83	0.00	0.00	0.00	#DIV/0!	0.00
27.	Chandigarh	0	0.00	0.00	0.00	0.00	#DIV/0!	#DIV/0!
28.	D & N Haveli	10	0.00	0.00	0.00	0.00	#DIV/0!	#DIV/0!
29.	Daman & Diu	10	5.00	0.00	0.00	0.00	#DIV/0!	0.00
30.	Delhi	0	25.00	0.00	0.00	0.00	#DIV/0!	0.00
31.	Lakshdweep	0	2.00	0.00	0.00	0.00	#DIV/0!	0.00
32.	Pondicherry	10	18.18	2.55	0.79	0.00	30.98	14.03
	Total		19451.28	1244.29	87.54	30.18	9.46	6.40

Statistical Tables

TABLE 1

Index Numbers of Agricultural Production

(Base : Triennium ending 1981-82 = 100)

	Weight	1970-71	1980-81	1990-91	1995-96	1996-97	1997-98	1998-99	1999-2000	2000-01*
A. Foodgrains	62.92	87.9	104.9	143.7	146.1	160.9	155.7	165.2	169.7	157.5
(a) Cereals	54.98	84.1	105.0	144.2	149.8	163.9	159.9	168.0	175.1	165.1
Rice	29.74	84.4	107.8	149.4	154.8	164.4	166.0	173.0	180.3	170.7
Wheat	14.45	67.7	103.2	156.6	176.4	197.0	188.5	202.5	217.0	195.4
Coarse Cereals	10.79	105.4	99.8	113.1	100.2	118.2	104.9	108.1	104.8	109.0
(b) Pulses	7.94	113.6	104.1	140.5	121.0	140.1	126.9	145.8	132.1	105.4
Gram	3.07	126.3	105.4	130.2	121.1	135.3	149.1	165.3	124.4	85.6
B. Non-foodgrains	37.08	82.6	97.1	156.3	185.4	200.9	181.6	199.4	185.6	174.8
(a) Oilseeds Total	12.64	97.1	95.1	179.5	212.1	231.3	198.2	224.9	193.7	175.4
Groundnut	5.60	101.8	83.4	125.3	126.4	144.1	122.9	149.7	87.7	103.7
Rapeseed and Mustard	2.41	97.2	113.0	256.3	294.0	326.3	230.5	277.6	283.7	206.2

(*Contd.*)

TABLE 1 (*Contd.*)

	Weight	1970-71	1980-81	1990-91	1995-96	1996-97	1997-98	1998-99	1999-2000	2000-01*
(b) Fibres	5.09	65.6	94.2	128.2	161.8	181.3	142.5	156.9	136.5	115.0
Cotton	4.37	63.4	93.2	130.9	171.0	189.2	144.3	163.4	153.3	128.3
Jute	0.55	76.5	100.8	122.6	118.8	154.2	154.2	136.8	26.3	25.8
Mesta	0.14	77.3	96.7	76.7	66.3	68.4	61.9	57.0	65.1	65.7
(c) Plantation Crops	2.29	73.2	76.0	144.9	176.5	182.4	186.2	188.6	188.1	188.1
Tea	1.46	74.7	101.6	132.3	139.1	144.5	144.5	144.5	143.6	143.6
Coffee	0.44	79.1	85.1	122.3	160.5	148.2	148.2	148.2	148.2	148.2
Rubber	0.39	60.8	101.1	217.2	334.6	362.6	385.3	399.3	399.3	399.3
(d) Others										
Sugarcane	8.11	81.2	98.8	154.3	179.9	177.6	178.9	184.8	191.6	191.5
Tobacco	1.12	75.5	100.2	115.8	111.5	128.7	132.9	153.3	100.2	100.2
Potato	2.09	50.2	103.9	163.3	202.4	260.1	189.5	253.6	265.0	239.2
C. All Commodities	100.00	85.9	102.1	148.4	160.7	175.7	165.3	177.9	175.6	163.9

* Provisional for plantation crops, tobacco, potato, non-foodgrain and all commodities.

Source: Directorate of Economics & Statistics, Department of Agriculture & Cooperation.

TABLE 2

Index Numbers of Area under Principal Crops

(Base : Triennium ending 1981-82 = 100)

	1970-71	1980-81	1990-91	1995-96	1996-97	1997-98	1998-99	1999-2000	2000-01*
A. Foodgrains	97.9	99.8	100.7	95.3	97.4	97.6	102.0	97.0	94.4
(a) Cereals	97.9	100.1	99.1	94.8	97.1	97.0	101.9	97.9	95.8
Rice	93.6	100.2	106.5	106.9	108.4	108.4	122.8	112.7	110.7
Wheat	82.2	100.4	108.9	112.7	116.7	120.3	124.0	123.9	113.0
Coarse Cereals	110.1	99.9	86.7	73.7	75.9	73.6	70.0	70.0	72.4
(b) Pulses	98.0	98.6	108.4	97.9	98.6	100.5	102.9	92.8	88.0
Gram	109.5	92.1	105.3	99.7	95.9	105.9	117.8	86.1	68.5
B. Non-foodgrains	91.1	99.4	120.0	131.7	134.6	133.6	134.9	130.9	127.4
(a) Oilseeds Total	94.2	98.5	122.9	136.9	138.9	137.0	139.3	129.9	125.6
Groundnut	102.8	95.4	116.6	105.6	106.6	99.5	103.8	96.4	94.5
Rapeseed and Mustard	84.8	102.2	143.7	162.7	162.7	175.0	161.9	149.8	111.2

(Contd.)

TABLE 2 (*Contd.*)

	1970-71	1980-81	1990-91	1995-96	1996-97	1997-98	1998-99	1999-2000	2000-01*
(b) Fibres	94.6	98.8	91.1	107.1	109.8	107.2	111.3	104.6	102.9
Cotton	95.1	97.7	92.9	112.8	113.9	110.8	116.7	108.8	107.1
Jute	86.4	108.5	89.7	85.0	103.5	104.6	97.9	97.7	95.4
Mesta	93.1	101.1	67.1	53.1	57.4	56.4	49.8	52.2	50.6
(c) Plantation Crops	79.8	100.5	122.5	139.6	140.9	142.7	146.9	144.2	161.8
Tea	93.2	100.5	110.3	113.1	113.8	113.8	113.8	113.8	115.3
Coffee	64.8	100.6	111.1	146.0	145.4	146.4	157.5	157.5	160.7
Rubber	73.0	100.4	158.2	184.0	188.8	194.7	199.9	188.8	253.6
(d) Others									
Sugarcane	91.5	94.4	130.4	146.8	147.7	139.1	143.5	149.3	152.0
Tobacco	101.5	102.5	93.3	89.7	97.2	105.3	105.3	105.3	97.7
Potato	62.2	100.6	128.6	152.4	171.7	165.8	176.0	183.8	168.7
C. All Commodities	96.3	99.7	105.2	103.8	106.0	105.9	109.6	104.8	102.0

* Provisional for plantation crops, tobacco, potato, non-foodgrain and all commodities.

Source: Directorate of Economics & Statistics, Department of Agriculture & Cooperation.

TABLE 3

Index Numbers of Yield of Principal Crops

(Base : Triennium ending 1981-82 = 100)

	1970-71	1980-81	1990-91	1995-96	1996-97	1997-98	1998-99	1999-2000	2000-01*
A. Foodgrains	93.2	105.1	137.8	143.1	154.5	148.4	146.8	159.8	153.8
(a) Cereals	89.9	104.9	139.3	146.3	156.7	152.0	148.3	162.3	158.2
Rice	90.2	107.7	140.2	144.8	151.7	153.1	140.8	160.0	154.2
Wheat	82.4	102.8	143.8	156.5	168.9	156.7	163.3	175.2	172.9
Coarse Cereals	97.0	100.2	128.8	131.9	151.3	137.8	148.9	143.0	145.1
(b) Pulses	114.4	106.6	128.1	120.3	139.1	123.1	136.2	139.6	118.1
Gram	115.3	114.3	123.6	121.5	141.1	140.7	140.4	144.5	125.0
B. Non-foodgrains	91.4	99.2	128.0	135.7	143.8	132.3	141.5	134.1	129.2
(a) Oilseeds Total	102.2	96.8	132.1	141.6	152.3	132.0	147.9	136.2	130.7
Groundnut	99.0	87.5	107.4	119.7	135.2	123.6	144.3	91.0	109.8
Rapeseed and Mustard	114.7	110.6	178.3	180.7	200.6	131.7	171.5	189.4	185.4

(Contd.)

TABLE 3 (*Contd.*)

	1970-71	1980-81	1990-91	1995-96	1996-97	1997-98	1998-99	1999-2000	2000-01*
(b) Fibres	69.5	95.1	139.9	150.1	163.6	131.8	139.6	129.3	110.7
Cotton	66.7	95.4	140.8	151.5	166.1	130.3	140.0	140.9	119.8
Jute	88.6	92.9	136.6	139.7	148.9	147.5	139.8	26.9	27.0
Mesta	83.1	95.6	114.3	124.7	119.1	109.7	114.5	124.6	129.7
(c) Plantation Crops	86.8	97.9	122.2	134.2	137.5	139.2	137.8	139.3	127.5
Tea	80.2	101.1	119.9	123.0	127.0	127.0	127.0	126.2	124.6
Coffee	122.0	84.6	110.2	110.0	101.9	101.2	94.1	94.1	92.2
Rubber	83.2	100.7	137.5	181.8	192.1	197.9	199.8	211.5	157.5
(d) Others									
Sugarcane	88.8	104.6	118.3	122.6	120.3	128.7	128.8	128.3	125.9
Tobacco	74.4	97.7	124.0	124.3	132.3	126.2	144.6	95.1	102.5
Potato	80.7	103.4	127.0	132.8	151.5	114.3	144.1	144.1	141.8
C. All Commodities	92.6	102.9	133.8	139.8	149.8	141.4	144.6	148.6	143.1

* Provisional for plantation crops, tobacco, potato, non-foodgrain and all commodities.

Source: Directorate of Economics & Statistics, Department of Agriculture & Cooperation.

TABLE 4

Production of Major Crops

(Million Units)

Group/Commodity	Unit	1960-61	1970-71	1980-81	1990-91	1994-95	1995-96	1996-97	1997-98	1998-99	1999-2000	2000-01
Foodgrains	Tonnes	82.0	108.4	129.6	176.4	191.5	180.4	199.4	192.3	203.6	209.8	195.9
Kharif	Tonnes	NA	68.9	77.7	99.4	101.1	95.1	103.9	101.6	102.9	105.5	103.4
Rabi	Tonnes	NA	39.5	51.9	77.0	90.4	85.3	95.5	90.7	100.7	104.3	92.5
Cereals	Tonnes	69.3	96.6	119.0	162.1	177.5	168.1	185.2	179.3	188.7	196.4	185.2
Kharif	Tonnes	NA	65.0	73.9	94.0	96.4	90.5	98.4	97.3	97.8	100.7	98.9
Rabi	Tonnes	NA	31.6	45.1	68.1	81.1	77.6	86.8	82.0	90.9	95.7	86.3
Pulses	Tonnes	12.7	11.8	10.6	14.3	14.1	12.3	14.2	13.0	14.9	13.4	10.7
Kharif	Tonnes	NA	3.9	3.8	5.4	4.7	4.6	5.5	4.3	5.1	4.8	4.5
Rabi	Tonnes	NA	7.9	6.8	8.9	9.4	7.7	8.7	8.7	9.8	8.6	6.2
Rice	Tonnes	34.6	42.2	53.6	74.3	81.8	77.0	81.7	82.5	86.1	89.7	84.9
Kharif	Tonnes	NA	39.5	50.1	66.3	72.6	67.9	71.3	72.5	72.7	77.5	73.4
Rabi	Tonnes	NA	2.7	3.5	8.0	9.2	9.1	10.4	10.0	13.4	12.2	11.5
Wheat	Tonnes	11.0	23.8	36.3	55.1	65.8	62.1	69.4	66.3	71.3	76.4	68.7

(*Contd.*)

TABLE 4 (*Contd.*)

Group/Commodity	Unit	1960-61	1970-71	1980-81	1990-91	1994-95	1995-96	1996-97	1997-98	1998-99	1999-2000	2000-01
Jowar	Tonnes	9.8	8.1	10.4	11.7	9.0	9.3	10.9	7.5	8.4	8.7	7.7
Kharif	Tonnes	NA	5.8	7.5	8.3	5.9	5.6	7.0	5.0	5.3	4.8	4.7
Rabi	Tonnes	NA	2.3	2.9	3.4	3.1	3.7	3.9	2.5	3.1	3.9	3.0
Maize	Tonnes	4.1	7.5	7.0	9.0	8.9	9.5	10.8	10.8	11.1	11.5	12.1
Bajra	Tonnes	3.3	8.0	5.3	6.9	7.2	5.4	7.9	7.6	7.0	5.8	7.1
Gram	Tonnes	6.3	5.2	4.3	5.4	6.4	5.0	5.6	6.1	6.8	5.1	3.5
Tur	Tonnes	2.1	1.9	2.0	2.4	2.1	2.3	2.7	1.8	2.7	2.7	2.3
Oilseeds*	Tonnes	7.0	9.6	9.4	18.6	21.3	22.1	24.4	21.3	24.7	20.7	18.4
Kharif	Tonnes	NA	7.0	5.0	9.8	11.9	13.1	14.4	14.1	15.8	12.5	11.8
Rabi	Tonnes	NA	2.6	4.4	8.8	9.4	9.0	10.0	7.2	8.9	8.2	6.6
Groundnut	Tonnes	4.8	6.1	5.0	7.5	8.1	7.6	8.6	7.4	9.0	5.3	6.2
Kharif	Tonnes	NA	NA	3.7	5.1	6.1	6.1	6.9	5.9	6.9	3.8	4.7
Rabi	Tonnes	NA	NA	1.3	2.4	2.0	1.5	1.7	1.5	2.1	1.5	1.5
Rapeseed and Mustard	Tonnes	1.4	2.0	2.3	5.2	5.8	6.0	6.7	4.7	5.7	5.8	4.2
Sugarcane	Tonnes	110.0	126.4	154.2	241.0	275.5	281.1	277.6	279.5	288.7	299.3	299.2

Cotton	Bales@	5.6	4.8	7.0	9.8	11.9	12.9	14.2	10.9	12.3	11.5	9.7
Jute and Mesta	Bales+	5.3	6.2	8.2	9.2	9.1	8.8	11.2	11.1	9.8	10.6	10.5
Jute	Bales+	4.1	4.9	6.5	7.9	8.0	7.7	10.0	10.0	8.8	9.4	9.3
Mesta	Bales+	1.1	1.3	1.7	1.3	1.1	1.1	1.2	1.1	1.0	1.2	1.2
Plantation Crops												
Tea	Tonnes	0.3	0.4	0.6	0.7	0.8	0.8	0.8	0.8	0.8	0.8	0.8
Coffee	Tonnes	Neg.	0.1	0.1	0.2	0.2	0.2	0.2	0.2	0.3	0.3	0.3
Rubber	Tonnes	Neg.	0.1	0.2	0.3	0.5	0.5	0.5	0.6	0.6	0.6	0.6
Potato	Tonnes	2.7	4.8	9.7	15.2	17.4	18.8	24.2	17.6	23.6	24.7	22.1

NA: Not Available.

* Include groundnut, rapeseed & mustard, sesamum, linseed, castorseed, nigerseed, safflower, sunflower and soyabean.

@ Bale of 170 Kgs.

+ Bale of 180 Kgs.

Neg. Negligible.

Sources: (1) Directorate of Economics & Statistics, Department of Agriculture & Cooperation.

(2) Ministry of Commerce & Industry.

TABLE 5

Gross Area under Major Crops

(Million hectares)

Group/Commodity	1960-61	1970-71	1980-81	1990-91	1994-95	1995-96	1996-97	1997-98	1998-99	1999-2000	2000-01
Foodgrains	115.6	124.3	126.7	127.8	123.7	121.0	123.6	123.8	125.2	123.1	119.8
Kharif	NA	82.3	83.2	80.8	75.0	73.6	75.4	74.1	74.0	73.2	75.2
Rabi	NA	42.0	43.5	47.0	48.7	47.4	48.2	49.7	51.2	49.9	44.6
Cereals	92.0	101.8	104.2	103.2	100.7	98.7	101.1	101.0	101.7	102.0	99.8
Kharif	NA	72.9	72.8	69.3	64.5	63.4	64.6	63.7	63.7	63.4	64.5
Rabi	NA	28.9	31.4	33.9	36.2	35.3	36.5	37.3	38.0	38.6	35.3
Pulses	23.6	22.6	22.5	24.7	23.0	22.3	22.4	22.9	23.5	21.1	20.0
Kharif	NA	9.5	10.4	11.5	10.5	10.2	10.7	10.5	10.3	9.8	10.7
Rabi	NA	13.1	12.1	13.2	12.5	12.1	11.7	12.4	13.2	11.3	9.3
Rice	34.1	37.6	40.1	42.7	42.8	42.8	43.4	43.4	44.8	45.2	44.3
Kharif	NA	36.0	38.4	39.7	39.4	39.4	39.8	39.8	40.5	41.0	40.5
Rabi	NA	1.6	1.7	3.0	3.4	3.4	3.6	3.6	4.3	4.2	3.8
Wheat	12.9	18.2	22.3	24.2	25.7	25.0	25.9	26.7	27.5	27.5	25.1
Jowar	18.4	17.4	15.8	14.4	11.5	11.3	11.4	10.8	9.8	10.2	10.0
Kharif	NA	10.9	10.2	8.6	5.9	5.7	5.7	5.2	5.0	4.8	4.9
Rabi	NA	6.5	5.6	5.8	5.6	5.6	5.7	5.6	4.8	5.4	5.1

Maize	4.4	5.8	6.0	5.9	6.1	6.0	6.3	6.3	6.2	6.4	6.6
Bajra	11.5	12.9	11.7	10.5	10.2	9.3	10.0	9 .7	9.3	8.9	9.8
Gram	9.3	7.8	6.6	7.5	7.5	7.1	6.8	7.6	8.5	6.2	4.9
Tur	2.4	2.7	2.8	3.6	3.3	3.4	3.5	3.4	3.4	3.4	3.7
Oilseeds*	13.8	16.6	17.6	24.1	25.3	26.0	26.3	26.1	26.2	23.2	22.3
Kharif	NA	10.8	10.2	14.0	15.0	15.7	16.0	15.5	15.9	15.3	16.0
Rabi	NA	5.8	7.4	10.1	10.3	10.3	10.3	10.6	10.3	7.9	6.3
Groundnut	6.5	7.3	6.8	8.3	7.8	7.5	7.6	7.1	7.4	6.9	6.7
Kharif	NA	NA	5.9	6.8	6.6	6.5	6.5	6.1	5.9	5.8	5.7
Rabi	NA	NA	0.9	1.5	1.2	1.0	1.1	1.0	1.5	1.1	1.0
Rapeseed and Mustard	2.9	3.3	4.1	5.8	6.1	6.5	6.5	7.0	6.5	6.0	4.5
Sugarcane	2.4	2.6	2.7	3.7	3.9	4.1	4.2	3.9	4.1	4.2	4.3
Cotton	7.6	7.6	7.8	7.4	7.9	9.0	9.1	8.9	9.3	8.7	8.6
Jute and Mesta	0.9	1.1	1.3	1.0	0.9	0.9	1.1	1.1	1.0	1.0	1.0
Jute	0.6	0.8	0.9	0.8	0.7	0.7	0.9	0.9	0.8	0.8	0.8
Mesta	0.3	0.3	0.4	0.2	0.2	0.2	0.2	0.2	0.2	0.2	0.2

(Contd.)

TABLE 5 (*Contd.*)

Group/Commodity	1960-61	1970-71	1980-81	1990-91	1994-95	1995-96	1996-97	1997-98	1998-99	1999-2000	2000-01
Plantation crops											
Tea (Total area)	0.3	0.4	0.4	0.4	0.4	0.4	0.4	0.4	0.4	0.4	NA
Coffee (Plucked area)	0.1	NA	0.2	0.2	0.2	0.2	0.3	0.3	0.3	0.3	0.3
Rubber (Tapped area)	0.1	0.1	0.2	0.3	0.3	0.4	0.4	0.5	0.5	0.5	0.6
Potato	0.4	0.5	0.7	0.9	1.1	1.1	1.2	1.2	1.3	1.3	1.2

NA: Not Available.

* Include groundnut, rapeseed & mustard, sesamum, linseed, castorseed, nigerseed, safflower, sunflower and soyabean.

Sources: (1) Directorate of Economics & Statistics, Department of Agriculture & Cooperation.

(2) Ministry of Commerce & Industry.

TABLE 6

Yield Per Hectare of Major Crops

(Kg./hectare)

Group/Commodity	1960-61	1970-71	1980-81	1990-91	1994-95	1995-96	1996-97	1997-98	1998-99	1999-2000	2000-01
Foodgrains	710	872	1023	1380	1548	1491	1614	1552	1627	1704	1636
Kharif	NA	837	933	1231	1341	1292	1379	1370	1391	1441	1376
Rabi	NA	942	1195	1635	1864	1799	1980	1825	1967	2091	2073
Cereals	753	949	1142	1571	1763	1703	1831	1775	1856	1926	2622
Kharif	NA	892	1015	1357	1486	1428	1523	1529	1536	1587	1535
Rabi	NA	1093	1434	2010	2260	2195	2376	2196	2391	2483	2445
Pulses	539	524	473	578	610	552	635	567	634	635	533
Kharif	NA	410	361	471	351	448	512	409	497	492	417
Rabi	NA	607	571	672	589	640	747	702	743	760	665
Rice	1013	1123	1336	1740	1911	1797	1882	1900	1921	1986	1913
Kharif	NA	1100	1303	1670	1841	1721	1773	1821	1798	1892	1810
Rabi	NA	1625	2071	2671	2731	2678	2856	2765	3073	2897	3002

(*Contd.*)

TABLE 6 (*Contd.*)

Group/Commodity	1960-61	1970-71	1980-81	1990-91	1994-95	1995-96	1996-97	1997-98	1998-99	1999-2000	2000-01
Wheat	851	1307	1630	2281	2559	2483	2679	2485	2590	2778	2743
Jowar	533	466	660	814	779	823	956	697	859	847	772
Kharif	NA	533	737	969	988	996	1214	954	1047	998	950
Rabi	NA	354	520	582	555	650	696	458	660	713	600
Maize	926	1279	1159	1518	1448	1595	1720	1711	1797	1792	1841
Bajra	286	622	458	658	700	577	788	791	748	650	719
Gram	674	663	657	712	853	700	813	811	803	833	720
Tur	849	709	689	673	644	670	756	551	787	786	616
Oilseeds*	507	579	532	771	843	851	926	816	944	892	826
Kharif	NA	649	492	698	797	835	902	913	992	813	737
Rabi	NA	449	588	872	910	876	963	675	868	1046	1051
Groundnut	745	834	736	904	1027	1007	1138	1040	1214	766	924
Kharif	NA	NA	629	751	913	928	1076	974	1174	655	817
Rabi	NA	NA	1444	1611	1650	1529	1490	1434	1370	1373	1563

Rapeseed and Mustard	467	594	560	904	950	916	1017	668	870	960	941
Sugarcane (tonnes/hect.)	46	48	58	65	71	68	66	71	71	71	69
Cotton	125	106	152	225	257	242	265	208	224	225	191
Jute and mesta	1049	1032	1130	1634	1760	1712	1818	1792	1722	1841	1852
Jute	1183	1186	1245	1833	1949	1875	1998	1978	1875	2005	2014
Mesta	742	684	828	988	1023	1078	1030	949	990	1078	1154
Plantation Crops											
Tea	971	1182	1491	1794	1770	1815	1875	1865	1995	1840	NA
Coffee @	448	NA	624	732	788	922	818	799	877	947	959
Rubber @	354	653	788	1076	1362	1422	1503	1549	1563	1576	1576
Potato (tonnes/hect.)	7	10	13	16	16	17	19	15	18	18	18

NA: Not Available.

* Include groundnut, rapeseed & mustard, sesamum, linseed, castorseed, nigerseed, safflower, sunflower and soyabean.

Sources: (1) Directorate of Economics & Statistics, Department of Agriculture & Cooperation.

(2) @ Ministry of Commerce and Industry.

TABLE 7

Three Largest Producing States of Important Crops during 1999-2000

(Production Million Tonnes)

Crops	States	Production	Per cent Share of Production to All India	Cumulative per cent of Production
I. Foodgrains				
Rice	West Bengal	13.95	15.59	15.59
	Uttar Pradesh	12.91	14.43	30.02
	Andhra Pradesh	10.49	11.72	41.74
Wheat	Uttar Pradesh	25.98	34.38	34.38
	Punjab	15.91	21.05	55.43
	Haryana	9.64	12.76	68.19
Maize	Karnataka	1.69	14.73	14.73
	Bihar	1.61	14.04	28.77
	Andhra Pradesh	1.4	12.21	40.98
Total Coarse Cereals	Maharashtra	6.45	21.16	21.16
	Karnataka	5.25	17.22	38.39
	Uttar Pradesh	3.75	12.30	50.69
Total Pulses	Madhya Pradesh	3.80	28.46	28.46
	Uttar Pradesh	2.60	19.48	47.94
	Maharashtra	2.19	16.40	64.34
Total Foodgrains	Uttar Pradesh	45.24	21.66	21.66
	Punjab	25.20	12.06	33.72
	Madhya Pradesh	21.02	10.06	43.79
II. Oilseeds				
Groundnut	Tamil Nadu	1.38	25.99	25.99
	Andhra Pradesh	1.12	21.09	47.08
	Karnataka	0.79	14.88	61.96

(Contd.)

TABLE 7 (*Contd.*)

Crops	States	Production	Per cent Share of Production to All India	Cumulative per cent of Production
Rapeseed & Mustard	Rajasthan	2.65	44.46	44.46
	Uttar Pradesh	1.09	18.29	62.75
	Madhya Pradesh	0.67	11.24	73.99
Soyabean	Madhya Pradesh	4.45	65.54	65.54
	Maharashtra	1.62	23.86	89.40
	Rajasthan	0.60	8.84	98.23
Sunflower	Andhra Pradesh	0.23	28.75	28.75
	Karnataka	0.21	26.25	55.00
	Maharashtra	0.21	26.25	81.25
Total Oilseeds	Madhya Pradesh	5.59	26.78	26.78
	Rajasthan	3.58	17.15	43.94
	Maharashtra	2.64	12.65	56.59
III. Other Cash Crops				
Sugarcane	Uttar Pradesh	115.42	38.57	38.57
	Maharashtra	53.14	17.76	56.33
	Karnataka	36.51	12.20	68.53
Cotton@	Maharashtra	3.10	26.63	26.63
	Gujarat	2.09	17.96	44.59
	Andhra Pradesh	1.60	13.75	58.33
Jute & Mesta$	West Bengal	7.68	72.93	72.93
	Bihar	1.28	12.16	85.09
	Assam	0.68	6.46	91.55
Potato	Uttar Pradesh	10.46	41.82	41.82
	West Bengal	7.48	29.93	71.75
	Bihar	1.72	6.88	78.63
Onion	Maharashtra	1.39	28.42	28.42
	Karnataka	0.59	12.14	40.56
	Andhra Pradesh	0.52	10.67	51.23

@ Production in million bales of 170 kgs. each.

$ Production in million bales of 180 kgs. each.

Source : Directorate of Economics & Statistics, Department of Agriculture & Cooperation.

TABLE 8

Irrigated Area under Different Crops

(Million hectares)

	1970-71	1980-81	1990-91	1994-95	1995-96	1996-97	1997-98
Rice	14.3	16.4	19.4	21.4	21.5	22.2	21.8
	(38.4)	(40.8)	(45.5)	(49.8)	(49.9)	(51.0)	(50.1)
Jowar	0.6	0.8	0.8	0.8	0.8	0.8	0.8
	(3.6)	(4.7)	(5.6)	(6.7)	(6.8)	(7.0)	(7.4)
Bajra	0.5	0.6	0.5	0.6	0.6	0.5	0.6
	(4.0)	(5.5)	(5.1)	(5.8)	(6.2)	(4.9)	(6.2)
Maize	0.9	1.2	1.2	1.3	1.4	1.3	1.4
	(15.9)	(20.1)	(19.7)	(21.3)	(22.6)	(20.3)	(21.9)
Wheat	9.9	15.6	19.5	22.0	21.6	22.4	22.7
	(54.3)	70.0	(81.1)	(84.9)	(85.8)	(86.2)	(85.0)
Barley	1.3	0.9	0.5	0.6	0.5	0.5	0.5
	(52.0)	(50.6)	(54.5)	(66.7)	(60.3)	(62.5)	(62.5)
Total Cereals	28.1	35.8	42.3	46.8	46.5	47.9	47.9

Total Pulses	2.0	2.0	2.6	3.1	3.0	3.0	2.8
	(8.8)	(9.0)	(10.5)	(12.8)	(12.9)	(12.9)	(12.0)
Total Foodgrains	30.1	37.8	44.9	49.9	49.5	50.8	50.7
	(24.1)	(29.7)	(35.1)	(39.6)	(40.1)	(40.6)	(40.6)
Oilseeds	1.1	2.3	5.8	6.8	7.3	7.4	7.0
	(7.4)	(14.5)	(22.9)	(25.0)	(26.0)	(26.2)	(24.3)
Cotton	1.4	2.1	2.5	2.7	3.2	3.3	3.2
	(17.3)	27.3	(32.9)	(33.8)	(35.0)	(35.9)	(35.9)
Sugarcane	1.9	2.4	3.4	3.6	3.9	3.9	3.9
	(72.4)	(81.3)	(86.9)	(83.7)	(87.4)	(88.6)	(90.7)

Notes : 1. Figures in parentheses represent percentages of irrigated area to total area under the crop.

2. Irrigated area under oilseeds denotes the area under groundnut, rapeseed & mustard, linseed, sesamum and others.

Source : Directorate of Economics & Statistics, Department of Agriculture & Cooperation.

TABLE 9

Net Availability, Procurement and Public Distribution of Foodgrains

(Million tonnes)

Year	Net production of foodgrains	Net imports	Net availability of foodgrains@	Procurement	Public distribution#	Col. 3 as per cent of Col. 4	Col. 5 as per cent of Col. 2	Col. 6 as per cent of Col. 4
1	2	3	4	5	6	7	8	9
1951	48.1	4.8	52.4	3.8	8.0	9.2	7.9	15.3
1952	48.7	3.9	52.0	3.5	6.8	7.5	7.2	13.1
1953	54.1	2.0	56.6	2.1	4.6	3.5	3.9	8.1
1954	63.3	0.8	63.9	1.4	2.2	1.3	2.2	3.4
1955	61.9	0.5	63.2	1.3	1.6	0.8	2.1	2.5
1956	60.7	1.4	62.6	Neg.	2.1	2.2	Neg.	3.4
1957	63.4	3.6	66.2	0.3	3.1	5.4	0.5	4.7
1958	58.3	3.2	61.8	0.5	4.0	5.2	0.9	6.5
1959	69.0	3.9	72.3	1.8	5.2	5.4	2.6	7.2
1960	67.5	5.1	71.2	1.3	4.9	7.2	1.9	6.9
1961	72.0	3.5	75.7	0.5	4.0	4.6	0.7	5.3
1962	72.1	3.6	76.1	0.5	4.4	4.8	0.7	5.7
1963	70.3	4.5	74.8	0.8	5.2	6.1	1.1	6.9
1964	70.6	6.2	78.1	1.4	8.7	8.0	2.0	11.1
1965	78.2	7.4	84.6	4.0	10.1	8.8	5.2	11.9
1966	63.3	10.3	73.5	4.0	14.1	14.0	6.3	19.2
1967	65.0	8.7	73.9	4.5	13.2	11.7	6.9	17.8

1968	83.2	5.7	86.8	6.8	10.2	6.5	8.2	11.8
1969	82.3	3.8	85.6	6.4	9.4	4.5	7.8	11.0
1970	87.1	3.6	89.5	6.7	8.8	4.0	7.7	9.9
1971	94.9	2.0	94.3	8.9	7.8	2.1	9.3	8.3
1972	92.0	(-)0.5	96.2	7.7	10.5	(-)0.5	8.3	10.9
1973	84.9	3.6	88.8	8.4	11.4	4.0	9.9	12.8
1974	91.6	5.2	97.1	5.6	10.8	5.3	6.2	11.1
1975	87.4	7.5	89.3	9.6	11.3	8.4	10.9	12.6
1976	105.9	0.7	95.8	12.8	9.2	0.7	12.1	9.6
1977	97.3	0.1	99.0	9.9	11.7	0.1	10.1	11.8
1978	110.6	(-)0.6	110.2	11.1	10.2	(-)0.5	10.0	9.2
1979	115.4	(-)0.2	114.9	13.8	11.7	(-)0.2	12.0	10.2
1980	96.0	(-)0.3	101.4	11.2	15.0	(-)0.3	11.6	14.8
1981	113.4	0.7	114.3	13.0	13.0	0.6	11.4	11.4
1982	116.6	1.6	116.9	15.4	14.8	1.4	13.2	12.6
1983	113.3	4.1	114.7	15.6	16.2	3.5	13.7	14.1
1984	133.3	2.4	128.6	18.7	13.3	1.8	14.0	10.4
1985	127.4	(-)0.4	124.3	20.1	15.8	(-)0.3	15.8	12.7
1986	131.6	0.5	133.8	19.7	17.3	0.4	15.0	12.9
1987	125.5	(-)0.2	134.8	15.7	18.7	(-)0.1	12.5	13.8
1988	122.8	3.8	130.8	14.1	18.6	2.9	11.5	14.2
1989	148.7	1.2	147.2	18.9	16.4	0.8	12.7	11.1
1990	149.7	1.3	144.8	24.0	16.0	0.9	16.0	11.0

(Contd.)

TABLE 9 (*Contd.*)

1	2	3	4	5	6	7	8	9
1991	154.3	(-)0.1	158.6	19.6	20.8	Neg.	12.7	13.1
1992	147.3	(-)0.4	148.5	17.9	18.8	(-)0.3	12.2	12.7
1993	157.5	3.1	149.8	28.1	16.4	2.1	17.9	10.9
1994	161.2	1.1	154.8	26.0	14.0	0.7	16.1	9.1
1995	167.6	(-)2.6	166.7	22.6	15.3	(-)1.6	13.5	9.0
1996	157.9	(-)3.1	163.3	19.8	18.3	(-)1.9	12.5	11.2
1997	174.5	(-)0.1	176.2	23.6	17.8	Neg.	13.5	10.1
1998	168.2	(-)2.5	159.6	26.3	18.6	(-)1.6	15.6	11.1
1999	178.2	(-)1.3	169.4	30.8	17.7	(-)0.8	17.3	9.9
2000	182.8	(-)1.4	167.5	35.5	12.8	(-)0.8	19.7	7.0
2001*	171.6	(-)2.7	156.3	42.2	11.3$	(-)1.7	24.6	6.6$

* Provisional. $ Upto November 2001.

Neg. Negligible.

@ Net availability = Net production+Net imports - changes in Government stocks.

\# Includes quantities released under the Food for Work Programme during the year 1978 to 1990.

Notes: 1. Production figures relate to agricultural year: 1951 figures correspond to 1950-51 and so on. Figures for procurement and public distribution relate to calendar years.

2. Net Imports from 1981 to 1994 are only on Government account and from 1995 onwards the Net Imports are total Imports and Export of the country.

Sources: 1. Department of Food and Public Distribution.

2. Directorate of Economics & Statistics, Department of Agriculture & Cooperation.

TABLE 10

Production, Imports and Consumption of Fertilizers

(Thousand tonnes of nutrients)

	1960-61	1970-71	1980-81	1990-91	1995-96	1996-97	1997-98	1998-99	1999-2000	2000-01	2001-02*
A. Nitrogenous fertilizers											
Production	98	830	2164	6993	8777	8599	10086	10480	10890	10962	10959
Imports	399	477	1510	414	1938	1155	1362	635	833	154	264 @
Consumption	210	1487	3678	7997	9823	10302	10901	11354	11592	10920	12197
B. Phosphatic fertilizers											
Production	52	229	841	2052	2558	2556	2976	3141	3399	3743	4082
Imports	—	32	452	1311	380	246	672	968	1503	396	415 @
Consumption	53	462	1214	3221	2898	2977	3914	4112	4799	4215	5198
C. Potassic fertilizers											
Imports	20	120	797	1328	1423	613	1140	1542	1739	1541	1271 @
Consumption	29	228	624	1328	1156	1029	1373	1332	1678	1567	1911
D. All fertilizers (NPK)											
Production	150	1059	3005	9045	11335	11155	13062	13621	14289	14705	15041
Imports	419	629	2759	2758	3955	1975	3174	3145	4075	2090	1590 @
Consumption	292	2177	5516	12546	13877	14308	16188	16798	18069	16702	19306

* Estimated. @ Upto November 2001.

Sources: (1) Ministry of Chemicals & Fertilizers, Department of Fertilizers.

(2) Department of Agriculture & Cooperation.

TABLE 11

Production of Major Livestock Products and Fish

Year	Milk (Million tonnes)	Eggs (Million Nos.)	Fish (Thousand tonnes)
1950-51	17.0	1832	752
1960-61	20.0	2881	1160
1970-71	22.0	6172	1756
1980-81	31.6	10060	2442
1981-82	34.3	10876	2444
1982-83	35.8	11454	2367
1983-84	38.8	12792	2506
1984-85	41.5	14252	2801
1985-86	44.0	16128	2876
1986-87	46.1	17310	2942
1987-88	46.7	17800	2959
1988-89	48.4	18980	3152
1989-90	51.4	20204	3677
1990-91	53.9	21100	3836
1991-92	55.7	21980	4157
1992-93	58.0	22930	4365
1993-94	60.6	24170	4644
1994-95	64.0	25980	4789
1995-96	66.2	27200	4949
1996-97	69.1	27500	5348
1997-98	71.9	28690	5388
1998-99	75.2	29476	5262
1999-2000 (P)	78.1	31501	5675
2000-01 (P)	81.0	32420	5656

(P) Provisional.

Source: Department of Animal Husbandry & Dairying.

TABLE 12

GDP, Agriculture and Foodgrains Growth Rates

(Per cent)

Year	GDP*	GDP Agri and Allied Sector*	Foodgrains Production
1992-93	5.1	5.8	6.6
1993-94	5.9	4.1	2.7
1994-95	7.3	5.0	3.9
1995-96	7.3	–0.9	–5.8
1996-97	7.8	9.6	10.5
1997-98	4.8	–2.4	–3.6
1998-99	6.5	6.2	5.9
1999-00	6.1	1.3	3.0
2000-01	4.0	–0.2	–6.6
2001-02**	5.4	5.7	6.8

*At 1993-1994 Prices. ** Advance Estimates.

TABLE 13

Foodgrains Production

(Million Tonnes)

Crop	1996-97	1997-98	1998-99	1999-2000	2000-01	2001-02*
Rice	81.7	82:5	86.1	89.7	84.9	91.0
Wheat	69.4	66.4	71.3	76.4	68.7	73.1
Coarse Cereals	34.1	30.4	31.3	30.3	31.6	31.9
Pulses	14.2	13.0	14.9	13.4	10.7	13.2
Foodgrains	199.4	192.3	203.6	209.8	195.9	209.2
Kharif	103.9	101.6	102.9	105.5	103.4	108.5
Rabi	95.5	90.7	100.7	104.3	92.5	100.7

* Advance Estimates.

TABLE 14

Commercial Crop Production

(Million Tonnes)

Crop	1996-97	1997-98	1998-99	1999-2000	2000-01	2001-02#
Groundnut	8.6	7.4	9.0	5.3	6.2	7.2
Rapeseed/ Mustard	6.7	4.7	5.7	5.8	4.2	5.2
Soyabean	5.4	6.5	7.1	7.1	5.3	5.9
Other oilseeds	3.7	2.7	2.9	2.5	2.7	2.8
Total nine oilseeds	24.4	21.3	24.7	20.7	18.4	21.1
Cotton*	14.2	10.9	12.3	11.5	9.7	12.0
Jute & Mesta**	11.1	11.0	9.8	10.6	10.5	10.7
Sugarcane	277.6	279.5	288.7	299.3	299.2	295.0

* Million bales of 170 kgs.

** Million bales of 180 kgs each.

Advance Estimates.

TABLE 15

Annual Compound Growth of Crop Area, Production and Productivity

(per cent)

Crop	1980-81 to 1989-90			1990-91 to 2000-01		
	Area	Production	Yield	Area	Production	Yield
Rice & Wheat	0.43	3.59	3.15	0.84	2.27	1.42
- Rice	0.41	3.62	3.19	0.63	1.79	1.16
- Wheat	0.47	3.57	3.10	1.21	3.04	1.81
Coarse Cereals	–1.34	0.40	1.62	–1.84	0.06	1.65
Pulses	–0.09	1.52	1.61	–1.02	–0.58	0.27
Total Foodgrains	–0.23	2.85	2.74	–0.20	1.66	1.34
Non-Food Crops	1.12	3.77	2.31	0.84	1.86	0.59
- Oilseeds	–1.51	5.20	2.43	0.44	0.66	0.61
- Sugarcane	1.44	2.70	1.24	1.72	2.62	0.89
- Cotton	–1.25	2.80	4.10	2.21	0.92	–1.26
All Crops	0.10	3.19	2.56	0.08	1.73	1.02

TABLE 16

Tea Production, Consumption and Trade

(Qty. : Million Kgs; Value : Rs. Crore)

Year	Production	Exports		Imports		Domestic
	Qty.	Qty.	Value	Qty.	Value	Consumption Qty.
1995-96	761	167	1,244	0.5	2.4	567
1996-97	787	169	1,301	1.3	6.2	585
1997-98	836	211	2,003	2.6	17.8	602
1998-99	855	206	2,192	8.9	64.7	620
1999-00	835	192	1,933	10.4	68.5	638
2000-01	848	204	1,890	15.2	95.5	658
2000-01 (April-Nov.)	733	144	1,349	9.7	60.3	—
2001-02 (Apr-Nov.)	742	125	1,107	10.8	59.8	—

TABLE 17

Production, Consumption and Export of Coffee

('000 Tonnes)

Year	Production	Export		Domestic
		Qty.	Value (Million $)	Consumption
1990-91	170	100	108	54
1996-97	205	181	452	55
1997-98	228	179	477	55
1998-99	265	212	431	50
1999-00	292	245	447	50
2000-01	301	247	333	55
2001-02	317*	120**	139**	—

* Post Blossom forecast.

** April-October, 2001.

TABLE 18

Natural Rubber-Consumption, Production and Yield

Year	Consumption	Production	Yield
	('000 Tonnes)		(Kg/Ha)
1996-97	560	550	1503
1997-98	570	580	1549
1998-99	590	610	1563
1999-00	630	620	1576
2000-01	630	630	1576
2001-02*	640	650	1580

*Estimated.

TABLE 19

Estimated Area and Production of Major Horticultural Crops

(Area : Million Hectares; Production : Million Tonnes)

Crop	1997-98		1998-99		1999-2000		2000-01*	
	Area	Production	Area	Production	Area	Production	Area	Production
Fruits	3.73	43.26	3.74	44.04	3.80	45.50	3.94	49.80
Apple	0.23	1.32	0.23	1.38	0.23	1.04	0.24	1.30
Banana	0.44	13.34	0.46	15.07	0.49	16.81	0.50	17.50
Citrus	0.48	4.31	0.48	4.57	0.52	4.65	0.53	4.80
Grapes	0.04	0.97	0.04	1.08	0.04	1.13	0.04	1.20
Guava	0.15	1.61	0.15	1.80	0.15	1.71	0.16	1.85
Litchi	0.05	0.45	0.05	0.43	0.05	0.43	0.06	0.45
Mango	1.38	10.23	1.40	9.78	1.48	10.50	1.50	11.40
Papaya	0.07	1.62	0.06	1.58	0.06	1.66	0.07	1.70
Pineapple	0.07	0.94	0.07	1.01	0.07	1.02	0.07	1.10
Sapota	0.04	0.44	0.05	0.68	0.06	0.80	0.07	0.90
Others	0.78	8.03	0.75	6.66	0.65	5.75	0.70	7.60
Vegetables	4.11	72.73	4.41	87.53	5.99	90.83	6.24	98.50
Brinjal	0.48	7.74	0.49	7.88	0.50	8.12	0.51	8.80

(Contd.)

TABLE 19 (*Contd.*)

Crop	1997-98		1998-99		1999-2000		2000-01*	
	Area	Production	Area	Production	Area	Production	Area	Production
Cabbage	0.23	5.32	0.24	5.62	0.26	5.90	0.28	6.10
Cauliflower	0.25	4.47	0.25	4.69	0.25	4.72	0.26	4.80
Okra	0.32	3.21	0.33	3.38	0.35	3.42	0.36	3.50
Onion	0.34	3.14	0.48	5.47	0.49	4.90	0.52	6.50
Pea	0.27	2.42	0.28	2.70	0.27	2.71	0.30	3.80
Potato	1.21	17.65	1.28	22.49	1.34	25.00	1.38	26.00
Tomato	0.41	6.18	0.47	8.27	0.46	7.43	0.50	8.40
Others	0.60	22.60	0.59	27.03	2.07	28.63	2.13	30.60
Flowers	0.07	0.37	0.07	0.42	0.09	0.52	0.10	0.55
Spices	NA	2.76	NA	2.87	NA	2.91	NA	3.00
Cashew nut	0.70	0.36	0.71	0.46	0.69	0.52	0.63	0.45
Arecanut	0.27	0.33	0.28	0.31	0.29	0.33	NA	NA
Coconut**	1.86	12.72	1.75	12.54	1.78	12.25	NA	NA
Other Horticultural crops	NA	1.50	NA	1.65	NA	1.75	NA	1.85

* Provisional. ** Production in thousand million nuts. NA: Not Available.

TABLE 20

Production and Per Capita Availability of Milk

Year	Milk Production (Million Tonnes)	Per Capita Availability (Gms/per day)
1950-51	17	124
1960-61	20	124
1970-71	22	112
1980-81	32	128
1990-91	54	176
1996-97	69	202
1997-98	72	203
1998-99	75	211
1999-00*	78	214
2000-01*	81	217

* Provisional.

TABLE 21

Production and Export of Fish and Marine Products

Year	Fish Production			Export of Marine Products	
	Marine	Inland	Total	Qty.	Value
	(Million Tonnes)			('000 Tonnes)	(Rs. crore)
1950-51	0.5	0.2	0.7	20	2
1960-61	0.9	0.3	1.2	20	4
1970-71	1.1	0.7	1.8	40	35
1980-81	1.5	0.9	2.4	80	235
1990-91	2.3	1.5	3.8	140	873
1996-97	3.0	2.4	5.4	380	4,121
1997-98	3.0	2.4	5.4	390	4,697
1998-99	2.7	2.6	5.3	300	4,627
1999-00*	2.9	2.8	5.7	300	5,116
2000-01*	2.8	2.8	5.6	430	6,318

* Provisional.

TABLE 22

Production/Distribution of Certified/Quality Seeds

Type	Unit	1997-98	1998-99	1999-2000	2000-01*	2001-02**
Breeder Seed	Qtls.	46,134	38,994	51,236	42,560	45,000
Foundation Seed	'000 Qtls.	684	675	466	590	—
Certified Quality seed distribution	'000 Qtls.	7,879	8,497	8,798	8,544	10,966

* Expected. ** Target.

TABLE 23

Consumption of Fertilizers

('000 Tonnes of nutrients)

Fertilizers	1997-98	1998-99	1999-2000	2000-01	2001-02*
Nitrogenous Fertilizers	10,901	11,354	11,592	10,920	12,197
Phosphatic Fertilizers	3,914	4,112	4,799	4,215	5,198
Potassic Fertilizers	1,373	1,332	1,678	1,567	1,911
All Fertilizers (NPK)	16,188	16,798	18,069	16,702	19,306
Percentage increase	13.14	3.77	7.57	–7.56	15.59

* Estimated.

TABLE 24

Season-wise Consumption of Fertilizers

Year	Kharif	Rabi	Total	Kharif	Rabi
	('000 Tonnes of nutrients)			(Per cent share)	
1980-81	2,138	3,378	5,516	38.8	61.2
1990-91	5,741	6,805	12,546	45.8	54.2
1996-97	6,920	7,388	14,308	48.4	51.6
1997-98	8,092	8,096	16,188	50.0	50.0
1998-99	7,834	8,964	16,798	46.6	53.4
1999-2000	8,861	9,208	18,069	49.0	51.0
2000-01	8,034	8,668	16,702	48.1	51.9
2001-02*	9,070	10,236	19,306	46.9	53.1

* Estimated.

TABLE 25

Fertilizer Production, Imports and Subsidy

Year	Production*		Imports*	Subsidy			
	Nitrogen	Phosphate	N+P+K	Imported Controlled Fertilizers	Domestic Controlled Fertilizers	Decontrolled Fertilizers	Total
	('000 Tonnes)			(Rs. crore)			
1960-61	98	52	419	—	—	—	—
1970-71	830	229	629	—	—	—	—
1980-81	2,164	841	2,759	335	170	—	505
1990-91	6,993	2,052	2,758	659	3,730	—	4,389
1996-97	8,599	2,556	1,975	1,163	4,743	1,672	7,578
1997-98	10,086	2,976	3,174	722	6,600	2,596	9,918
1998-99	10,480	3,141	3,145	124	7,473	3,790	11,387
1999-2000	10,890	3,399	4,075	74	8,670	4,500	13,244
2000-01	10,962	3,743	2,090	1	9,480	4,319	13,800
2001-02 (BE)	10,959	4,082	1,950**	500	7,956	5,714	14,170

* In nutrient terms. (BE) — Budget Estimate. ** Up to November 2001.

TABLE 26

Selling Prices of Fertilizer Products

(Rs./Tonne)

Type of Fertilizer	Selling Price
Urea	4,600
Di-Ammonium Phosphate	8,900
Muriate of Potash	4,255
Complex Fertilizers	6,620-8,520
Single Super Phosphate	Varies from State to State

TABLE 27

Number of Tractors and Power Tillers Sold

States	Tractors		States	Power Tillers	
	1999-2000	2000-01		1999-2000	2000-01
Uttar Pradesh	69,665	68,354	West Bengal	5,270	5,161
Punjab	27,679	24,397	Tamil Nadu	2,644	2,125
Madhya Pradesh	28,815	23,099	Karnataka	1,649	1,623
Bihar	13,230	18,031	Assam	1,506	1,514
Haryana	21,100	17,978	Kerala	1,536	1,194
Andhra Pradesh	16,911	17,958	Orissa	970	1,150
Maharashtra	18,742	16,733	Maharashtra	477	603
Rajasthan	26,664	15,447	Andhra Pradesh	1,142	469
Gujarat	17,747	12,365	Gujarat	290	460
Karnataka	8,245	11,801	Tripura	289	288
Other States/UTs and Export etc.	24,383	28,662	Other States/UTs and Export etc.	1,118	1,431
All India	**273,181**	**254,825**	**All India**	**16,891**	**16,018**

TABLE 28
Flow of Institutional Credit to Agriculture

(Rs. crore)

Institutions	1997-98	1998-99	1999-2000#	2000-01$	2001-2002@
Co-operative Banks	14,085	15,957	18,429	21,909	27,080
Short-term	10,895	12,571	14,648	17,700	21,542
Medium/ Long-term	3,190	3,386	3,781	4,209	5,538
Regional Rural Banks	2,040	2,460	3,329	3,807	4,956
Short-term	1,396	1,710	2,517	2,778	3,415
Medium/ Long-term	644	750	812	1,029	1,541
Commercial Banks	15,831	18,443	22,854	27,788	34,735
Short-term	8,349	9,622	11,697	14,222	17,778
Medium/ Long-term	7,482	8,821	11,157	13,566	16,957
Total	31,956	36,860	44,612	53,504	66,771
Per cent increase	21	15	21	20	25

Provisional. $ Estimated. @ Projections.

TABLE 29

Number of Kisan Credit Cards Issued and Amount Sanctioned

(Rs. crore)

Agency	1998-1999		1999-2000		2000-2001		2001-02 (up to Nov. 2001)		Comulative Progress (up to Nov. 2001)	
	Cards Issued ('000)	Amount Sanc-tioned	Cards Issued ('000)	Amount Sanc-tioned	Cards Issued ('000)	Amount Sanc-tioned	Cards Issued ('000)	Amount Sanc-tioned	Cards Issued ('000)	Amount Sanc-tioned
Coop. Banks	155	826	3,595	3,606	5,614	9,412	4,148	12,465	13,512	26,309
RRBs	7	11	173	405	648	1,400	566	1,528	1,394	3,344
Commercial Banks	445	1,247	1,366	3,537	2,390	5,615	1,309*	3,340*	5,510*	13,739*
Total	607	2,084	5,134	7,548	8,652	16,427	6,023	17,333	20,416	43,392

* Position upto September 2001.

TABLE 30

Performance of the National Agricultural Insurance Scheme

Particulars	Rabi 1999-2000	Kharif 2000	Rabi 2000-2001*
Farmers covered (No.)	579,940	8,409,419	2,079,109
Sum Insured (Rs. Crore)	356.41	6,903.47	1,525.15
Premium (Rs. Crore)	5.42	206.51	27.45
Area Coverage (in million ha.)	780	13,000	3,092
Claims (Rs. Crore)	7.69	1,179.49	41.90

* as on December 18, 2001.

TABLE 31

Livestock Insurance

Year	No. of animals Insured (Million)	Premium Collected (Rs. cr.)	Incurred Claims Amount (Rs. cr.)	Claims to premium ratio
1995-96	15.3	113.39	74.05	65
1996-97	14.7	122.54	74.83	61
1997-98	6.3	143.45	80.11	56
1998-99	7.9	152.02	126.08	83
1999-00	9.8	137.14	114.28	83
2000-01	7.9	145.53	127.97	88

TABLE 32

Capital Formation in Agriculture

(at 1993-94 prices)

(Rs. Crore)

Year	Total	Public	Private	Per cent share		Investment in Agriculture as Per cent of GDP
				Public	Private	
1993-94	13,523	4,467	9,056	33.0	67.0	1.6
1994-95	14,969	4,947	10,022	33.0	67.0	1.6
1995-96	15,690	4,849	10,841	30.9	69.1	1.6
1996-97	16,176	4,668	11,508	28.9	71.1	1.5
1997-98	15,942	3,979	11,963	25.0	75.0	1.4
1998-99	14,895	3,869	11,026	26.0	74.0	1.3
1999-00	16,582	4,112	12,470	24.8	75.2	1.3
2000-01*	16,545	4,007	12,538	24.2	75.8	1.3

* Quick Estimates.

TABLE 33

India's Exports of Principal Agricultural Products

(US $ million)

Products	1998-1999	Per cent of Agri. Exports	1999-2000	Per cent of Agri. Exports	2000-2001	Per cent of Agri. Exports
1. Tea	538	8.9	412	7.3	433	7.2
2. Coffee	411	6.8	331	5.9	259	4.3
3. Cereals	1,495	24.8	724	12.9	744	12.4
4. Tobacco	181	3.0	233	4.2	191	3.2
5. Spices	388	6.4	408	7.3	354	5.9
6. Cashew	387	6.4	567	10.1	411	6.8
7. Sesame and Niger Seeds	78	1.3	86	1.5	131	2.2
8. Guargum Meal	173	2.9	188	3.4	132	2.2
9. Oil meals	462	7.7	378	6.7	448	7.5
10. Fruits & Vegetables	184	3.0	209	3.7	248	4.1
11. Processed Fruits & Vegetables	69	1.1	86	1.5	122	2.0
12. Meat & Meat Preparations	187	3.1	189	3.4	322	5.4
13. Marine Products	1,038	17.2	1,183	21.1	1,394	23.2
14. Others	446	7.4	614	11.0	815	13.6
Agri-Exports	6,037	100.0	5,608	100.0	6,004	100.0
Per cent of Agri. to Total Exports	18.2	—	15.2	—	13.5	—
Total Exports	33,218		36,822		44,560	

TABLE 34

Agriculture Imports

(US $ million)

Commodity	1998-1999		1999-2000		2000-2001	
	Value	Per cent to total Agri. Imports	Value	Per cent to total Agri. Imports	Value	Per cent to total Agri. Imports
Cereal	288	9.9	222	7.8	19	1.0
Pulses	169	5.8	82	2.9	109	5.9
Milk & cream	3	0.1	25	0.9	2	0.1
Cashew nuts	230	7.9	276	9.7	211	11.3
Nuts & fruits	159	5.5	136	4.8	175	9.4
Sugar	264	9.0	256	9.0	7	0.4
Oil seeds	2	0.1	4	0.1	2	0.1
Veg. Oils	1,804	61.8	1,857	65.0	1,334	71.8
Total Agri. Imports	2,919	100.0	2,858	100.0	1,858	100.0
Per cent of Agri. to Total Imports	6.9	—	5.8	—	3.7	—
Total Country Imports	42,389		49,671		50,536	

TABLE 35

Import Duty on Agri. Products

Commodity	Bound Rate (as on January 1, 2001)	Import Duty (per cent)		
		Applied Rate Prior to 2001-02 Budget	Announced in 2001-02 Budget	Revised rate (if any) subsequent to 2001-02 Budget
Nuts				
Almonds	Rs. 35/kg	Rs. 35/kg	Rs. 35/kg	—
Arecanut	112	100	100	—
Cashewnut (in shell)	112	Zero	Zero	—
Cashewnut (shelled)	112	44	40	—
Foodgrains				
Rice	70 & 80	70 & 80	70 & 80	—
Wheat	80-100	0-50	0-50	—
Millets	70	50	50	—
Pulses	100	0	5	—
Fruits				
Apple	50	50	50	—
Fresh Grapes	40	38.5	35	—
Oranges	40	38.5	35	—
Plantations Crops				
Coffee	150	38.5	70	—
Tea	100	38.5	70	—
Natural Rubber in other forms	25	25	25	—
Silk other than silk waste	100	38.5	35	—

(Contd.)

TABLE 35 (*Contd.*)

Commodity	Bound Rate (as on January 1, 2001)	Import Duty (per cent): Applied Rate Prior to 2001-02 Budget	Import Duty (per cent): Announced in 2001-02 Budget	Import Duty (per cent): Revised rate (if any) sub-sequent to 2001-02 Budget
Edible Oil				
Refined Palm Oil	300	71.6	92.4	—
Refined Soya Oil	45	50.8	50.8	—
Crude Palm Oil (for Vanaspati)	300	25	75	65 (w.e.f. Oct. 30, 2001)
Crude Palm Oil (other than Vanaspati)	300	55	75	65 (w.e.f. Oct. 30, 2001)
Others				
Sugar	150	60	60	—
Cotton (Raw cotton)	100	5.5	5	10 (w.e.f. Oct. 30, 2001)
Skimmed Milk Powder	60	60	60	—
		15 (under TRQ)	15 (under TRQ)	—
		60 (out side TRQ)	60 (out side TRQ)	—

Note : In August 3, 2001 the Government imposed a fixed tariff value of \$337/tonne on CPO and \$351/tonne on RBD Palm Oil which were revised downwards to \$286/tonne and \$295/tonne respectively with effect from October 9, 2001.